Modern Black Nationalism

Edited by William L. Van Deburg

MODERN BLACK

NATIONALISM

FROM MARCUS GARVEY

TO LOUIS FARRAKHAN

New York University Press   *New York and London*

NEW YORK UNIVERSITY PRESS
New York and London

Library of Congress Cataloging-in-Publication Data
Modern Black nationalism : from Marcus Garvey to Louis Farrakhan /
edited by William L. Van Deburg.
p.   cm.
Includes bibliographical references and index.
ISBN 0-8147-8788-6 (cloth : alk. paper).—ISBN 0-8147-8789-4
(pbk. : alk. paper)
1. Black nationalism—United States—History—20th century-
–Sources.   2. Black power—United States—History—20th century-
–Sources.   3. Afro-Americans—Politics and government—Sources.
4. Back to Africa movement—History—20th century.   I. Van Deburg,
William L.
E185.61.M676   1997
323.1'196073—dc20   96-36071
                    CIP

New York University Press books are printed on acid-free paper,
and their binding materials are chosen for strength and durability.

Manufactured in the United States of America

10   9   8   7   6   5   4   3   2   1

*To three Pan-African practitioners
of the historian's activist art:*

Cheikh Anta Diop

Walter Rodney

Chancellor Williams

Contents

Two Black Nationalism in the Black Power Era

Acknowledgments

Typically, historical research begins as a solitary pursuit. Over time, it is transformed into a communal activity. *Modern Black Nationalism* is a perfect example of this phenomenon. A project that started with a single individual and his trusty word processor, a rough outline, and a stack of photocopies eventually came to involve a fairly substantial number of people. I call them "enablers." Believing there was merit in the attempt to introduce a new generation of students to the major figures, tenets, and tendencies of African American nationalism, they pitched in with sound advice, wry observations, and more file cabinet digging, fact checking, and telephone networking than one has a right to expect from busy professionals. Any short list of these helpful souls would have to include Sandy Adell, John Cooper, manuscript reviewer James Cone, Stanlie James, Gerda Lerner, Nellie McKay, Ron Radano, Richard Ralston, my wife, Diane Sommers, Mike Thornton, Tim Tyson, and Craig Werner. Kudos of the highest order go to Jim Danky, whose work on behalf of the State Historical Society of Wisconsin's African American Newspapers and Periodicals Bibliography Project is fast becoming the stuff of legend. At New York University Press, Tim Bartlett, Despina Papazoglou Gimbel, Lisa Lepson, and Eve Stotland have constituted a most winning editorial team. I am indebted to each of these "enablers" as well as to the authors and publishers who have facilitated the reprinting of these seminal documents.

Introduction

Attempting to gain a clear understanding of twentieth-century black nationalism is a bit like trying to eat Jell-O with chopsticks. Just when you think the situation is under control, wisdom slips away. Then, if too much time elapses before one returns to the topic, one risks being left with no more than a colorful puddle of partial truths—perhaps a few cryptic quotes resonant with street corner rage or an unsatisfying collection of desert-dry literary scraps best left for political philosophers gifted with long attention spans. Why does it have to be so hard?

Certainly, the complexity of this subject can bring manifold complications. But its interpreters' foibles and idiosyncrasies also add to the confusion. Many U.S. history texts—at all levels—practice avoidance. Guided by the old-fashioned notion that there exists but a single, undifferentiated national historical pageant, some sacrifice diversity for interpretive unity or pseudo-patriotic puffery. Here, at best, black nationalist champions like Marcus Garvey or Malcolm X merit a "gray box" or two. Although succinctly encapsulated and artfully inserted, their stories fall well outside the obvious concerns of the main narrative. As a result, the messages and meanings of their lives are lost in a never-never land of special interest factoids.

Other textbooks are directed toward noble multicultural ends, but provide only the most basic of introductions to a veritable cavalcade of competing regional, ethnic, generational, and gender-specific experiences. In-depth treatment of weighty issues or multifaceted ideologies specific to any one group tend to be sacrificed on the altar of inclusiveness as the author focuses on historical figures to which any member of the rising rainbow coalition can feel comfortable pledging allegiance. In the worst-case scenario, coverage of black nationalist initiatives is juxtaposed with photos of riot-torn 1960s ghettoscapes, suffering Vietnamese refugees, and bra-burning feminists. In the end, too much becomes too little.

More specialized works, especially those penned by confirmed ideologues, bring additional problems. For example, if heavily laden with sectarian baggage, they may seek to recount all of nationalist history in the first person—or at least make it appear that theirs is the only ideological variant worth considering. Part and parcel of a deeply rooted in-house doctrinal debate, such accounts avoid avoidance, but either denigrate or deny black nationalism's characteristic diversity and breadth of expression. Although engaging, these tub-thumping texts can be factually facetious and frustratingly incomplete. In some cases, a true believer's overcommitment to the cause generates more heat than light and results in the worst obscurantist pedantry imaginable.

The present documentary anthology seeks to chart a course between these hazardous pedagogical alternatives—neither ignoring nor overstating the case for any one of Afro-America's historically important nationalisms. It posits the notion that black Americans have experienced an ongoing love-hate relationship with these belief systems; that if not always noted for its front-page immediacy, black nationalism's attractive power has remained remarkably vital over time; and that a wide-ranging documentary survey of the subject will assist all interested parties in fathoming the meaning(s) of African American nationalism for today. Here, originality and continuity, maleability and conviction are not considered polar opposites. Rather, they are viewed as complementary attributes that have contributed to black nationalism's longevity and serve to enhance its relevance for the twenty-first century.

The basic concept of nationalism is easy to fathom. Throughout world history nationalistic ideologies have competed for the hearts and minds of commoners and kings, plebeians and parliamentarians. They have flourished in the most unlikely of places and have fueled social movements from the Golden Age of Greece to modern-day Ireland, Palestine, and Francophone Canada. A common denominator of these robust nationalistic expressions is the high value placed on self-definition and self-determination. Whether their nationalism is expressed in demands for territorial cession, political empowerment, or increased cultural autonomy, confirmed nationalists believe that the ethnic, religious, or linguistic group to which they are most intimately attached is undervalued and oppressed by "outsiders." Typically, such feelings are spawned by unfavorable geopolitical circumstances and may be communicated to fellow sufferers via appeals based on a common historical background or cultural heritage. Denied what they perceive to be a rightful share of resources or respect, aggrieved nationalists throw down an ideological gauntlet, repudiating the imposed power others hold over them.

In order to convince comfortable or complacent countrymen that the current state of affairs warrants such action, the nationalists must in some way combine their appeal with a critique of competing ideologies. Students of collective behavior identify the most important of these ideologies as assimilationism and pluralism.

Assimilationists, it is said, view the collective expression of grievances as a short-term strategy for ultimate absorption into a mainstream melting pot. Not deeply concerned with altering the basic values of society or initiating fundamental institutional changes, the assimilationist merely hopes, through group action, to win greater participation in existing societal institutions.

Pluralists, on the other hand, view the social world as being composed of various ethnic and interest groups, all of whom are competing with one another for goods and services. This is fine, they say, as long as equal opportunities, privileges, and respect are accorded to all. Unlike assimilation, an amicable coexistence of diverse constituencies would allow each subculture to remain relatively intact. Granted equal access to power and continually strengthened and renewed through their unique cultural roots, the groups would form a multicultural society in which each component supported and enriched all others.

Nationalists, by comparison, are determined skeptics. They are suspicious of claims that radically divergent groups can live in peace and on a basis of equality while inhabiting the same territory or participating in the same societal institutions. Inevitably, they say—often from painful personal experience—one component of the social matrix comes to dominate and oppress the others. In the process, important subgroup mores may be altered or eradicated. To escape assimilation by fiat, nationalists seek to strengthen in-group values while holding those promoted by the larger society at arm's length. Withdrawing from the body politic as much as practicable, they strive to win and maintain sociocultural autonomy.

It goes without saying that such encouragements to group solidarity may, on occasion, backfire—actually decreasing the level of unity and national consciousness within a targeted community. Potential in-group supporters turned off by the nationalists' theoretical assumptions, operational agenda, or overzealous promotional efforts may opt to cling ever tighter to a competing belief system. At such times, nationalist recruiting agents can take comfort in the fact that they are attempting to "sell" an ideology, not a magazine subscription or an overpriced time-share condo. As with any such intellectual construction, nationalism can be blended with a host of related "isms" and approaches—to better address the specific needs of individual adherents or to more easily adapt to changed social conditions. Nationalists can lean either to the right or to the left of their customary place on the political spectrum. They can be "classical" or "modern"—sometimes even "neo" or "proto." Their issue orientation may tend toward territorial, religious, economic, or cultural concerns. Nevertheless, if it can be determined that a person's predominant passion is both galvanized by and rooted in fundamental nationalist tenets, it is likely that the individual in question will be considered for membership in the grand and honorable nationalist confraternity.

Some roguish types stray across stated ideological boundaries so frequently that demarcations between opposing camps become muddied and indistinct. Plural nationalist and revolutionary nationalist hybrids are the most obvious examples. Here, in order to avoid confusion, we may apply the following rule of thumb: Since most people are known primarily by their deeds, if someone looks, speaks, writes, and acts like a nationalist, others may be justified in treating them as such until compelling evidence to the contrary is produced. As is the case with the racial self-identification section on census questionnaires, each of us in a sense *becomes* what we claim to be. Unfortunately, there is no foolproof litmus test for use in nationalist accreditation.

Attaching "black" to "nationalism" also seems to perplex many otherwise astute Americans. Vague, tabloid press nomenclature has only made matters worse. "To what group(s) of black people in what part(s) of the world does such a term apply?" ask the confused and the curious. "Is a 'Pan-Africanist' or 'Pan-Negroist' a nationalist?" "How about a 'black revolutionary' or a garden-variety 'black militant'?" "How can a tax-paying, MasterCard-carrying U.S. citizen pledge loyalty to a 'national' entity other than the United States and not consider themselves a traitor?" In truth, such questions are less difficult than they appear at first glance. (Suggested responses are (1) not just South Africans; (2) usually; (3) possibly; (4) with surprising ease.) All manner of black nationalists, past and present, are located somewhere within the gnarled, sprawling expanse of the nationalist family tree.

Adapting traditional nationalist tenets to their own situation as members of a racially defined minority population, most African American nationalists equate "racial" with "national" identities and goals. Bound together by ties of history, culture, and kinship, they conceptualize themselves as being differentiated and (at least potentially) separated from competing social and ethnic groups. At various times and under certain conditions, these deep-rooted feelings of racial consanguinity may be manifested in overt political movements arguing for the creation of an autonomous nation-state or a transnational union of states grounded in shared experiences.

Whenever the prime movers of such movements manage to make themselves heard over the clamorous din of everyday life, one definitely should pause, ponder, and marvel. What has occurred is a noteworthy accomplishment. Against considerable odds—and in the face of almost all popular cultural and mainstream socialization—some activist leader or group within the black community has succeeded in convincing their compatriots to claim more for themselves than second-class citizenship. Hoping to turn presumed racial deficits (skin color, cultural forms and traits) into wellsprings of strength, these nationalist alchemists strive to bring about a unifying, self-defining revolution in racial consciousness that will ultimately lead to revolutionary advances in the area of black self-determination.

No one knows the identity of the first black American slave whose heartfelt longings for familiar West African scenes and loved ones were eased by the belief that it still might be possible to realize one's personal and group destiny—to separate bondsman from presumed master, leaving each to flourish, as it were, "under their own vine and fig tree." Surely, essential groundwork for the development of black nationalist thought was laid whenever an unwilling exile began to (1) question and then reject their presumed status as "inferior" vis-à-vis the whites; (2) recognize the need for intraracial solidarity; (3) proclaim their intellectual independence; and (4) employ shared experiences with bondage, caste, and folk culture to shape countervisions of the racial future. But could this series of exacting mental exercises produce tangible benefits? The historical record provides numerous proof texts.

Although raised in an environment that was ill suited to the development of self-esteem and unified action, African American slaves somehow managed to forge an alternative worldview capable of supporting either a spiritual or "national" liberation movement. The process began with the collection of accurate information about their group history and culture. Those who were very young when separated from their parents often found it difficult even to determine their own birthdate. But a well-placed question from an inquiring mind often yielded a surprising amount of useful data. Future abolitionist Frederick Douglass used this approach to uncover his heritage. When he was a youngster on an isolated Maryland plantation, Douglass's initial inquiries into the origin and nature of slavery were frustrated because his questions were put to children only a little older and better informed than himself. In attempting to solve the mystery "Why am I a slave?" he was told that God had made all things, that blacks were created to be servants of white masters, and that the Heavenly Father knew what was best for all His creatures. Nevertheless, by questioning somewhat older members of the slave community, the skeptical seven-year-old discovered that several could relate in detail the experience of their enslavement in Africa. Armed with this new information, he concluded that it was "not *color,* but *crime,* not *God,* but *man*" who had shaped the origins of black bondage.[1] Wrenching themselves from the white-good, black-bad dichotomy favored by the planters, bondsmen like Douglass were well on their way to the realization that race was a social variable that cut both ways. As employed by most white people, it facilitated and justified the African's enslavement. But it also provided black folk with an organizational mechanism that could be of inestimable value both in unifying fellow sufferers and in defining and charting a black "national" future.

Such heartfelt longings and hard-won understandings were by no means limited to the enslaved portion of the African American population. Nationalist tendencies have been present in all eras. They have percolated through all class-, age-, and gender-based divisions within the black community. Indeed, the persistence of black nationalist ideologies and institutions is reflective of young Douglass's unwillingness to accept any proposition that "came, point blank, against all my notions of goodness."[2] For example, before the Civil War, noteworthy elaborations on black nationalist themes were evident in the writings and speeches of free blacks who—conscious of their shared experiences and cultural traits—formed fraternal, mutual aid, and cooperative organizations to promote black solidarity, do battle with Anglo-Saxon assumptions of superiority, and aid in racial survival. In militant fashion, their reform conventions and activist scholarship made it clear that black people would represent themselves and fight their own battles. For many, this remained true no matter what the odds, irrespective of the cost.

Clearly differentiating "us" from "them," some took great pleasure in trumpeting the accomplishments of heroic ancestors (who were said to include the Egyptians, Babylonians, and Phoenicians; Plato, Augustine, and Hannibal) while denigrating their white countrymen's forebears. When black African civilization was "filling the world with amazement," said Presbyterian minister/abolitionist Henry Highland Garnet, the Anglo-Saxon "abode in caves under ground, either naked or covered with the skins of wild beasts." The most degraded creatures imaginable, these wretched beings made the nighttime "hideous" with savage shouts and darkened European skies with the smoke from their altars of human sacrifice. It was held that only a relatively recent loss of power occasioned by European technological advancements and slave-holding greed could account for the African Americans' devolution to servile status. Nevertheless, it was hoped that through individual self-affirmation and group self-determination, oppressed blacks could regain their lost heritage and once again achieve greatness as a people.[3]

In order to accomplish these cherished goals (and to serve as good role models as the process of liberation unfolded), early black nationalist spokespersons stood tall. Employing language as a weapon of liberation, they were determined to name themselves and their organizations according to group standards—demanding to be called "African" or "colored" rather than some slurred variant of the Portuguese os negros. Convinced that they were a black and beautiful people, they dared compare their physical characteristics with those of whites. It was no contest. By the time white people had been created, said one antebellum commentator, "nature was pretty well exhausted." The sharp-featured, lank-haired Euro-American was but a pale imitation of nature's crown of creation.[4]

Energized by these subversive notions, outspoken African Americans broadcast the spirit of group loyalty throughout the land. Responding vigorously to whites who would presume to "think for, dictate to, and know better what suited colored people, than they knew for themselves," black activists told it like it was—from a critical, nationalist political perspective. The nation's Constitution was "a sepulchre of whited lies," its religious institutions seedbeds of heathenism. Certainly, they said, revealing their disagreement with mainstream "patriotism," the "clanking of chains" made "sounds of strange discord" on Liberty's plains.[5] "America, it is to thee, /Thou boasted land of liberty," wrote black separatist poet James M. Whitfield, "It is to thee I raise my song, /Thou land of blood, and crime, and wrong."[6] How long, such impassioned voices seemed to be asking, could the proud men and women of Afro-America remain imprisoned within this perverted white republic? "Not a single moment longer" was the immediate, nationalist response.

Slave-era militants put both exploitative plantation owners and elected officials (often the same individuals) on notice that Virginia's state motto, "Death to Tyrants," would be adapted to radical antislavery purposes if the nation's system of racial bondage was not abolished.

Printed or embroidered, Garnet's militant slogan, "RATHER DIE FREE-MEN, THAN LIVE TO BE SLAVES," graced many a parlor wall, while Boston pamphleteer David Walker's boldly stated proposition that it was no worse to kill an oppressor than "to take a drink of water when thirsty" caused numerous black heads to nod in agreement.[7] When similarly disposed delegates to black conventions debated issues such as whether or not to aid slave insurrection movements or to instruct their children in "the act of war," some were so bold as to defend the affirmative position. Physical violence, they claimed, *always* was justified in self-defense.[8] Indeed, those who saw no hope of black national redemption without the shedding of blood saw nothing wrong with elevating insurrectionists Nat Turner, Gabriel Prosser, Joseph Cinque, and Denmark Vesey to the rank of racial demigods. "If the American revolutionaries had excuse for shedding one drop of blood," noted these race-conscious voices, "then have the American slaves for making blood flow 'even unto the horsebridles.' "[9] Revered because they dared wage unceasing war against tyranny, slave-era revolutionaries—and their memorialists—served as vivid reminders of Afro-America's collective determination to be free, to gain and exercise national power.

Other somewhat less strident advocates of black freedom and nationhood preached a territorial separatist alternative to American exclusivism, discrimination, and violence. Certainly, Afro-America's cold-shouldered rejection of the white-initiated Liberian colonization movement did not signal universal disapproval of the notion that black people could improve their lot in life by joining together to form a separate, independent state. The concept of establishing a powerful, black-governed nation outside the United States was formulated well before the Civil War by black emigrationists such as the late eighteenth-century Masonic lodge organizer Prince Hall, the crusading Pittsburgh physician and newspaper editor Martin Delany, and members of Henry Highland Garnet's 1850s-era African Civilization Society.[10]

Believing that black America constituted an oppressed "nation within a nation," activists such as these drafted ambitious plans for a self-repatriation that would join concerns about their own second-class citizenship with the often-stated desire to elevate the status of indigenous African populations. Because they were wedded to the notion that all peoples of the Afroworld—those separated from their roots by the slave trade's involuntary diaspora as well as those still resident within the ancestral homeland—should work together for their mutual benefit,

Pan-African nationalists evidenced a keen interest in "redeeming" the continent. With the twin engines of Christianity and commerce propelling their idealized ship of state forward, antebellum nationalist visionaries eagerly anticipated the day and hour when a black-controlled African nation or league of nation-states finally succeeded in amassing such economic and political clout that whites no longer could view *any* black person with "feelings of commiseration, sorrow and contempt." [11] Perhaps, they also mused, such a development might even provide the diplomatic or military instrument that at long last would remove the manacles from every slave in the so-called civilized world. Until that glorious day of Jubilee, nationalists would scour the globe for a suitable piece of land. In addition to the mother continent, various locales in Central and South America, the West Indies, and Canada were suggested as potential sites for large-scale, voluntary African American resettlement.

Short of actually departing for one of these far-flung destinations, nationalist-oriented blacks could and did continue to rail against majoritarian proscription and to demand recognition of their full American citizenship rights. Even while held captive within the white-governed "colony," they worked to invigorate and strengthen their communities through "Free African Societies" and other benevolent, fraternal, and religious organizations. Some initiated symbolic protests against white usurpation of God-given black freedoms. Martin and Catherine Delany, for example, made the family's nationalist politics known to all by naming their children after black historical, political, and cultural luminaries: Toussaint L'Ouverture, the father of Haitian independence; French writer Alexandre Dumas; abolitionist orator Charles Lenox Remond; and the Egyptian pharaoh Rameses. Others, like Henry Bibb, an outspoken advocate of emigration to Canada, urged blacks of the early 1850s to establish a network of "free labor stores" where purchases of nonslave-produced goods would, bit by bit, erode the economic foundation of black bondage. Still others sought to cement both the historical and hoped-for Pan-African connection deep within their group's collective memory by recounting folkloric stories of New World chattels who tolerated white oppression as long as they could and then simply rose up and flew back to Africa.[12] Whatever the specific mechanism for establishing their activist credentials, intellectual independence, and racial identity, such individuals made it clear that passivity, submissiveness, dependence, and fatalism had no place in a nationalist's vocabulary.

"Our elevation must be the result of *self-efforts,* and work of our *own hands,*" they said. "These are the proper and only means of elevating ourselves and attaining equality in this country or any other."[13]

By the opening of the twentieth century, these sentiments had been echoed time and again in the minutes of meetings held by postbellum emigrationist organizations such as the South Carolina-based Liberian Exodus Joint Stock Steamship Company, ex-slave Benjamin Singleton's United Transatlantic Society, and the International Migration Society promoted by African Methodist Episcopal Church bishop Henry McNeal Turner; in the correspondence of black Southerners who journeyed westward during the late nineteenth century to establish all-black towns—certain of which drafted restrictive (no whites) covenants—in Oklahoma and the Plains States; and in surviving accounts of the multi-(black) national Pan-African Conference held in London during the summer of 1900.[14] Obviously, black freedom did not obviate the need for black nationalism. Indeed, for many of those disillusioned by the dashed expectations and failed promises of postbellum American life, this race-specific ideology served as an ideological lifeline, an empowering source of strength for the ongoing fight against segregation, disfranchisement, and Ku Klux Klan-sponsored terrorism.

As reflected in (1) its level of meaningful engagement with grassroots issues; (2) its degree of acceptance within black America; and (3) its general visibility outside the Afroworld, twentieth-century African American nationalism can be said to have experienced two peak periods of activity. These, in turn, were surrounded on either side by valley-like troughs of relative calm. The first high point coincides with the post–World War I organizational efforts of Marcus Garvey and the Universal Negro Improvement Association (UNIA). The second appeared as Black Power movement activists worked to transform black life and culture during the mid-1960s and early 1970s.

Son of a Jamaican stonemason descended from the Maroons—runaway slaves who had defied the island's plantation overlords by forming virtually independent black communities in remote mountain regions—Marcus Mosiah Garvey came to the United States in 1916. Within a year he made Harlem the epicenter of UNIA activism. A defiantly pro-black, anticolonial organization that could claim over a thousand branch chapters worldwide during the mid-1920s, the UNIA tapped into post-war discontent with the status quo in race relations. Garvey's dramatic call-to-assembly, "Up you mighty Race! You can accomplish what you will!" caught the ear of those who could wait no longer for the fulfillment of wartime promises concerning the extension and safeguarding of democracy. Said to number in the millions, loyal Garveyites would, at the first opportunity, unfurl the red, black, and green nationalist flag and follow their Pan-African shepherd to a new promised land in Africa.[15]

Given the failure of Garvey's emigration plans to get off dry land, it was fortunate that the UNIA's appeal was broad-based. Certainly, the organization's stated aims and objectives offered something for everyone. As initially outlined, they were

> To establish a Universal Confraternity among the race; to promote the spirit of pride and love; to reclaim the fallen; to administer to and assist the needy; to assist in civilizing the backward tribes of Africa; to assist in the development of Independent Negro nations and communities; to establish a central nation for the race, where they will be given the opportunity to develop themselves; to establish Commissaries and Agencies in the principal countries and cities of the world for the representation of all Negroes; to promote a conscientious Spiritual worship among the native tribes of Africa; to establish Universities, Colleges, Academies and Schools for racial education and culture of the people; to improve the general conditions of Negroes everywhere.[16]

For economic nationalists, the UNIA provided a cooperative network of grocery stores, laundries, and restaurants as well as the Negro Factories Corporation, the Black Star Line Steamship Corporation, the Black Cross Navigation and Trading Company, and even a (black) doll factory, a printing plant, and a fleet of moving vans.

Religious nationalists undoubtedly were pleased to learn that many Garveyites worshipped a "Black Man of Sorrows" and had their own *Universal Negro Catechism* and *Universal Negro Ritual*. Here, black nationalism was seen as the fulfillment of prophecy and Garvey apotheosized as "the reincarnated Angel of Peace come from Heaven to dispense Political Salvation" to an oppressed people. If, during his lifetime, this objective was not met, the UNIA leader pledged to rise from the dead to help create an autonomous black world.[17]

Educational nationalists could send their children to one of several UNIA branch-sponsored elementary schools, attend classes at New York's Booker T. Washington University or at Liberty University in Claremont, Virginia, and receive both fellowship and in-service instruction through UNIA auxiliaries such as the Universal African Black Cross Nurses and the Juvenile Black Cross Nurses.

Cultural nationalists reaffirmed and deepened their commitment to blackness whenever they attended a concert, dance, or play at one of the organization's Liberty Hall auditoriums; read the race-conscious historical and poetic works published in Garveyite papers such as the *Negro World* and the *Daily Negro Times;* or honored outstanding race champions by helping initiate them into the noble order of the Knights of the Nile.

Politically oriented types kept their hopes for the realization of Pan-African nationhood alive via periodic International Conventions of the Negro Peoples of the World (which, in 1920, attracted twenty-five thousand delegates from some twenty-five countries to New York's Madison Square Garden); through frequent utilization of inspirational slogans such as "Africa for the Africans," "Princes Shall Come Out of Egypt," and "One God! One Aim! One Destiny!"; and by helping recruit new members for one of the UNIA's paramilitary units, the African Legion, the Garvey Militia, the Ladies Brigade, the Black Eagle Flying Corps, and the Universal African Motor Corps.

To this interconnected assemblage of committed black nationalists, "UNIA" was an acronym for "United, Nothing can Impede your Aspirations." By way of contrast, the integration-oriented National Association for the Advancement of Colored People (NAACP) was said to stand for "Nothing Accomplished After Considerable Pretence."[18] Surely, thirty-five cents per month in dues was a minuscule price to pay for membership in an activist organization that in the early 1920s seemed well on its way to converting the burden of race into a positive tool for worldwide black liberation.

All too soon, however, an unfortunate series of personal and institutional setbacks dimmed this anticipatory vision of a redeemed, self-governing Afroworld. First, Garvey's flamboyant racial chauvinism and the UNIA's avowedly separatist agenda provoked a series of acrimonious ideological feuds with other black advocacy groups. The resulting plague of intraracial name-calling and general rancor alienated many potential allies. Then, after the poorly managed Black Star Line ceased operations — its four-ship, less-than-completely-seaworthy fleet awash in red ink — financial and legal difficulties mounted. Long a subject of government surveillance and harassment, Garvey was arrested, tried, and found guilty of using the mails to defraud investors in his ill-fated maritime venture. In November 1927, after he had served two years of a five-year prison term, his sentence was commuted by President Calvin Coolidge. Early the next month, the head of the now-bankrupt UNIA was deported as an undesirable alien. Until his death in 1940 at age fifty-two, Garvey directed the affairs of the once grand and glorious organization from exile; he continued to organize international conferences and promote the Pan-African ideal through a variety of Jamaican and London-based nationalist publications.

As the documents in this book reveal, twentieth-century black nationalism was neither buried with its best-known patron saint nor destined to remain forever time-encapsulated in the 1920s Garveyite mold. The still attractive, unifying core of nationalist belief was both strong and malleable enough to ward off such potentially fatal blows. Its followers were steeled for a season of organizational fragmentation, character assassination, and what they characterized as integration-minded Afro-America's mad stampede toward certain assimilation. If it can be said that black nationalist ideology suffered a lengthy post-Garvey "eclipse" in terms of presence, popularity, and power, it also should be noted that his proud "race first" legacy never ceased to serve as a reservoir of hope and of belief in race and self. Certainly, during these years none knew the exact hour of Africa's redemption, but as the faithful confidently asserted, "It is in the wind. It is coming. One day, like a storm, it will be here." [19]

By the end of 1966, it seemed to many that the fateful hour was at hand. During the summer, the Black Power movement had arrived on the national news scene, its angry birth cries reverberating throughout the popular media. Although initially the concept seemed unfamiliar and somewhat foreboding, Black Power's ideological roots ran deep. Inextricably intertwined with Afro-America's historical struggles for freedom, its essential spirit was the product of generations of black people confronting powerlessness—and surviving. While not all who participated in the movement can be considered committed, by-the-book nationalists, many were. Countless others found black nationalism's major tenets compatible with their own, somewhat more pluralistic, beliefs. It was an era of experimentation, and activists sampled freely, formulating numerous pluralist and revolutionary nationalist combinations.

But why the sudden interest in "Black Power"? What was wrong with the "One Man, One Vote" or "Freedom Now" rallying cries of the early 1960s civil rights activists? Certainly, the ultimate concerns of the two groups were similar. In many ways, Black Power was a logical extension of the earlier movement. Nevertheless, by mid-decade many African Americans had reached an intellectual and emotional impasse that caused them to consider adopting an approach to black liberation that was both more "radical" and more "nationalistic" than the prevailing civil rights mind-set allowed. Some had become skeptical of the white liberals' value to the freedom movement in the South. Others had lost faith in the ability of black moderates to spur economic renewal in Northern ghettos. Still others had begun to question whether the federal government *ever* would become an effective promoter and protector of legal equality. Collectively, these civil rights crusaders were tired, perplexed, and mad as hell at white America. Driven to near the breaking point by governmental foot-dragging, increasingly sophisticated legal evasions, widespread poverty, de facto segregation, and the inability of Martin Luther King's crusade of love and nonviolence to put an end to white-sponsored terrorism, many turned their backs on the integrationist ethic and embraced Black Power via one of the variants of black nationalism.

While equating attempts to integrate the societal mainstream with an unconscionable ideological drift toward assimilationism and the debasement of racial culture, Black Power–era nationalists were careful to distinguish between segregation and separatism. In the former, noted Harry Edwards, organizer of the 1968 Olympic Games boycott movement, the dominant majority "pushes the minority into a corner—exploits, brutalizes and colonizes them." As was all too evident in places like Harlem, segregation resulted in inferior public schools, rat-infested housing, and joblessness. But with black separatism, said Edwards, "we're talking about people moving out on their own to gain their destiny."[20]

The black nationalist worldview of these tumultuous years can be encapsulated as follows: White Power, as manifested in the workings of U.S. institutional life, had long been a major impediment to the African American's attainment of the good life. In order to challenge and ultimately dissolve this oppressive monopoly, blacks had to mobilize, close ranks, and build group strength. This difficult process involved all aspects of black life—political, economic, psychological, and cultural. Once unity had been achieved in these areas, blacks would form a significant power bloc and move toward realizing the ideal expressed in the concept "consent of the governed." Able to exercise true freedom of choice for the first time, they might then choose to go it alone, either in "liberated" urban enclaves, in a separate black-run nation-state, or simply in the realm of the psyche.[21]

Whatever the specific nationalist format, the New Black American would be a transformed, self-actualized individual. Central to the Black Power/black nationalist experience, the concept of self-definition was a fundamental component of the "revolution of the mind" that many activists believed was a prerequisite for the successful implementation of their (numerous and varied) plans for revolutionizing society. To become self-directed, to be assertive, to take pride in skin color and heritage was to remove the negative connotations of race that had long served as a constraining psychological and social force. Whites, of course, might still factor supposed racial limitations into their own plans for continued societal domination, but black people endowed with a "national" consciousness no longer would agree to play by the old rules. Instead of meekly responding to white stimuli or linking arms with paternalistic white liberals, they would dare to be pro-black—to look, feel, be, and *do* black. It was the nationalists' hope and expectation that this revolutionary psychological process of *becoming* black would initiate and support a social revolution of considerable magnitude.[22]

The belief that this could be accomplished—that widespread identity transformation was capable of mobilizing and unifying Afro-America in common cause—buoyed the spirits of all manner of nationalists during the Black Power years. This widely expressed desire to preserve and honor racial distinctiveness, to define the world in black terms, and to experience the soul-satisfying joys of individual empowerment and group autonomy reaffirmed the teachings of those earlier generations of strivers whose determined efforts in support of nationalist agendas were held up as behavioral benchmarks.

Today, more than twenty years after headlines such as "Where Are the Revolutionaries?" "What Happened to the Black Movement?" and "The Failure of Black Separatism" began to supercede those that somewhat prematurely had announced "The Coming of the Black Ghetto-State," the residual influence of Black Power–era nationalism can be seen whenever black folk band together to contest what Student Nonviolent Coordinating Committee (SNCC) leader Stokely Carmichael once termed "the dictatorship of definition, interpretation and consciousness."[23] Beset by internal dissension, U.S. counterintelligence intrigues, bad press, the death, exile, or defection of key spokespersons, tactical errors, squandered opportunities, societal inertia, ingrained prejudices, and entrenched bureaucracies, black nationalists of the 1960s and early 1970s may have been unable to implement their programs in full, but their labors were not in vain. As the concluding section of this volume reveals, the Black Power militants' work on behalf of national liberation has informed the efforts of contemporary activists who, gifted with the same irrepressible, combative spirit, have sought self-definition through various types and degrees of separation from the white mainstream.

Given the nation's racial history, the continuing divergence between Afro- and Euro-American cultures and experiences, and our current unresolved backlog of race-based social problems, it is likely that this ages-old contest for control of institutions and identities will continue far into the next century. If the black nationalist future remains consistent with its past, each new generation will seek to traverse new frontiers without totally severing emotional and ideological roots—to send forth committed leaders who are unafraid to step out from the crowd to lend encouragement with a ringing "Up you mighty Race! You can accomplish what you will!" Providing both an ideological and symbolic basis for group cohesiveness as well as a much-needed stimulus to political mobilization, black nationalist ideologies will be with us as long as there is a perceived need to employ their self-defining qualities against the regressive forces of sociocultural diffusion and co-optation.

Notes

1. Frederick Douglass to Thomas Auld, 3 September 1848, in *Anti-Slavery Bugle,* 29 September 1848; idem, *My Bondage and My Freedom* (Urbana: University of Illinois Press, 1987 [1855]), 60–61.

2. Douglass, *My Bondage,* 60.

3. Henry Highland Garnet, "The Past and the Present Condition and the Destiny of the Colored Race, Troy, 1848," in Earl Ofari, *"Let Your Motto Be Resistance": The Life and Thought of Henry Highland Garnet* (Boston: Beacon, 1972), 166.

4. "The Boston Massacre, March 5, 1770: Commemorative Festival in Faneuil Hall," *Liberator,* 12 March 1858, 42.

5. Martin Robison Delany, *The Condition, Elevation, Emigration, and Destiny of the Colored People of the United States* (New York: Arno Press and the New York Times, 1969 [1852]), 8, 10; Joseph C. Holly, "Injustice—not Law," in *Freedom's Offering, A Collection of Poems* (Rochester: Charles H. McDonnell, 1853), 27; Frances Ellen Watkins, "Bible Defense of Slavery" and "Eliza Harris," in *Poems on Miscellaneous Subjects* (Philadelphia: Merrihew and Thompson, 1857), 9, 11.

6. James M. Whitfield, "America," in *Early Black American Poets,* ed. William H. Robinson, Jr. (Dubuque: William C. Brown, 1969 [1853]), 40.

7. "Declaration of Sentiments of the Colored Citizens of Boston on the Fugitive Slave Bill," *Liberator,* 11 October 1850, 162; Henry Highland Garnet, *An Address to the Slaves of the United States of America* (New York: Arno Press

and the New York Times, 1969 [1848]), 96; David Walker, *Walker's Appeal in Four Articles* (New York: Arno Press and the New York Times, 1969 [1829]), 37.

8. Howard H. Bell, "Expressions of Negro Militancy in the North, 1840–1860," *Journal of Negro History* 45 (January 1960): 14–15; *Proceedings of the National Convention of Colored People* (Troy, NY: J. C. Kneeland, 1847), 17.

9. "Fugitive Slave Convention," *National Anti-Slavery Standard*, 5 September 1850, 58.

10. Many Pan-African nationalists of this era viewed white-led groups like the American Colonization Society (ACS) as "deportation" associations—intent on forcibly removing free blacks from the United States in order to protect the institution of slavery. By way of contrast, emigration was conceptualized as a black-led, voluntary movement grounded in antislavery principles. See Floyd J. Miller, *The Search for a Black Nationality: Black Emigration and Colonization, 1787–1863* (Urbana: University of Illinois Press, 1975). On Hall, see Charles H. Wesley, *Prince Hall: Life and Legacy* (Washington, DC: United Supreme Council, Southern Jurisdiction, Prince Hall Affiliation, 1977). On Delany, see Cyril E. Griffith, *The African Dream: Martin R. Delany and the Emergence of Pan-African Thought* (University Park: Pennsylvania State University Press, 1975). On Garnet, see Joel Schor, *Henry Highland Garnet: A Voice of Black Radicalism in the Nineteenth Century* (Westport, CT: Greenwood, 1977).

11. Delany, *Condition, Elevation*, 43.

12. On the Delanys' nationalistic naming practices, see Victor Ullman, *Martin R. Delany: The Beginnings of Black Nationalism* (Boston: Beacon, 1971), 50–51. On Bibb, see Roger W. Hite, "Voice of a Fugitive: Henry Bibb and Antebellum Black Separatism," *Journal of Black Studies* 4 (March 1974): 269–84. On slaves "flying" to Africa, see Work Projects Administration, Savannah Unit, Georgia Writers' Project, *Drums and Shadows: Survival Studies among the Georgia Coastal Negroes* (Garden City, NY: Doubleday, 1972 [1940]), 16, 26, 74, 101–2, 143.

13. Delany, *Condition, Elevation*, 45–46.

14. On the Pan-African emigrationist movements of this era, see Edwin S. Redkey, *Black Exodus: Black Nationalist Movements, 1890–1910* (New Haven: Yale University Press, 1969); Wilson Jeremiah Moses, *The Golden Age of Black Nationalism, 1850–1925* (Hamden, CT: Archon, 1978). On Afro-American emigration to the Plains States, see Nell Irvin Painter, *Exodusters: Black Migration to Kansas after Reconstruction* (New York: Alfred A. Knopf, 1976); Robert G. Athearn, *In Search of Canaan: Black Migration to Kansas, 1879–80* (Lawrence: Regents Press of Kansas, 1978); Norman L. Crockett, *The Black Towns* (Lawrence: Regents Press of Kansas, 1979). On the early twentieth-century Pan-African conferences, see Imanuel Geiss, *The Pan-African Movement: A History of Pan-Africanism in America, Europe and Africa* (New York: Africana, 1974).

15. In an autobiographical piece published in *Current History* (September 1923), Garvey wrote that the UNIA had "an approximate membership of 6,000,000." Although most would revise this tally downward, neither contemporary observers nor latter-day historians have agreed on a more precise figure.

In the UNIA tricolor, red stood for the blood shed in liberation struggles, black for the skin color of the African race, and green for the luxuriant vegetation of the Motherland.

16. Amy Jacques Garvey, *Garvey and Garveyism* (New York: Collier, 1970), 11.

17. Randall K. Burkett, *Garveyism as a Religious Movement: The Institutionalization of a Black Civil Religion* (Metuchen, NJ: Scarecrow Press and the American Theological Library Association, 1978), 29–32, 82–88; Tony Martin, *Race First: The Ideological and Organizational Struggles of Marcus Garvey and the Universal Negro Improvement Association* (Westport, CT: Greenwood, 1976), 69–70.

18. "Report of the Convention, 31 August 1920," in *The Marcus Garvey and Universal Negro Improvement Association Papers,* ed. Robert A. Hill (Berkeley: University of California Press, 1983), 2:647.

19. *Philosophy and Opinions of Marcus Garvey,* ed. Amy Jacques Garvey (New York: Atheneum, 1974 [1923]), 1:10.

20. Peter Goldman, *Report from Black America* (New York: Simon and Schuster, 1971), 29.

21. Representative encapsulations of these concepts may be found in Stokely Carmichael and Charles V. Hamilton, *Black Power: The Politics of Liberation in America* (New York: Random House, 1967), 44–47; Richard C. Tolbert, "A New Brand of Black Nationalism," *Negro Digest* 16 (August 1967): 20–23; Solomon P. Gethers, "Black Power: Three Years Later," *Negro Digest* 19 (December 1969): 4–10, 69–81.

22. For representative statements affirming the need for black cultural self-definition, see James Turner, "The Sociology of Black Nationalism," *Black Scholar* 1 (December 1969): 18–27; Calvin C. Hernton, *Coming Together: Black Power, White Hatred and Sexual Hang-Ups* (New York: Random House, 1971), 33–37; Alvin F. Poussaint, "A Psychiatrist Looks at Black Power," *Ebony* 24 (March 1969): 142.

23. Stokely Carmichael, "Toward Black Liberation," *Massachusetts Review* 7 (autumn 1966): 639.

Suggestions for Further Reading

Nationalism

Anderson, Benedict. *Imagined Communities: Reflections on the Origin and Spread of Nationalism.* New York: Verso, 1991.

Deutsch, Karl W. *Nationalism and Social Communication: An Inquiry into the Foundations of Nationality.* Cambridge: MIT Press, 1966.

Gellner, Ernest. *Nations and Nationalism.* Ithaca: Cornell University Press, 1983.

Hobsbawm, E. J. *Nations and Nationalism since 1780: Programme, Myth, Reality.* Cambridge: Cambridge University Press, 1992.

Smith, Anthony D. *National Identity.* Reno: University of Nevada Press, 1991.

Pre-Garvey Black Nationalism

Geiss, Imanuel. *The Pan-African Movement: A History of Pan-Africanism in America, Europe and Africa.* New York: Africana, 1974.

Miller, Floyd J. *The Search for a Black Nationality: Black Emigration and Colonization, 1787–1863.* Urbana: University of Illinois Press, 1975.

Moses, Wilson Jeremiah. *The Golden Age of Black Nationalism, 1850–1925.* Hamden, CT: Archon, 1978.

Redkey, Edwin, S. *Black Exodus: Black Nationalist Movements, 1890–1910.* New Haven: Yale University Press, 1969.

Stuckey, Sterling. *Slave Culture: Nationalist Theory and the Foundations of Black America.* New York: Oxford University Press, 1987.

Marcus Garvey

Cronon, E. David. *Black Moses: The Story of Marcus Garvey and the Universal Negro Improvement Association.* Madison: University of Wisconsin Press, 1955.

Lewis, Rupert. *Marcus Garvey: Anti-Colonial Champion.* Trenton, NJ: Africa World Press, 1988.

Martin, Tony. *Race First: The Ideological and Organizational Struggles of Marcus Garvey and the Universal Negro Improvement Association.* Westport, CT: Greenwood, 1976.

Stein, Judith. *The World of Marcus Garvey: Race and Class in Modern Society.* Baton Rouge: Louisiana State University Press, 1986.

Vincent, Theodore G. *Black Power and the Garvey Movement.* Berkeley: Ramparts Press, 1971.

Post-Garvey Black Nationalism

Essien-Udom, E. U. *Black Nationalism: A Search for an Identity in America.* Chicago: University of Chicago Press, 1962.

Hall, Raymond L. *Black Separatism in the United States.* Hanover, NH: University Press of New England, 1978.

Pinkney, Alphonso. *Red, Black, and Green: Black Nationalism in the United States.* Cambridge: Cambridge University Press, 1976.

Van Deburg, William L. *New Day in Babylon: The Black Power Movement and American Culture, 1965–1975.* Chicago: University of Chicago Press, 1992.

Weisbord, Robert G. *Ebony Kinship: Africa, Africans, and the Afro-American.* Westport, CT: Greenwood, 1973.

Bibliographies

Bentley, G. Carter. *Ethnicity and Nationality: A Bibliographic Guide.* Seattle: University of Washington Press, 1981.

Davis, Lenwood G., and Janet L. Sims. *Marcus Garvey: An Annotated Bibliography.* Westport, CT: Greenwood, 1980.

Herod, Agustina, and Charles C. Herod. *Afro-American Nationalism: An Annotated Bibliography of Militant Separatist and Nationalist Literature.* New York: Garland, 1986.

Jenkins, Betty Lanier, and Susan Phillis. *Black Separatism: A Bibliography.* Westport, CT: Greenwood, 1976.

Williams, Michael W. *Pan-Africanism: An Annotated Bibliography.* Pasadena, CA: Salem Press, 1992.

PART ONE

*Foundations of Modern
Black Nationalism*

1 Marcus Garvey and the Universal Negro Improvement Association

Consisting of a preamble, twelve causes for complaint, and a list of fifty-four specific demands, the Declaration of Rights of the Negro Peoples of the World was the chief policy statement produced at the first of the Universal Negro Improvement Association's (UNIA) annual conventions. Adopted on 13 August 1920, following a series of reports on injustices prevailing throughout the black world, the document was signed by 122 delegates and observers. Thereafter, it was reproduced periodically in the association's official news organ, the *Negro World*. Elements of the declaration—which was described as the Magna Carta of the race—also appeared in the *Universal Negro Catechism*. To Marcus Garvey, the document was "the property of every Negro in every corner of the world" and left no doubt as to the determination of race-conscious blacks to preserve their "manhood rights . . . at all costs." Pan-African in its conceptualization and scope, the declaration reflected an interesting mix of nationalistic and universal concerns. Demonstrating that black separatism was consonant with the ongoing African American struggle for civil rights, it provided the UNIA membership with a nationalist anthem (Article 40), a flag (Article 39), and a rationale for protesting post–World War I public policy decisions such as the League of Nations' mandate assigning oversight of the former German colonies in Africa to France and Great Britain (Articles 15 and 45). The text reproduced here is from *Philosophy and Opinions of Marcus Garvey*, vol. 2, ed. Amy Jacques Garvey (New York: Universal Publishing House, 1925; reprint, New York: Atheneum, 1974), by permission.

1920 Declaration of Rights of the Negro Peoples of the World

Universal Negro Improvement Association

Be it Resolved, That the Negro people of the world, through their chosen representatives in convention assembléd in Liberty Hall, in the City of New York and United States of America, from August 1 to August 31, in the year of our Lord, one thousand nine hundred and twenty, protest against the wrongs and injustices they are suffering at the hands of their white brethren, and state what they deem their fair and just rights, as well as the treatment they propose to demand of all men in the future.

We complain:

I. That nowhere in the world, with few exceptions, are black men accorded equal treatment with white men, although in the same situation and circumstances, but, on the contrary, are discriminated against and denied the common rights due to human beings for no other reason than their race and color.

We are not willingly accepted as guests in the public hotels and inns of the world for no other reason than our race and color.

II. In certain parts of the United States of America our race is denied the right of public trial accorded to other races when accused of crime, but are lynched and burned by mobs, and such brutal and inhuman treatment is even practised upon our women.

III. That European nations have parcelled out among themselves and taken possession of nearly all of the continent of Africa, and the natives are compelled to surrender their lands to aliens and are treated in most instances like slaves.

IV. In the southern portion of the United States of America, although citizens under the Federal Constitution, and in some states almost equal to the whites in population and are qualified land owners and taxpayers, we are, nevertheless, denied all voice in the making and administration of the laws and are taxed without representation by the state governments, and at the same time compelled to do military service in defense of the country.

V. On the public conveyances and common carriers in the Southern portion of the United States we are jim-crowed and compelled to accept separate and inferior accommodations and made to pay the same fare charged for first-class accommodations, and our families are often humiliated and insulted by drunken white men who habitually pass through the jim-crow cars going to the smoking car.

VI. The physicians of our race are denied the right to attend their patients while in the public hospitals of the cities and states where they reside in certain parts of the United States.

Our children are forced to attend inferior separate schools for shorter terms than white children, and the public school funds are unequally divided between the white and colored schools.

VII. We are discriminated against and denied an equal chance to earn wages for the support of our families, and in many instances are refused admission into labor unions, and nearly everywhere are paid smaller wages than white men.

VIII. In Civil Service and departmental offices we are everywhere discriminated against and made to feel that to be a black man in Europe, America and the West Indies is equivalent to being an outcast and a leper among the races of men, no matter what the character and attainments of the black man may be.

IX. In the British and other West Indian Islands and colonies, Negroes are secretly and cunningly discriminated against, and denied those fuller rights in government to which white citizens are appointed, nominated and elected.

X. That our people in those parts are forced to work for lower wages than the average standard of white men and are kept in conditions repugnant to good civilized tastes and customs.

XI. That the many acts of injustice against members of our race before the courts of law in the respective islands and colonies are of such nature as to create disgust and disrespect for the white man's sense of justice.

XII. Against all such inhuman, unchristian and uncivilized treatment we here and now emphatically protest, and invoke the condemnation of all mankind.

In order to encourage our race all over the world and to stimulate it to a higher and grander destiny, we demand and insist on the following Declaration of Rights:

1. Be it known to all men that whereas, all men are created equal and entitled to the rights of life, liberty and the pursuit of happiness, and because of this we, the duly elected representatives of the Negro peoples of the world, invoking the aid of the just and Almighty God do declare all men women and children of our blood throughout the world free citizens, and do claim them as free citizens of Africa, the Motherland of all Negroes.

2. That we believe in the supreme authority of our race in all things racial; that all things are created and given to man as a common possession; that there should be an equitable distribution and apportionment of all such things, and in consideration of the fact that as a race we are now deprived of those things that are morally and legally ours, we believe it right that all such things should be acquired and held by whatsoever means possible.

3. That we believe the Negro, like any other race, should be governed by the ethics of civilization, and, therefore, should not be deprived of any of those rights or privileges common to other human beings.

4. We declare that Negroes, wheresoever they form a community among themselves, should be given the right to elect their own representatives to represent them in legislatures, courts of law, or such institutions as may exercise control over that particular community.

5. We assert that the Negro is entitled to even-handed justice before all courts of law and equity in whatever country he may be found, and when this is denied him on account of his race or color such denial is an insult to the race as a whole and should be resented by the entire body of Negroes.

6. We declare it unfair and prejudicial to the rights of Negroes in communities where they exist in considerable numbers to be tried by a judge and jury composed entirely of an alien race, but in all such cases members of our race are entitled to representation on the jury.

7. We believe that any law or practice that tends to deprive any African of his land or the privileges of free citizenship within his country is unjust and immoral, and no native should respect any such law or practice.

8. We declare taxation without representation unjust and tyrannous, and there should be no obligation on the part of the Negro to obey the levy of a tax by any law-making body from which he is excluded and denied representation on account of his race and color.

9. We believe that any law especially directed against the Negro to his detriment and singling him out because of his race or color is unfair and immoral, and should not be respected.

10. We believe all men entitled to common human respect, and that our race should in no way tolerate any insults that may be interpreted to mean disrespect to our color.

11. We deprecate the use of the term "nigger" as applied to Negroes, and demand that the word 'Negro' be written with a capital "N".

12. We believe that the Negro should adopt every means to protect himself against barbarous practices inflicted upon him because of color.

13. We believe in the freedom of Africa for the Negro people of the world, and by the principle of Europe for the Europeans and Asia for the Asiatics; we also demand Africa for the Africans at home and abroad.

14. We believe in the inherent right of the Negro to possess himself of Africa, and that his possession of same shall not be regarded as an infringement on any claim or purchase made by any race or nation.

15. We strongly condemn the cupidity of those nations of the world who, by open aggression or secret schemes, have seized the territories and inexhaustible natural wealth of Africa, and we place on record our most solemn determination to reclaim the treasures and possession of the vast continent of our forefathers.

16. We believe all men should live in peace one with the other, but when races and nations provoke the ire of other races and nations by attempting to infringe upon their rights, war becomes inevitable, and the attempt in any way to free one's self or protect one's rights or heritage becomes justifiable.

17. Whereas, the lynching, by burning, hanging or any other means, of human beings is a barbarous practice, and a shame and disgrace to civilization, we therefore declare any country guilty of such atrocities outside the pale of civilization.

18. We protest against the atrocious crime of whipping, flogging and overworking of the native tribes of Africa and Negroes everywhere. These are methods that should be abolished, and all means should be taken to prevent a continuance of such brutal practices.

19. We protest against the atrocious practice of shaving the heads of Africans, especially of African women or individuals of Negro blood, when placed in prison as a punishment for crime by an alien race.

20. We protest against segregated districts, separate public conveyances, industrial discrimination, lynchings and limitations of political privileges of any Negro citizen in any part of the world on account of race, color or creed, and will exert our full influence and power against all such.

21. We protest against any punishment inflicted upon a Negro with severity, as against lighter punishment inflicted upon another of an alien race for like offense, as an act of prejudice and injustice, and should be resented by the entire race.

22. We protest against the system of education in any country where Negroes are denied the same privileges and advantages as other races.

23. We declare it inhuman and unfair to boycott Negroes from industries and labor in any part of the world.

24. We believe in the doctrine of the freedom of the press, and we therefore emphatically protest against the suppression of Negro newspapers and periodicals in various parts of the world, and call upon Negroes everywhere to employ all available means to prevent such suppression.

25. We further demand free speech universally for all men.

26. We hereby protest against the publication of scandalous and inflammatory articles by an alien press tending to create racial strife and the exhibition of picture films showing the Negro as a cannibal.

27. We believe in the self-determination of all peoples.

28. We declare for the freedom of religious worship.

29. With the help of Almighty God, we declare ourselves the sworn protectors of the honor and virtue of our women and children, and pledge our lives for their protection and defense everywhere, and under all circumstances from wrongs and outrages.

30. We demand the right of unlimited and unprejudiced education for ourselves and our posterity forever.

31. We declare that the teaching in any school by alien teachers to our boys and girls, that the alien race is superior to the Negro race, is an insult to the Negro people of the world.

32. Where Negroes form a part of the citizenry of any country, and pass the civil service examination of such country, we declare them entitled to the same consideration as other citizens as to appointments in such civil service.

33. We vigorously protest against the increasingly unfair and unjust treatment accorded Negro travelers on land and sea by the agents and employees of railroad and steamship companies and insist that for equal fare we receive equal privileges with travelers of other races.

34. We declare it unjust for any country, State or nation to enact laws tending to hinder and obstruct the free immigration of Negroes on account of their race and color.

35. That the right of the Negro to travel unmolested throughout the world be not abridged by any person or persons, and all Negroes are called upon to give aid to a fellow Negro when thus molested.

36. We declare that all Negroes are entitled to the same right to travel over the world as other men.

37. We hereby demand that the governments of the world recognize our leader and his representatives chosen by the race to look after the welfare of our people under such governments.

38. We demand complete control of our social institutions without interference by any alien race or races.

39. That the colors, Red, Black and Green, be the colors of the Negro race.

40. Resolved, That the anthem 'Ethiopia, Thou Land of Our Fathers,' etc., shall be the anthem of the Negro race.

The Universal Ethiopian Anthem
(Poem by Burrell and Ford.)

I

Ethiopia, thou land of our fathers,
Thou land where the gods loved to be,
As storm cloud at night suddenly gathers
Our armies come rushing to thee.
We must in the fight be victorious
When swords are thrust outward to gleam;

For us will the vict'ry be glorious
When led by the red, black and green.

Chorus

Advance, advance to victory,
Let Africa be free;
Advance to meet the foe
With the might
Of the red, the black and the green.

II

Ethiopia, the tyrant's falling,
Who smote thee upon thy knees,
And thy children are lustily calling
From over the distant seas.
Jehovah, the Great One has heard us,
Has noted our sighs and our tears,
With His spirit of Love he has stirred us
To be One through the coming years.

CHORUS —Advance, advance, etc.

III

O Jehovah, thou God of the ages
Grant unto our sons that lead
The wisdom Thou gave to Thy sages
When Israel was sore in need.
Thy voice thro' the dim past has spoken,
Ethiopia shall stretch forth her hand,
By Thee shall all fetters be broken,
And Heav'n bless our dear fatherland.

CHORUS —Advance, advance, etc.

41. We believe that any limited liberty which deprives one of the complete rights and prerogatives of full citizenship is but a modified form of slavery.

42. We declare it an injustice to our people and a serious impediment to the health of the race to deny to competent licensed Negro physicians the right to practise in the public hospitals of the communities in which they reside, for no other reason than their race and color.

43. We call upon the various governments of the world to accept and acknowledge Negro representatives who shall be sent to the said governments to represent the general welfare of the Negro peoples of the world.

44. We deplore and protest against the practice of confining juvenile prisoners in prisons with adults, and we recommend that such youthful prisoners be taught gainful trades under humane supervision.

45. Be it further resolved, that we as a race of people declare the League of Nations null and void as far as the Negro is concerned, in that it seeks to deprive Negroes of their liberty.

46. We demand of all men to do unto us as we would do unto them, in the name of justice; and we cheerfully accord to all men all the rights we claim herein for ourselves.

47. We declare that no Negro shall engage himself in battle for an alien race without first obtaining the consent of the leader of the Negro people of the world, except in a matter of national self-defense.

48. We protest against the practice of drafting Negroes and sending them to war with alien forces without proper training, and demand in all cases that Negro soldiers be given the same training as the aliens.

49. We demand that instructions given Negro children in schools include the subject of "Negro History," to their benefit.

50. We demand a free and unfettered commercial intercourse with all the Negro people of the world.

51. We declare for the absolute freedom of the seas for all peoples.

52. We demand that our duly accredited representatives be given proper recognition in all leagues, conferences, conventions or courts of international arbitration wherever human rights are discussed.

53. We proclaim the 31st day of August of each year to be an international holiday to be observed by all Negroes.

54. We want all men to know we shall maintain and contend for the freedom and equality of every man, woman and child of our race, with our lives, our fortunes and our sacred honor.

These rights we believe to be justly ours and proper for the protection of the Negro race at large, and because of this belief we, on behalf of the four hundred million Negroes of the world, do pledge herein the sacred blood of the race in defense, and we hereby subscribe our names as a guarantee of the truthfulness and faithfulness hereof in the presence of Almighty God on the 13th day of August, in the year of our Lord one thousand nine hundred and twenty.

2 Federal Surveillance of "Negro Agitators"

During World War I, the Justice Department's Bureau of Investigation, the forerunner of the FBI, initiated surveillance activities in order to ascertain African American attitudes toward the draft and to investigate rumors of subversion. The "Red Scare" of the immediate postwar years encouraged the belief that bolshevism was spreading rapidly within urban centers—perhaps accounting for the race riots that shook dozens of U.S. cities in 1917 and 1919.

In this letter, J. Edgar Hoover, the twenty-four-year-old chief of the Justice Department's General Intelligence Division, communicates his belief that black nationalism—in the person of Marcus Garvey—was creating a bit too much "excitement" for such troubled times. As a result, the UNIA became the focus of extensive federal surveillance and infiltration activities. Reflecting the acute paranoia that surfaced whenever the future (1924–72) FBI director encountered "Negro agitators," Hoover tried unsuccessfully to prove that Garvey was a foreign agent and a white slaver. Finally, in 1923, he secured the mail fraud indictment that led to the black leader's imprisonment and eventual deportation. The letter is reprinted from Ward Churchill and Jim Vander Wall, eds., *The COINTELPRO Papers: Documents from the FBI's Secret Wars against Domestic Dissent* (Boston: South End Press, 1990), by permission.

1919 **Memorandum to Special Agent Ridgely**

J. Edgar Hoover

Department of Justice,
Washington, D.C. October 11, 1919.

Memorandum for Mr. Ridgely

I am transmitting herewith a communication which has come to my attention from the Panama Canal, Washington office, relative to the activities of MARCUS GARVEY. Garvey is a West-Indian negro and in addition to his activities in endeavoring to establish the Black Star Line Steamship Corporation he has also been particularly active among the radical elements in New York City in agitating the negro movement. Unfortunately, however, he has not as yet violated any federal law whereby he could be proceeded against on the grounds of being an undesirable alien, from the point of view of deportation. It occurs to me, however, from the attached clipping that there might be some proceeding against him for fraud in connection with his Black Star Line propaganda and for this reason I am transmitting the communication to you for your appropriate attention.

The following is a brief statement of Marcus Garvey and his activities;
Subject a native of the West Indies and one of the most prominent negro agitators in New York;
He is a founder of the Universal Negro Improvement Association and African Communities League;
He is the promulgator of the Black Star Line and is the managing editor of the Negro World;
He is an exceptionally fine orator, creating much excitement among the negroes through his steamship proposition;
In his paper the "Negro World" the Soviet Russian Rule is upheld and there is open advocation of Bolshevism.

Respectfully,
J.E. Hoover

3 Cyril Briggs and the African Blood Brotherhood

Founded in 1919 by Cyril V. Briggs, a native of St. Kitts whose controversial notions about establishing a "colored autonomous State" in the American West had cost him his job as associate editor of New York's *Amsterdam News,* the African Blood Brotherhood (ABB) was a tight-knit "revolutionary secret Order" which possessed both fraternal and paramilitary characteristics. Organized through a system of "posts" located throughout the black world, the brotherhood alternately courted and sparred with members of Marcus Garvey's UNIA. Attractive to African Americans with socialist leanings and a desire to promote armed self-defense, the organization peaked in the early 1920s with a dues-paying membership approaching seven thousand. As "paramount chief" of the supreme executive council, Briggs moved the ABB ever closer to a sympathetic alliance with American communists. This was accomplished in 1924–25 as the brotherhood was dissolved and replaced by the American Negro Labor Congress with Briggs as its national secretary. In 1929, Briggs was elected to the central executive committee of the Communist Party of the United States (CPUSA), which, ten years later, expelled the black leader because of his "Negro nationalist way of thinking." He rejoined the party in 1948 and was active in its West Coast initiatives until his death at the age of seventy-eight in 1966.

In the first selection from the ABB's monthly journal, the *Crusader,* Briggs outlines the group's organizational structure and hoped-for role in effecting "the redemption of the Negro race." Clearly stated is his willingness to embrace major tenets of both nationalist ("patronize race enterprises"; "kill the caste idea") and leftist ("don't mind being called 'Bolsheviki' "; "make the cause of other oppressed peoples your cause") ideologies. Nevertheless, as the second selection from Briggs's magazine reveals, members of the pioneering left-wing black nationalist organization possessed a sense of "race patriotism" that would not be diluted through "alien education" of any kind. The documents are reprinted from the June 1920 and September 1918 issues of the *Crusader,* by permission.

1920 The African Blood Brotherhood

Cyril V. Briggs

The African Blood Brotherhood is probably the first Negro *secret* organization to be effected in the Western world, having as its sole purpose the liberation of Africa and the redemption of the Negro race.

The organization now numbers over 1,000 men and women of African blood. It is confined to persons of African blood. Its organization has been carried out along lines similar to secret fraternal orders and societies. It has a ritual of its own, with degrees, pass-words, signs, etc., and a formal initiation ceremony when a solemn oath is taken. Membership is at present by voluntary enlistment, subject to acceptance or rejection at the discretion of the body. Appropriate regalias and uniforms are under consideration. Post commands have been established in various cities of the United States, in the West Indies, Central and South America and in West Africa.

The government of the African Blood Brotherhood is by a supreme council or war college of five, which controls the appointment and tenure of office of the commanders of the various posts and formulates the policies and directs the activities and movements of the organization. There are two sets of other officers—the secretaries, treasurers, chaplains, etc., of the various posts, and the international officers. These are all elected by the members, with all members participating in the election of the international officers. These officers are subject to the rulings and decrees of the supreme council or war college.

Under the rules of the organization, the word of the council, when issued in the form of "instructions," must be considered as law by the members of the brotherhood. When issued in the form of "suggestions" it is expected to command at least respectful and careful consideration.

There are at present no stipulated fees or membership dues. These are left to the patriotism and financial ability of each member. As not enough money could be raised for the work the brotherhood has in view, by the medium of fees and dues, unless these were made so large as to be prohibitive to the great mass of the race, the expedient was adopted of allowing each member to fix his own dues, by pledging himself a monthly donation. This amount may be 25 cents a month, 50 cents, one dollar or whatever sum the individual can give under the patriotic rule of "Give till it hurts."

Two-thirds of all donations are allocated to the war chest as a central fund for general operations of the organization. The other one-third is placed at the disposal of the post through which it was received, to be used, within the rulings of the war college, for the work of local training in the essential industries, in science, etc.

The following "suggestions" have been issued for the guidance of members and for the race in general:

Affiliate yourself with the liberal, radical and labor movements. Don't mind being called "Bolsheviki" by the same people who call you "nigger." Such affiliation in itself won't solve our problems, but it will help immensely.

Patronize race enterprises and study the cooperative spirit. But discriminate between good and bad, honest and dishonest enterprises.

Encourage the Universal Negro Improvement Association movement as the biggest thing so far effected in surface movements.

Reject all allegiance that carries no corresponding rights and privileges, and remember that such rights and privileges should always precede allegiance and patriotism.

Make the cause of other oppressed peoples your cause, that they may respond in kind, and so make possible effective co-ordination in one big blow against tyranny.

Find possibilities for the study of modern warfare, aeronautics and the artillery branch in particular.

Learn a trade. Get into the essential industries where possible. Study modern agricultural methods, horticulture, medicine, chemistry, etc. Encourage those studying in any of these lines.

Adopt the policy of race first, without, however, ignoring useful alliances with other groups.

Help propagate the "race first idea" by first studying the subject and then using your knowledge to enlighten your fellows.

Invest in race enterprises, but follow your money with your active, personal interest.

Kill the caste idea. Stop dividing the race into light and dark. Stop harping about West Indians, Southerners, Northerners, and so forth. Let the line of cleavage fall between true Negroes and false Negroes.

Help build up a strong public opinion against the serviles of the race, against ignorance, against immorality and race debasement.

Wage war against the alien education that is being taught our children in the white man's schools. Demand the true facts concerning the grand achievements of the Negro race.

Inculcate race pride in the little ones by instructing them at home in the facts of Negro achievement.

Organize literary clubs for the discussion and study of Negro history and problems.

Ask your ministers to teach race history from the pulpit, in the Sunday schools and lyceums.

Don't leave everything to your officers and leaders. Get into the fight yourself. Do your bit financially, orally and in every possible way.

1918   Race Catechism

(Teach it to the little ones, learn and practise
it yourself)

Cyril V. Briggs

QUESTION: How do you consider yourself in relation to your Race?

ANSWER: I consider myself bound to it by a sentiment which unites all.

QUESTION: What is it?

ANSWER: The sentiment that the Negro Race is of all races the most
favored by the Muses of Music, Poetry and Art, and is possessed of those
qualities of courage, honor and intelligence necessary to the making of
the best manhood and womanhood and the most brilliant development
of the human species.

QUESTION: What are one's duties to the Race?

ANSWER: To love one's Race above one's self and to further the common
interests of all above the private interests of one. To cheerfully sacrifice
wealth, ease, luxuries, necessities and, if need be, life itself to attain for
the Race that greatness in arms, in commerce, in art, the three combined
without which there is neither respect, honor nor security.

QUESTION: How can you further the interests of the Race?

ANSWER: By spreading Race Patriotism among my fellows; by unfolding
the annals of our glorious deeds and the facts of the noble origin,
splendid achievements and ancient cultures of the Negro Race to those
whom Alien Education has kept in ignorance of these things; by combatting the insidious, mischievous and false teachings of school histories
that exalt the white man and debase the Negro, that tell of the white
man's achievements but not of his ignominy while relating only that part
of the Negro's story that pertains to his temporary enslavement and
partial decadence; by helping Race industries in preference to all others;
by encouraging Race enterprise and business to the ends of an ultimate
creation of wealth, employment and financial strength within the Race;
by so carrying myself as to demand honor and respect for my Race.

QUESTION: Why are you proud of your race?

ANSWER: Because in the veins of no human being does there flow more generous blood than in our own; in the annals of the world the history of no race is more resplendent with honest, worthy glory than that of the Negro Race, members of which founded the first beginning of civilization upon the banks of the Nile, developing it and extending it southward to Ethiopia and westward over the smiling Sudan to the distant Atlantic, so that the Greeks who came to learn from our fathers declared that they were "the most just of men, the favorites of the gods".

4   W. E. B. Du Bois and Pan-Africanism

Believing fervently that black people were destined to make a significant and lasting contribution to world history, Harvard-educated scholar and activist W. E. B. Du Bois played an important role in linking long-separated diaspora communities in common cause. Between 1919 and 1927, he convened four Pan-African Congresses (1919, Paris; 1921, London, Brussels, and Paris; 1923, London and Lisbon; 1927, New York). Here, an international assembly of intellectuals, politicians, and other "race leaders" called for "the development of Africa for the Africans and not merely for the profit of Europeans." Du Bois's determined anti-imperialist stance and his unequivocal demand for recognition of "the absolute equality of races,—physical, political and social" make him a key figure in the evolution of Pan-Africanist conceptualizations of national liberation. Just prior to his death at the age of ninety-five, the former Atlanta University professor and longtime editor of the NAACP's *Crisis* became a citizen of Ghana. He was honored by a state funeral and buried in Accra in 1963.

Du Bois's "Manifesto" is reprinted from the *Crisis* (November 1921), by permission. It was adopted by the Second Pan-African Congress in 1921 and provided the intellectual and ideological framework for a petition that he later presented to the League of Nations in Geneva. As conference participant Jessie Fauset noted, those in attendance considered Du Bois's resolutions "bold and glorious . . . couched in winged, unambiguous words." Upon their approval, she wrote, the American representatives "clasped hands with our newly found brethren and departed, feeling that it was good to be alive and most wonderful to be colored. Not one of us but envisaged in his heart the dawn of a day of new and perfect African brotherhood."

A similar sense of ecstasy is evident in the second selection, as Du Bois describes his first trip to Africa. Here, the black intellectual is nearly overwhelmed by emotion. "I'm all impatience," he writes in anticipation of visiting the land of his "stolen forefathers." The roseate picture he subsequently draws of Liberia testifies to the potency of the "spell" the continent is capable of casting on receptive Pan-Africanists. The document is excerpted from W. E. B. Du Bois, "Africa," *Crisis* (April 1924), by permission.

1921　To the World

(Manifesto of the Second Pan-African Congress)

W. E. B. Du Bois

The absolute equality of races,—physical, political and social—is the founding stone of world peace and human advancement. No one denies great differences of gift, capacity and attainment among individuals of all races, but the voice of science, religion and practical politics is one in denying the God-appointed existence of super-races, or of races naturally and inevitably and eternally inferior.

That in the vast range of time, one group should in its industrial technique, or social organization, or spiritual vision, lag a few hundred years behind another, or forge fitfully ahead, or come to differ decidedly in thought, deed and ideal, is proof of the essential richness and variety of human nature, rather than proof of the co-existence of demi-gods and apes in human form. The doctrine of racial equality does not interfere with individual liberty, rather, it fulfils it. And of all the various criteria by which masses of men have in the past been prejudged and classified, that of the color of the skin and texture of the hair, is surely the most adventitious and idiotic.

It is the duty of the world to assist in every way the advance of the backward and suppressed groups of mankind. The rise of all men is a menace to no one and is the highest human ideal; it is not an altruistic benevolence, but the one road to world salvation.

For the purpose of raising such peoples to intelligence, self-knowledge and self-control, their intelligentsia of right ought to be recognized as the natural leaders of their groups.

The insidious and dishonorable propaganda, which, for selfish ends, so distorts and denies facts as to represent the advancement and development of certain races of men as impossible and undesirable, should be met with widespread dissemination of the truth. The experiment of making the Negro slave a free citizen in the United States is not a failure; the attempts at autonomous government in Haiti and Liberia are not proofs of the impossibility of self-government among black men; the experience of Spanish America does not prove that mulatto democracy will not eventually succeed there; the aspirations of Egypt and India are not successfully to be met by sneers at the capacity of darker races.

We who resent the attempt to treat civilized men as uncivilized, and who bring in our hearts grievance upon grievance against those who lynch the untried, disfranchise the intelligent, deny self-government to educated men, and insult the helpless, we complain; but not simply or primarily for ourselves—more especially for the millions of our fellows, blood of our blood, and flesh of our flesh, who have not even what we have—the power to complain against monstrous wrong, the power to see and to know the source of our oppression.

How far the future advance of mankind will depend upon the social contact and physical intermixture of the various strains of human blood is unknown, but the demand for the interpenetration of countries and intermingling of blood has come, in modern days, from the white race alone, and has been imposed upon brown and black folks mainly by brute force and fraud. On top of this, the resulting people of mixed race have had to endure innuendo, persecution, and insult, and the penetrated countries have been forced into semi-slavery.

If it be proven that absolute world segregation by group, color or historic affinity is best for the future, let the white race leave the dark world and the darker races will gladly leave the white. But the proposition is absurd. This is a world of men, of men whose likenesses far outweigh their differences; who mutually need each other in labor and thought and dream, but who can successfully have each other only on terms of equality, justice and mutual respect. They are the real and only peacemakers who work sincerely and peacefully to this end.

The beginning of wisdom in interracial contact is the establishment of political institutions among suppressed peoples. The habit of democracy must be made to encircle the earth. Despite the attempt to prove that its practice is the secret and divine gift of the few, no habit is more natural or more widely spread among primitive people, or more easily capable of development among masses. Local self-government with a minimum of help and oversight can be established tomorrow in Asia, in Africa, in America and in the Isles of the Sea. It will in many instances need general control and guidance, but it will fail only when that guidance seeks ignorantly and consciously its own selfish ends and not the people's liberty and good.

Surely in the 20th century of the Prince of Peace, in the millennium of Buddha and Mahmoud, and in the mightiest Age of Human Reason, there can be found in the civilized world enough of altruism, learning and benevolence to develop native institutions for the native's good, rather than continue to allow the majority of mankind to be brutalized and enslaved by ignorant and selfish agents of commercial institutions, whose one aim is profit and power for the few.

And this brings us to the crux of the matter: It is the shame of the world that today the relation between the main groups of mankind and their mutual estimate and respect is determined chiefly by the degree in which one can subject the other to its service, enslaving labor, making ignorance compulsory, uprooting ruthlessly religion and customs, and destroying government, so that the favored Few may luxuriate in the toil of the tortured Many. Science, Religion and Philanthropy have thus been made the slaves of world commerce and industry, and bodies, minds, souls of Fiji and Congo, are judged almost solely by the quotations on the Bourse.

The day of such world organization is past and whatever excuse be made for it in other ages, the 20th century must come to judge men as men and not as material and labor.

The great industrial problem which has hitherto been regarded as the domestic problem of culture lands, must be viewed far more broadly, if it is ever to reach just settlement. Labor and capital in England, France and America can never solve their problem as long as a similar and vastly greater problem of poverty and injustice marks the relations of the whiter and darker peoples. It is shameful, unreligious, unscientific and undemocratic that the estimate, which half the peoples of earth put on the other half, depends mainly on their ability to squeeze profit out of them.

If we are coming to recognize that the great modern problem is to correct maladjustment in the distribution of wealth, it must be remembered that the basic maladjustment is in the outrageously unjust distribution of world income between the dominant and suppressed peoples; in the rape of land and raw material, and monopoly of technique and culture. And in this crime white labor is *particeps criminis* with white capital. Unconsciously and consciously, carelessly and deliberately, the vast power of the white labor vote in modern democracies has been cajoled and flattered into imperialistic schemes to enslave and debauch black, brown and yellow labor, until with fatal retribution, they are themselves today bound and gagged and rendered impotent by the resulting monopoly of the world's raw material in the hands of a dominant, cruel and irresponsible few.

And, too, just as curiously, the educated and cultured of the world, the well-born and well-bred, and even the deeply pious and philanthropic, receive their training and comfort and luxury, the ministrations of delicate beauty and sensibility, on condition that they neither inquire into the real source of their income and the methods of distribution or

To the World (Manifesto of the Second Pan-African Congress)   43

interfere with the legal props which rest on a pitiful human foundation of writhing white and yellow and brown and black bodies.

We claim no perfectness of our own nor do we seek to escape the blame which of right falls on the backward for failure to advance, but *noblesse oblige,* and we arraign civilization and more especially the colonial powers for deliberate transgressions of our just demands and their own better conscience.

England, with her Pax Britannica, her courts of justice, established commerce and a certain apparent recognition of native law and customs, has nevertheless systematically fostered ignorance among the natives, has enslaved them and is still enslaving some of them, has usually declined even to try to train black and brown men in real self-government, to recognize civilized black folks as civilized, or to grant to colored colonies those rights of self-government which it freely gives to white men.

Belgium is a nation which has but recently assumed responsibility for her colonies, and has taken some steps to lift them from the worst abuses of the autocratic regime; but she has not confirmed to the people the possession of their land and labor, and she shows no disposition to allow the natives any voice in their own government, or to provide for their political future. Her colonial policy is still mainly dominated by the banks and great corporations. But we are glad to learn that the present government is considering a liberal program of reform for the future.

Portugal and Spain have never drawn a legal caste line against persons of culture who happen to be of Negro descent. Portugal has a humane code for the natives and has begun their education in some regions. But, unfortunately, the industrial concessions of Portuguese Africa are almost wholly in the hands of foreigners whom Portugal cannot or will not control, and who are exploiting land and re-establishing the African slave trade.

The United States of America after brutally enslaving millions of black folks suddenly emancipated them and began their education; but it acted without system or forethought, throwing the freed men upon the world penniless and landless, educating them without thoroughness and system, and subjecting them the while to lynching, lawlessness, discrimination, insult and slander, such as human beings have seldom endured and survived. To save their own government, they enfranchised the Negro and then when danger passed, allowed hundreds of thousands of educated and civilized black folk to be lawlessly disfranchised and subjected to a caste system; and, at the same time, in 1776, 1812, 1861, 1897, and 1917, they asked and allowed thousands of black men to offer up their lives as a sacrifice to the country which despised and despises them.

France alone of the great colonial powers has sought to place her cultured black citizens on a plane of absolute legal and social equality with her white and given them representation in her highest legislature. In her colonies she has a widespread but still imperfect system of state education. This splendid beginning must be completed by widening the political basis of her native government, by restoring to the indigenes the ownership of the soil, by protecting native labor against the aggression of established capital, and by asking no man, black or white, to be a soldier unless the country gives him a voice in his own government.

The independence of Abyssinia, Liberia, Haiti and San Domingo, is absolutely necessary to any sustained belief of the black folk in the sincerity and honesty of the white. These nations have earned the right to be free, they deserve the recognition of the world; notwithstanding all their faults and mistakes, and the fact that they are behind the most advanced civilization of the day, nevertheless they compare favorably with the past, and even more recent, history of most European nations, and it shames civilization that the treaty of London practically invited Italy to aggression in Abyssinia, and that free America has unjustly and cruelly seized Haiti, murdered and for a time enslaved her workmen, overthrown her free institutions by force, and has so far failed in return to give her a single bit of help, aid or sympathy.

What do those wish who see these evils of the color line and racial discrimination and who believe in the divine right of suppressed and backward peoples to learn and aspire and be free?

The Negro race through its thinking intelligentsia is demanding:

I—The recognition of civilized men as civilized despite their race or color

II—Local self government for backward groups, deliberately rising as experience and knowledge grow to complete self government under the limitations of a self governed world

III—Education in self knowledge, in scientific truth and in industrial technique, undivorced from the art of beauty

IV—Freedom in their own religion and social customs, and with the right to be different and non-conformist

V—Co-operation with the rest of the world in government, industry and art on the basis of Justice, Freedom and Peace

To the World (Manifesto of the Second Pan-African Congress)   45

VI—The ancient common ownership of the land and its natural fruits and defence against the unrestrained greed of invested capital

VII—The establishment under the League of Nations of an international institution for the study of Negro problems

VIII—The establishment of an international section in the Labor Bureau of the League of Nations, charged with the protection of native labor.

The world must face two eventualities: either the complete assimilation of Africa with two or three of the great world states, with political, civil and social power and privileges absolutely equal for its black and white citizens, or the rise of a great black African state founded in Peace and Good Will, based on popular education, natural art and industry and freedom of trade; autonomous and sovereign in its internal policy, but from its beginning a part of a great society of peoples in which it takes its place with others as co-rulers of the world.

In some such words and thoughts as these we seek to express our will and ideal, and the end of our untiring effort. To our aid we call all men of the Earth who love Justice and Mercy. Out of the depths we have cried unto the deaf and dumb masters of the world. Out of the depths we cry to our own sleeping souls.

The answer is written in the stars.

1924 *From* **Africa**

W. E. B. Du Bois

December 20

It is Thursday. Day after tomorrow I shall put my feet on the soil of
Africa. As yet I have seen no land, but last night I wired to Monrovia by
way of Dakar—"President King—Monrovia—Arrive Saturday, *Hen-
ner*—DuBois." I wonder what it all will be like? Meantime it's getting
hot—*hot,* and I've put on all the summer things I've got.

December 20

Tonight the sun, a dull gold ball, strange shaped and rayless sank before
a purple sky into a bright green and sinking turned the sky to violet blue
and grey and the sea turned dark. But the sun itself blushed from gold
to shadowed burning crimson, then to red. The sky above, blue-green;
the waters blackened and then the sun did not set—it died and was not.
And behind gleamed the pale silver of the moon across the pink efful-
gence of the clouds.

December 21

Tomorrow—Africa! Inconceivable! As yet no sight of land, but it was
warm and we rigged deck chairs and lay at ease. I have been reading
that old novel of mine—it has points. Twice we've wired Liberia. I'm all
impatience.

December 22

Waiting for the first gleam of Africa. This morning I photographed the
officers and wrote an article on Germany. Then I packed my trunk and
big bag. The step for descending to the boat had been made ready. Now
I read and write and the little boat runs sedately on.

3:22 P.M.—I see Africa—Cape Mount in two low, pale semi-circles,
so pale it looks a cloud. So my great great grandfather saw it two
centuries ago. Clearer and clearer it rises and now land in a long low
line runs to the right and melts dimly into the mist and sea and Cape
Mount begins Liberia—what a citadel for the capital of Negrodom!

When shall I forget the night I first set foot on African soil—I, the sixth generation in descent from my stolen forefathers. The moon was at the full and the waters of the Atlantic lay like a lake. All the long slow afternoon as the sun robed itself in its western scarlet with veils of misty cloud, I had seen Africa afar. Cape Mount—that mighty headland with its twin curves, northern sentinel of the vast realm of Liberia gathered itself out of the cloud at half past three and then darkened and grew clear. On beyond flowed the dark low undulating land quaint with palm and breaking sea. The world darkened. Africa faded away, the stars stood forth curiously twisted—Orion in the zenith—the Little Bear asleep and the Southern Cross rising behind the horizon. Then afar, ahead, a lone light, straight at the ship's fore. Twinkling lights appeared below, around and rising shadows. "Monrovia" said the Captain. Suddenly we swerved to our left. The long arms of the bay enveloped us and then to the right rose the twinkling hill of Monrovia, with its crowning star. Lights flashed on the shore—here, there. Then we sensed a darker shadow in the shadows; it lay very still. "It's a boat," one said. "It's two boats." Then the shadow drifted in pieces and as the anchor roared into the deep five boats outlined themselves on the waters—great ten-oared barges black with men swung into line and glided toward us. I watched them fascinated.

Nine at Night

It was nine at night—above, the shadows, there the town, here the sweeping boats. One forged ahead with the stripes and lone star flaming behind, the ensign of the customs floating wide and bending to the long oars, the white caps of ten black sailors. Up the stairway clambered a soldier in khaki, aide-de-camp of the President of the Republic, a custom house official, the clerk of the American legation—and after them sixty-five lithe, lean black stevedores with whom the steamer would work down to Portuguese Angola and back. A few moments of formalities, greetings and goodbyes and I was in the great long boat with the President's Aide—a brown major in brown khaki. On the other side the young clerk and at the back the black, bare-legged pilot. Before us on the high thwarts were the rowers: men, boys, black, thin, trained in muscle and sinew, little larger than the oars in thickness, they bent their strength to them and swung upon them.

One in the centre gave curious little cackling cries to keep the rhythm, and for the spurts, the stroke, a bit thicker and sturdier, gave a low guttural command now and then and the boat, alive, quivering, danced beneath the moon, swept a great curve to the bar to breast its narrow teeth of foam—"t'chick-a-tickity, t'chik-a-tickity" sang the boys and we glided and raced, now between boats, now near the landing—now oars aloft at the dock. And lo! I was in Africa!

December 25

Christmas eve and Africa is singing in Monrovia. They are Krus and Fanti—men, women and children and all the night they march and sing. The music was once the music of revival hymns. But it is that music now transformed and the silly words hidden in an unknown tongue—liquid and sonorous. It is tricked and expounded with cadence and turn. And this is that same trick I heard first in Tennessee 38 years ago: The air is raised and carried by men's strong voices, while floating above in obligato, come the high mellow voices of women—it is the ancient African art of part singing so curiously and insistently different.

And so they come, gay apparelled, lit by a transparency. They enter the gate and flow over the high steps and sing and sing and sing. They saunter round the house, pick flowers, drink water and sing and sing and sing. The warm dark heat of the night steams up to meet the moon. And the night is song.

Christmas day, 1923. We walk down to the narrow, crooked wharves of Monrovia, by houses old and grey and steps like streets of stone. Before is the wide St. Paul river, double mouthed, and beyond, the sea, white, curling on the sand. Before is the isle—the tiny isle, hut-covered and guarded by a cotton tree, where the pioneers lived in 1921. We circle round—then up the river.

Great bowing trees, festoons of flowers, golden blossoms, star-faced palms and thatched huts; tall spreading trees lifting themselves like vast umbrellas, low shrubbery with grey and laced and knotted roots—the broad, black, murmuring river. Here a tree holds wide fingers out and stretches them over the water in vast incantation; bananas throw their wide green fingers to the sun. Iron villages, scarred clearings with grey, sheet-iron homes staring grim and bare at the ancient tropical flood of green.

The river sweeps wide and the shrubs bow low. Behind, Monrovia rises in clear, calm beauty. Gone are the wharves, the low and clustered houses of the port, the tight-throated business village, and up sweep the villas and the low wall, brown and cream and white, with great mango and cotton tree, with light house and spire, with porch and pillar and the green and color of shrubbery and blossom.

We climbed the upright shore to a senator's home and received his wide and kindly hospitality—curious blend of feudal lord and modern farmer—sandwiches, cake and champagne.

Again we glided up the drowsy river—five, ten, twenty miles and came to our hostess. A mansion of five generations with a compound of endless native servants and cows under the palm thatches. The daughters of the family wore, on the beautiful black skin of their necks, the exquisite pale gold chains of the Liberian artisan and the slim, black little granddaughter of the house had a wide pink ribbon on the thick curls of her dark hair, that lay like sudden sunlight on the shadows. Double porches one above the other, welcomed us to ease. A native man, gay with Christmas and a dash of gin, danced and sang and danced in the road. Children ran and played in the blazing sun. We sat at a long broad table and ate duck, chicken, beef, rice, plantain and collards, cake, tea, water and Madeira wine. Then we went and looked at the heavens, the uptwisted sky—Orion and Cassiopeia at zenith; the Little Bear beneath the horizon, new unfamilar sights in the Milky Way—all awry, a-living—sun for snow at Christmas, and happiness and cheer.

5 Black Nationalism and the Harlem Renaissance

Rejecting the shiftless "coon" persona that was so popular with white audiences, black creative artists of the 1920s worked to create a national network of playwrights, poets, and painters who could capture the essence of "what it means to be colored in America." Striving for authenticity, this Harlem Renaissance or "New Negro" generation looked to the folk tradition and to contemporary issues in black life for their subject matter. They spoke of an end to accommodation and of a new day coming when African Americans would wield power sufficient to invalidate forever white America's presumption of racial supremacy. If more often ideologically wedded to pluralism than to nationalism, the Harlem Renaissance artists' rejection of white formulae, their enthusiastic promotion of black cultural distinctiveness, and their commitment to heightening black self-esteem mirrored the celebration of blackness displayed by many culturally attuned Garveyites. These individuals provided a rich, activist legacy for the cultural nationalists of the 1960s and 1970s.

One such writer was the accomplished and prolific Langston Hughes. In a seminal essay entitled "The Negro Artist and the Racial Mountain," the "poet laureate of Harlem" challenged black creative artists and others imbued with the pluralists' legendary "double consciousness" (the ability to conceive of oneself as being both black and American at the same instant) to glory in their blackness and refuse to "run away spiritually" from their racial heritage.

Taking note of Hughes's pride-filled sentiments, Amy Jacques Garvey—the UNIA president general's second wife, principal aide, and key Garveyite propagandist—elaborated on this "black is beautiful" theme. Adding her own nationalist spin to Hughes's description of the "white is best" mind-set, she termed it a remnant of slavery and urged all UNIA members to shun any ideology that would impede black America's steady advance "to nationhood and to power." The Hughes piece is reprinted from the *Nation,* 23 June 1926, by permission. Garvey's "I Am a Negro—and Beautiful" is reprinted from *Negro World,* 10 July 1926, by permission.

1926 The Negro Artist and the Racial Mountain

Langston Hughes

One of the most promising of the young Negro poets said to me once, "I want to be a poet—not a Negro poet," meaning, I believe, "I want to write like a white poet"; meaning subconsciously, "I would like to be a white poet"; meaning behind that, "I would like to be white." And I was sorry the young man said that, for no great poet has ever been afraid of being himself. And I doubted then that, with his desire to run away spiritually from his race, this boy would ever be a great poet. But this is the mountain standing in the way of any true Negro art in America this urge within the race toward whiteness, the desire to pour racial individuality into the mold of American standardization, and to be as little Negro and as much American as possible.

But let us look at the immediate background of this young poet. His family is of what I suppose one would call the Negro middle class: people who are by no means rich yet never uncomfortable nor hungry—smug, contented, respectable folk, members of the Baptist church. The father goes to work every morning. He is a chief steward at a large white club. The mother sometimes does fancy sewing or supervises parties for the rich families of the town. The children go to a mixed school. In the home they read white papers and magazines. And the mother often says "Don't be like niggers" when the children are bad. A frequent phrase from the father is, "Look how well a white man does things." And so the word white comes to be unconsciously a symbol of all the virtues. It holds for the children beauty, morality, and money. The whisper of "I want to be white" runs silently through their minds. This young poet's home is, I believe, a fairly typical home of the colored middle class. One sees immediately how difficult it would be for an artist born in such a home to interest himself in interpreting the beauty of his own people. He is never taught to see that beauty. He is taught rather not to see it, or if he does, to be ashamed of it when it is not according to Caucasian patterns.

For racial culture the home of a self-styled "high-class" Negro has nothing better to offer. Instead there will perhaps be more aping of things white than in a less cultured or less wealthy home. The father is perhaps a doctor, lawyer, landowner, or politician. The mother may be a social worker, or a teacher, or she may do nothing and have a maid.

Father is often dark but he has usually married the lightest woman he could find. The family attend a fashionable church where few really colored faces are to be found. And they themselves draw a color line. In the North they go to white theaters and white movies. And in the South they have at least two cars and a house "like white folks." Nordic manners, Nordic faces, Nordic hair, Nordic art (if any), and an Episcopal heaven. A very high mountain indeed for the would-be racial artist to climb in order to discover himself and his people.

But then there are the low-down folks, the so-called common element, and they are the majority—may the Lord be praised! The people who have their nip of gin on Saturday nights and are not too important to themselves or the community, or too well fed, or too learned to watch the lazy world go round. They live on Seventh Street in Washington or State Street in Chicago and they do not particularly care whether they are like white folks or anybody else. Their joy runs, bang! into ecstasy. Their religion soars to a shout. Work maybe a little today, rest a little tomorrow. Play awhile. Sing awhile. O, let's dance! These common people are not afraid of spirituals, as for a long time their more intellectual brethren were, and jazz is their child. They furnish a wealth of colorful, distinctive material for any artist because they still hold their own individuality in the face of American standardizations. And perhaps these common people will give to the world its truly great Negro artist, the one who is not afraid to be himself. Whereas the better-class Negro would tell the artist what to do, the people at least let him alone when he does appear. And they are not ashamed of him—if they know he exists at all. And they accept what beauty is their own without question.

Certainly there is, for the American Negro artist who can escape the restrictions the more advanced among his own group would put upon him, a great field of unused material ready for his art. Without going outside his race, and even among the better classes with their "white" culture and conscious American manners, but still Negro enough to be different, there is sufficient matter to furnish a black artist with a lifetime of creative work. And when he chooses to touch on the relations between Negroes and whites in this country with their innumerable overtones and undertones, surely, and especially for literature and the drama, there is an inexhaustible supply of themes at hand. To these the Negro artist can give his racial individuality, his heritage of rhythm and warmth, and his incongruous humor that so often, as in the Blues, becomes ironic laughter mixed with tears. But let us look again at the mountain.

A prominent Negro clubwoman in Philadelphia paid eleven dollars to hear Raquel Meller sing Andalusian popular songs. But she told me a few weeks before she would not think of going to hear "that woman," Clara Smith, a great black artist, sing Negro folksongs. And many an upper-class Negro church, even now, would not dream of employing a spiritual in its services. The drab melodies in white folks' hymnbooks are much to be preferred. "We want to worship the Lord correctly and quietly. We don't believe in 'shouting.' Let's be dull like the Nordics," they say, in effect.

The road for the serious black artist, then, who would produce a racial art is most certainly rocky and the mountain is high. Until recently he received almost no encouragement for his work from either white or colored people. The fine novels of Chesnutt go out of print with neither race noticing their passing. The quaint charm and humor of Dunbar's dialect verse brought to him, in his day, largely the same kind of encouragement one would give a side-show freak (A colored man writing poetry! How odd!) or a clown (How amusing!).

The present vogue in things Negro, although it may do as much harm as good for the budding colored artist, has at least done this: it has brought him forcibly to the attention of his own people among whom for so long, unless the other race had noticed him beforehand, he was a prophet with little honor. I understand that Charles Gilpin acted for years in Negro theaters without any special acclaim from his own, but when Broadway gave him eight curtain calls, Negroes, too, began to beat a tin pan in his honor. I know a young colored writer, a manual worker by day, who had been writing well for the colored magazines for some years, but it was not until he recently broke into the white publications and his first book was accepted by a prominent New York publisher that the "best" Negroes in his city took the trouble to discover that he lived there. Then almost immediately they decided to give a grand dinner for him. But the society ladies were careful to whisper to his mother that perhaps she'd better not come. They were not sure she would have an evening gown.

The Negro artist works against an undertow of sharp criticism and misunderstanding from his own group and unintentional bribes from the whites. "O, be respectable, write about nice people, show how good we are," say the Negroes. "Be stereotyped, don't go too far, don't shatter our illusions about you, don't amuse us too seriously. We will pay you," say the whites. Both would have told Jean Toomer not to write "Cane." The colored people did not praise it. The white people did not buy it.

Most of the colored people who did read "Cane" hate it. They are afraid of it. Although the critics gave it good reviews the public remained indifferent. Yet (excepting the work of Du Bois) "Cane" contains the finest prose written by a Negro in America. And like the singing of Robeson, it is truly racial.

But in spite of the Nordicized Negro intelligentsia and the desires of some white editors we have an honest American Negro literature already with us. Now I await the rise of the Negro theater. Our folk music, having achieved world-wide fame, offers itself to the genius of the great individual American Negro composer who is to come. And within the next decade I expect to see the work of a growing school of colored artists who paint and model the beauty of dark faces and create with new technique the expressions of their own soul-world. And the Negro dancers who will dance like flame and the singers who will continue to carry our songs to all who listen—they will be with us in even greater numbers tomorrow.

Most of my own poems are racial in theme and treatment, derived from the life I know. In many of them I try to grasp and hold some of the meanings and rhythms of jazz. I am sincere as I know how to be in these poems and yet after every reading I answer questions like these from my own people: Do you think Negroes should always write about Negroes? I wish you wouldn't read some of your poems to white folks. How do you find anything interesting in a place like a cabaret? Why do you write about black people? You aren't black. What makes you do so many jazz poems?

But jazz to me is one of the inherent expressions of Negro life in America: the eternal tom-tom beating in the Negro soul—the tom-tom of revolt against weariness in a white world, a world of subway trains, and work, work, work; the tom-tom of joy and laughter, and pain swallowed in a smile. Yet the Philadelphia clubwoman is ashamed to say that her race created it and she does not like me to write about it. The old subconscious "white is best" runs through her mind. Years of study under white teachers, a life-time of white books, pictures, and papers, and white manners, morals, and Puritan standards made her dislike the spirituals. And now she turns up her nose at jazz and all its manifestations—likewise almost everything else distinctly racial. She doesn't care for the Winold Reiss portraits of Negroes because they are "too Negro." She does not want a true picture of herself from anybody. She wants the artist to flatter her, to make the white world believe that all Negroes are as smug and as near white in soul as she wants to be. But, to my mind, it is the duty of the younger Negro artist, if he accepts any duties at all from outsiders, to change through the force of his art that old whispering "I want to be white," hidden in the aspirations of his people, to "Why should I want to be white? I am a Negro—and beautiful!"

So I am ashamed for the black poet who says, "I want to be a poet, not a Negro poet," as though his own racial world were not as interesting as any other world. I am ashamed, too, for the colored artist who runs from the painting of Negro faces to the painting of sunsets after the manner of the academicians because he fears the strange un-whiteness of his own features. An artist must be free to choose what he does, certainly, but he must also never be afraid to do what he might choose.

Let the blare of Negro jazz bands and the bellowing voice of Bessie Smith singing Blues penetrate the closed ears of the colored near-intellectuals until they listen and perhaps understand. Let Paul Robeson singing Water Boy, and Rudolph Fisher writing about the streets of Harlem, and Jean Toomer holding the heart of Georgia in his hands, and Aaron Douglas drawing strange black fantasies cause the smug Negro middle class to turn from their white, respectable, ordinary books and papers to catch a glimmer of their own beauty. We younger Negro artists who create now intend to express our individual dark-skinned selves without fear or shame. If white people are pleased we are glad. If they are not, it doesn't matter. We know we are beautiful. And ugly too. The tom-tom cries and the tom-tom laughs. If colored people are pleased we are glad. If they are not, their displeasure doesn't matter either. We build our temples for tomorrow, strong as we know how, and we stand on top of the mountain, free within ourselves.

1926   I Am a Negro—and Beautiful

Amy Jacques Garvey

Too much cannot be said in denouncing the class of "want-to-be-white" Negroes one finds everywhere. This race destroying group are dissatisfied with their mothers and with their creator—mother is too dark "to pass" and God made a mistake when he made black people. With this fallacy uppermost in their minds, they peel their skins off, and straighten their hair in mad effort to look like their ideal type. To what end, one asks? To the end that they may be admitted to better jobs, moneyed circles, and, in short, share the blessings of the prosperous white race. They are too lazy to help build a prosperous Negro race, but choose the easier route—crossing the racial border. It is the way of the weakling, and in their ignorance and stupidity they advise others to do likewise. As if 400,000,000 Negroes could change their skins over night. And if they could, would they? Seeing that the bulk of Negroes are to be found on the great continent of Africa, and they, thank Heaven, are proud of their black skins and curly hair. The "would-be-white" few are fast disappearing in the Western world, as the entire race, through the preachments of Marcus Garvey, has found its soul, and is out to acquire for itself and its posterity all that makes other races honored and respected.

This urge for whiteness is not just a mental gesture. It is a slavish complex, the remnant of slavery, to look like "Massa," to speak like him, even to cuss and drink like him. In last week's issue of the Nation Magazine, Langston Hughes, a poet, wrote a splendid article on the difficulties facing the Negro artist, in which, he described the racial state of mind of a Philadelphia club woman, which is typical of the group under discussion. He states:

"The old subconscious 'white is best' runs through her mind. Years of study under white teachers, a lifetime of white books, pictures, and papers, and white manners, morals, and Puritan standards made her dislike the spirituals. And now she turns up her nose at jazz and all its manifestations—likewise almost everything else distinctly racial. She doesn't care for the Winold Reiss portraits of Negroes because they are 'too Negro.' She does not want a true picture of herself from anybody. She wants the artist to flatter her, to make the white world believe that all Negroes are as smug and as near white in soul as she wants to be."

We are delighted with the frank statement of Mr. Hughes in a white magazine; we do not know if he is a registered member of the Universal Negro Improvement Association; in any event his closing paragraph marks him as a keen student of Garveyism, and with stamina enough to express its ideals:

"To my mind, it is the duty of the younger Negro artist, if he accepts any duties at all from outsiders, to change through the force of his art that old whispering 'I want to be white,' hidden in the aspirations of his people, to 'Why should I want to be white? I am a Negro—and beautiful!' . . . We younger Negro artists who create now intend to express our individual dark-skinned selves without fear or shame. If white people are pleased we are glad. If they are not, it doesn't matter."

Bravo, Mr. Hughes! From now on under your leadership we expect our artists to express their real souls, and give us art, that is colorful, full of ecstasy, dulcet and even tragic, for has it not been admitted by those who would undervalue us that the Negro is a born artist. Then let the canvas come to life with dark faces; let poetry charm the muses with the hopes and aspirations of our race; let the musicians drown our sorrows with the merry jazz; while a race is in the making, and steadily moving on to nationhood and to power.

Play up, boys, and let the world know "we are Negroes and beautiful."

6   Depression-Era Communists and Self-Determination in the Black Belt

Eager to win the trust of the black masses, guard the "revolutionary integrity" of the Communist Party, and prove conclusively that bigotry was a capitalist trait, white Depression-era communists were careful to police the social attitudes of their comrades. "Chauvinist tendencies" were to be exposed and the delinquent party member suitably chastened by being brought to trial before a workers' jury. In this selection, CPUSA prosecutor Clarence A. Hathaway bolsters the case against one such malefactor—August Yokinen—by restating his organization's support for black self-determination in the American South.

Although critical of Marcus Garvey's back-to-Africa approach to the establishment of a "Negro Zion," American communists recognized the mass appeal of the UNIA's race-conscious nationalist program. In 1928, the Sixth Comintern Congress decreed that African Americans living in the Southern Black Belt constituted a colonized "nation" in need of liberation. As can be seen in the concluding section of Hathaway's remarks, such impassioned appeals often were compromised by the white radicals' assumption that *they*, rather than blacks, would lead the struggle to create an independent Negro Soviet Republic in the South. Striving to be all things to all potential comrades, the CPUSA long continued to advocate proletarian unity even as it treated black self-determination as a "national" question. The selection is taken from the CPUSA pamphlet, *Race Hatred on Trial* (New York: Workers Library, 1931) as reprinted in *American Communism and Black Americans: A Documentary History, 1930-1934*, ed. Philip S. Foner and Herbert Shapiro (Philadelphia: Temple University Press, 1991), by permission.

1931   *From* Speech on Black Self-Determination

Clarence A. Hathaway

What About the Party?

... The Communist Party, not only in the United States, but in all countries, stands everywhere for the equality of all peoples. And to prove this assertion I only want to quote one short sentence here from Comrade Lenin, to show that the position of our Party on the Negro question is not something that we have worked out here in the United States alone. The position of our Party on the Negro question is the position of the international Communist movement in regard to all peoples oppressed by imperialism, by the capitalists. He states:

> The victory over capitalism cannot be fully achieved and carried to its ulti-mate goal unless the proletariat and the toiling masses of all nations of the world rally of their own accord in a harmonious and close union.

This is the international policy of the Communist Party. On the basis of this fundamental principle that was given to us, that has been given to all its Sections by the Communist International, the Communist Party here worked out its program on the Negro question in the United States. And we state categorically and unconditionally, that the Communist Party stands for complete and unconditional equality for the Negroes. We do not add any "ifs" or "buts," we do not make any qualifications— we say full equality, and this we mean—*full equality.* We propose the abolition of all laws or practices that prevent the Negro masses from enjoying any right or any practices that are, or will be given to the whites now or at any future time in the United States.

For Full Equality

Comrade Bill Dunne, a member of the Central Committee of the Com-munist Party, U.S.A., made a speech a few months ago in the South, and in the South, as you know, it is a little dangerous to speak on the Negro question, but he chose as his subject, "The Position of the Communist Party on the Negro Question." During his speech somebody asked: "Mr. Dunne, would you want your sister to marry a nigger?" And Comrade Bill Dunne replied, that he would sooner have his sister marry a militant, fighting Negro, determined to secure equality, than any yellow-bellied white chauvinist. *(Applause.)* They then tried to organize a walk-out.

Most of them were white workers—they succeeded in getting only fifteen to leave the hall, and five or six came back.

And I say again that all laws which in any way discriminate against Negroes, whether they be marriage laws, or other practices, must be eliminated by joint struggle of the Negro and white workers and by wiping out of the minds of every white worker especially, all traces of white chauvinism.

The Communist Party not only declares its support for social, economic and political equality—for complete unconditional equality—for the Negroes, but the Communist Party fights for equality for the Negroes. We organize the fight everywhere to get equality for the Negroes with the whites. In the South we also fight for equality for the Negroes, but we do not merely fight for equality in the abstract; we do not merely chatter and talk about equality in the South at some future time. In the South we make our fight for equality in terms of concrete demands for the Negro masses, so that when these are won, it actually means real equality and not equality on paper.

The Land for the Negroes

In the Black Belt of the South Negroes constitute the overwhelming majority of the population, and how can these Negroes ever have equality there so long as the white landowners who have persecuted them for centuries continue to rule? We say that the land belongs to the farmers, to the Negro tenants and share-croppers, and the Communist Party fights to confiscate this land that is today held by the white landowners and operated by the Negroes. The cotton is produced in the South today by the sweat and blood of the Negro masses and not by the white landowners. We say that the Negroes who are tilling the land, who are raising the cotton are entitled to this land. This is their land and the first step toward winning equality is to take this land away from the white exploiters and give it to the Negroes.

For State Unity of the Black Belt

Secondly, we say that the Negroes in the Black Belt of the South can never get equality under the rule, domination and State power of the southern landowners. We say, immediately fight to establish the State unity of the Black Belt of the South. The Black Belt now runs across several States. We say, unite this territory into one State and then hold new elections there and give the Negro masses there the freedom, not to be dominated by the rule and the persecution of the white ruling classes, but to rule themselves in their own State, under such a form of government as they desire in the South.

For Self-Determination

Furthermore, we say that the Negro masses in the Black Belt must have the complete and unrestricted right to determine for themselves the kind of government that they will have, and their relationship to the government of the United States, to the other States and to foreign governments. We say that they must be given the opportunity if they wish to completely separate themselves from the United States, to establish their own rule here without any restrictions imposed upon them by any foreign power.

There have been Negro leaders such as Garvey who have come forward with the proposal that all the Negroes be loaded into boats and sent back to Africa. We say that the Negro masses have helped to build this country, to establish its institutions and to create its wealth. These Negro masses today are just as much American as any one of us here. They have a right to live in this country on terms of complete freedom. *(Applause.)*

So we do not propose to load all the Negroes on boats and send them to Africa or any place else. We propose that in the first place, the white working class take up the fight to establish the right of the Negroes to remain in the United States. *(Applause.)*

The Party furthermore declares that it is the duty of the working class, the white workers especially, and also the Negroes fighting together with the white workers, to take such steps as are necessary to defeat the practice of lynching in the United States. *(Applause.)* We demand that the death penalty be administered to all lynchers. We say that the workers must not tolerate any more the lynchers. We say that the white workers especially must organize to meet the lynch gangs and prevent lynchings from taking place, by meeting the frenzied lynch mobs with the organized mass power of the workers. *(Applause.)*

Not Mere Promises

Our program is not a program of phrases, not a program of resolutions, not a program of promises. Our whole program is a program of struggle, and comrades, the policy of the Communist Party in all sections of the country has been to carry through in action the program put forth in our resolutions.

In order to show that the program I have put forth is not merely my program, or my interpretation of the program, I want to read a couple of excerpts from the resolutions of the Party, published in our official monthly organ, *The Communist:*

> The slogan of equal rights of the Negroes *without a relentless struggle in practice against all manifestations of Negrophobia on the part of the American bourgeoisie can be nothing but a deceptive liberal gesture of a sly owner or his agent. This slogan is in fact repeated by "socialist" and many other bourgeois politicians and philanthropists, who want to get publicity for themselves by appealing to the "sense of justice" of the American bourgeoisie in the individual treatment of the Negroes, and thereby side-track attention from the one effective struggle against the shameful system of "white superiority": from the class struggle against the American bourgeoisie.* The struggle for equal rights for the Negroes is, in fact, one of the most important parts of the proletarian class struggle of the United States. . . .
>
> In the struggle for equal rights for the Negro, however, it is the duty of the *white* workers to march *at the head* of this struggle. They must everywhere make a breach in the walls of segregation and Jim-Crowism which have been set up by bourgeois slave-market morality. They must most ruthlessly unmask and condemn the hypocritical reformists and bourgeois "friends of Negroes" who, in reality, are only interested in strengthening the power of the enemies of the Negroes. *They, the white workers, must boldly jump at the throat of the 100 percent bandits who strike a Negro in the face. This Struggle will be the test of real international solidarity of the American white workers.*

Merely to make promises is not worth a dime. That the Negro masses have found out through many bitter experiences. The Democrats, the Republicans, the Socialists, the American Federation of Labor, have all made promises; but their promises were empty words. This has embittered the Negro masses and strengthened the distrust born of years of persecution and oppression. So we say to our Party members, promises in words only strengthen the bourgeoisie. We impress upon them the necessity in action, *in struggle,* of strengthening the bonds of class unity.

7   Uncovering a "National" Past

The Harlem Renaissance years witnessed considerable nationwide growth in black historical awareness and concern. Encouraged by the Association for the Study of Negro Life and History's (ASNLH) promotion of Negro History Week beginning in 1926, "New Negroes" sought to express their spiritual emancipation by honoring the heroes of a previously "buried" racial past. Unfortunately, this socially useful view of African American history could be found only with great difficulty in the lecture halls and seminar rooms of the nation's "white" colleges and universities. The situation was hardly more promising at certain historically black schools. Here, as noted by Langston Hughes in 1934, "old and mossbacked presidents, orthodox ministers or missionary principals" controlled course content—burdening their institutions with liberal arts curricula based largely on conventional Euro-American models. Given this widespread lack of appreciation for the notion that a course of study constructed for a majority population may be completely inadequate for minority group students, educators committed to promoting the "Negro history gospel" often had to work outside the educational "establishment," fund their own research, and publish their own books.

The most prolific of these crusading "outsider" historians was J. A. Rogers. The Jamaican-born black history researcher and freelance journalist was largely self-educated, but traveled extensively and maintained a voluminous private library at his Harlem residence. While most of his works were self-published, they circulated widely in black communities. He wrote regularly for Marcus Garvey's *Negro World* and for many years produced an illustrated feature, "Your History," for the *Pittsburgh Courier*. Titles such as *World's Greatest Men of African Descent* (1930); *100 Amazing Facts about the Negro* (1934); and *Nature Knows No Color-Line* (1952) reveal Rogers's commitment to uncovering and highlighting the inspiring record of black achievement. In "The Suppression of Negro History," reprinted by permission from the *Crisis* (May 1940), Rogers seeks to protect the "good name" of his people while discrediting white assumptions of racial superiority. Unafraid of making controversial claims—especially if they would combat "the preaching of defeatism"—Joel Augustus Rogers had a telling influence on later generations of nationalist-oriented historians.

1940   The Suppression of Negro History

J. A. Rogers

History, or what is said of us nationally, racially, socially, or individually, is often the most important factor in our lives. The most effective way of keeping down a people, regardless of race, and forcing it to sell its labor in the lowest market is continually to publish bad things about it. He who robs me of my good name, said Shakespeare, leaves me poor indeed.

Of this art of debasing a whole people, the American slaveholders were the past masters. Using the Bible as their authority, they painted such an awful picture of Negro ancestry that even some of the Virginia aristocrats had a lively time side-stepping charges of being touched with the tar brush. George Washington, in his diary, January 12, 1760, tells how one haughty Virginia colonel, Catesby Cocke, walked out of Washington's home 'disgusted' because he saw there "an old Negro" who resembled him strongly. Colonel George William Fairfax, Washington's bosom friend, was another. Fairfax, who was nephew of Lord Fairfax, Virginia's richest landowner, was born in the West Indies, it was said, of a black Negro mother. Most of the native-born West Indian whites, then as well as now, had a touch of the tar-brush, more or less evident. "In view of his distinguished ancestry this scandal was particularly annoying" to the colonel, who moreover hoped to inherit his uncle's title and estates. He went to England, it is said, to prove to his uncle that he wasn't a Negro; nevertheless, the property went to another. (Rupert Hughes. Life of Washington, Vol. I, p. 183; Vol. II, p. 21).

Still another who was "accused" of being a Negro was Thomas Jefferson. In his case, however, it was clearly pure politics. Jefferson had a fondness for fair black femininity, quite unconcealed, particularly for Sally Hemings, the celebrated Black Sal, and Jefferson's enemies argued that one so fond of Negroes must be of Negro strain himself.

With this as typical of the spirit of the time anything about the achievements of the Negro was simply out of the question. Indeed, any history that did not paint Africans as cannibals and savages who had been dragged out of Africa to save their souls would be almost downright atheism. Solemn-faced divines from Massachusetts to Georgia pounded the Bible at the command of the tobacco-growers to prove that the Negro "was descendant of Ham and thus doomed to be a hewer of wood and a drawer of water for the white race, forever." To talk of

Hannibal, Esop, Delphos, Buddha, Akhenaton, or Christ, as being Negroes, was equivalent to flying in the face of the Almighty. Negro history had no more chance than the proverbial cockroach at the roosters' ball. In short, the black man was entirely cut off from his past and liberally dosed with white religion to make him a cross of something between a faithful dog and a grinning mule.

The American slave-holder did not stop there. Like the average white southerner of today he was an ardent propagandist abroad of his doctrines of white superiority. He took his racial creed to England, along with his slaves, and succeeded in reviving Negro slavery, which had been abolished there by Chief Justice Holt in 1707. In short, the American slave holding interests made such a thorough black-out of everything favorable to the Negro in literature that now, centuries later, it functions as almost brand new.

Negro History a Reality

Nevertheless, "Negro history" was a reality even as the so-called New World was there despite its absence from maps of the world prior to Columbus. Mankind has been living on this planet not less than half a million years and there is ever increasing proof that the first human beings were Negroes, and that all the other human varieties, including the proud Aryan, are their offspring. Professor W. K. Gregory in "Our Face From Fish to Man" traces on a chart the evolution of man from the Tasmanian Negro. And there are many other scientists from Schopenhauer onwards who have done similarly. Of course, for many Nordics, it is easier to believe that their ancestor was an ape rather than a Negro.

In the dawn of history we find the whites idealizing the blacks. It is possible to produce much painstaking authority to prove that all or nearly all the earliest gods and messiahs from Japan to Mexico, including Jehovah, Christ and the Virgin Mary were what are now called Negroes. The earliest gods of even Ancient Greece were black. Homer tells how the Greek gods used to go to Ethiopia, their ancestral home, to feast and enjoy themselves at intervals. Even the curling of the hair so common among the later Greeks might have been done in imitation of the Negroes. Apollo's face is distinctly Caucasian but his hair is artificially curled until it is a tight pepper-corn. Now the founder of the famous Delphic oracle, the rites of Apollo, was Delphos, a full-blooded, woolly-haired Negro whose effigy appears on a Greek coin of 500 B.C. (C. T.

Seltman: Athens, Its History and Coinage, pp. 97,200. 1924). The Christ on a gold coin of Justinian II, Byzantine emperor, has the same peppercorn hair, a distinctive characteristic of the Negro of the purest type, as the Bushman and the Andaman Islander. The Venus of Willendorf, the oldest known statuary of the human form, of about 10,000 to 15,000 B.C., has the same kind of hair.

George Washington in his Barbados Journal told how the white ladies "affect the Negro style." In Europe I saw white women got up to look like black ones, particularly during the Paris Colonial Exposition of 1931. Some white women had their hair so tightly curled and skin so darkened by sunlight or lotions that it was a distinct surprise to see them later in low neck dresses with the white streak left by the shoulder-straps of the bathing suit.

There is so much of Negro history to be garnered that I am convinced after thirty years of research that it would take several industrious historians a lifetime to gather it. Gerald Massey rightly says, "To the despised black race we have at length to turn for the birth of language, the beginnings of all human creation, and as the Arabic saying puts it let us 'honor the first although the followers do better.' "

Historians Have Blind Spot

So heavy was the black-out laid down by the slave interests, however, that almost none of this Negro history glimmers into the histories written for popular white consumption, including Wells' Outline of History. The popular white writer has actually developed a blind spot where the Negro is concerned.

The following incident will illustrate my point. I must insist in advance that though it sounds most ridiculous I am telling it just as it happened. Some years ago I attended a lecture on Brazil given by a professor from one of New York's most enlightened colleges and with a reputation for being radical. During the question period I brought up the subject of the Negro strain in John VI, who once ruled Portugal from Brazil. The professor said, "Impossible! He was not a Negro. He was a Bourbon!" In reply I quoted from the Duchess d'Abrantès, one of France's greatest women writers, and wife of the French ambassador to John's court at Lisbon. She said of John VI, "his enormous head with its Negro hair, which, moreover, was quite in harmony with his thick lips, his African nose, and the color of his skin." (Son enorme tête, surmontée d'une chevelure de nègre, qui, au reste, était bien en harmonie avec ses lèvres épaisses, son nez africain, et la couleur de sa peau." Memoires, p. 200, Paris, 1837.) I added that a large proportion of the Portuguese population was then Negro, that John's portrait bears out the Duchess' description, and that the Duchess knew the Negro type as she had lived in Haiti. Still the professor held to his point. "No," he said, "he was not a Negro. *He had adenoids!*"

Equally amazing is the case of Professor Arnold J. Toynbee of London university. If Toynbee's work is an index of his mind he must be utterly free from color prejudice; nevertheless, like H. G. Wells, he is also a victim of the slaveholders' blackout. In his study of history (Vol. I, pp. 232–238), Toynbee flatly asserts that the Negro has made no contribution to past civilization. He says, "When we classify mankind by colour the only one of the primary races given by this classification which has not made a contribution to any of our twenty-one civilizations is the Black Race. . . .

"Within the first six thousand years the Black Race has not helped to create any civilization while the Polynesian has helped to create one civilization; the Brown Race, two; the Yellow Race, three; the Red Race and the Nordic White Race, four apiece; the Alpine White Race, nine; and the Mediterranean White Race, ten."

Four Deleted Words

Match this with what Sir Arthur Evans, one of the greatest archaeologists has said. In his presidential address to the British Association for the Advancement of Science, 1916 (p. 15), he says, as regards even Western Europe, "We must never lose sight of the fact that from the earliest Aurignacian Period onwards a Negroid culture in the broadest sense of the word shared in this artistic culture as seen on both sides of the Pyrenees." What also of the researches of Dieulafoy in Persia, not to mention others!

Yet another illustration. F. A. Wright, in his introduction to the works of Liudprand, Bishop of Cremona, (p. 11) omits mention of the color of Nicephorus Phocas, Byzantine emperor. He quotes Liudprand's whole description of Nicephorus except the four small words "in color a Negro." In place of these he has three dots. Nicephorus Phocas was an Arab. Liudprand visited him in his capital at Constantinople. There was much Negro strain in the Byzantines. The southern part of their empire, Greece, was dominated for years by Negro sea-rovers, who landed in Thessaly in fifty-four ships in 904 A.D. (Schlumberger: Un empereur byzantin, p. 34–35.) The Byzantine emperors took their title of Basileus from the Ethiopians.

Still another case of the hundreds I could cite is that of Robert Browning. Browning was of West Indian ancestry. Frederick J. Furnivall, a contemporary of Browning and head of the Browning Society, after a lengthy discussion of Browning's ancestry, said Browning's Negro strain was a "certainty" to him. (Browning Society Papers, Feb. 28, 1890, Vol. III, pp. 31, 36. London). Thomas Carlyle almost spoke of Browning's dark skin. Nevertheless, many of Browning's admirers and biographers, most of whom have never seen Browning have almost frothed at the mouth at Furnivall's statement.

For unblushing, barefaced suppression of Negro history the palm, as in so many other cases where truth is involved, goes to Hollywood. Cleopatra, who is known throughout history, was at least a mulatto woman, becomes a pale Nordic. So are all of the Three Wise Men, one of whom is depicted in all or nearly all, the great paintings as a Negro. Frank Morgan plays Alessandro de' Medici, Duke of Florence, and mulatto son of Pope Clement VII, in the most approved Hitler complexion. Quite different are the films of Italian make. In D'Annunzio's film Cabiria, Massinissa, celebrated King of Numidia, was played by a Negro. Massinissa provided the balance of power whereby Rome defeated Carthage.

Radicals No Better

So much for the conservative white people. What of the radical economic whites? Are they any better? Personally I have found them to be even narrower. While the conservative whites consider Negro history to be "social equality," the radicals denounce it as "black chauvinism" even while some of them talk about self-determination in the black belt. A book on great Negroes is dubbed "inferiority complex" by the radical whites and some of their Negro converts. Was it a sense of inferiority that inspired Plutarch to write his Lives? Radicals keep their nose so close to the economic grindstone; they talk so much about the belly that one would imagine it is the only organ in the body, except when it comes to laudation of their own leaders. They would put these economic blinders on the Negro, too. Most of the literature they get out about him is defeatist. Reason: the Negroes will be discouraged in their own leadership and become easier tools. The stressing of crime, degeneracy, and injustice at the expense of the more favorable aspects of the Negro's life serves to make many Negroes feel that the economic nostrums of these radicals are their only salvation.

White publishers, too, complain that Negroes will not buy books about themselves. Most of these books tend to hold the Negro just where he has always been. After three centuries of the preaching of defeatism one needs inspiration. People who have been thrust into dark holes crave sunlight.

The Negro Lends Aid

And speaking of crime and defeatism that brings us to the subject of what the Negroes, themselves, do to suppress the favorable in their own history. My experiences on this alone would fill a book. The chief offender in this respect is the Negro press, whose policy, broadly speaking, is almost identical with that of the white press, namely, to give crime and scandal precedence over achievement.

Some years ago at a press conference in Chicago, a Negro reporter took the white editors to task for mentioning color in the case of Negro offenders.

The late Victor Lawson, publisher of the *Daily News* quietly asked, "If we did not carry the color of the offender where would the Negro press get its news? Besides while we give the matter only a paragraph or two, you make a headline of it." After that the Negroes were as mum as mice. I was working on a Negro paper at the time and this was its precise policy. Our editor, and he was no different from the rest, felt that week lost when some Negro did not kill another or some Negro minister or other big shot was not mixed up in a scandal. Negro journalism has come a long way—a very long way—since John Brown Russwurm and Frederick Douglass. Today it is only a job.

Negro journalism is also far more personal than white. Some of the editors are more touchy than a dictator of a small Latin-American state or a petty African chief and will order to be suppressed news of those individuals who differ with them however slightly. The younger crop of Negro newspapermen too, know, as a rule, little or nothing of Negro history and hate to be corrected. In 1937, a leading Negro newspaper, copying from a white one, said that Sergeant Wanton of Washington, D. C., was the first and only Negro to win the Congressional Medal of Honor. I sent four typewritten lines to the paper saying that instead of one there were forty-one Negroes to win this highest honor. The article was never published. I called at the office and left a stamp for its return. The stamp disappeared, too.

Then there is the rivalry in the camp of the Negro historians. There are the Brahmins and the Sudras, or the fellows from the big white colleges with big degrees and those who have none. The Brahmins, in turn, are divided. In short, the researches of none of the groups mix, or are endorsed by the others, even when drawn from the same sources.

Again, any number of Negroes also resent hearing that this and that great man were Negroes. They had been taught that they were white and hate to have their ideas changed. They much prefer to sit back in the easy chair of their own inferiority. I have several times been attacked in print or conversation because I said from the extensive documentation I have on the subject, that Christ was originally worshipped as black, or that Beethoven, according to the description of him by his contemporaries, must have been a dark mulatto. In 1919 when I was writing sketches of Negroes as General Dumas, Antar, Bilal, Kafur, one Aframerican wrote from Germany to a Negro newspaper saying I was talking all fable. Of course, his white professor had never told him so, ergo, it couldn't be so.

Latin America "Touchy"

In the suppression of Negro history, Latin America comes a close second to England and America. Most of the peoples of these lands are of mixed Indian, Negro and white ancestry, and sometimes very much offended at candid photos that show up their Negro strains, a fact also true of the British West Indian. Dr. Francia of Paraguay, most terrible of the Latin-American dictators, had a blue-blooded Spaniard, who had once snubbed him, shot because he took him for a mulatto, which Francia probably was. Francia further decreed that white Spaniards in Paraguay should marry only Negroes and Indians. Hence most of the great Latin-Americans, including even San Martin and Sucre are doctored up to look like white movie stars of the technicolor.

Some Mexicans in California once protested because I said that Vicente Guerrero, liberator of Mexico and its third president, was a mulatto, my authority being Biographie Universelle, Larousse, and Guerrero's less idealized portrait. Similar it was with what I said of Bolivar, the George Washington of South America. Now comes a distinguished authority on Latin-Americans, S. G. Inman, who says in his book, "Latin America" published in 1937, page 46, "The two most gifted men of

Latin America, ranking high among the geniuses of the nineteenth century, were born in the Caribbean—Simon Bolivar of Venezuela and Ruben Dario of Nicaragua. Both probably had Negro blood although it is often considered unpatriotic to say so—this, no doubt because of the desire to appear well in the eyes of the European and the North American."

If you don't want a fight on your hands don't mention "Negro" blood to the average Cuban or Porto Rican in the United States even if he is three-fourths black. He wants to be white.

In the matter of hushing up Negro ancestry, the South African is even worse. Some of the oldest and most aristocratic families of the Cape are the descendants of white men and native women, who were made "white by law" in order to clamp down more effectively the exploitation of the native blacks.

Negro ancestry will come into its own, and Negro history is the means that will bring it about. All peoples were once despised, even the English, chief despisers of the Negro. Macaulay says, "In the time of Richard I, the ordinary imprecation of a Norman gentleman was, 'May I become an Englishman.' His ordinary form of indignant denial was, 'Do you take me for an Englishman?' "

8 A. Philip Randolph and the March on Washington Movement

"All Negro and pro-Negro," the March on Washington Movement (MOWM) of World War II mobilized the black masses in support of increased opportunity in the industrial workplace. Initially hoping to pressure federal officials into monitoring the hiring practices of defense contractors by threatening a massive protest demonstration in the nation's capital, the March on Washington brain trust soon expanded its list of demands to address a broad range of racial concerns. As noted by the group's chief spokesperson, African American labor leader and longtime socialist A. Philip Randolph, not even Franklin Roosevelt's June 1941 executive order requiring that defense contracts contain a nondiscrimination clause could silence the ever-vigilant, ever-skeptical black activists. Executive Order 8802 had "only scratched the surface" of a very thorny set of problems. As a result, Randolph remained an unofficial compliance watchdog and refused to stop pushing for enactment of the entire MOWM program. Fearful of Communist Party infiltration, he also maintained the group's racial distinctiveness in the hope that its members would develop "a sense of self-reliance with Negroes depending upon Negroes in vital matters." MOWM held its last national conference in Chicago in October 1946. The source of the text is A. Philip Randolph, "Why Should We March?" *Survey Graphic* (November 1942), reprinted by permission.

1942 Why Should We March?

A. Philip Randolph

Though I have found no Negroes who want to see the United Nations lose this war, I have found many who, before the war ends, want to see the stuffing knocked out of white supremacy and of empire over subject peoples. American Negroes, involved as we are in the general issues of the conflict, are confronted not with a choice but with the challenge both to win democracy for ourselves at home and to help win the war for democracy the world over.

There is no escape from the horns of this dilemma. There ought not to be escape. For if the war for democracy is not won abroad, the fight for democracy cannot be won at home. If this war cannot be won for the white peoples, it will not be won for the darker races.

Conversely, if freedom and equality are not vouchsafed the peoples of color, the war for democracy will not be won. Unless this double-barreled thesis is accepted and applied, the darker races will never wholeheartedly fight for the victory of the United Nations. That is why those familiar with the thinking of the American Negro have sensed his lack of enthusiasm, whether among the educated or uneducated, rich or poor, professional or nonprofessional, religious or secular, rural or urban, north, south, east or west.

That is why questions are being raised by Negroes in church, labor union and fraternal society; in poolroom, barbershop, schoolroom, hospital, hair-dressing parlor; on college campus, railroad, and bus. One can hear such questions asked as these: What have Negroes to fight for? What's the difference between Hitler and that "cracker" Talmadge of Georgia? Why has a man got to be Jim Crowed to die for democracy? If you haven't got democracy yourself, how can you carry it to somebody else?

What are the reasons for this state of mind? The answer is: discrimination, segregation, Jim Crow. Witness the navy, the army, the air corps; and also government services at Washington. In many parts of the South, Negroes in Uncle Sam's uniform are being put upon, mobbed, sometimes even shot down by civilian and military police, and on occasion lynched. Vested political interests in race prejudice are so deeply entrenched that to them winning the war against Hitler is secondary to preventing

Negroes from winning democracy for themselves. This is worth many divisions to Hitler and Hirohito. While labor, business, and farm are subjected to ceilings and floors and not allowed to carry on as usual, these interests trade in the dangerous business of race hate as usual.

When the defense program began and billions of the taxpayers' money were appropriated for guns, ships, tanks and bombs, Negroes presented themselves for work only to be given the cold shoulder. North as well as South, and despite their qualifications, Negroes were denied skilled employment. Not until their wrath and indignation took the form of a proposed protest march on Washington, scheduled for July 1, 1941, did things begin to move in the form of defense jobs for Negroes. The march was postponed by the timely issuance (June 25, 1941) of the famous Executive Order No. 8802 by President Roosevelt. But this order and the President's Committee on Fair Employment Practice, established thereunder, have as yet only scratched the surface by way of eliminating discriminations on account of race or color in war industry. Both management and labor unions in too many places and in too many ways are still drawing the color line.

It is to meet this situation squarely with direct action that the March on Washington Movement launched its present program of protest mass meetings. Twenty thousand were in attendance at Madison Square Garden, June 16; sixteen thousand in the Coliseum in Chicago, June 26; nine thousand in the City Auditorium of St. Louis, August 14. Meetings of such magnitude were unprecedented among Negroes. The vast throngs were drawn from all walks and levels of Negro life—businessmen, teachers, laundry workers, Pullman porters, waiters, and red caps; preachers, crapshooters, and social workers; jitterbugs and Ph.D's. They came and sat in silence, thinking, applauding only when they considered the truth was told, when they felt strongly that something was going to be done about it.

The March on Washington Movement is essentially a movement of the people. It is all Negro and pro-Negro, but not for that reason anti-white or anti-Semitic, or anti-Catholic, or anti-foreign, or anti-labor. Its major weapon is the non-violent demonstration of Negro mass power. Negro leadership has united back of its drive for jobs and justice. "Whether Negroes should march on Washington, and if so, when?" will be the focus of a forthcoming national conference. For the plan of a protest march has not been abandoned. Its purpose would be to demonstrate that American Negroes are in deadly earnest, and all out for their full rights. No power on earth can cause them today to abandon their fight to wipe out every vestige of second class citizenship and the dual standards that plague them.

A community is democratic only when the humblest and weakest person can enjoy the highest civil, economic, and social rights that the biggest and most powerful possess. To trample on these rights of both Negroes and poor whites is such a commonplace in the South that it takes readily to anti-social, anti-labor, anti-Semitic and anti-Catholic propaganda. It was because of laxness in enforcing the Weimar constitution in republican Germany that Nazism made headway. Oppression of the Negroes in the United States, like suppression of the Jews in Germany, may open the way for a fascist dictatorship.

By fighting for their rights now, American Negroes are helping to make America a moral and spiritual arsenal of democracy. Their fight against the poll tax, against lynch law, segregation, and Jim Crow, their fight for economic, political, and social equality, thus becomes part of the global war for freedom.

Program of the March on Washington Movement

1. We demand, in the interest of national unity, the abrogation of every law which makes a distinction in treatment between citizens based on religion, creed, color, or national origin. This means an end to Jim Crow in education, in housing, in transportation and in every other social, economic, and political privilege; and especially, we demand, in the capital of the nation, an end to all segregation in public places and in public institutions.

2. We demand legislation to enforce the Fifth and Fourteenth Amendments guaranteeing that no person shall be deprived of life, liberty or property without due process of law, so that the full weight of the national government may be used for the protection of life and thereby may end the disgrace of lynching.

3. We demand the enforcement of the Fourteenth and Fifteenth Amendments and the enactment of the Pepper Poll Tax bill so that all barriers in the exercise of the suffrage are eliminated.

4. We demand the abolition of segregation and discrimination in the army, navy, marine corps, air corps, and all other branches of national defense.

5. We demand an end to discrimination in jobs and job training. Further, we demand that the FEPC be made a permanent administrative agency of the U.S. Government and that it be given power to enforce its decisions based on its findings.

6. We demand that federal funds be withheld from any agency which practices discrimination in the use of such funds.

7. We demand colored and minority group representation on all administrative agencies so that these groups may have recognition of their democratic right to participate in formulating policies.

8. We demand representation for the colored and minority racial groups on all missions, political and technical, which will be sent to the peace conference so that the interests of all people everywhere may be fully recognized and justly provided for in the post-war settlement.

---

9   Richard B. Moore and the
       Pan-Caribbean Movement

A naturalized U.S. citizen who had immigrated from Barbados as a teenager in 1909, Richard B. Moore served as educational director of the African Blood Brotherhood and was a fellow traveler with Cyril Briggs in the CPUSA of the Depression years. He too was expelled from the party because of his "extreme nationalist tendencies." Thereafter, the bibliophile and student of black history devoted his energies to organizing New York City's West Indian community in support of independence and self-determination for Caribbean nations. During the 1960s and 1970s, he also employed his well-honed oratorical skills in a campaign to popularize use of the racial designation "Afro-American" (as opposed to "Negro" or "Black").

In this 1953 address to British dignitaries assembled at the Hotel Theresa in Harlem, Moore attempts to marshall support for the establishment of a Pan-Caribbean federation of English-speaking states; his appeal is based on (1) classical natural rights philosophy; (2) Lenin's analysis of the national and colonial questions; and (3) the black historical record. African peoples, he noted, had created "powerful . . . well organized and administered" nation-states in the past. Afro-Caribbean peoples were equally well equipped to do so in the present and by all rights should be released from their bondage to "external imperial powers." Political independence for the Caribbean would, he felt, inspire considerable dignity and pride in all peoples of the black diaspora.

Moore's Caribbean commonwealth became a short-lived reality in 1958 as the islands of Barbados, Jamaica, Trinidad and Tobago, Antigua, Montserrat, St. Kitts-Nevis-Anguilla, Dominica, Grenada, St. Lucia, and St. Vincent united to form the West Indies Federation. After Jamaica opted for its own independence in 1962, the federal experiment unraveled quickly. Nevertheless, Moore refused to relinquish his belief that a self-governing federation was essential for the optimum economic development of the region and the best possible defense against balkanization and neocolonialist intrigue. He succumbed to cancer in 1978 and was buried in Barbados. The speech is reprinted from *Richard B. Moore, Caribbean Militant in Harlem: Collected Writings, 1920–1972,* ed. W. Burghardt Turner and Joyce Moore Turner (Bloomington: Indiana University Press, 1988), by permission.

1953 Speech on Caribbean Federation
at the Luncheon Meeting for Lord Listowel

Richard B. Moore

I should like to make a few observations so our distinguished visitor will realize the trend of thought among people of Caribbean origin here, and also among other interested persons born in these United States, in respect to the important question of Federation of the Caribbean People in the islands and mainland areas now governed as colonies by the British government.

This question of federation now assumes very great importance in view of the forthcoming Conference scheduled to be held in London during the month of April.

The view prevailing among the majority of those especially interested here has been set forth in a Memorandum addressed to the Caribbean Labour Congress which convened in Kingston, Jamaica, on September 2nd to 9th, 1947. This Memorandum I shall now present to Lord Listowel so this more ample statement will be before him and may reach those of weight and influence to whom it may come.

Federation is here considered in its proper meaning and strict sense. As stated in the Memorandum, "federation is the union of independent sovereign states, hence there can be no federation worthy of the name where there is no recognition or achievement of actual independence and sovereignty."

It is recognized, of course, that the term federation has been loosely applied to denote the bringing together of colonies for the purpose of administering them as a single political unit. This improper and misleading usage has been noted by Algernon Aspinall as quoted in the Memorandum:

> The terms "confederation" and "federation" are strictly only applicable to the federal union of independent sovereign states: but they have been freely used to indicate the policy of bringing together colonies or groups of colonies into some form of union.

It should be clear, then, that when we speak of federation, this term is used only in its proper, precise, political significance as the union of sovereign, independent states. This excludes altogether any process of joining together colonies in what Mr. Malliet has referred to as "a glorified crown colony," a phrase which I first heard in this connection from an elder statesman of the Caribbean, the Hon. T. Albert Marryshow of Grenada, when he visited us here a few years ago.

Those of us who have given serious thought to this paramount question are deeply interested in genuine federation with complete self-government. This means that the Caribbean people would then enjoy the status of a self-governing Dominion within the British Commonwealth of Nations. By self-governing Dominion is meant a political status such as that of Canada, Australia, or India. I do not speak of Ceylon, because while there are those who deem Ceylon to be a fully self-governing Dominion, there are also those who hold that there are treaty agreements and other arrangements which detract from the status of full self-government.

From this clear and precise view, federation is the *sine qua non* of progress for the Caribbean people. It is the essential means whereby they can move forward to a solution of the many and grievous problems of economic poverty, political retardation, and social depression with which they are now gravely confronted, and in fact, seriously menaced. Moreover, from any adequate view of the situation, such genuine federation of the Caribbean people is clearly and palpably long overdue.

It is the stated aim and proclaimed purpose of British colonial policy to prepare and to fit the peoples whom they rule for self-government. Quite obviously, the Caribbean people are among the oldest colonies ruled by the British government. Standing high upon the list in point of time are such colonies as the Bahamas, Barbados, St. Christopher, and the other colonies of the Caribbean and mainland areas. After several centuries of such rule, the people of the Caribbean must certainly now be ready for self-government.

Still more important is the fact that the indigenous people of these Caribbean areas, for a considerable period, have been executing most of the work in the actual administration and government of these colonies, except for the few topmost officials appointed by the British government and the overriding control of the British colonial office. There can be no valid question, then, as to their ability or fitness for self-government.

Considerable confusion has arisen, though, over this vital question of federation, chiefly because of the Rance Report, or to give its formal title, the British Caribbean Standing Closer Association Committee 1948–1949 Report. This Report proposes to reserve large powers to the Crown on the score of finance. Significantly, this Report also fails to approach the question of finance with any consideration of the historical flow of wealth from the Caribbean people to Britain. So great are the powers reserved to the British Crown, that the people of some areas in the Caribbean would lose important powers that they have already gained and now possess.

As a result, and because of certain propaganda also, there has developed considerable reluctance in British Guiana and British Honduras, as well as decided reservations in other areas, toward joining in what is misnamed a "federation" in view of the proposals of this Report. For such proposals do not constitute a plan for genuine federation on the basis of full self-government, nor even any appreciable advance toward self-government, but in fact a retrogression for some areas in very vital aspects of political and financial power.

A plan for genuine federation, however, would dispel this confusion, reluctance, and reservation. There are those, we know, in positions of power who still question the ability of the Caribbean people to govern themselves. But in addition to what has already been said in refutation of this purblind notion, which arises only out of partisan and short-sighted self-interest, it should be obvious that as it is only possible to learn to swim by striking out in the water, so it is possible to learn to govern only by actually governing.

Besides, it is well known that the majority of the people in the Caribbean areas are the descendants of people brought from Africa. It is not so well known, but nevertheless an established fact of history, that the African peoples governed themselves for centuries before the European invasion of Africa which began in the middle of the fifteenth century. Any unbiased estimate, based upon the facts of that historical situation, must acknowledge that over vast areas and from remote times the Africans did quite well at the task of governing themselves.

The distinguished anthropologist, Leo Frobenius, and several other scholars have pointed to the facts which demonstrate that Africans had achieved great cultures. They had developed powerful states well organized and administered, flourishing industries, exquisite crafts, great arts. If, on the other hand, we consider objectively the record of the results of government by external imperial powers whether in Africa, the Caribbean, Asia, or anywhere else in the world, and if we accurately assess the plight of the world today, we cannot but conclude that government imposed by any nation upon another people has in no case been just, or alike beneficial, or conducive to the peace and progress of mankind.

Despite all this, there still remains this meretricious theory of the necessity of continuing "guardianship." But the question arises: Who will guard the guardians; who will civilize the civilizers?

The right of the Caribbean people, as indeed of all peoples, to self-determination and self-government is an inalienable, human, democratic right. This fundamental right is deemed to be most vital for themselves by powerful nations which proclaim democracy while imposing imperial rule upon other peoples. Clearly, there is a gap and a contradiction between the theory and the practice.

It is evident, however, that we have now reached a stage in human affairs when the denial of these democratic rights can no longer be maintained with any prospect of peace, security, or well-being for any of the peoples of the earth. Any attempt forcibly to retain the Caribbean people, or any other peoples, in the status of colonial subjection, can only engender hostility in the minds of these peoples against those who impose such imperial rule.

The forthright recognition of this right to self-determination, and to federation with self-government, is the primary condition for that voluntary union which is the only basis for peaceful relations and mutually beneficial advancement. The Caribbean people will thus be enabled to take their rightful place among the other nations of the Commonwealth, and so achieve amicable, proper, and mutually advantageous relations with the people of the United Kingdom, with the other nations of this hemisphere, and with all the peoples of the world.

10   Carlos Cooks and the African Nationalist Pioneer Movement

An officer in Marcus Garvey's Universal African Legion at the age of nineteen, Carlos A. Cooks was influenced greatly by the UNIA's program. Following Garvey's death in 1940, Cooks founded the African Nationalist Pioneer Movement (ANPM), an "educational, inspirational, instructive, constructive and expansive society" devoted to "bringing about a progressive, dignified, cultural, fraternal and racial confraternity amongst the African peoples of the world." Thereafter, the fiery Harlem street orator took particular interest in organizing "Buy Black" initiatives. Here, African American consumers practiced the basic tenets of economic nationalism by refusing to patronize stores owned by "alien" merchants. The following selection describes the fundamentals of "buying black." It also highlights two of Cooks's other major areas of concern: promotion of natural hairstyles and condemnation of the "ominous appellation" "Negro." Viewing nationalism as a racial survival mechanism, Cooks criticized any economic or cultural practice that turned proud black people into "zombified," white-controlled "Caste creatures." He died after suffering a stroke in 1966. The text is taken from speeches delivered between May and December 1955 as transcribed by ANPM member Robert Harris and reprinted in *Carlos Cooks and Black Nationalism from Garvey to Malcolm*, ed. Robert Harris, Nyota Harris, and Grandassa Harris (Dover, MA: Majority Press, 1992), by permission.

1955 Speech on the "Buy Black" Campaign

Hair Conking; Buy Black

Carlos Cooks

Let's stand! Repeat after me, "One Cause, One Goal, One Destiny."

Fellow Nationalists and members of the race, the Negro is being used as a stooge for the Jews and other non-Blacks who are exploiting Black people. The Negro is a manufactured "wrongo." He is made to do wrong. He cannot do right. It is the devout policy of white supremacists to make Negroes out of every Black man, woman and child. As we constantly point out, the word, Negro, is a weapon and scheme of whites to disassociate Black people from the human family and their homeland, Africa.

Slavery cut Black people in the western world adrift from Africa. In the western world, Black people were oriented towards an alien culture and were forbidden to practice their African culture. The penalty meant death. They underwent the most macabre, diabolical and consistent application of mental and physical torture the world has ever known.

With physical torture being insufficient in converting the African into useful assets for the slave system, the Christian church was called upon to destroy the Black people's minds and turn them into Negroes.

I have written an article in *The Street Speaker* magazine under the title "American Traditions Veto Integration." It will give you a scientific, detailed breakdown on how Africans were converted into Negroes. The proud, aggressive, courageous, resourceful, and clannish Black people descended into degraded, miserable, fawning, flunky, Caste creatures now known as Negroes—manufactured "wrongoes."

Nature, habit and opinions are the three strongest forces in the world. Black people in the western world have been under the habits and opinions of "Negroism" ever since they were brought here. With the exception of Booker T. Washington and his Tuskegee movement, all efforts of Black people in the USA were towards integration and better "Negroism."

As Negroes, Black people have been converted into zombified Caste creatures whose loyalty is permanently married to the white race; whose God and idolatry status is white; whose standards of beauty, sense of decency and opinions on all matters are based on the set concepts laid down by white people.

As Negroes, Black people are the stoutest defenders of white supremacy and the loudest defamers of Africa and everything pertaining to it.

Integration has been made the target of the Negroes' focus. The concentric pull of this fallacious doctrine has such a revolting effect on the behavior of Negroes that we find them at war with nature. They are disgusted with their color, hair, and physique to such a nauseating extent that they employ the use of harsh and potent chemicals to efface the handiwork of nature. Negroes are convinced that if they simulate the hair, color and general mannerisms of the white race, they would be accepted by white society.

The Negro man conks his hair in his faggot, cowardly attempt to have his hair simulate the white man's hair. Hair conking is a lucrative business in the Negro communities. All your big time Negro entertainers, sports figures and many of your Negro preachers conk their hair. These are your role models in the Negro communities.

This big, Black zombie takes his hard earned money and goes to a conking shop, where another Negro is waiting on him. The Negro operating the conking shop invites his patron to take a seat and tells him he will "straighten" him. He reaches down and gets a bottle of lye mixed with some grease and begins covering the Negro's head with it. The ignorant Negro begins squirming as the lye burns his head. After ten or fifteen minutes of this torture, the operator leads the Negro to a sink where he applies water to the Negro's head to cool it, and washes the lye mixture out. He then leads the Negro back to the chair to finish the conking process.

During the ten to fifteen tortuous minutes that the Negro is waiting with that conking mixture on his head, he twists, turns, squirms and sometimes soils his underwear. The operator cautions him. "Steady! Steady! You will be sharp and straight in a minute. Steady! Steady!"

When the operator leads the stupid, jackass Negro back to the chair to finish the conking process, he dries the Negro's head, covers it with grease and sets it in a simulated European style. He gives his patron two toothpicks to scratch his hair as some of the lye mixture remains on the Negro's head and burns him from time to time. You see the faggot Negro elegantly scratching his hair with the toothpicks as if he is presenting an example of accomplishment. A more ignorant, stupid, inferior, backwards jackass the world has never known.

In the case of the Negro woman, she goes to a so-called "beauty parlor" where another Negress is waiting for her. The "beautician" invites this Aunt Jemima Negress to take a seat and tells her that shortly she will be "straightened".

The ignorant, sadistic "beautician" covers the head of the stupid masochistic Negress with grease, reaches for an iron comb, and puts it into a towel. If the iron is not hot enough to burn the towel, it is put back into the fire to get hotter. She waits until it gets hot enough to brand a cattle, then she rakes it over Aunt Jemima's hair until the hair is straightened.

The laws of science say that you can take something and make nothing out of it, but you cannot take nothing and make something out of it. In the case of Black people's hair, you have live, woolly, curly, human hair where harsh chemicals and heat are applied to kill the hair until it lays in ruin like the white people's or dogs' hair. You took something and made nothing out of it. But there is no known chemical or application of heat that can change the dead, straight hair of white people to the live, lovely curly hair of Black people. You cannot take nothing and make something out of it.

As Negroes, the Black people give up the best to ape the less. The Negro's hair has more sense than the Negro. After two or three weeks under the conk and hot comb applications, the hair says, "To hell with this. I am going back to Africa," and it goes back to its natural state. The Negro has to go through the conk and hot comb all over again.

The Negro is the greatest enemy of Black opportunities and racial solidarity in the path of the onward march of African Nationalism.

The constant drip of water on the hardest granite will ultimately make an impression. Likewise, the constant application of Orthodox African Nationalism to the cement mentality of the Negro will ultimately make an impression.

We must be rid of that word, Negro, as a racial classification of the African people. Negro is not an authentic, scientific classification of our racial group, but it is a Caste name. We will begin referring to all Black people who answer to Negro as a Caste people until we establish our true racial identity—Black people or Africans.

On our agenda is a call to a convention for the African people of the world. The major item on the agenda will be to get rid of that word, Negro, as a racial classification for our people, and to demand that we be addressed with the same dignity and respect extended to all other races and national groups.

The problem, as it projects itself upon the African people in the

Americas, is economical and psychological, and we must approach it as such. It takes an economical antidote to solve an economic problem and a psychological antidote to solve a psychological problem.

As we have stated earlier, we are philosophically committed to the ideals of Marcus Garvey—African Nationalism and self-determination.

For an antidote to our economic problem, Marcus Garvey founded the African Communities League to acquire the land, buildings, machines, tools, technology and personnel to win, control and dominate the commerce, business life and body politic in all communities where Black people are the majority population.

The faults of the Black people, as Negroes, are that they rely on supernatural powers to bring about material salvation based on a misguided concept of world society. They display extreme gullibility and naivete in accepting other people's ideas. Plus they disdain and scorn everything Black, African or symbolic of racial unity. The results are misery, social leprosy and political vassalage.

We find the solution to the above problem in the philosophy of the African Communities League, which is as follows—when and wherever we live in a community and are the majority population, we must own, control and dominate the commerce, business life and body politic of that community.

I have drawn up a concise, clear-cut and positive program of action that will implement the above philosophy. This program is the "Buy Black" campaign. It demands Black consumers to adhere to this program of racial economic necessity, and is dramatized by a reorientation of our shopping habits to the extent that we patronize those people belonging to our ethnic group.

The "Buy Black" campaign is the key. It will scientifically transfer the commerce, business life and body politic of the alien parasite to its rightful owner, the Black communities.

The "Buy Black" campaign demands that the Black consumer be as clannish in their patronage as all other racial groups are.

New York City is a cosmopolitan city, meaning that it has different racial and ethnic groups. We have Chinese, Italians, Germans, Jews, Latinos, etc. Each group has its own communities. These Chinese have a community known as Chinatown, where Chinese are the majority population. The Italians have a community known as Little Italy where Italians are the majority population. The Irish have a community known as Hell's Kitchen where the Irish are the majority population. The Germans have a community known as Germantown where the Germans are the majority population. The Jews have communities in Forest Hills, Queens, and on the Grand Concourse in the Bronx where Jews are the majority population.

The African Nationalist Pioneer Movement has made a complete survey of all homogeneous communities in New York City. Our findings show that in the Chinese community, the business life is controlled by the resident majority, Chinese. In the Italian community, the same pattern follows. In the Jewish community all the businesses are controlled by Jews. In the Puerto Rican settlements, the majority of businesses are controlled by Latinos. However, when we come to the Black communities, we find everybody but the Black people owning and controlling the businesses in these localities.

The "Buy Black" campaign will correct the situation, and make the Black community behave like the other racial and ethnic groups. It will have Blacks own and control the businesses in Black neighborhoods.

Whereas the other racial and ethnic groups realize that the basic action governing their welfare and survival is economic cooperation among and within their respective groups, the Black people (as Negroes), so far, have resisted all efforts to do likewise.

"Buy Black" is the key. It will transfer businesses in the Black communities from present alien parasites to their rightful owners—Black people.

Black consumers hold the key. They have the answer in their pockets and must be convinced to only patronize Black businesses. This will remove the non-Black enterprises from Black sections and replace these operations with Black community owned businesses.

The Black consumer is a Negro in the overwhelming majority of cases and therefore the biggest enemy to the "Buy Black" campaign. Yet, the success of the "Buy Black" campaign rests upon our ability to have Black consumers patronize only businesses owned by members of their race.

A thirty to sixty day boycott of non-Black businesses in Black communities will be sufficient to cause these enterprises to leave Black localities.

The Negro is not acting from a lack of information. He has been, and still is, exposed to as much information as all the other people. All that is missing in having the Negro behave like other racial ethnic groups is "a little touch of force," a little activity from the Lead Pipe Brigade.

This is the basic reason that we need the African Legion. With a 2,000 man African Legion, we can guarantee the success of the "Buy Black" campaign.

Along with meetings, picketing and handing out of circulars, close surveillance will be made on Black consumers patronizing the non-Black, businesses. This will be followed by appeals and warnings.

It is definitely an inhumane and criminal activity to rob a people of their commerce, business life and body politic. In communities where they are the majority population, Blacks are denied this fundamental basic requirement to a normal and secure life.

Knowingly or unknowingly, controlled or free will, consciously or unconsciously, all who take part in the above criminal activity must remember the universal cardinal principle. "Where there is crime, there must be punishment."

Black consumers are committing the unforgivable crime and sin. By refusing to patronize only Black businesses in Black communities, they are making themselves fit candidates for just punishment. Since the crime is committed against the Black community, the punishment should be implemented by this victim.

Therefore, if a Black soldier confronts a chronic Uncle Tom or Aunt Jemima Negro or Negress and makes a peaceful appeal to this person, the Negro or Negress will probably ignore this gesture. Angie usually hollers, "I spend my money where I want," or the jackass, Uncle Tom Negro will say, "I don't believe in that." The Black soldier withdraws and the Surveillance Squad takes over at that point.

The Surveillance Squad takes close observation of the Black consumer committing the crime of buying non-Black, nothing more.

The Tactical Squad takes over at this point. They are better known as the Lead Pipe Brigade. They do not bother Angie or move on the alien's businesses. As the criminal Black consumer walks or arrives home, the Lead Pipe Brigade moves in, destroys the merchandise, breaks a rib or two, or cracks the Negro's or Negress' head open slightly. In a short span of time a psychological metamorphosis will take place. The Black consumer will be convinced to patronize only Black businesses in Black communities.

Neither the white man nor anybody has a more effective media outlet than Mose and Angie when they realize that pain and punishment will automatically follow the criminal and traitorous act of not patronizing only the Black businesses in Black communities. I can hear Angie holler-ing, "Child, you better not go in them alien stores in our communities. You can get hurt that way. Someone kicked Beulah's ribs and rear end out of shape, and broke two ribs. I am 'Buying Black' in Black communi-ties, and you better too, unless you want what Beulah got."

Unfortunately, the present Black businesses are owned mostly by Negroes who are enemies to the "Buy Black" campaign. As stupid as that is, it is nonetheless true. The backward, ignorant, Negro businessman will tell you, "That's segregation. I have white and Black customers. I ain't prejudiced." You remind the stupid Negro that there are no white people in the community. This unbelievable jackass answers, "When the Pepsi-Cola or beer men deliver the merchandise, they always buy a soda or a beer."

We are passionately fascinated with the excellence of our African origin; therefore, we believe in finding the answers to all our problems from ourselves.

The cooperative corporations within this European, capitalistic system legally permit African people to practice truly African, democratic, communal, economic life. The businesses will be collectively owned by every member of the community and every member will have equal say and equal vote about the direction and management of businesses, regardless of their amount invested.

We must convince the present and potential Black businesses of great opportunities for expanding into larger markets with dedicated and regular customers. The "Buy Black" campaign will automatically bring this advantage.

African Nationalism is a philosophy and program that Black people must accept and implement if they are to measure up to the exacting standards set by the world today—and if they are to survive.

A universal mass movement for the freedom, dignity, security, progress and advancement of Black people everywhere, this is the source of the power, clout, and leverage that will allow African Nationalism to materialize. The key is the organization of the masses of African people all over the world. This organization must be committed and dedicated to the scientific implementation of Marcus Garvey's ideal, African Nationalism.

In essence, the philosophies of Marcus Garvey were:

1. A universal racial organization;
2. The emancipation of the African people of the world;
3. The redemption of Africa for Africans, those at home and those abroad;
4. The United States of Africa as a Black super power committed and dedicated to the welfare and security of Black people all over the world.

We are dedicated and committed to the scientific accomplishment of the above ideals, regardless of obstacles.

The "Buy Black" campaign is the primary, fundamental and necessary activity that will give the Black people the logistics required to implement Marcus Garvey's ideals, African Nationalism and self-determination.

The masses of Blacks all over the world must embrace and support the "Buy Black" campaign. This is where the gains from this activity and program will go.

The "Buy Black" campaign is a program of action for, by and of the African people of the world.

The "Buy Black" campaign will universally allow Blacks to taste real freedom after a long period of being denied this natural, sweet and righteous status.

The "Buy Black" campaign will rid Black people of alien parasites in Black communities, and will prevent the outflow of the community's expenditures. Retained expenditures will go for budgets that will eliminate unemployment, poverty, crime, perversion and alien exploitation in Black communities.

We believe in the principle of self-determination for all races. We submit that the people in Harlem and all other homogeneous African communities have the same moral and natural right to be as clannish in their patronage as other people have dramatized that they are. We advocate as a matter of sound racial economy the "Buy Black" campaign. Patronize your own race. Build a solvent foundation for your children. Help create employment and independence for your race.

One Cause, One Goal, One Destiny!

11 Robert F. Williams and "Armed Self-Reliance"

A former Monroe, North Carolina, NAACP leader and longtime proponent of "armed self-reliance," Robert F. Williams lived abroad in Cuba, China, and Tanzania between 1961 and 1969. He was being sought by the FBI on kidnapping charges leveled in the wake of an armed confrontation that had pitted Klansmen and their supporters against a handful of civil rights demonstrators. Granted asylum by Fidel Castro, Williams broadcast weekly encouragements to armed resistance over "Radio Free Dixie" and contributed equally spirited copy outlining effective guerrilla warfare techniques to his monthly newsletter, the *Crusader*. "America is a house on fire," he warned stateside listeners. "FREEDOM NOW, or let it burn, let it burn. Praise the Lord and pass the ammunition." Williams's impassioned rhetoric served as inspiration for 1960s groups such as the Deacons for Defense and Justice, a Louisiana-based federation of black activists committed to the protection of civil rights workers against the attacks of white racists; the Revolutionary Action Movement (RAM), which called for worldwide black revolution to overthrow Western imperialism; and the Republic of New Africa (RNA), which made Williams its president-in-exile. The following selection is taken from a Radio Free Dixie broadcast as transcribed in the July-August 1963 issue of the *Crusader*, by permission.

1963 Speech from Radio Free Dixie

Robert F. Williams

GREETINGS MY BROTHERS AND SISTERS:

The violence and the oppressive tyranny of racist ofays sweep across the USA like an uncontrollable firestorm. Police brutality and terror cast a dark and foreboding shadow over our people like a ghastly raven. Daily, the situation becomes more tense. No relief is in sight. Terrifying bombs are resounding in the night like thunder and electrifying the darkness of night like lightning. Mobs are howling in the streets like hungry wolf packs driven to the low lands in search of helpless prey by drought and famine.

Our people are being herded to prison like cattle driven to stock yards. The so-called courts of justice have initiated mass production trials based upon assembly line techniques. Chronic unemployment is becoming a way of life for many of our dehumanized people. Yes, savage cops have become so brutal that they are shooting our women in the back on public streets. Yes, our women and children are being gunned down like rabbits, felled by the blazing guns of hunters on Thanksgiving day. The lives of our women and children are less respected than those of common street dogs.

While the lives of our people are being savagely snuffed out by vicious racists for no other reason than that they were born black in the racist so-called FREE WORLD of the USA, our boys are being sent to fight and die in foreign campaigns. While all of these heinous crimes are being committed against our people, while all of this oppression and tyranny is being directed at us, slick John Kennedy pledges to the world that the U.S. will defend what he calls democracy around the world. What is this democracy that slick John pledges to defend? What is this democracy that the USA finds necessary to force on the people of South Viet-nam with armed might? Why will the racist USA force an unwanted so-called democracy on foreign peoples while black Americans beg and pray in vain for simple justice and human rights?

The so-called democracy of the savage USA is a racist democracy. It is a democracy of brutal exploitation and misery. It has no respect, whatever, for the rights of black people. What is the nature of a people who have constructed such a society? What is the nature of a people who support and tolerate such a society? It is time for Americans who plead innocence to these crimes against humanity to prove their innocence by open opposition to this barbaric tyranny.

Collectively and individually mankind is responsible for the type of society in which he lives. Those who share in the spoils of folly must be prepared to share the eventual results of folly. He who witnesses, with no more than a sigh, unjust brutality visited upon his fellowman is a party to the crime and must be prepared to share the harvest of such bitter seed. The USA is passing the final milestone along the road to the point of no return. Already her streets are becoming stained with the blood of freedom martyrs, already her jails are buldging with the most noble of the land, already the first winds of a hurricane gather over the sea of discontent and black men's heartbeats quicken to the tempo of war drums.

My brothers and sisters, where is our recourse? Where is our redress? And where is our hope? The choice has been thrust upon us. We have not chosen to be slaves, we have not chosen to be brutally dehumanized. No, we have not chosen not to live in peace, but our oppressors have chosen to make war on us. In peace and humility we have humbly asked for our natural and legal right to human dignity. They have answered our peaceful petition with terror and violence. They have tightened their noose around our necks, they have opened fire on our women and children. They have invested in ferocious dogs the power to block our path to freedom.

There are some among us who exhort us not to defend ourselves. There are some who exhort us to invoke the power of love and nonviolence. Yes, they would have us to turn the other cheek even as our women and children are being defiled. Is not self preservation the first law of nature? There are some among us who preach that violent self defense is immoral. Who are these pious, self-righteous people who consider themselves qualified to pass judgement on the morality of the great liberators of the world and the violent struggles they lead and have led? Who are these self-righteous people who propose to pass judgement on those who live in the noble tradition of the glorious patriots of the American Revolution?

My brothers and sisters, there is no justice for the black American in the racist USA. A common street dog has more police protection than our despised and abused people. U.S. Courts are no more than cesspools of racial injustice and persecution. The antics we are watching of those apes in the Congress and Senate are ample proof that the USA is a social jungle of race hate. These racist maniacs and their fellow traveling goon squads are determined to block our path to freedom. We say freedom now, but they say never! While we speak of human rights, they speak nobly of property rights. They speak of the right of the racist states to scoff at and scorn the 14th Amendment to the U.S. Constitution. We may put more stock in our hope for a fool than in the possibility of a change of heart in these savage, racist maniacs. The only hope we can possibly have is that which is forged and created by our own determination.

Our oppressors are beasts. They are devoid of human conscience. But even the beast of the jungle respects force and violence. Our dignity demands that we defend ourselves. Our self preservation requires us to FIGHT BACK! Yes, a dark and foreboding shadow hovers over our people like a ghastly raven. Violence and terror sweep the land like a firestorm. We have no recourse but to raise our battle cry. Let every street become a battle field and every fist strike a blow. Let every stone become a weapon and every black man, woman and child become a soldier and patriot in our cause of liberty. My brothers and sisters, it is now or never. We must overcome at any price. No, we are not afraid, for it is better to die than to survive as a subhuman. It is better to live just 30 seconds in full and beautiful dignity of manhood than to live a thousand years crawling and dragging our chains at the feet of our brutal oppressors. In the spirit of Lexington and Concord, LET OUR BATTLE CRY BE HEARD AROUND THE WORLD, FREEDOM! FREEDOM! FREEDOM NOW OR DEATH!!!

12   Elijah Muhammad and the Nation of Islam

The territorial nationalist stance of the Nation of Islam has been made clear to adherents since its founding in the midst of the Great Depression. Patriarch Elijah Muhammad taught that all Americans of African descent belonged to an "Asian black nation," more specifically to the tribe of Shabazz. It was the mission of the North American branch of this ancient clan to redeem the Black Nation from centuries of unjust white rule. Short of divine intervention, the best solution to black people's problems was thought to be relocation to a state of their own. Separation—"either on this continent or elsewhere"—would enable African Americans to escape the "mental poisoning" of their "400-year-old enemies." Freed from the "blue-eyed devils'" impositions, they would work to create a vibrant Islamic civilization "beyond the white world."

According to the political economy of the Nation, much could be accomplished even before the achievement of full-blown statehood. Members were to pool their resources, spend money among themselves, and create their own institutions. To encourage such endeavor, Muhammad instituted a communalistic tithing/taxation system known as the "Duty." Other trappings of sovereignty included an Islamic flag, said to be several trillion years old; the University of Islam—primarily an elementary and high school system; a paramilitary self-defense corps, the Fruit of Islam; and a wide-ranging economic infrastructure of businesses, factories, and farms.

Foundational to all group economic and cultural activities was a unique messianic theology that transcended normal religious boundaries. To the devout, Elijah Muhammad was the "last Messenger" of a black creator God. Sometime before the year 2000, Allah would reappear, signaling the beginning of a new and glorious epoch in which black people would inherit power over all of creation. Prior to that day, members of the Nation were duty-bound to help protect and sustain other "so-called Negroes" by promoting territorial separatism and economic nationalism.

In the following excerpts, reprinted by permission from Elijah Muhammad's *Message to the Blackman in America* (Chicago: Muhammad's Temple No. 2, 1965), the Nation of Islam leader speaks of separatism as (1) a reflection of self-love; (2) a way to combat the "white devils' " wiles; and (3) an essential step in the quest for black dignity, unity, and independence.

1965 Know Thyself

Elijah Muhammad

It is knowledge of self that the so-called Negroes lack that which keeps them from enjoying freedom, justice and equality. This belongs to them divinely as much as it does to other nations of the earth.

It is Allah's (God's) will and purpose that we shall know ourselves. Therefore He came Himself to teach us the knowledge of self. Who is better knowing of who we are than God, Himself? He has declared that we are descendants of the Asian black nation and of the tribe of Shabazz.

You might ask, who is this tribe of Shabazz? Originally, they were the tribe that came with the earth (or this part) 60 trillion years ago when a great explosion on our planet divided it into two parts. One we call earth and the other moon.

This was done by one of our scientists, God; who wanted the people to speak one language, one dialect for all, but was unable to bring this about. He decided to kill us by destroying our planet, but still He failed. We were lucky to be on this part, earth, which did not lose its water in the mighty blasting away of the part called moon.

We, the tribe of Shabazz, says Allah (God), were the first to discover the best part of our planet to live on. The rich Nile Valley of Egypt and the present seat of the Holy City, Mecca, Arabia.

The origin of our kinky hair, says Allah, came from one of our dissatisfied scientists, 50,000 years ago, who wanted to make all of us tough and hard in order to endure the life of the jungles of East Asia (Africa) and to overcome the beasts there. But he failed to get the others to agree with him.

He took his family and moved into the jungle to prove to us that we could live there and conquer the wild beasts, and we have. So, being the first and the smartest scientist on the deportation of our moon and the one who suffered most of all, Allah (God) has decided to place us on the top with a thorough knowledge of self and his guidance.

We are the mighty, the wise, the best, but do not know it. Being without the knowledge, we disgrace ourselves, subjecting ourselves to suffering and shame. We could not get the knowledge of self until the coming of Allah. To know thyself is to know all men, as from us came all and to us all will return.

I must keep warning you that you should give up the white race's names and religion in order to gain success. Their days of success are over. Their rule will last only as long as you remain asleep to the knowledge of self.

Awake and know that Allah has revealed the truth. Stop believing in something coming to you after you are physically dead. That is untrue, and no one can show any proof of such belief.

Again, know that Jesus was only a prophet and cannot hear you pray any more than Moses or any other dead prophet. Know too, that this white race was created to be the enemy of black mankind for 6,000 years, which makes their number to be six. That is not your number or mine. We do not have a number, because we have no birth record. Do not let anyone fool you. This is the separation and the War of Armageddon.

1965 *From* The Making of Devil

Elijah Muhammad

You have learned, from the reading of history, that a nation's permanent success depends on its obedience to Allah. We have seen the white race (devils) in heaven, among the righteous, causing trouble (making mischief and causing bloodshed), until they were discovered.

They made trouble for six months, right in heaven, deceiving the ancient original people who were holy. But, when they learned just who was causing the trouble; they, as you have learned, cast the troublemakers out into the worst and poorest part of our planet earth.

They were punished by being deprived of divine guidance, for 2,000 years which brought them almost into the family of wild beasts—going upon all fours; eating raw and unseasoned, uncooked food; living in caves and tree tops, climbing and jumping from one tree to the other.

Even today, they like climbing and jumping. The monkeys are from them. Before their time, there were no such things as monkeys, apes and swine. Read the Holy Qur-an (Chapter 18) entitled: "The Cave." The Holy Qur-an mentions them as being turned into apes and swine as a divine curse, because of their disbelief in Moses.

We do know that both of these animals are loved and befriended by the white race, along with the dog. But, all of the divine curses sent upon the white race in these days are not enough to serve as a warning to that race. They rose up from the caves and hillsides of Europe, went back to Asia, and have ruled nine-tenths of that great continent.

Muhammad set the devils back for 1,000 years. They were released on the coming of Columbus, and his finding of this Western Hemisphere. They have been here now over 400 years. Their worst and most unpardonable sins were the bringing of the so-called Negroes here to do their labor.

The so-called Negroes have not only given free labor, but have given their lives on the soil of their masters and, all over the earth wherever his hateful and murdering slave-master wants them to go. Now, the slave wants better treatment. They are fast learning today, that these are the children of those who made merchandise out of their fathers. The devil is the "devil" regardless of place and time.

They deceived our fathers and are now deceiving the children, under many false disguises, (as though they want to be friends of the black man) such as integration and intermarriage.

The devil said to Allah: "I shall certainly come upon them from before them and from behind them; and from their right and from their left; and Thou wilt not find most of them thankful" (Holy Qur-an 7:17). This is being fulfilled before our very eyes today. The devils are doing both.

They come to the so-called Negroes as friends and as open enemies. They go before them, changing the truth into false; and come behind the Truth-bearer to the so-called Negroes, speaking evil of the truth. They threaten the so-called Negroes with poverty and imprisonment, and make rosy promises to them, only to deceive.

They are telling the so-called Negroes that they realized that they used to mistreat the Negroes, but now they are going to do better and forget the past. "Let us live like brothers for we are all from God."

Along with such smooth lies is an offer of one of the devils' women. The poor so-called Negroes fall victim and the devil men raid the neighborhood of the so-called Negro women, day and night, to make all desirous of hell fire.

This is the way they have planned to beat Allah to the so-called Negroes. What should you do? The answer: Stay away from sweethearting with devils. Surely this is the end of their time, on our planet. Allah said to the devil: "Get out of it despised, and driven away. Whoever of them (the Negroes) will follow you, I will certainly fill hell with you all" (7:18). So remember, your seeking friendship with this race of devils means seeking a place in their hell.

From **A Program for Self-Development**

Elijah Muhammad

We must remember that we just cannot depend on the white race ever to do that which we can and should do for self. The American so-called Negroes are like the Bible story of Lazarus and the rich man, the story that Jesus must have foreseen at the time. This Bible beggar was charmed by the wealth of the rich man to whom he was a servant, and he could not make up his mind to go seek something for self.

This beggar was offered a home in Paradise but could not make up his mind to leave the gate of his master, the rich man, wishing for that which God had in store for destruction along with its owner. The beggar's eyes could not turn from that perishable wealth. So it is with the American Negroes; they are charmed by the luxury of their slave-master, and cannot make up their minds to seek for self something of this good earth, though hated and despised by the rich man and full of sores caused by the evil treatment of the rich man. On top of that he is chased by the rich man's dogs and still remains a beggar at the gate, though the gates of Paradise were ever open to him and the gates of hell were open to receive his rich master.

The American Negroes have the same gates of Paradise open to them but are charmed by the wealth of America and cannot see the great opportunity that lies before them. They are suffering untold injustices at the hands of the rich; they have been and still are being lynched and burned; they and their women and children are beaten all over the country, by the rich slave-masters and their children. The slaves' houses and churches are bombed by the slave-masters; their girls are used as prostitutes and at times are raped in public. Yet the Negroes are on their knees begging the rich man to treat them as the rich man treats himself and his kind. The poor beggar kindly asks for the crumbs, a job and a house in the neighborhood of the rich man.

The Negro leaders are frightened to death and are afraid to ask for anything other than a job. The good things of this earth could be theirs if they would only unite and acquire wealth as the masters and the other independent nations have. The Negroes could have all of this if they could get up and go to work for self. They are far too lazy as a Nation — 100 years up from slavery and still looking to the master to care for them and give them a job, bread and a house to live in on the master's land. You should be ashamed of yourselves, surely the white race has been very good in the way of making jobs for their willing slaves, but this cannot go on forever; we are about at the end of it and must do something for SELF or else.

The slave-master has given you enough education to go and do for self, but this education is not being used for self; it is even offered back to the slave-masters to help them to keep you a dependent people looking to them for support. Let us unite every good that is in us for the uplifting of the American so-called Negroes to the equal of the world's independent nations. Ask for a start for self and the American white people, I believe, are willing to help give us a start if they see you and I are willing to do for self. It would remove from them not only the worry of trying to give jobs and schools to a lazy people but also would get them honor and sincere friendship all over the Asiatic world and God, Himself, would prolong their time on the earth.

We must stop relying upon the white man to care for us. We must become an independent people. So-called Negroes should:

1. Separate yourselves from the "slave-master."
2. Pool your resources, education and qualifications for independence.
3. Stop forcing yourselves into places where you are not wanted.
4. Make your own neighborhood a decent place to live.
5. Rid yourselves of the lust of wine and drink and learn to love self and your kind before loving others.
6. Unite to create a future for yourself.
7. Build your own homes, schools, hospitals, and factories.
8. Do not seek to mix your blood through racial integration.
9. Stop buying expensive cars, fine clothes and shoes before being able to live in a fine home.
10. Spend your money among yourselves.
11. Build an economic system among yourselves.
12. Protect your women.

Stop allowing the white men to shake hands or speak to your women anytime or anywhere. This practice has ruined us. They wink their eye at your daughter after coming into your home—but you cannot go on the North side and do the same with his women.

No black man feels good—by nature—seeing a white man with a Negro woman. We have all colors in our race—red, yellow, brown and jet black—why should we need a white person?

Africans would not dare allow their women to be the targets that we allow ours to be.

If I were not protected by Allah (God), how would I be able to stand before this white man unafraid and speak as I do.

13 Malcolm X and the Organization of Afro-American Unity

Born into a Garveyite family in 1925, Malcolm Little was converted to the teachings of Elijah Muhammad during the late 1940s while serving a prison sentence for burglary. The Black Muslim "X" replaced his "slave name" and he became a minister of the Nation of Islam shortly after his release in 1952. Over the next decade, Malcolm X became the best-known evangelist for the separatist Muslim faith, organizing temples from coast to coast and recruiting thousands of new members. Eventually, however, a series of theological, intellectual, stylistic, personal, and political issues created tension between the prophet and his disciple. In March 1964, Malcolm X quit the Nation, converted to orthodox Islam, and denounced his spiritual father as a "religious faker." This increasingly open and bitter conflict led to his assassination while he was addressing a rally at New York's Audubon Ballroom.

At the time of his death, Malcolm X—now also known by his Sunni Muslim name, El-Hajj Malik El-Shabazz—was intimately involved in building support for the Organization of Afro-American Unity (OAAU). Founded shortly after he left Muhammad's fold, the OAAU provided Malcolm with an organizational platform on which he could work out the details of his post-Nation political evolution. Only eight months old when its chief attractive force and major financial contributor was murdered, the OAAU survived, but in attenuated form. Even before the assassination it could claim no more than a few hundred members.

The following document was drafted by an OAAU committee and approved by Malcolm X early in 1965. Designed to "galvanize the black masses of Harlem to become the instruments of their own liberation," the Basic Unity Program was to have been introduced to the membership at a 15 February rally. Unfortunately, the Valentine's Day firebombing of Malcolm's home caused the program's presentation to be postponed a week. It was at this 21 February session that the OAAU leader was killed. As can be seen from the text, the OAAU's vision was expansive.

Its program embraced a variety of what soon would be termed "Black Power" beliefs and initiatives. The document is reprinted from George Breitman, *The Last Year of Malcolm X: The Evolution of a Revolutionary* (New York: Schocken Books, 1968), by permission.

1965 *From* Basic Unity Program
Organization of Afro-American Unity
Malcolm X

Pledging unity . . .
Promoting justice . . .
Transcending compromise . . .
We, Afro-Americans, people who originated in Africa and now reside in America, speak out against the slavery and oppression inflicted upon us by this racist power structure. We offer to downtrodden Afro-American people courses of action that will conquer oppression, relieve suffering and convert meaningless struggle into meaningful action.

Confident that our purpose will be achieved, we Afro-Americans from all walks of life make the following known:

Establishment

Having stated our determination, confidence and resolve, the Organization of Afro-American Unity is hereby established on the 15th day of February, 1965, in the city of New York.

Upon this establishment, we Afro-American people will launch a cultural revolution which will provide the means for restoring our identity that we might rejoin our brothers and sisters on the African continent, culturally, psychologically, economically and share with them the sweet fruits of freedom from oppression and independence of racist governments.

1. The Organization of Afro-American Unity welcomes all persons of African origin to come together and dedicate their ideas, skills and lives to free our people from oppression.

2. Branches of the Organization of Afro-American Unity may be established by people of African descent wherever they may be and whatever their ideology—as long as they be descendants of Africa and dedicated to our one goal: Freedom from oppression.

3. The basic program of the Organization of Afro-American Unity which is now being presented can and will be modified by the member-

ship, taking into consideration national, regional and local conditions that require flexible treatment.

4. The Organization of Afro-American Unity encourages active participation of each member since we feel that each and every Afro-American has something to contribute to our freedom. Thus each member will be encouraged to participate in the committee of his or her choice.

5. Understanding the differences that have been created amongst us by our oppressors in order to keep us divided, the Organization of Afro-American Unity strives to ignore or submerge these artificial divisions by focusing our activities and our loyalties upon our one goal: Freedom from oppression.

Basic Aims and Objectives

Self-Determination

We assert that we Afro-Americans have the right to direct and control our lives, our history and our future rather than to have our destinies determined by American racists . . .

We are determined to rediscover our true African culture which was crushed and hidden for over four hundred years in order to enslave us and keep us enslaved up to today . . .

We, Afro-Americans—enslaved, oppressed and denied by a society that proclaims itself the citadel of democracy, are determined to rediscover our history, promote the talents that are suppressed by our racist enslavers, renew the culture that was crushed by a slave government and thereby—to again become a free people.

National Unity

Sincerely believing that the future of Afro-Americans is dependent upon our ability to unite our ideas, skills, organizations and institutions . . .

We, the Organization of Afro-American Unity pledge to join hands and hearts with all people of African origin in a grand alliance by forgetting all the differences that the power structure has created to keep us divided and enslaved. We further pledge to strengthen our common bond and strive toward one goal: Freedom from oppression.

The Basic Unity Program

The program of the Organization of Afro-American Unity shall evolve from five strategic points which are deemed basic and fundamental to our grand alliance. Through our committees we shall proceed in the following general areas:

I. Restoration

In order to enslave the African it was necessary for our enslavers to completely sever our communications with the African continent and the Africans that remained there. In order to free ourselves from the oppression of our enslavers then, it is absolutely necessary for the Afro-American to restore communications with Africa.

The Organization of Afro-American Unity will accomplish this goal by means of independent national and international newspapers, publishing ventures, personal contacts and other available communications media.

We, Afro-Americans, must also communicate to one another the truths about American slavery and the terrible effects it has upon our people. We must study the modern system of slavery in order to free ourselves from it. We must search out all the bare and ugly facts without shame for we are still victims, still slaves—still oppressed. Our only shame is believing falsehood and not seeking the truth.

We must learn all that we can about ourselves. We will have to know the whole story of how we were kidnapped from Africa, how our ancestors were brutalized, dehumanized and murdered and how we are continually kept in a state of slavery for the profit of a system conceived in slavery, built by slaves and dedicated to keeping us enslaved in order to maintain itself.

We must begin to reeducate ourselves and become alert listeners in order to learn as much as we can about the progress of our Mother-land—Africa. We must correct in our minds the distorted image that our enslaver has portrayed to us of Africa that he might discourage us from reestablishing communications with her and thus obtain freedom from oppression.

II. Reorientation

In order to *keep* the Afro-American enslaved, it was necessary to limit our thinking to the shores of America—to prevent us from identifying our problems with the problems of other peoples of African origin. This made us consider ourselves an isolated minority without allies anywhere.

The Organization of Afro-American Unity will develop in the Afro-American people a keen awareness of our relationship with the world at large and clarify our roles, rights and responsibilities as human beings. We can accomplish this goal by becoming well informed concerning world affairs and understanding that our struggle is part of a larger world struggle of oppressed peoples against all forms of oppression. We must change the thinking of the Afro-American by liberating our minds through the study of philosophies and psychologies, cultures and languages that did not come from our racist oppressors. Provisions are being made for the study of languages such as Swahili, Hausa and Arabic. These studies will give our people access to ideas and history of mankind at large and thus increase our mental scope.

We can learn much about Africa by reading informative books and by listening to the experiences of those who have traveled there, but many of us can travel to the land of our choice and experience for ourselves. The Organization of Afro-American Unity will encourage the Afro-American to travel to Africa, the Caribbean and to other places where our culture has not been completely crushed by brutality and ruthlessness.

III. Education

After enslaving us, the slavemasters developed a racist educational system which justified to its posterity the evil deeds that had been committed against the African people and their descendants. Too often the slave himself participates so completely in this system that he justifies having been enslaved and oppressed.

The Organization of Afro-American Unity will devise original educational methods and procedures which will liberate the minds of our children from the vicious lies and distortions that are fed to us from the cradle to keep us mentally enslaved. We encourage Afro-Americans themselves to establish experimental institutes and educational workshops, liberation schools and child-care centers in the Afro-American communities.

We will influence the choice of textbooks and equipment used by our children in the public schools while at the same time encouraging qualified Afro-Americans to write and publish the textbooks needed to liberate our minds. Until we completely control our own educational institutions, we must supplement the formal training of our children by educating them at home.

IV. Economic Security

After the Emancipation Proclamation, when the system of slavery changed from chattel slavery to wage slavery, it was realized that the Afro-American constituted the largest homogeneous ethnic group with a common origin and common group experience in the United States and, if allowed to exercise economic or political freedom, would in a short period of time own this country. Therefore racists in this government developed techniques that would keep the Afro-American people economically dependent upon the slavemasters—economically slaves— twentieth century slaves.

The Organization of Afro-American Unity will take measures to free our people from economic slavery. One way of accomplishing this will be to maintain a Technician Pool: that is, a Bank of Technicians. In the same manner that blood banks have been established to furnish blood to those who need it at the time it is needed, we must establish a Technician Bank. We must do this so that the newly independent nations of Africa can turn to us who are their Afro-American brothers for the technicians they will need now and in the future. Thereby, we will be developing an open market for the many skills we possess and at the same time we will be supplying Africa with the skills she can best use. This project will therefore be one of mutual cooperation and mutual benefit.

V. Self-Defense

In order to enslave a people and keep them subjugated, their right to self-defense must be denied. They must be constantly terrorized, brutalized and murdered. These tactics of suppression have been developed to a new high by vicious racists whom the United States government seems unwilling or incapable of dealing with in terms of the law of this land. Before the Emancipation it was the black man who suffered humiliation, torture, castration, and murder. Recently our women and children, more and more, are becoming the victims of savage racists whose appetite for blood increases daily and whose deeds of depravity seem to be openly encouraged by all law enforcement agencies. Over 5,000 Afro-Americans have been lynched since the Emancipation Proclamation and not one murderer has been brought to justice!

The Organization of Afro-American Unity, being aware of the increased violence being visited upon the Afro-American and of the open sanction of this violence and murder by the police departments throughout this country and the federal agencies—do affirm our right and obligation to defend ourselves in order to survive as a people.

We encourage all Afro-Americans to defend themselves against the wanton attacks of racist aggressors whose sole aim is to deny us the guarantees of the United Nations Charter of Human Rights and of the Constitution of the United States.

The Organization of Afro-American Unity will take those private steps that are necessary to insure the survival of the Afro-American people in the face of racist aggression and the defense of our women and children. We are within our rights to see to it that the Afro-American people who fulfill their obligations to the United States government (we pay taxes and serve in the armed forces of this country like American citizens do) also exact from this government the obligations that it owes us as a people, or exact these obligations ourselves. Needless to say, among this number we include protection of certain inalienable rights such as life, liberty and the pursuit of happiness.

In areas where the United States government has shown itself unable and/or unwilling to bring to justice the racist oppressors, murderers, who kill innocent children and adults, the Organization of Afro-American Unity advocates that the Afro-American people insure ourselves that justice is done—whatever the price and *by any means necessary.*

National Concerns

General Terminologies

We Afro-Americans feel receptive toward all peoples of goodwill. We are not opposed to multi-ethnic associations in any walk of life. In fact, we have had experiences which enable us to understand how unfortunate it is that human beings have been set apart or aside from each other because of characteristics known as "racial" characteristics.

However, Afro-Americans did not create the prejudiced background and atmosphere in which we live. And we must face the facts. A "racial" society does exist in stark reality, and not with equality for black people; so we who are non-white must meet the problems inherited from centuries of inequalities and deal with the present situations as rationally as we are able.

The exclusive ethnic quality of our unity is necessary for self-preservation. We say this because: Our experiences backed up by history show that African culture and Afro-American culture will not be accurately recognized and reported and cannot be respectably expressed nor be secure in its survival if we remain the divided, and therefore the helpless, victims of an oppressive society.

We appreciate the fact that when the people involved have real equality and justice, ethnic intermingling can be beneficial to all. We must denounce, however, all people who are oppressive through their policies or actions and who are lacking in justice in their dealings with other people, whether the injustices proceed from power, class, or "race." We must be unified in order to be protected from abuse or misuse.

We consider the word "integration" a misleading, false term. It carries with it certain implications to which Afro-Americans cannot subscribe. This terminology has been applied to the current regulation projects which are supposedly "acceptable" to some classes of society. This very "acceptable" implies some inherent superiority or inferiority instead of acknowledging the true source of the inequalities involved.

We have observed that the usage of the term "integration" was designated and promoted by those persons who expect to continue a (nicer) type of ethnic discrimination and who intend to maintain social and economic control of all human contacts by means of imagery, classifications, quotas, and manipulations based on color, national origin, or "racial" background and characteristics.

Careful evaluation of recent experiences shows that "integration" actually describes the process by which a white society is (remains) set in a position to use, whenever it chooses to use and however it chooses to use, the best talents of non-white people. This power-web continues to build a society wherein the best contributions of Afro-Americans, in fact of all non-white people, would continue to be absorbed without note or exploited to benefit a fortunate few while the masses of both white and non-white people would remain unequal and unbenefited.

We are aware that many of us lack sufficient training and are deprived and unprepared as a result of oppression, discrimination, and the resulting discouragement, despair, and resignation. But when we are not qualified, and where we are unprepared, we must help each other and work out plans for bettering our own conditions as Afro-Americans. Then our assertions toward full opportunity can be made on the basis of equality as opposed to the calculated tokens of "integration." Therefore, we must reject this term as one used by all persons who intend to mislead Afro-Americans.

Another term, "negro," is erroneously used and is degrading in the eyes of informed and self-respecting persons of African heritage. It denotes stereotyped and debased traits of character and classifies a whole segment of humanity on the basis of false information. From all intelligent viewpoints, it is a badge of slavery and helps to prolong and perpetuate oppression and discrimination.

Persons who recognize the emotional thrust and plain show of disrespect in the southerner's use of "nigra" and the general use of "nigger" must also realize that all three words are essentially the same. The other two: "nigra" and "nigger" are blunt and undeceptive. The one representing respectability, "negro," is merely the same substance in a polished package and spelled with a capital letter. This refinement is added so that a degrading terminology can be legitimately used in general literature and "polite" conversation without embarrassment.

The term "negro" developed from a word in the Spanish language which is actually an adjective (describing word) meaning "black," that is, the *color* black. In plain English, if someone said or was called *A* "black" or *A* "dark," even a young child would very naturally question: "*A* black what?" or "*A* dark what?" because adjectives do not name, they describe. Please take note that in order to make use of this mechanism, a word was transferred from another language and deceptively changed in function from an adjective to a noun, which is a naming word. Its application in the nominative (naming) sense was intentionally used to portray persons in a position of objects or "things." It stamps the article as being "all alike and all the same." It denotes: a "darkie," a slave, a sub-human, an ex-slave, a *"negro."*

Afro-Americans must re-analyze and particularly question our own use of this term, keeping in mind all the facts. In light of the historical meanings and current implications, all intelligent and informed Afro-Americans and Africans continue to reject its use in the noun form as well as a proper adjective. Its usage shall continue to be considered as unenlightened and objectionable or deliberately offensive whether in speech or writing.

We accept the use of Afro-American, African, and Black Man in reference to persons of African heritage. To every other part of mankind goes this measure of just respect. We do not desire more nor shall we accept less.

PART TWO

*Black Nationalism
in the Black Power Era*

14 The Student Nonviolent Coordinating Committee and Black Empowerment

The Student Nonviolent Coordinating Committee (SNCC, pronounced "snick") was formed in 1960 to help facilitate nonviolent direct action civil rights demonstrations throughout the South. Its idealistic, committed, interracial activists participated in numerous early 1960s sit-in, jail-in, freedom ride, and voting rights campaigns. By mid-decade, however, black-white tensions within the organization and the growing attraction of nationalism as an ideology and organizational tool caused SNCC leaders such as Stokely Carmichael (now Kwame Ture) and H. Rap Brown (now Jamil Abdullah Al-Amin) to conclude that their work would be made easier if nonblacks were excluded from participation. In 1966, whites were expelled as SNCC adopted an openly separatist orientation. "The only way we gonna stop them white men from whuppin' us is to take over," noted Carmichael. "We been saying freedom for six years and we ain't got nothin'. What we gonna start saying now is Black Power!" As the group's militant chairperson told his former ally, Martin Luther King, Jr., SNCC now believed that "power is the only thing respected in this world, and we must get it at any cost." The following position paper, first published in the *New York Times* of 5 August 1966 and reprinted by permission, provides a multifaceted rationale for these controversial policy shifts.

1966 Position Paper on Black Power

Student Nonviolent Coordinating Committee

The myth that the Negro is somehow incapable of liberating himself, is lazy, etc., came out of the American experience. In the books that children read, whites are always "good" (good symbols are white), blacks are "evil" or seen as savages in movies, their language is referred to as a "dialect," and black people in this country are supposedly descended from savages.

Any white person who comes into the movement has these concepts in his mind about black people if only subconsciously. He cannot escape them because the whole society has geared his subconscious in that direction.

Miss America coming from Mississippi has a chance to represent all of America, but a black person from either Mississippi or New York will never represent America. So that white people coming into the movement cannot relate to the black experience, cannot relate to the word "black," cannot relate to the "nitty gritty," cannot relate to the experience that brought such a word into being, cannot relate to chitterlings, hog's head cheese, pig feet, hamhocks, and cannot relate to slavery, because these things are not a part of their experience. They also cannot relate to the black religious experience, nor to the black church unless, of course, this church has taken on white manifestations.

Negroes in this country have never been allowed to organize themselves because of white interference. As a result of this, the stereotype has been reinforced that blacks cannot organize themselves. The white psychology that blacks have to be watched, also reinforces this stereotype. Blacks, in fact, feel intimidated by the presence of whites, because of their knowledge of the power that whites have over their lives. One white person can come into a meeting of black people and change the complexion of that meeting, whereas one black person would not change the complexion of that meeting unless he was an obvious Uncle Tom. People would immediately start talking about "brotherhood," "love," etc; race would not be discussed.

If people must express themselves freely, there has to be a climate in which they can do this. If blacks feel intimidated by whites, then they are not liable to vent the rage that they feel about whites in the presence of whites—especially not the black people whom we are trying to organize, i.e., the broad masses of black people. A climate has to be created whereby blacks can express themselves. The reason that whites must be excluded is not that one is anti-white, but because the efforts that one is trying to achieve cannot succeed because whites have an intimidating effect. Ofttimes the intimidating effect is in direct proportion to the amount of degradation that black people have suffered at the hands of white people.

It must be offered that white people who desire change in this country should go where that problem (of racism) is most manifest. The problem is not in the black community. The white people should go into white communities where the whites have created power for the express [purpose] of denying blacks human dignity and self-determination. Whites who come into the black community with ideas of change seem to want to absolve the power structure of its responsibility of what it is doing, and saying that change can come only through black unity, which is only the worst kind of paternalism. This is not to say that whites have not had an important role in the movement. In the case of Mississippi, their role was very key in that they helped give blacks the right to organize, that role is now over, and it should be.

People now have the right to picket, the right to give out leaflets, the right to vote, the right to demonstrate, the right to print.

These things which revolve around the right to organize have been accomplished mainly because of the entrance of white people into Mississippi, in the summer of '64. Since these goals have now been accomplished, their (whites') role in the movement has now ended. What does it mean if black people, once having the right to organize, are not allowed to organize themselves? It means that blacks' ideas about inferiority are being reinforced. Shouldn't people be able to organize themselves? Blacks should be given this right. Further (white participation) means in the eyes of the black community that whites are the "brains": behind the movement and blacks cannot function without whites. This only serves to perpetuate existing attitudes within the existing society, i.e., blacks are "dumb," "unable to take care of business," etc. Whites are "smart," the "brains" behind everything.

How do blacks relate to other blacks as such? How do we react to Willie Mays as against Mickey Mantle? What is our response to Mays hitting a home run against Mantle performing the same deed? One has to come to the conclusion that it is because of black participation in baseball. Negroes still identify with the Dodgers because of Jackie Robinson's efforts with the Dodgers. Negroes would instinctively champion all-black teams if they opposed all-white or predominantly white teams. The same principle operates for the movement as it does for baseball: a mystique must be created whereby Negroes can identify with the movement.

Thus an all-black project is needed in order for the people to free themselves. This has to exist from the beginning. This relates to what can be called "coalition politics." There is no doubt in our minds that some whites are just as disgusted with this system as we are. But it is meaningless to talk about coalition if there is no one to align ourselves with, because of the lack of organization in the white communities. There can be no talk of "hooking up" unless black people organize blacks and white people organize whites. If these conditions are met then perhaps at some later date—and if we are going in the same direction—talks about exchange of personnel, coalition, and other meaningful alliances can be discussed.

In the beginning of the movement, we had fallen into a trap whereby we thought that our problems revolved around the right to eat at certain lunch counters or the right to vote or to organize our communities. We have seen, however, that the problem is much deeper. The problem of this country, as we had seen it, concerned all blacks and all whites (and therefore) if decisions were left to the young people, then solutions would be arrived at. But this negates the history of black people and whites. We have dealt stringently with the problem of "Uncle Tom," but we have not yet gotten around to Simon Legree. We must ask ourselves who is the real villain? Uncle Tom or Simon Legree? Everybody knows Uncle Tom but who knows Simon Legree?

So what we have now (in S.N.C.C.) is a closed society. A clique. Black people cannot relate to S.N.C.C., because of its unrealistic, nonracial atmosphere; denying their experiences of America as a racist society. In contrast, S.C.L.C. [the Rev. Dr. Martin Luther King Jr.'s Southern Christian Leadership Conference] has a staff that at least maintains a black facade. The front office is virtually all-black, but nobody accuses S.C.L.C. of being racist.

If we are to proceed toward true liberation, we must cut ourselves off from white people. We must form our own institutions, credit unions, co-ops, political parties, write our own histories.

To proceed further, let us make some comparisons between the Black Movement of the (early) 1900's and the movement of the 1960's—the N.A.A.C.P. [the National Association for the Advancement of Colored People] with S.N.C.C. Whites subverted the Niagara movement [the fore-runner of the N.A.A.C.P.] which, at the outset, was an all-black movement. The name of the new organization was also very revealing, in that it pre-supposed blacks have to be advanced to the level of whites. We are now aware that the N.A.A.C.P. has grown reactionary, is controlled by the black power structure itself, and stands as one of the main roadblocks to black freedom. S.N.C.C., by allowing the whites to remain in the organization, can have its efforts subverted in the same manner, i.e., through having them play important roles such as community organizers, etc. Indigenous leadership cannot be built with whites in the positions they now hold.

These facts do not mean that whites cannot help. They can participate on a voluntary basis. We can contract work out to them, but in no way can they participate on a policy-making level.

The charge may be made that we are "racists," but whites who are sensitive to our problems will realize that we must determine our own destiny.

In an attempt to find a solution to our dilemma, we propose that our organization (S.N.C.C.) should be black-staffed, black-controlled and black-financed. We do not want to fall into a similar dilemma that other civil rights organizations have fallen. If we continue to rely upon white financial support we will find ourselves entwined in the tentacles of the white power complex that controls this country. It is also important that a black organization (devoid of cultism) be projected to our people, so that it can be demonstrated that such organizations are viable.

More and more, we see black people in this country being used as a tool of the white liberal establishment. Liberal whites have not begun to address themselves to the real problem of black people in this country; witness their bewilderment, fear and anxiety when nationalism is mentioned concerning black people. An analysis of their (white liberal) reaction to the word alone (nationalism) reveals a very meaningful attitude of whites of any ideological persuasion toward blacks in this country. It means previous solutions to black problems in this country have been made in the interests of those whites dealing with these problems and not in the best interests of black people in this country. Whites can only subvert our true search and struggle for self-determination, self-identification, and liberation in this country. Re-evaluation of the white and black roles must NOW take place so that whites no longer designate roles that black people play but rather black people define white people's roles.

Too long have we allowed white people to interpret the importance and meaning of the cultural aspects of our society. We have allowed them to tell us what was good about our Afro-American music, art and literature. How many black critics do we have on the "jazz" scene? How can a white person who is not a part of the black psyche (except in the oppressor's role) interpret the meaning of the blues to us who are manifestations of the songs themselves?

It must also be pointed out that on whatever level of contact that blacks and whites come together, that meeting or confrontation is not on the level of the blacks but always on the level of the whites. This only means that our everyday contact with whites is a reinforcement of the myth of white supremacy. Whites are the ones who must try to raise themselves to our humanistic level. We are not, after all, the ones who are responsible for a genocidal war in Vietnam; we are not the ones who are responsible for neocolonialism in Africa and Latin America; we are not the ones who held a people in animalistic bondage over 400 years. We reject the American dream as defined by white people and must work to construct an American reality defined by Afro-Americans.

One of the criticisms of white militants and radicals is that when we view the masses of white people we view the over-all reality of America, we view the racism, the bigotry, and the distortion of personality, we view man's inhumanity to man: we view in reality 180 million racists. The sensitive white intellectual and radical who is fighting to bring about change is conscious of this fact but does not have the courage to admit this. When he admits this reality, then he must also admit his involvement because he is a part of the collective white America. It is only to the extent that he recognizes this that he will be able to change this reality.

Another concern is how does the white radical view the black community and how does he view the poor white community in terms of organizing. So far, we have found that most white radicals have sought to escape the horrible reality of America by going into the black community and attempting to organize black people while neglecting the organization of their own people's racist communities. How can one clean up someone else's yard when one's own yard is untidy? Again we feel that S.N.C.C. and the civil rights movement in general is in many aspects similar to the anticolonial situations in the African and Asian countries. We have the whites in the movement corresponding to the white civil servants and missionaries in the colonial countries who have worked with the colonial people for a long period of time and have developed a paternalistic attitude toward them. The reality of the colonial people taking over their own lives and controlling their own destiny must be faced. Having to move aside and letting this natural process of growth and development take place must be faced.

These views should not be equated with outside influence or outside agitation but should be viewed as the natural process of growth and development within a movement; so that the move by the black militants and S.N.C.C. in this direction should be viewed as a turn toward self-determination.

It is very ironic and curious how aware whites in this country can champion anticolonialism in other countries in Africa, Asia, and Latin America, but when black people move toward similar goals of self-determination in this country they are viewed as racists and anti-white by these same progressive whites. In proceeding further, it can be said that this attitude derives from the overall point of view of the white psyche as it concerns the black people. This attitude stems from the era of the slave revolts when every white man was a potential deputy or sheriff or guardian of the state. Because when black people got together among themselves to work out their problems, it became a threat to white people, because such meetings were potential slave revolts.

It can be maintained that this attitude or way of thinking has perpetuated itself to this current period and that it is part of the psyche of white people in this country whatever their political persuasion might be. It is part of the white fear-guilt complex resulting from the slave revolts. There have been examples of whites who stated that they can deal with black fellows on an individual basis but become threatened or menaced by the presence of groups of blacks. It can be maintained that this attitude is held by the majority of progressive whites in this country.

A thorough re-examination must be made by black people concerning the contributions that we have made in shaping this country. If this re-examination and re-evaluation is not made, and black people are not given their proper due and respect, then the antagonisms and contradictions are going to become more and more glaring, more and more intense until a national explosion may result.

When people attempt to move from these conclusions it would be faulty reasoning to say they are ordered by racism, because, in this country and in the West, racism has functioned as a type of white nationalism when dealing with black people. We all know the habit that this has created throughout the world and particularly among nonwhite people in this country.

Therefore any re-evaluation that we must make will, for the most part, deal with identification. Who are black people, what are black people; what is their relationship to America and the world?

It must be repeated that the whole myth of "Negro citizenship," perpetuated by the white elite, has confused the thinking of radical and progressive blacks and whites in this country. The broad masses of black people react to American society in the same manner as colonial peoples react to the West in Africa, and Latin America, and had the same relationship—that of the colonized toward the colonizer.

15 Frantz Fanon: Raising the Consciousness of the Colonized

The ideological underpinnings of the Black Power movement owed a great deal to the conceptualizations of Frantz Fanon, a black psychiatrist from Martinique who had joined a career as physician/scholar with that of a political militant in service of the Algerian revolution. Fanon, whose work *Les damnés de la terre* (The wretched of the earth) was published shortly before he died of leukemia in 1961, provided black American activists with a compelling analysis of the consciousness and situation of "colonized" peoples everywhere. Chief among his teachings was that violence in support of political and cultural liberation was a positive force, one that was both psychologically empowering and tactically sound. Forceful opposition to an oppressive regime was said to reaffirm the humanity of the oppressed, allowing them to "experience themselves as men." Armed with this wisdom, mid-sixties activist intellectuals began to speak of Afro-America as an internal colony at war with the forces of cultural degradation and assimilation. By adopting variants of Fanon's conceptualization, rank-and-file Black Power militants were able to identify with the colonized of the Third World even as they affirmed the notion that violent acts could lead to both mental catharsis and meaningful political change at home. By the end of 1970, the black psychiatrist's book had sold some 750,000 copies and, to many, had become the bible of the black liberation movement. The following selection is taken from the 1968 Grove Press edition of *The Wretched of the Earth*, by permission.

1961 *From* Concerning Violence

Frantz Fanon

National liberation, national renaissance, the restoration of nationhood to the people, commonwealth: whatever may be the headings used or the new formulas introduced, decolonization is always a violent phenomenon. At whatever level we study it—relationships between individuals, new names for sports clubs, the human admixture at cocktail parties, in the police, on the directing boards of national or private banks—decolonization is quite simply the replacing of a certain "species" of men by another "species" of men. Without any period of transition, there is a total, complete, and absolute substitution. It is true that we could equally well stress the rise of a new nation, the setting up of a new state, its diplomatic relations, and its economic and political trends. But we have precisely chosen to speak of that kind of *tabula rasa* which characterizes at the outset all decolonization. Its unusual importance is that it constitutes, from the very first day, the minimum demands of the colonized. To tell the truth, the proof of success lies in a whole social structure being changed from the bottom up. The extraordinary importance of this change is that it is willed, called for, demanded. The need for this change exists in its crude state, impetuous and compelling, in the consciousness and in the lives of the men and women who are colonized. But the possibility of this change is equally experienced in the form of a terrifying future in the consciousness of another "species" of men and women: the colonizers.

Decolonization, which sets out to change the order of the world, is, obviously, a program of complete disorder. But it cannot come as a result of magical practices, nor of a natural shock, nor of a friendly understanding. Decolonization, as we know, is a historical process: that is to say that it cannot be understood, it cannot become intelligible nor clear to itself except in the exact measure that we can discern the movements which give it historical form and content. Decolonization is the meeting of two forces, opposed to each other by their very nature, which in fact owe their originality to that sort of substantification which results from and is nourished by the situation in the colonies. Their first encounter was marked by violence and their existence together—that is to say the exploitation of the native by the settler—was carried on by dint of a great array of bayonets and cannons. The settler and the native are old acquaintances. In fact, the settler is right when he speaks of knowing "them" well. For it is the settler who has brought the native into existence and who perpetuates his existence. The settler owes the fact of his very existence, that is to say, his property, to the colonial system.

Decolonization never takes place unnoticed, for it influences individuals and modifies them fundamentally. It transforms spectators crushed with their inessentiality into privileged actors, with the grandiose glare of history's floodlights upon them. It brings a natural rhythm into existence, introduced by new men, and with it a new language and a new humanity. Decolonization is the veritable creation of new men. But this creation owes nothing of its legitimacy to any supernatural power; the "thing" which has been colonized becomes man during the same process by which it frees itself.

In decolonization, there is therefore the need of a complete calling in question of the colonial situation. If we wish to describe it precisely, we might find it in the well-known words: "The last shall be first and the first last." Decolonization is the putting into practice of this sentence. That is why, if we try to describe it, all decolonization is successful.

The naked truth of decolonization evokes for us the searing bullets and bloodstained knives which emanate from it. For if the last shall be first, this will only come to pass after a murderous and decisive struggle between the two protagonists. That affirmed intention to place the last at the head of things, and to make them climb at a pace (too quickly, some say) the well-known steps which characterize an organized society, can only triumph if we use all means to turn the scale, including, of course, that of violence.

You do not turn any society, however primitive it may be, upside down with such a program if you have not decided from the very beginning, that is to say from the actual formulation of that program, to overcome all the obstacles that you will come across in so doing. The native who decides to put the program into practice, and to become its moving force, is ready for violence at all times. From birth it is clear to him that this narrow world, strewn with prohibitions, can only be called in question by absolute violence.

The colonial world is a world divided into compartments. It is probably unnecessary to recall the existence of native quarters and European quarters, of schools for natives and schools for Europeans; in the same way we need not recall apartheid in South Africa. Yet, if we examine closely this system of compartments, we will at least be able to reveal the lines of force it implies. This approach to the colonial world, its ordering and its geographical layout will allow us to mark out the lines on which a decolonized society will be reorganized.

The colonial world is a world cut in two. The dividing line, the frontiers are shown by barracks and police stations. In the colonies it is the policeman and the soldier who are the official, instituted go-betweens, the spokesmen of the settler and his rule of oppression. In capitalist societies the educational system, whether lay or clerical, the structure of moral reflexes handed down from father to son, the exemplary honesty of workers who are given a medal after fifty years of good and loyal service, and the affection which springs from harmonious relations and good behavior—all these aesthetic expressions of respect for the established order serve to create around the exploited person an atmosphere of submission and of inhibition which lightens the task of policing considerably. In the capitalist countries a multitude of moral teachers, counselors and "bewilderers" separate the exploited from those in power. In the colonial countries, on the contrary, the policeman and the soldier, by their immediate presence and their frequent and direct action maintain contact with the native and advise him by means of rifle butts and napalm not to budge. It is obvious here that the agents of government speak the language of pure force. The intermediary does not lighten the oppression, nor seek to hide the domination; he shows them up and puts them into practice with the clear conscience of an upholder of the peace; yet he is the bringer of violence into the home and into the mind of the native.

The zone where the natives live is not complementary to the zone inhabited by the settlers. The two zones are opposed, but not in the service of a higher unity. Obedient to the rules of pure Aristotelian logic, they both follow the principle of reciprocal exclusivity. No conciliation is possible, for of the two terms, one is superfluous. The settlers' town is a strongly built town, all made of stone and steel. It is a brightly lit town; the streets are covered with asphalt, and the garbage cans swallow all the leavings, unseen, unknown and hardly thought about. The settler's feet are never visible, except perhaps in the sea; but there you're never close enough to see them. His feet are protected by strong shoes although the streets of his town are clean and even, with no holes or stones. The settler's town is a well-fed town, an easygoing town; its belly is always full of good things. The settlers' town is a town of white people, of foreigners.

The town belonging to the colonized people, or at least the native town, the Negro village, the medina, the reservation, is a place of ill fame, peopled by men of evil repute. They are born there, it matters little where or how; they die there, it matters not where, nor how. It is a world without spaciousness; men live there on top of each other, and their huts are built one on top of the other. The native town is a hungry town, starved of bread, of meat, of shoes, of coal, of light. The native town is a crouching village, a town on its knees, a town wallowing in the mire. It is a town of niggers and dirty Arabs. The look that the native turns on the settler's town is a look of lust, a look of envy; it expresses his dreams of possession—all manner of possession: to sit at the settler's table, to sleep in the settler's bed, with his wife if possible. The colonized man is an envious man. And this the settler knows very well; when their glances meet he ascertains bitterly, always on the defensive, "They want to take our place." It is true, for there is no native who does not dream at least once a day of setting himself up in the settler's place.

This world divided into compartments, this world cut in two is inhabited by two different species. The originality of the colonial context is that economic reality, inequality, and the immense difference of ways of life never come to mask the human realities. When you examine at close quarters the colonial context, it is evident that what parcels out the world is to begin with the fact of belonging to or not belonging to a given race, a given species. In the colonies the economic substructure is also a superstructure. The cause is the consequence; you are rich because you are white, you are white because you are rich. This is why Marxist analysis should always be slightly stretched every time we have to do with the colonial problem.

Everything up to and including the very nature of precapitalist society, so well explained by Marx, must here be thought out again. The serf is in essence different from the knight, but a reference to divine right is necessary to legitimize this statutory difference. In the colonies, the foreigner coming from another country imposed his rule by means of guns and machines. In defiance of his successful transplantation, in spite of his appropriation, the settler still remains a foreigner. It is neither the act of owning factories, nor estates, nor a bank balance which distinguishes the governing classes. The governing race is first and foremost those who come from elsewhere, those who are unlike the original inhabitants, "the others."

The violence which has ruled over the ordering of the colonial world, which has ceaselessly drummed the rhythm for the destruction of native social forms and broken up without reserve the systems of reference of the economy, the customs of dress and external life, that same violence will be claimed and taken over by the native at the moment when, deciding to embody history in his own person, he surges into the forbidden quarters. To wreck the colonial world is henceforward a mental picture of action which is very clear, very easy to understand and which may be assumed by each one of the individuals which constitute the colonized people. To break up the colonial world does not mean that after the frontiers have been abolished lines of communication will be set up between the two zones. The destruction of the colonial world is no more and no less than the abolition of one zone, its burial in the depths of the earth or its expulsion from the country.

16 COINTELPRO and "Black Nationalist Hate Groups"

Between 1967 and 1971, the FBI, assisted by other law enforcement agencies, conducted an extensive covert action campaign against so-called black nationalist hate groups. In the hope of preventing "the rise of a messiah who could unify and electrify the militant nationalist movement," J. Edgar Hoover's COINTELPRO program sought to limit the growth of such groups, discourage cooperation between them, and discredit their leaders. In pursuit of these goals, U.S. counterintelligence operatives engaged in a wide array of repressive tactics. Detailed "Rabble Rouser" and "Agitator" indices, a Racial Calendar, and a Black Nationalist Photograph Album were compiled and circulated. Black militant groups were subjected to numerous harassment arrests and increased tax surveillance by the Internal Revenue Service. Informants infiltrated the movement, spreading rumors about the "disloyalty" of bona fide members, exacerbating existing intragroup tensions, and supplying authorities with inside information useful in conducting police raids. The press and electronic media were manipulated shamelessly. In sum, COINTELPRO had the potential to create what one seasoned activist characterized as "beaucoup dissention and disunity," to impede recruitment of new members, and to drain the capacity of the militants to sustain insurgency. The following 1967 directive announcing the new counterintelligence initiative is taken from Ward Churchill and Jim Vander Wall, eds., *The COINTELPRO Papers: Documents from the FBI's Secret Wars against Domestic Dissent* (Boston: South End Press, 1990), by permission.

1967   Memorandum to Special Agent in Charge, Albany, New York

J. Edgar Hoover

SAC, Albany   August 25, 1967

COUNTERINTELLIGENCE PROGRAM
BLACK NATIONALIST—HATE GROUPS
INTERNAL SECURITY

Offices receiving copies of this letter are instructed to immediately establish a control file, captioned as above, and to assign responsibility for
following and coordinating this new counterintelligence program to an
experienced and imaginative Special Agent well versed in investigations
relating to black nationalist, hate-type organizations. The field office
control file used under this program may be maintained in a pending
inactive status until such time as a specific operation or technique is
placed under consideration for implementation.

*The purpose of this new counterintelligence endeavor is to expose,
disrupt, misdirect, discredit, or otherwise neutralize the activities of
black nationalist, hate-type organizations and groupings, their leadership, spokesmen, membership, and supporters, and to counter their
propensity for violence and civil dis*order. The activities of all such
groups of intelligence interest to this Bureau must be followed on a
continuous basis so we will be in a position to promptly take advantage
of all opportunities for counterintelligence and to inspire action in instances where circumstances warrant. The pernicious background of
such groups, their duplicity, and devious maneuvers must be exposed to
public scrutiny where such publicity will have a neutralizing effect.
Efforts of the various groups to consolidate their forces or to recruit new
or youthful adherents must be frustrated. No opportunity should be
missed to exploit through counterintelligence techniques the organizational and personal conflicts of the leaderships of the groups and where
possible an effort should be made to capitalize upon existing conflicts
between competing black nationalist organizations. When an opportunity is apparent to disrupt or neutralize black nationalist, hate-type
organizations through the cooperation of established local news media
contacts or through such contact with sources available to the Seat of
Government, in every instance careful attention must be given to the

proposal to insure the targeted group is disrupted, ridiculed, or discredited through the publicity and not merely publicized. Consideration should be given to techniques to preclude violence-prone or rabble-rouser leaders of hate groups from spreading their philosophy publicly or through various mass communication media.

Many individuals currently active in black nationalist organizations have backgrounds of immorality, subversive activity, and criminal records. Through your investigation of key agitators, you should endeavor to establish their unsavory backgrounds. Be alert to determine evidence of misappropriation of funds or other types of personal misconduct on the part of militant nationalist leaders so any practical or warranted counterintelligence may be instituted.

Intensified attention under this program should be afforded to the activities of such groups as the Student Nonviolent Coordinating Committee, the Southern Christian Leadership Conference, Revolutionary Action Movement, the Deacons for Defense and Justice, Congress of Racial Equality, and the Nation of Islam. Particular emphasis should be given to extremists who direct the activities and policies of revolutionary or militant groups such as Stokely Carmichael, H. "Rap" Brown, Elijah Mohammad, and Maxwell Stanford.

At this time the Bureau is setting up no requirement for status letters to be periodically submitted under this program. It will be incumbent upon you to insure the program is being afforded necessary and continuing attention and that no opportunities will be overlooked for counterintelligence action.

This program should not be confused with the program entitled "Communist Party, USA, Counterintelligence Program, Internal Security—C," (Bufile 100-3-104).

17   Black Power Politics

Convinced that increased political power would bring with it the ability to influence the workings of those institutions, agencies, and programs that most tellingly affected the lives of black people, African American political activists viewed government control as a prerequisite to meaningful progress in areas such as economics and education. Evidencing the fact that they were tired of being a third-class influence within a two-party system that seemed to operate largely for the benefit of a single racial group, the demands forwarded by these black politicos often surpassed the bounds of what the existing system could be reasonably expected to deliver. They called on the government to boost funding for community development corporations, increase the minimum wage, expand federally assisted child care centers, create new public service jobs, establish a system of national health insurance and a guaranteed minimum annual income, abolish the death penalty, and institute a system of proportionate black representation on juries and in Congress.

For some, to make such demands was sufficiently cathartic. Others labored to build functioning political organizations. At gatherings such as the national black political conventions held in Gary, Indiana, in 1972 and in Little Rock, Arkansas, in 1974, delegates debated political strategy and sought to develop new techniques of community mobilization. They established guidelines for endorsing candidates and discussed ways of pressuring white officeholders into supporting black initiatives. Motivated by inspirational speeches and slogans such as "Black Unity without Uniformity," delegates returned to their home districts with new insight into the inadequacies of the existing system and a heightened desire to institutionalize their Black Power programs.

The 2,700 delegates and 4,000 alternates and observers who attended the March 1972 National Black Political Convention in Gary heard presentations on dozens of key policy issues. In May, a position paper containing lengthy "action agendas" for both voters and officeholders was released. Optimistically noting that "all things are possible," it called for the creation of a new black political movement—one that would be grounded in and energized by "an independent Black spirit." The first selection, "The Gary Declaration," places the work of the convention in a sociopolitical context. The second is the model pledge of accountability developed by the delegates. Both documents are reprinted from *The National Black Political Agenda* (Washington, DC: National Black Political Convention, 1972), by permission.

The final selection is a speech delivered by poet and playwright Amiri Baraka (formerly LeRoi Jones) to delegates attending the September 1970 meeting of the Congress of African Peoples in Atlanta. Here, the coordinator of the congress's political liberation workshop details the role a nationalist-oriented political party could play as a preliminary organizational vehicle for the creation of an "African World State." In concluding his talk with a poem, Baraka evidences the connection many activists of the day made between nationalist cultural concepts and political ideas. According to this conceptualization, black America was "a cultural nation striving to seize the power to become a political nation." In order to reach this goal, the politically minded had to become "culturally aware." For their part, culturally attuned blacks were obliged to create a pragmatic, politically involved art that would convey the nationalist political message across the length and breadth of black America. The document is reprinted from *African Congress: A Documentary of the First Modern Pan-African Congress*, ed. Amiri Baraka (New York: William Morrow, 1972), by permission.

1972   The Gary Declaration

Black Politics at the Crossroads

National Black Political Convention

Introduction

The Black Agenda is addressed primarily to Black people in America. It rises naturally out of the bloody decades and centuries of our people's struggle on these shores. It flows from the most recent surgings of our own cultural and political consciousness. It is our attempt to define some of the essential changes which must take place in this land as we and our children move to self-determination and true independence.

The Black Agenda assumes that no truly basic change for our benefit takes place in Black or white America unless we Black people organize to initiate that change. It assumes that we must have some essential agreement on overall goals, even though we may differ on many specific strategies.

Therefore, this is an initial statement of goals and directions for our own generation, some first definitions of crucial issues around which Black people must organize and move in 1972 and beyond. Anyone who claims to be serious about the survival and liberation of Black people must be serious about the implementation of the Black Agenda.

What Time Is It?

We come to Gary in an hour of great crisis and tremendous promise for Black America. While the white nation hovers on the brink of chaos, while its politicians offer no hope of real change, we stand on the edge of history and are faced with an amazing and frightening choice: We may choose in 1972 to slip back into the decadent white politics of American life, or we may press forward, moving relentlessly from Gary to the creation of our own Black life. The choice is large, but the time is very short.

Let there be no mistake. We come to Gary in a time of unrelieved crisis for our people. From every rural community in Alabama to the high-rise compounds of Chicago, we bring to this Convention the agonies of the masses of our people. From the sprawling Black cities of Watts and Nairobi in the West to the decay of Harlem and Roxbury in the East, the testimony we bear is the same. We are the witnesses to social disaster.

Our cities are crime-haunted dying grounds. Huge sectors of our youth—and countless others—face permanent unemployment. Those of us who work find our paychecks able to purchase less and less. Neither the courts nor the prisons contribute to anything resembling justice or reformation. The schools are unable—or unwilling—to educate our children for the real world of our struggles. Meanwhile, the officially approved epidemic of drugs threatens to wipe out the minds and strength of our best young warriors.

Economic, cultural, and spiritual depression stalk Black America, and the price for survival often appears to be more than we are able to pay. On every side, in every area of our lives, the American institutions in which we have placed our trust are unable to cope with the crises they have created by their single-minded dedication to profits for some and white supremacy above all.

Beyond These Shores

And beyond these shores there is more of the same. For while we are pressed down under all the dying weight of a bloated, inwardly decaying white civilization, many of our brothers in Africa and the rest of the Third World have fallen prey to the same powers of exploitation and deceit. Wherever America faces the unorganized, politically powerless forces of the non-white world, its goal is domination by any means necessary—as if to hide from itself the crumbling of its own systems of life and work.

But Americans cannot hide. They can run to China and the moon and to the edges of consciousness, but they cannot hide. The crises we face as Black people are the crises of the entire society. They go deep, to the very bones and marrow, to the essential nature of America's economic, political, and cultural systems. They are the natural end-product of a society built on the twin foundations of white racism and white capitalism.

So, let it be clear to us now: The desperation of our people, the agonies of our cities, the desolation of our countryside, the pollution of the air and the water—these things will not be significantly affected by new faces in the old places in Washington, D.C. This is the truth we must face here in Gary if we are to join our people everywhere in the movement forward toward liberation.

White Realities, Black Choice

A Black political convention, indeed all truly Black politics must begin from this truth: *The American system does not work for the masses of our people, and it cannot be made to work without radical fundamental change.* (Indeed, this system does not really work in favor of the humanity of anyone in America.)

In light of such realities, we come to Gary and are confronted with a choice. Will we believe the truth that history presses into our face—or will we, too, try to hide? Will the small favors some of us have received blind us to the larger sufferings of our people, or open our eyes to the testimony of our history in America?

For more than a century we have followed the path of political dependence on white men and their systems. From the Liberty Party in the decades before the Civil War to the Republican Party of Abraham Lincoln, we trusted in white men and white politics as our deliverers. Sixty years ago, W. E. B. Du Bois said he would give the Democrats their "last chance" to prove their sincere commitment to equality for Black people—and he was given white riots and official segregation in peace and in war.

Nevertheless, some twenty years later we became Democrats in the name of Franklin Roosevelt, then supported his successor Harry Truman, and even tried a "non-partisan" Republican General of the Army named Eisenhower. We were wooed like many others by the superficial liberalism of John F. Kennedy and the make-believe populism of Lyndon Johnson. Let there be no more of that.

Both Parties Have Betrayed Us

Here at Gary, let us never forget that while the times and the names and the parties have continually changed, one truth has faced us insistently, never changing: Both parties have betrayed us whenever their interests conflicted with ours (which was most of the time), and whenever our forces were unorganized and dependent, quiescent and compliant. Nor should this be surprising, for by now we must know that the American political system, like all other white institutions in America, was designed to operate for the benefit of the white race: It was never meant to do anything else.

That is the truth that we must face at Gary. If white "liberalism" could have solved our problems, then Lincoln and Roosevelt and Kennedy would have done so. But they did not solve ours nor the rest of the nation's. If America's problems could have been solved by forceful, politically skilled and aggressive individuals, then Lyndon Johnson would have retained the presidency. If the true "American Way" of unbridled monopoly capitalism, combined with a ruthless military imperialism could do it, then Nixon would not be running around the world, or making speeches comparing his nation's decadence to that of Greece and Rome.

If we have never faced it before, let us face it at Gary: The profound crisis of Black people and the disaster of America are not simply caused by men nor will they be solved by men alone. These crises are the crises of basically flawed economics and politics, and of cultural degradation. None of the Democratic candidates and none of the Republican candidates—regardless of their vague promises to us or to their white constituencies—can solve our problems or the problems of this country without radically changing the systems by which it operates.

The Politics of Social Transformation

So we come to Gary confronted with a choice. But it is not the old convention question of which candidate shall we support, the pointless question of who is to preside over a decaying and unsalvageable system. No, if we come to Gary out of the realities of the Black communities of this land, then the only real choice for us is whether or not we will live by the truth we know, whether we will move to organize independently, move to struggle for fundamental transformation, for the creation of new directions, towards a concern for the life and the meaning of Man. Social transformation or social destruction, those are our only real choices.

If we have come to Gary on behalf of our people in America, in the rest of this hemisphere, and in the Homeland—if we have come for our own best ambitions—then a new Black Politics must come to birth. If we are serious, the Black Politics of Gary must accept major responsibility for creating both the atmosphere and the program for fundamental, far-ranging change in America. Such responsibility is ours because it is our people who are most deeply hurt and ravaged by the present systems of society. That responsibility for leading the change is ours because we live in a society where few other men really believe in the responsibility of a truly humane society for anyone anywhere.

We Are the Vanguard

The challenge is thrown to us here in Gary. It is the challenge to consolidate and organize our own Black role as the vanguard in the struggle for a new society. To accept that challenge is to move independent Black politics. There can be no equivocation on that issue. History leaves us no other choice. White politics has not and cannot bring the changes we need.

We come to Gary and are faced with a challenge. The challenge is to transform ourselves from favor-seeking vassals and loud-talking, "militant" pawns, and to take up the role that the organized masses of our people have attempted to play ever since we came to these shores: That of harbingers of true justice and humanity, leaders in the struggle for liberation.

A major part of the challenge we must accept is that of redefining the functions and operations of all levels of American government, for the existing governing structures—from Washington to the smallest county—are obsolescent. That is part of the reason why nothing works and why corruption rages throughout public life. For white politics seeks not to serve but to dominate and manipulate.

We will have joined the true movement of history if at Gary we grasp the opportunity to press Man forward as the first consideration of politics. Here at Gary we are faithful to the best hopes of our fathers and our people if we move for nothing less than a politics which places community before individualism, love before sexual exploitation, a living environment before profits, peace before war, justice before unjust "order", and morality before expediency.

This is the society we need, but we delude ourselves here at Gary if we think that change can be achieved without organizing the power, the determined national Black power, which is necessary to insist upon such change, to create such change, to seize change.

Towards a Black Agenda

So when we turn to a Black Agenda for the seventies, we move in the truth of history, in the reality of the moment. We move recognizing that no one else is going to represent our interests but ourselves. *The society we seek cannot come unless Black people organize to advance its coming.* We lift up a Black Agenda recognizing that white America moves towards the abyss created by its own racist arrogance, misplaced priorities, rampant materialism, and ethical bankruptcy. Therefore, we are certain that the Agenda we now press for in Gary is not only for the future of Black humanity, but is probably the only way the rest of America can save itself from the harvest of its criminal past.

So, Brothers and Sisters of our developing Black nation, we now stand at Gary as people whose time has come. From every corner of Black America, from all liberation movements of the Third World, from the graves of our fathers and the coming world of our children, we are faced with a challenge and a call: Though the moment is perilous we must not despair. We must seize the time, for the time is ours.

We begin here and now in Gary. We begin with an independent Black political movement, an independent Black Political Agenda, an independent Black spirit. Nothing less will do. We must build for our people. We must build for our world. We stand on the edge of history. We cannot turn back.

1972 **Model Pledge**

For Black Candidates

National Black Political Convention

As a Candidate seeking the approval of the National Black Political Convention:

I pledge, that as I campaign, and if I am elected, I will conduct the daily affairs and decision making of my activity, and/or office, so as to reflect the actual, explicit desires and concerns of the Black Community beyond question. In this manner I will constantly act out my accountability to the manifest interests of the Black Community, as revealed, at present, through the National Black Political Convention and whatever instrument(s) this Convention will establish as a means of follow-through.

In regard to this pledge, I will do the following:

1. Without fear I will raise controversial issues, when the raising of such issues will serve the needs and interests of the Black Community.
2. I will constantly seek to expose the corrupt aspects of the system, as such exposure will raise the level of awareness in the Black Community.
3. I will take any steps necessary to increase power for the Black Community when such steps are not in conflict with this Convention's Agenda and the programs of its follow-up mechanisms.
4. I will support the right of the Black Community to control its own areas and the institutions thereof as this principle of control relates to Political Empowerment, Economic Empowerment, Human Development, International Policy and Black People, Communications, Rural Development, Environmental Protection and Self-determination for the District of Columbia.

I make this pledge in dedication to a commitment to serve the Black Community, of which I am unquestionably a part, and I do so without reservation or intimidation.

_____   _____

Witness   Date

                                                              _____

                                                              Signature

Speech to the Congress of African Peoples

Amiri Baraka

Habari Gani, Asalaam Alaikum. How are you doing?

I'm sorry a lot of our people are at home but I can dig it's been a long weekend. Everybody is ready to go back. I hope when we go back we don't forget to take something back with us in terms of some of the things that hopefully we've gotten together here in these four or five historic days. Congress of African Peoples is a very historic kind of occasion if you can really think about it, really see it. It's very hard to think in America, especially Black people, because our nervous system is in the hands of our enemies. Very hard for a human being, a body, to think without a nervous system. But what the congress is trying to do is draw all the many different kinds of Black people together. All the different parts of the nervous system, the body, so that it understands again that it is a single body, like a man's body, and all the different African peoples all over this world are just part of that single African Nation, the African Nation which is rising again.

What we came out of the Political Workshop with was first of all the idea that what we wanted is a political party. A political party that would service the needs of Black people wherever they are. A political party that could deal internationally everywhere Black people were. What we are talking about is a national, international, nationalist, Pan-Africanist political party. A political party which will be the model for the nation becoming.

The problem is, usually, that the systems that we make to try to liberate us are usually not good models. Many times you know that Black people have these little organizations—they in the organization and the organization are supposed to be dedicated to steering Black people—but, meanwhile, everybody in the organization is living in exactly the opposite way necessary to free Black people. In other words, people are always saying one thing and doing another. Negroes are always talking Black, but living Negro. Like Sékou Touré says, "We're always talking new things but we always moving like old things." So what the congress is trying to do is find out what our new ideas are and then make us live by them. Commit us to live, be the best element of our ideas. It's very hard, because in America you are magnetized by America. You see, that is what Einstein was trying to tell you with his dimwitted relativity theory—several thousand years after Black people had said that—that bodies tend to magnetize things. So the more bodies you have the more things are magnetized toward those bodies. So if you have a whole lot of bodies that are practicing evil, then everything is magnetized toward evil. Can you understand that? So that in order to get away from the evil magnetism you have to begin practicing a more positive, a more *positive*, philosophy and ideology. And by the example that you create you will begin to magnetize Black people to you, in your various cities; in your various countries.

This political party we want to set up, that is set up, should be a model for the *nation becoming.* The Black political party must be an example of what we want the nation to be *now*, not in the future. We should not live as if we believe what the white boy says: that we would never be liberated. We must live on the one hand as if we were liberated people of a high value system; then more Black people will be magnetized to it and the larger our *nation becoming* will be.

A political party has to function in four areas. A lot of times Black people—because of the television and movies and radios and comic books, controlled by our enemies—believe that revolution is another thing. They believe it has to do with television fantasy or movies that's got something to do with "Up-Tight" or the "Lost Man" or that it has to do with some kind of instantaneous, overnight revolution where you emerge in flame and victory immediately. But that's not the case, Brothers and Sisters. There is no such thing as instant revolution. In the Russian Revolution or the Lenin revolution which was supposed to be an overnight revolution, the majority took control from the minority, captured the means of production. But it the United States of America the so-called minority mentality is the majority mentality. We are not the majority of people; we cannot overnight take power. We must build organizations in the four areas of political power. We must build people who are able to run for public office; we must build community organizations; we must make alliances and coalitions with people all around the world; and we must become skilled in the arts of disruption. We must have a political party that can do all four of those things, not just one unskillfully.

Many think that once they get a .22 rifle and go and shoot once a month that they are skillful enough to overtake and overthrow the United States Government which is the most powerful force on this planet. But that is not the case. Just being angry at white people will not overthrow them. I hope you understand that. Many of our brothers and sisters think that just because they are angry at the crackers, that the crackers will get frightened of them and die, they will dry up and blow away. There is no such thing as instant revolution. Free people are people who deserve to be free. You are slaves because you want to be slaves, because you deserve to be slaves! Can you understand that? You are slaves because you have not done anything that will enable you not to be slaves. You are not free people because you are not qualified to be free people. If you are qualified to be free, you would be free. That's hard to take, ain't it? If you had the skills, if you had the skills to overthrow the white man, you could overthrow the white man. If you were efficient enough, you could do it; if you were dedicated enough, you could do it; if you were disciplined and trained enough, you could do it; but you are none of these and most of you refuse to deal with the realities of becoming skilled and efficient enough to do it. It is not a little dream game where they give you a gift for being Black that you will be free. It is something that will have to be achieved through science and study and dedication and training. These are the things that we wanted to begin to talk about here at this congress; and even so, it's very difficult to get people to stay long enough—to get them to sit down in a chair long enough—to find out some information.

But the party that we want to see is a Black, a World African Political Party. A political party that will function in South Africa like it will function in Chicago, where you know that if you are in Surinam or Jamaica, or New York City this World African Party will be functioning to get power, to bring about self-determination for Black people. Our enemies work along these lines. Many of our brothers, yesterday for instance, in Political Liberation Workshop, wanted to come out and make a lot of condemnations of our enemies. Some of the brothers for instance wanted to come out and denounce super-Jew—come down on them—naming the Zionists as our enemies. But the problem is this. We are a people without an army, without a communication system, with no means of relaying what our brain has conceived to our arms and legs and our muscles. We are a body whose muscles do not even know they belong to the body that the head belongs to, and yet we want to neophyte on our enemies. You cannot achieve political power by talking bad to white people. You can only achieve political power by organizing well enough to take political power, and this is the point. That's a humbling thing, I know, that's humiliating sometimes to have to face that reality—that you are powerless. The nigger would rather talk like he has power, make those great Arab statements without Chinese power.

He would rather neophyte, and say how bad he is; what the police ain't going to do and, "We got these guns, hunky," and hunky come in and wipe them out. The nigger talking about a nation and can't even keep a storefront from being overrun by overweight policemen. Now let us face these realities: a nigger wants to put down the Zionist and the Zionists control the radio, the television, the movies, the education, the intellectual life of the United States, the morality of the United States—Judeo-Christian ethics. The minute you condemn them publicly, you die. They will declare a war on you forever.

The point would be getting strong enough to overthrow your enemies, not broadcasting your hatred for them. Also, there is no revolution without the people. All you leaders and vanguarders, all you niggers who think you going to single-handedly, super-duper nigger style bring freedom to all Black people—you can forget that, there is no such thing as that. Only the people can achieve national liberation. I say national liberation instead of revolution because a whole lot of long-haired white boys are singing about revolution, so I know that can't be the same thing I'm talking about. I'm talking about national liberation. There is no revolution without the people because it is the people themselves who are the only ones that have the power to make revolution. Only the nation itself has the power to change its life. No few bloods high on marijuana and white women are going to change the life style of Black people. There is no national liberation without the nation, without you belonging to a nation: a people with a specific way of life. You must see, as part of that nation, that you evolve to consciousness in that you become politically conscious enough to achieve liberation. If the people are too slow—like the nigger nationalist says—the people are backward because if you're supposed to be the smart, how come you haven't found a way to organize? If you're supposed to be super smart, how come you can't get them—if they so slow—organized into the direction they should go? You are the backward ones; not the people. It is the people that must make revolution, not the so-called vanguard.

Also, we say nationalism because, finally, what are we doing? Who are we trying to bring the power to? Who are we willing to die for? We are willing to die for our mothers and fathers and sisters and brothers, ourselves, our nation, our memory, our future, our past, not abstractions. It is nationalism. Once you become a nation then you can become international. What is so weird is that certain peoples always get niggers to fight harder for them than they fight for niggers. For instance, the radicals, the Jewish radicals have bloods willing to die to see Jews get political power (and that's not an anti-Semitic statement, I think it's a very congratulatory statement). I would like to get somebody to go out and do our dying for us, to run around getting slaughtered so that we could get famous, so that we could get to be free on the expense of some other people. But there is no other people dumb enough to do that for us. There are Jewish lawyers getting famous for losing cases for niggers. There are certain radical revolutionaries who are getting famous while our brothers are waiting in jail to be executed. You understand that? You can make alliances and coalitions with people of color, you can make alliances with people of color, Third World peoples, because they have the same destiny. But we say a political party that can move in four areas, that can move through public office in a Black community, should be nationalist or controlled by nationalists. If that is not the case, and you think you're a nationalist, you jivin'. If there's a nigger in your community running who is truly just a nigger, a tom, a white boy with a mask on, you are jiving. You are supposed to be the smart. Any candidate that runs in the Black community must face a nationalist candidate and the nationalist must soon become powerful enough to win. If you do not deal with that level of politics, by default, the white boy will take it over, as he always has, and his stooges. And Black people will respond to them because they can supply them with goods and services. No matter what our people say, when they get hungry they go where the food is. When they want a place to sleep, they go to the person who's giving out houses. When they need a job, they go to where the jobs are given out. No matter what they say, even the so-called revolutionaries do that.

You must control everything in the community that needs to be controlled. Anything of value: any kind of anti-poverty program, politicians, celebrities, anything that brings money, resources into your community, you should control it. You understand that? Anything of value in your community, you have to control it because if you don't control it, the white boy controls it. It's no need in you saying for instance that the anti-poverty program is jive, of course it's jive. It is designed by your enemy. Take it over, take it over, control it, control everything. The schools are jive. We know the schools are jive. Do you think you are going to keep Black people from sending their children to school? You can say, "This is the white man's education. You getting all these white symbols and they brainwashing you sisters and you shouldn't send your children to school," and she will say, "Yes, you right, Brother, you right, Brother," and tomorrow morning at eight-thirty they getting their faces washed and they're on their way to school. Now the point is: You must control the institutions that already exist in your community, through public office, community organization, coalitions and alliances. Make alliances with people of color in your community, Puerto Ricans. Negroes walk around saying Puerto Ricans, well, they think they're white. There is probably more niggers that think they are white than Puerto Ricans because there are more niggers. People could say that about us. But in your community where there's Mexicans, Puerto Ricans, Indians, you must make alliances with them as if you were a nation. Do not be brainwashed into thinking you just a slave or you will be a slave. Begin to function as if you were a nation—make alliances. You used to do it when you were in the gang. Make alliances with other groups. This extends your power.

In NewArk we made an alliance with the Puerto Ricans, with the Young Lords—a Mutual Assistance Pact—because Anthony Imperiale attacked the Young Lords. A bomb was thrown into their headquarters and burned it out. So we made a statement that said, "An attack on the Puerto Rican community is an attack on the Black community. An attack on the Black community is an attack on the Puerto Rican community." In other words, if you attack the Puerto Ricans you attack us. Imperiale made a statement a couple of days later that he was going to the state attorney general to see what he could do about this "Pact" that we had made because it must be illegal. In other words, here's a man who makes his living murder-mouthing Black people. And once we declared our mutual assistance that we would meet anything at the level it was delivered—Black and Puerto Ricans together—then he wanted to know how come this Pact existed and wasn't it illegal. Because we had expanded our force and it wasn't just Black people that he had to be frightened of, but the Black people and the Puerto Rican people. And understand this, that if Negroes only want to be Negroes and to not evolve to become the African mind of Black men again, then it will be all the peoples around the world that will kill us when they kill the white boy. It will be you like a butler in the white boy's house when all the people come to burn down the house, the nigger still opening the door letting folks in so he can burn too. Either you will help burn it down or you will burn with it. This is a place where the so-called slaves can ride in Cadillacs; where the so-called revolutionaries can hang out with the enemy; where anybody who is supposed to represent anything has usually been bought and paid for by the time you even hear it. This is the most degenerate place on this earth, and either we will separate ourselves or minds first from this degeneracy, or we will go down with it. Either we will step away from this dying body or we will die with it. Either we will form alternatives to these dead institutions or we will die with these institutions.

The Negro don't have to be immortal. The dinosaurs didn't think they would be extinct either. The dinosaur used to be happy walking around eating off the tops of trees and then the climate changed and it wasn't no trees anymore. It was valleys and it was dry and the dinosaur was too stupid to get down lower and eat close to the earth and so he passed away and a new species came on the planet, that was better adapted. Now either we will be a species of people strong enough to transcend our enslavement or we will pass away with this epoch. Either we will be strong enough to survive into the next epoch or we pass away with this one.

This is not China, this is not nineteenth-century Russia, this is not Cuba, this is not Vietnam, this is not any of those kind of revolutions you can read about easily from the drugstore turntable of books. There is no literature really written on this revolution, on this struggle for national liberation. You cannot get it easily and talk about it at literary cocktail parties. This liberation has to be achieved through efforts and work. You must do enough work so that when the time comes when the bloodletting really comes down, that you are prepared to do it. In 1972, for instance, when they come back around the same cycle that went down in 1967. When it comes back around and the bloodletting comes back, what will you be prepared to do? Negroes have sold white people wolf tickets for the last decade. All of the sixties everybody has sold the white boy wolf tickets, and now he believes that we mean to kill him; we have convinced him for ten years that we want to kill him and now he believes it. Now that he believes it and is getting ready to receive your terrible onslaught, with what are you going to attack him? You understand that? Where is our army? We are talking about going up against the armies of the United States, most of which are Niggers, your brothers. You haven't even convinced your brother not to be in the army, yet, of your enemy, and you are getting ready to attack him. Most Black people are involved with white mythology. They have pictures of Jesus Christ, Marilyn Monroe or the Beatles up on they walls. They are involved, whether with Beethoven or the Rolling Stones. They like Joe DiMaggio or Mozart. One of those scales—it's the same folks. They either trying to tell you about Marx and Lenin, one group of white boys, or George Washington, Thomas Jefferson, another group of white boys. They are all hooked up with white life.

Where is an army that would fight for the struggle and survival of the Black Nation? Niggers are talking about *now* revolutionaries; that they are not nationalists; they don't represent any nation; they don't represent any culture, they are cultureless; they drop from the sky and even if they did drop from the sky, that would be their culture—sky drops. We must not become the peasant army for the rising tide of Jewish political power. Napoleon had a concept of a peasant army. You hip to it? You can get a whole lot of peasants and talk to them about the international struggle and he would get them lined up with some pitchforks and some brooms and some stones, you see. And they would be facing the standup stomp German-Russian elite. And he would get all these farmers and peasants unarmed, unskilled, to run down in the way of the cavalry. And he would run groups of them down in front of the cavalry and they would fall out and be trying to kill the horses with the pitchforks. And they would be taking those muskets in they heads, and they would be screaming Napoleon's slogans, and Napoleon would be sitting on a hill with his cavalry. And he would wait until the peasants' army had taken the first wave, had disorganized the troops, had caused so much disruption, that the cavalry of the Germans couldn't function. And then he would come zooming down off of that mountain and would ease up and might become Governor of New York, might get on the Supreme Court, or might become a famous lawyer, as famous as William Kunstler.

But the point is this, our struggle must be a struggle that is organically connected to our lives. No one can pin a revolution button on you, an ideology, and say now, blood, you know about revolution, here's your copy of the "Red Book." It has to come out of the lives of the people themselves. I would rather make a coalition with Roy Wilkins or Whitney Young—with any of the most backwards upside-down Negroes in the world, because even they must be, in they jivist moment, committed to change. There are more Black people involved with Roy Wilkins than are involved with the Congress of African Peoples. There are more niggers who think like Whitney Young than think like we do. We have to co-opt these people because they exist in our communities. You cannot merely say, "You're corny, nigger." You got to get him and embrace him and make him be with you. If white people have created some nigger stars and giant civil rights figures, we must love them and embrace them, we must unify with them in brotherhood. I hope you understand. Because it's like coming into this room. If there was Black people and white people in here and you come running in the room and you say, "All you Black folks," the white people got they foot on your neck—and they really would. They would all be standing up and they would have they feet on their necks. But what you have forgotten is that they have developed a relationship after these three hundred years and a lot of bloods *like* that. They feel more uncomfortable with you trying to take the foot off their necks than with the foot on their necks. You have to be able to deal with every area of the Black community. If you so bad and revolutionary that you have hostilized every element of the Black community then you are isolated from the Black community and they will shoot you at random, knowing that there will be no retaliation from the Black community. You must get in with the people; that is your only defense—the people, the community. You must get in with the N.A.A.C.P. and the Urban League and the nigger fraternities and sororities. You must surround yourself with them and function with them.

The nationalist must be the spine of the body of the Black nation. What the nation does the nationalist must make him do a little better, a little faster. If it's slow it's because we slow. You understand that? But the minute you put yourself away from the people (no matter how backward and corny you might think they are), then you are isolated, standing there by yourself—and you will get killed. You will get killed. We are not interested in suicide; it is not about suicide. The white boy is in the death syndrome, the death struggle. We want to live. We want a new life. We want a life that we remember vaguely, sometimes in the back of our heads, as a liberated African people. We do not want to die when white people die. I'm not interested in being killed when Richard Nixon is killed or being destroyed when Fifth Avenue goes up in flames. That's not my idea of what we are about.

So in NewArk what we are trying to do is create a sympathetic atmosphere in which to develop a strong organized understanding of what the struggle is. How we must win. How can we win? Everything of value in the Black community we must control. Whoever runs for public office must be a nationalist or be accountable to nationalists. Anybody that speaks using the Black community as his base must refer and deal with nationalism and Pan-Africanism. All our politicians must do as much for us and Africans all over the world as Javits does for the Jews. Have you ever seen a Jewish congressman jump and denounce Israel? How long do you think he will be a congressman? How long do you think Javits would be a senator if he jumped up and denounced Israel? But niggers can jump up and denounce Africa all day and all night and be elected to anything by Africans. Because you are unconscious like a piece of wood, like a vegetable trying to become a human being, like a human being trying to become something spiritual. That's the kind of evolution we going through, but it is slow. Some of us would rather be animals, some of us would rather be vegetables and some of us would rather be minerals.

I hope that everybody here has gotten something out of the congress. We mean to reconvene, sometime, probably in October. Some of the brothers are coming over to address the U.N. in October. So that in New York City we will probably have a reconvening of those committees of twenty-five in New York City—probably the middle or late October—to hear one of the outstanding philosophers from the African continent, one of the leaders of state, and also to go over our first work, the beginnings of our work. I hope some of you will not get so tripped out by tomorrow's re-emergence into the white world as to forget what we said and did while we were here. I know it's hard to be Black in a world controlled by white folks. Du Bois said we always have the double consciousness. We trying to be Black and meanwhile you got a white ghost hovering over your head that says if you don't do this you get killed, if you don't do this you won't get no money, if you don't do this nobody will think you're beautiful, if you don't do this nobody will think you're smart. That's the ghost, you tryin' to be Black and the ghost is telling you to be a ghost. We hope you won't submit.

I lost my voice, I don't think I'll be able to read the poem but I'm s'posed to read it.

In NewArk when we greet each other on the street we say, "What time is it?" We always say, "It's Nation time!" We say, "What's gonna happen?" We say, "The land is gonna change hands!" Say: "What time is it?" "Nation time," and what's gonna happen? "The land is gonna change hands." Now you think about that. Like Malcolm said, you want some land, look down at your feet. The African concept of who owns the land is who is standing on it. Who uses it owns the land. If somebody could sell you the concept of an absentee landlord, you're really a sucker—they could be on the moon and sell you the land! The land belongs to the people who are standing on it. And if there is enough of you standing on it you ought to claim it. The African Nation is wherever there are enough Africans to take it. The African Nation is wherever there are enough Africans who are willing to take it. You understand that? By *any* means, by *any* means, *any* way you can conceive to do it, *any* way you can conceive. Think about Malcolm, read that. Listen to that record again. I don't mean at a cocktail party, I mean by yourself. Listen to it. By *any* means. It's about land. If you're a revolutionary—WHAT? Black Nationalism. Listen to Malcolm what he said, it's about land. You want some land? What are you standing on? If there's enough of you standing on it, take it. That's what it's about. Nationalism is about land and Nation. A way of life, trying to free itself. So the next time somebody ask you what time is it you tell 'em, "IT'S NATION TIME, Brother!"

IT'S NATION TIME

Time to get
together
time to be one strong fast black energy space
     one pulsating positive magnetism, rising
time to get up and
be
come
be
come, time to
        be come
        time to
        get up be come
        black genius rise in spirit muscle
        sun man get up rise heart of universes to be
future of the world
the black man is the future of the world
be come
rise up
future of the black genius spirit reality
      move
      from crushed roach back
      from dead snake head
      from wig funeral in slowmotion
      from dancing teeth and coward tip
      from jibberbabber patme boss patme smmich
when the brothers strike niggers come out
come out niggers
      when the brothers take over the school
      help niggers
      come out niggers
      all niggers negroes must change up
      come together in unity unify
      for nation time

Speech to the Congress of African Peoples   155

it's nation time. . . . .
Boom
Booom
BOOOOM
Dadadadadadadadadadada
Boom
Boom
Boom
Boom
Dadadadadaad adadadad
                    Hey aheee (soft)
                    Hey ahheee (loud)
Boom
Boom
Boom
sing a get up time to nationfy
sing a miracle fire light
sing a airplane invisibility for the jesus niggers
    come from the grave
for the jesus niggers dead in the cave, rose up,
    passst jewjuice on shadow world
raise up christ nigger
Christ was black
Krishna was black Shango was black
        Black jesus nigger come out and strike
            come out and strike boom boom
            Heyahheeee come out
        strike close ford
            close prudential burn the policies
        tear glasses off dead statue puppets
            they just imitating life
                shango buddha black
            hermes rasis black
                moses krishna
                            black
When the brothers wanna stop animals
come out niggers come out
come out niggers niggers niggers come out
help us stop the devil
help us build a new world

Niggers come out, brothers are we
        with you and your sons your daughters are ours
        and we are the same, all the blackness from one black Allah

when the world is clear you'll be with us
come out niggers come out
come out niggers come out
It's nation time eye ime
chant with bells and drum
it's nation time
It's nation time, get up santa claus
get up Roy Wilkins
get up Diana Ross
Get up Jimmy Brown
It's nation time, build it
get up muffet dragger
get up rastus for real to be rasta farari
ras jua, get up nigger, get up nigger
come over here
take a bow
nigger
It's Nation
Time!

18 Black Power in Education

Black Power activists evidenced a deep concern for educational reform at all levels. Some focused on making the public schools community-based and -controlled centers of individual and group empowerment. Treating black children as creative, educable beings (rather than as aberrant or dysfunctional ones), these revamped institutions would emphasize racial and cultural difference in a positive way—by nurturing a youngster's sense of self and instilling respect for collective responsibility and action. Others remained skeptical that sweeping reforms could be instituted swiftly and without undue compromise. As a result, they opted to create alternative institutions that would be sure to counteract the "socialization in whiteness" carried out through traditional schooling. Here, black students were to be instructed in group values and immersed in black culture before being sent forth to make their way in the larger society. Still others sought to transform both black and predominantly white college campuses into strongholds of liberation and laboratories for the study of the African American experience. Recognizing that knowledge was power and that higher education had a great deal to do with the ordering of societal power relationships, campus militants demanded major curriculum reforms and sought early retirement for "colonial" or "Uncle Tom" administrators. Here, as elsewhere, increased control of the learning environment and the creation of a "relevant" course of study were key agenda items.

In the following selection, Nathan Hare shares his ideas on Black Power–era educational reform. Appointed chair of San Francisco State College's pioneering black studies department in 1968, the outspoken sociologist held that any black studies curriculum that was not revolutionary and nationalistic was, by definition, "quite profoundly irrelevant." He also recognized the importance of combining course work with community involvement. Such a union of town and gown, he said, contributed to the development of a broad-based racial consciousness. It also would encourage students to commit themselves to the task of revitalizing (rather than fleeing) the community upon graduation.

Nathan Hare's article is reprinted from the *Massachusetts Review* (autumn 1969), by permission. It focuses on a series of interrelated issues that were the subject of frequent, heated debate during the formative years of black studies. The second document was produced by the education workshop that Hare chaired at the Third International Conference on Black Power at Philadelphia in 1968. The various components of the resolution reflect participants' sentiments on the future direction of black, community-controlled education. The selection is reprinted from *Black Power Conference Reports* (New York: Afram Associates, 1970), by permission.

1969 Questions and Answers about Black Studies

Nathan Hare

1. *What would a sample curriculum or program of black studies look like?*

A black studies program may be divided into two phases—the expressive and the pragmatic. The expressive phase refers to the effort to build in black youth a sense of pride or self, of collective destiny, a sense of pastness as a springboard in the quest for a new and better future. It also refers to the effort to deracicize white students. It revolves around such courses as black history and black art and culture but hinges on applicability ("relevance") to the black community and its needs.

The pragmatic phase operates specifically to prepare black students to deal with their society. The student's ultimate use of his pragmatic skills can be directed toward overcoming (or, if need be, overthrowing) his handicaps in dealing with his society. The pragmatic phase, in either case, is highly functional: courses producing socio-economic skills (black politics, black economics, black science, black communications, and so forth), extensive field work and community involvement in collaboration with classroom activities.

For instance, students in a course even so abstract and non-functional (in the conventional view) as black history would have as a requirement some participation in panel discussions for younger children in church basements or elementary and junior high schools. A class project might be the establishment of a black history club. The possibilities are even greater, of course, for such subjects as black economics, black politics, black journalism and the like, where students additionally should do apprenticeships and field work in connection with classroom discussions. Thus the student gets a more "relevant" education, testing out theories learned (in the laboratory of life against experiences and observations and experimentation in his community). As education is made more relevant to the black community and its needs, the community is, so to speak, made more relevant to (or involved in) the educational process.

The mere presence of a black college student in the black slum, tutoring black youth and engaged in course-connected activities, would provide role models for youth who ordinarily would not come into intimate contact with college students and their orientation.

Here follows a sample black studies curriculum, already approved by the California State College Trustees and instituted at San Francisco State College. Bear in mind that these courses and their descriptions are experimental and subject to change, as in the case of any new curriculum. Also, the curriculum was influenced heavily by the current necessity for approval by liberal-moderate administrators. And yet that is no real handicap here. In any case, a revolutionary program could be written but taught by a squad of Uncle Toms and we would still wind up with a "chitlin education." The key to success resides in the professors and, accordingly, in who has the power to hire and fire them.

A student receiving the bachelor's degree in black studies would be required to take the six core courses, to choose electives (24 units) in his area of concentration within the black studies program, and nine electives from throughout the college, on advisement from the black studies department. The rest of his units, some 76 or more in most colleges, would consist of general electives.

Core Courses:

101. BLACK HISTORY (3 units). African cultures from the Iron Age to the present; European colonization, contemporary nationalism; black cultural and scientific contributions, African and American. Political, economic, and social aspects of slavery and the contemporary black movement.

102. BLACK MATH. (3). Presentation of mathematics as a way of thinking, a means of communication and an instrument of problem solving, with special reference to the black community, using references from black experiences where possible for illustrative and reading-problem material. Deductive, inductive, and heuristic methods of mathematics are developed and used with special attention to application to the black community's needs.

103. BLACK PSYCHOLOGY (3). Introduction to the basic concepts of psychology with emphasis on their application to the life problems of black Americans. The scientific study of black behavior.

104. BLACK SCIENCE (3). Introduction to scientific development stressing the contributions of black scientists. Emphasis on the application of fundamental concepts and methods of science to the environment of black Americans.

105. BLACK PHILOSOPHY. The foundations of black philosophies as related to theories of knowledge and thought considered within the social and political context.

106. BLACK ARTS AND HUMANITIES (3). Introduction to, and exploration of, primary works by black artists and writers with special attention to values expressed in their works and values held by black students. Formation and development of black culture.

Black Arts Concentration:

107. LITERATURE OF BLACKNESS (3). A beginning course in the study of black literature, including methods of evaluation and analysis essential for understanding and appreciation.

108. BLACK WRITERS' WORKSHOP (6). Advanced composition with special reference to the portrayal of the black experience. Group discussions as well as supervision of individual projects, apprenticeships, and class project.

109. BLACK INTELLECTUALS (3). Major social and political thought within the black race from ancient Africa to the present. Analysis of the historical and cultural context with in-depth analysis of major black thinkers.

110. BLACK FICTION (3). Major contributions to black fiction, considered in relation to the development of poetic traditions and prose styles, with special reference to the history of black intellectuals. Examination of the style and techniques of representative black writers.

111. BLACK POETRY (3). Examination of structure, style, and techniques of representative black poets.

112. THE PAINTING OF BLACKNESS (3). Fundamental concepts of the black aesthetic orientation and the black experience. Work with color, light, space, and motion in relation to major styles in black painting.

113. THE MUSIC OF BLACKNESS (3). Analysis of styles and techniques of major traditions in black music. Fundamentals of music reading and theory applied through development of basic skills in singing, conducting, and playing black music.

114. BLACK DRAMA. Introduction to the art of acting, including theory and technique with emphasis upon resources, methods, characterization,

stage movement and business, using the social and art influences affecting black people as a frame of reference. Individual projects in selected aspects.

115. BLACK RADIO, TELEVISION, FILM (6). Special problems of radio, television, and/or film production in relation to black persons and the black community. Work on various programs with direct faculty supervision.

116. BLACK JOURNALISM (6). The history, social role, function, and organization of the print and broadcast media in relation to black Americans. Field experience, apprenticeships, and supervised projects.

117. BLACK ORATORY (6). Oratory as part of the black American political, social, and intellectual history; issues, ideas, spokesmen, and method of advocacy. Supervised study and experience.

118. BLACK CLASSICS (3). Society, literature, thought, and art and their interrelationships in ancient and modern Africa, early and current America. Intensive humanistic study of black works in literature, the fine arts, history, philosophy, and the sciences of man.

Behavioral and Social Sciences Concentration

119. SOCIOLOGY OF BLACKNESS (6). Major features of black American society. Application of the principles and concepts of sociology and social change to analysis of movements for black parity.

120. BLACK POLITICS (6). The political values, structure and behavior of black Americans. Theories, problems, and issues relating to the political behavior of black Americans. Apprenticeships and supervised practicum.

121. ECONOMICS OF THE BLACK COMMUNITY (6). Economic and social development of the black community from the slave trade to the present. Problems and growth of black economic enterprise, with field experience and supervised practicum.

122. GEOGRAPHY OF BLACKNESS (3). Location and geographic distribution of black people and black political and economic activities. Relationship of physical environment, population, and social-political factors of the black community. Special attention to the urban geography of blackness.

123. SOCIAL ORGANIZATION OF BLACKNESS (6). Applications of the concepts of social organization to black institutions and interrelationships of black organizations. The social structure of the black community covering organizational patterns, leadership, cleavage and conflict, and planning and development of the black community, with field experience, apprenticeships, and practicum.

124. DEVELOPMENT OF BLACK LEADERSHIP (6). Analysis of the black community power structure; changing patterns of the leadership, influence, and decision-making in the black community with supervised individual and group projects.

125. BLACK COUNSELING (6). The counseling process and counseling problems will be considered in relation to the black child as well as the dynamics of black-white relations; issues and legal aspects of counseling the black child. Clinical practicum and experience.

126. DEMOGRAPHY OF BLACKNESS (3). Changes in quantity, composition, and distribution of black population throughout the world with special emphasis on the United States. The implications for the black race and its development will be stressed along with application of theory and methods of population analysis to the black race.

127. BLACK NATIONALISM AND THE INTERNATIONAL COMMUNITY (3). Analysis of the sources of black nationalism and its nature; major concepts, nomenclature, and symbols in relation to the rise of the black race in the international arena. The effect of international relations and its effect on international relations will be explored.

128. THE ANTHROPOLOGY OF BLACKNESS (6). An examination of the peoples of Africa and blacks in other lands with emphasis upon the arts, customs, industries and social structure. Cultural origins and influences upon the western world, and the United States in particular, will be examined.

129. BLACK CONSCIOUSNESS (3). Analysis of the nature and trends of black consciousness through history. Intensive study of the psychology and sociology of the process and development of thinking black.

130. BLACK STATISTICS: SURVEY AND METHOD (6). Analysis of the pitfalls and safeguards in statistical research on matters of race. Techniques of measuring, tabulating, analyzing, and interpreting statistical

data, using examples and illustrative materials from the black community. Apprenticeships and supervised projects.

131. BLACK ECONOMIC WORKSHOP (6). The structure, behavior and results of black economic enterprise and the policies appropriate to black social objectives. Apprenticeships and supervised projects.

132. BLACK POLITICAL WORKSHOP (6). Direct investigation, analysis, and evaluation of political activities of black Americans. Current developments and issues concerning basic approaches to the acquisition of political power. Individual involvement in politics through group and organizational affiliations. Field work in local government offices and community services.

2. *Should the aim of every Black Studies Program be to serve and transform the black community? If so, how is that aim best achieved: by, let us say, high-powered research institutes, "think-tank" centers, experimental and innovative programs that include extensive field work and relations with the black community, changing the usual degree or credential requirements, "beefing up" or ignoring traditional notions of academic soundness in black studies courses?*

While we have no wish to appear disdainful of research in any form, it is our considered judgment that enough research has already been done to suit our current needs. There are studies on "Negroes and Potato Growing in South Georgia," "Negroes and the Consumption of Watermelons in Maine." And yet people still maintain their ignorance of what is wrong—or even that there is really something wrong—let alone about what we need to do about it. Four major white universities this year received $1 million from the Ford Foundation alone to study "the Negro." We believe that they have been studying the wrong man. We want $10 million from Ford to study the white man.

Actually, the problem is one of application of the knowledge we already have. The late great W. E. B. Du Bois, who was the father of the modern scientific study of the black condition, eventually came to the realization that knowledge is not enough, that people know pretty much what needs to be done if they would only act. And so, he switched, in his own words, "from science to propaganda."

The notion that "academic soundness" would suffer is basically a racist apprehension, a feeling that any deviation on the part of blacks away from white norms and standards inevitably would dip downward. It also is based, perhaps, on the naive notion that traditional education is value-free and, because it is based on the ideology of the existing political forces, is blessed with "the end of ideology." That is, most emphatically, not the case. The whole need for black studies grows out of the current lack of true academic soundness in the educational system as we know it now. A key test of soundness for any structure is whether or not it works. Obviously our current educational system does not work for a growing number of black and oppressed "minorities" whose backgrounds and experiences have not coincided with those of white suburbia.

The matter of "qualifications" particularly is often farcical. The fact that even I.Q. tests, let alone achievement tests, too clearly fail to measure precisely what they purport to measure is now well known even among academicians. Besides, many persons eventually find success in a field outside their college field of studies. Even when they do achieve success within their own fields they are likely to be lifted out of that endeavor and made administrators over their inferiors who actually work in that field. Few public administrators are trained in public administration and few politicians or public officials have had more than the ordinary number of courses in political science. Most of what people learn in college is irrelevant to the actual performance of their specialty anyway. This observation was corroborated by the survey described in the book, *The Miseducation of American Teachers,* where a national cross-sample of teachers admitted that their courses even in the methodology of teaching had not prepared them for teaching, a skill they had to learn on the job.

Yet, despite the fact that most teachers report learning how to teach on the job, from tips culled from co-workers, most major school systems seldom honor more than five or six years of the teaching experience of teachers recruited from other cities. Recently, a black teacher from the District of Columbia applied to teach in San Francisco. Although she had been named by the Junior Chamber of Commerce previously as the Outstanding Young Educator for the District of Columbia, she was told by the personnel clerk that only persons of high quality are hired in San Francisco. She indicated that she had a master's degree plus thirty hours beyond and had taught for twelve years in such places as Chicago, the District of Columbia, Oklahoma and Virginia. She then was told she would have to pass the National Teachers Exam, whereupon she replied that she had passed that exam both in her special field and one other. She was informed that she would only be able to teach in San Francisco after she had taken five additional courses such as California history!

3. *Should admission to Black Studies Programs be limited to black students? What then will likely be the effect of a recent HEW memorandum warning college officials they risk losing federal funds if they sanction such exclusion?*

Admission to Black Studies in general should not be limited to black students; though, where there are not sufficient facilities to cover everybody, black students should receive priority because for them black studies are doubly therapeutic. However, a racist society cannot be healed merely by solving the problems of its black victims alone. The black condition does not exist in a vacuum; we cannot solve the problems of the black race without solving the problems of the society which produced and sustains the predicament of blacks. At the same time as we transform the black community, through course-related community activities, white students duplicating this work in their communities— predominantly—may operate to transform the white community and thus a racist American society.

White students also need educational relevance. For example, in place of foreign languages they seldom use, even when they learn them well enough, they might better be required to take courses in law along with their "civics" and English, algebra, geometry, trigonometry and the like. This would not put lawyers out of business anymore than algebra and trigonometry and French now put mathematicians and interpreters out of business. But it would seem to be more relevant to their lives as well as their performance in their various occupations. More particularly, an education which largely ignores the study of the black race and its problems, one of the gravest problems facing America, if not the entire world, is gravely irrelevant. No solution to the world's problems can come about without a solution to the problems of color conflict. White students frequently seem to know this intuitively, even if their learned elders pretend to be ignorant of this fact. They cry to get into black studies courses, not the least because they find their traditional courses typically so empty.

Understand me, black studies is based ideally on the ideology of revolutionary nationalism; it is not based on any form of racism, black or white, though it is dedicated, of course, to the destruction of white racism. Which may be why the establishment seems so determined (chiefly by way of its mass media) to confuse black students into a search for tangential, ultra-separatist goals such as separate dormitories, chitterlings in the cafeteria, and similar diversions having little to do with changing seriously the power relations of blacks and whites, let alone the nature of education. The media rush to play up such demands as "militant," leading black students who identify with militant blackness to seek divergent ends. Once students fall into this trap, the government (through HEW) rushes in with its "opposition" to such ultra-separatist goals. This sidetracks us onto insignificant battlefields.

This is no simple game; the quest for liberation cannot be based on absolutist notions, symbolic aspirations which enslave one's strategy, nor any other reaction-formation to the methods of white oppression. Black studies is nationalistic, not separatist. All separatists in a sense are nationalists but not all nationalists are separatists. Separatism or cultural nationalism may be a first stage of revolutionary nationalism, but it tends too often to be preoccupied with molding a cultural nexus and is therefore likely to get bogged down in that effort. Revolutionary nationalism by contrast seeks to transfer power, at least a portion thereof, to an oppressed group, and in that effort is more tolerant of white radicals.

4. *Should black teachers for programs in white institutions be recruited from southern Negro colleges? What role can and should the Negro college play?*

Black students do have a deep and abiding need for black professors as role models, particularly in black studies. Where these professors come from is not so important as what kind of professors they are. We hear much these days about a so-called "brain drain on Negro colleges." Just what brains they refer to I do not know. It is conceivable that these brains have been lying dormant all this time, but it is not likely in any case that they will suddenly come alive and function in an altogether different manner just because they migrate North to a white college. It is interesting to me that many of the same persons who once said that Negro colleges should not steal or pull away potentially token blacks from white colleges now wail that white colleges should not pull blacks from Negro colleges.

Ideally, Negro colleges should play the role of devising a new black ideology and a new black ethics (had we forgotten that academic "disciplines" teach ethics?). Negro colleges should be setting the pace and providing models of scholarly excellence and inquiry into the problems of color—the "problem of the twentieth century"—comprising laboratories for experimentation in the techniques and tactics of revolutionary change. But we do not believe in miracles. The Negro college is glued to the mores of its missionary origins. It is located invariably in the South, cemented to the prevailing cake of conservatism, and less free politically even than the typical white college there. Rather than address itself seriously to the solution of the problems of academia, the Negro college has been more inclined to ape and compound white trivia and miseducation.

We do not have any more time for dreams that already have been contaminated by the elements of nightmare. What happens to the Negro college ultimately is a matter for history to relate. Meanwhile, we cannot be anchored in excessive, time-consuming lamentation over decaying bodies. The Negro colleges, let us not forget, were established by the southern power structure. One doubts that the motivation was revolution for blacks in the South, let alone the North.

5. *What, if any, may be the role of the white scholar in such programs (in such fields, say, as race relations, or Negro history and literature, where a person has made or continues to make important contributions; or in courses that require specialists the black community may not be able to supply; or courses that don't necessarily require a black experience as part of the person's qualification)?*

There is going to be a need for some white scholars (who can qualify emotionally and ideologically) to help teach black education to white students. They would be more attuned to the white community and better able to arrange the relevant field work experiences there for white students in the white community.

The primary reluctance to admit white professors to the black studies program—aside from the present need for black role models on college faculties and the relative inability of white professors to operate within the framework of revolutionary-compensatory-black-nationalism—is the tendency for whites, because of their recent socio-historical conditioning, to be inclined to take over whenever they take part in black enterprises.

Still, we need not be sidetracked into the refusal to hire a single white professor, resisting the government's policy of tokenism prematurely and unnecessarily. If the white race can perpetuate white racism by hiring a black now and then, we can fight racism and mold, compensatorily, our own nationalism by adhering to the policy of tokenism as well.

6. Where and how should control of the program be vested? Should there be complete autonomy within schools? Should there be specially appointed Trustees or overseers? How do state schools and private ones differ?

The control of black studies programs must, of course, be vested in the black community just as the control over white education—indeed both Negro and white education—is presently vested in the white community. Special trustees or review boards may be established if necessary, but when revolutionary black nationalists call for a department of black studies they do not mean a separate department but a distinct or autonomous one. Nay more: self-determination or ultimate authority in determining their educational destiny.

Too often of course they are given black studies programs which merely represent black carbon copies of conventional education when they are given any autonomy at all. There must be complete autonomy at least, if not clear sovereignty. Autonomy gives the right to independence from one's oppressor and his institutions, the chance to establish one's own institutions alongside his, generally leaving political power and hence control over one's autonomous institutions in his hands. Sovereignty, or self-determination, implies supreme rank or authority. We must have sovereignty because, with mere autonomy, we would not be permitted to diverge too far from the norms and practices of existing white institutions without the probability of the sovereign axe of the oppressor falling upon our heads.

Yet the oppressor's institutional norms and practices were the source of the cry for black autonomy in the first place! It is not very reasonable, anyway, to assume that the same racist institutions (self-defined as such by the Kerner report) will suddenly reverse their present course and extend freedom where before they oppressed. It would be necessary first to reverse its norms and values, its regulations, even if it could.

This goes for private colleges as well. Their relative freedom, when it does exist, is only a matter of small degree. Many persons have advocated private schools as more realistic places to begin the implementation of black studies. But realism is a matter of definition and perception. What one perceives as reality not only may differ from person to person but neither may accord with objective reality. Why have private colleges not taken the lead? Notre Dame's president contrarily took a notoriously hard line in the other direction; the liberal University of Chicago has not stood out among recent responses to student demands; nor has Northwestern.

We can only conclude that a change has got to come within colleges as a whole; that any genuine and significant change will be resisted to the death by the powers that be; and that those of us concerned with the salvation of the black race and humanity have a lot of work to do.

1968 Report of the Workshop on Education

Third International Conference on Black Power

WHEREAS, Black people know more about their needs than anybody else;

WHEREAS, schools in Black communities controlled by whites have failed to provide the kind of education Black children need;

WHEREAS, the entire system of education has mitigated against Black persons;

WHEREAS, white racist learning has produced Black persons with white minds to undermine, aid and abet the suppression of Black people;

WHEREAS, there is a vital need to rehabilitate and salvage the battered ego, white-washed soul, spirit and culture of many of our Black citizenry;

WE RESOLVE:

Move immediately to effect total Black control of hiring, firing, retention and promotion of all Black school personnel.

Develop coalitions among diverse Black groups to promote responsibility to the Black community.

Develop specific strategies for physically taking over schools and classrooms, disrupting racist learning, whenever the situation demands.

Develop techniques for redirecting and guiding Black professionals to take responsible stances which are consistent with the aims and goals of the Black community.

Black control of school necessitates Black control over all school personnel.

Black "experts" must be accountable to the Black community and able to give schools the service they have given the power structure in the past.

Demand the waiver of all tests standardized on white middle-class urban experiences or give equal weight to the Black experience.

Go into the community and find out how the citizens view their schools and, in turn, assist them in evaluating the relevance and irrelevance of the schools to their lives.

Secure data with which to confront those Brothers and Sisters (and other relatives) who are unsympathetic to the Black interest.

Find ways to organize parents so they will know what is happening to their children.

Explain and illustrate to the community how the schools are not fulfilling their obligation to Black children and the Black community.

Begin to differentiate between such concepts as tokenism and total victory, reform and revolution, nationalism and assimilationism.

Corps of Black revolutionaries should be constantly evaluating and reassessing the Black community.

Each local Black community should have a Black information and clearing house.

The community should demand teacher orientations conducted by the Black community.

Establish Black nurseries and pre-school studies for Black children.

Disregard the George Washington birthday holiday and replace it with a Black Winter Break, beginning with February 21, to commemorate the death of Malcolm X and ending with February 23, the birthday of W. E. B. Du Bois, the late Black scholar.

Establish Black cultural centers in each locality.

Establish Black libraries and mobile Black library units in each neighborhood.

Infiltrate the Sunday Schools as a part of the effort to rejuvenate the Black child's soul, spirit and personality.

Assist in the formation and strengthening of Black parents' councils in each locality, region and neighborhood.

Form textbook evaluation corps for criticism and production of books relevant to the Black condition.

Extend "Negro History Week" the year round and replace it with a "White History Week" for a special week's concentration on the study and exposure of the science of white racism and its history. This also is a year round concern.

Establish Black scholarly and academic journals.

Provide conferences to educate those Brothers and Sisters who express curiosity about the meaning of Blackness, Black Power and the like.

Work toward redefining all pertinent values and standards toward building a Black morality relevant to the Black reality.

Establish a "captive action" week commemorating the day our Black forefathers were abducted and transported in chains to the abominable American colonialists.

Every Black person who knows something must find one or two Black Brothers and Sisters to teach.

Require that all teachers in Black schools undergo a year's in-service de-brainwashing program administered by the Black community.

Revive the national anthem "Lift Every Voice and Sing" to replace the singing of the "Star Spangled Banner" in morning devotional exercises in Black schools.

Develop techniques for converting colleges and institutions, now Black in name only and color composition only, into true Black institutions.

Continue efforts to build Black universities.

Organize intelligence squads to infiltrate each educational institution, white or "Negro."

Assist in the establishment of a Black Studies or Afro-American studies curriculum at each institution.

Continue to promote the establishment of several model Black universities. (An Association of Afro-American Educators proposal is submitted at the request of David Kent, Lincoln University, in charge of information for the AAAE.)

19   Roy Innis and the Congress
of Racial Equality

Founded in Chicago during World War II as a nonviolent, direct-action protest organization, the Congress of Racial Equality (CORE) gained national recognition during the 1960s for its Southern "freedom ride" campaign and for conducting demonstrations at the 1964 New York World's Fair. By 1965, CORE chapters also had become engaged in a variety of community development projects. Recognizing that the nation's central cities faced staggering problems against which their traditional antidiscrimination, equal opportunity emphasis seemed hopelessly ineffective, the organization's leaders began organizing ghetto residents. CORE helped form tenants' councils and launch rent strikes. Community centers were opened, offering tutoring, sports, and craft programs, job counseling, and information on family planning, health care, and voter registration. Some chapters assisted black workers in demanding better pay and work conditions and lobbied for increased grassroots representation on local antipoverty commissions.

CORE's shift away from direct-action demonstrations to the more tedious work of community organizing was accompanied by a significant growth in black membership and increased African American representation on leadership councils. Both developments were conducive to the flowering of a Black Power perspective. In the summer of 1968, CORE officially excluded whites from membership, becoming "once and for all" a black nationalist organization with "separation" as its goal. National director Roy Innis deemed this course of action "a necessary and pragmatic way of organizing two separate and distinct races of people." The following document is a distillation of Innis's ideas on economic nationalism, community control, and the "new social contract" that, if implemented in full, would radically redefine both American capitalism and black-white relations. It is reprinted from *Black Economic Development,* ed. William F. Haddad and G. Douglas Pugh (Englewood Cliffs, NJ: Prentice-Hall, 1969), by permission.

1969 *From* **Separatist Economics**

A New Social Contract

Roy Innis

There exists today a crisis of immense proportions within the boundaries of the United States of America. This crisis is the direct result of the breakdown of the relationship between black and white people in our society. It was scarcely a good relationship to begin with. For blacks it has been degrading and dehumanizing; for whites, it has been abrasive, guilt-ridden, and a perpetual thorn. Over the decades, the problem has festered and spread to the point where it now threatens to destroy the entire political organism in which it is rooted.

Even at this late date, we can provide an alternative to the collision course of whites and blacks in this country. But to do so, we must develop entirely new solutions to the massive problems of the past. The present programs and plans offered by well-meaning agencies, groups, and individuals are entirely insufficient. Aside from the fundamental lack of understanding in the past of the nature and degree of racism in this country, there has been a failure to coordinate the multiplicity of suggested "solutions." Such solutions, in any case, have never been structured by black people. They have always been structured by whites who interpreted our needs and in many cases designed these solutions to accommodate their own needs.

Where the collision of black and white is concerned, we have falsely assumed in America that a contract or constitution designed for a dominant majority, with distinct attributes, self-interests, and needs, could simply be adapted, by minor modifications, to fit the needs of a significant minority with different attributes, interests, and needs. Obviously, this has not worked. A crucial weakness has been the lack of control by black people over the institutions that surround them: institutions that not only establish imposed values for them but also control the flow of goods and services within their communities, thereby shaping the quality of their lives. The black community sees these institutions in the hands of people with interests too often at odds with their own. Thus, schools in black neighborhoods too often do not teach, sanitation departments do not protect, employment departments do not find jobs, welfare departments do not give adequate relief, housing departments do not give decent housing. Most ironic of all, human rights departments do not guarantee human rights.

The obvious solution, then in a *new social contract,* to be drawn in the mutual interest of both parties. This contract must redefine the relationship between blacks and whites, to the extent that black people are recognized as a major interest group. While this redefinition is in progress, there are palpable changes to be implemented.

Large, densely populated black areas, especially in urban centers, must have a change in status. They must become political sub-divisions of the state, instead of sub-colonial appendages of the cities. Blacks must manage and control the institutions that service their areas, as has always been the case for other interest groups. There is an immediate need in the institutions of education, health, social service, sanitation, housing, protection, etc. Black people must be able to control basic societal instruments in the social, political, and economic arenas.

Definitions

In short, black people must seek liberation from the dominance and control of white society. Nothing less than this liberation will allow black people to determine their own destinies.

Perhaps, at this point, a few definitions are in order. There is always a controversy as to whether our tactics, our objectives, are reformist or revolutionary. In my own view, black people at this stage of their development are not and should not be talking about some romantic thing called revolution, but rather a more pragmatic and necessary step called liberation. There is a difference between the two. A revolution, of course, occurs where one class of a national group rebels against another class of that same group, as in the Russia of 1917, the France of the late 18th Century. Liberation comes about in a setting of two distinct groups, where one is suppressing the other. Jews caught in Egypt in the time of the Pharaohs did not talk about revolution against what was the most powerful and formidable military machine of the time. They talked about liberation—separating themselves from Egyptians.

We black nationalists, too, must speak of separating ourselves. We live in a setting where one group—not our own—controls the institutions, and the flow of goods and services. We can change our condition by liberating ourselves and placing these vital instruments of social and economic destiny in our own hands. This is what we mean by separation—quite a different matter from segregation, which is the condition that now exists, in fact, throughout the United States.

Separation is a more equitable way of organizing the society. The important distinction is that in such a society the control of goods and services flowing through a distinct geographical area inhabited by a distinct population group would be in the hands of those indigenous to the area. In other words, if we have a clearly defined sociological unit called Harlem, New York City, the people of Harlem will control the flow of goods and services there. The same would hold true for the white areas of New York City: the whites would control their own "action."

In the struggle toward self-determination, there has been a great deal of argument about the order of steps to be taken. Should we be talking first about politics, about culture, or should we be talking about economics? Let me suggest that we can resolve this dilemma by understanding first of all that these three stages of liberation are virtually inseparable. There must be some sort of socio-cultural renaissance if there is to be movement in any other direction. There must be some sort of politico-economic development if the cultural movement is to have any base on which to acquire significance.

My feeling is that we have already begun part of this movement. That is, black people have begun revitalizing their culture, recreating their values. We must now phase in the element of economic growth. The failure of many of the past economic measures—community action, training and hiring programs, and the like—is that they have been little more than board games, depending on some sort of arithmetic progression. What we need to do now is to find the geometric factor that can speed up this process. And that is why we turn to the control of institutions. But some further definition is needed.

Capitalism or Development

In the new focus on economic control, there has been much talk about something called "black capitalism." Many of our people have been deluded into endless debates centered around this term. There is no such animal. Capitalism, like socialism, is an economic and political philosophy that describes the experience of Europeans and their descendants—Americans. Blacks must innovate, must create a new ideology. It may include elements of capitalism, elements of socialism, or elements of neither: that is immaterial. What matters is that it will be created to fit our needs.

So then black people are not talking about black capitalism. Black people are talking about economic development. We are talking about the creation and the acquisition of capital instruments by means of which we can maximize our economic interests. We do not particularly try to define styles of ownership; we say that we are willing to operate pragmatically and let the style of ownership fit the style of the area or its inhabitants.

The question of autonomy is critical. Any reliable sociological analysis will indicate that we live in natural units called communities. Where whites are concerned, these natural sociological units then become natural political units—political subdivisions of county, state, or federal government. This does not happen with black communities, so that extensive areas like Harlem in New York, Roxbury in Boston, Watts in Los Angeles, exist as colonial appendages of the urban center. In fact, government programs almost always deal with us as part of urban centers, and in terms of the overall condition of those centers. This is something we must resist strenuously, for there is a fundamental conflict of interest between our communities—the so-called ghettos—and the urban centers in which they are situated. The urban centers are managed by political and institutional barons who include our piece of "turf" in their domain. And we see that whenever we make any attempt to change that relationship—political, social, or economic—we meet the massive resistance of these barons. This sort of frustration has led and will continue to lead to disastrous confrontations between blacks and whites.

We understand also that the urban setting, throughout history, has been the energizer of mankind, thus the cradle of change. It is there that blacks, too, will have to find their solutions. We cannot go off to conduct a masquerade of change in newly created little rural centers. But if we are to develop in the urban centers, our position must be newly understood.

There is a very striking similarity between the so-called underdeveloped countries and our underdeveloped black communities. Both have always been oppressed; almost always there is an unfavorable balance of trade with the oppressors or exploiters; both suffer from high unemployment, low income, scarce capital, and we can point to a series of other similarities. But let me point to at least one vital difference. In every so-called underdeveloped country, the people have a measure of sovereignty. They have a vastly greater amount of autonomy compared with the black communities across this country. It seems to me, then, that a natural impetus for our communities is to move to gain that missing ingredient—sovereignty, or at least a greater degree of autonomy and self-determination.

In other words, I am saying there is no way we can divorce economic development from political imperatives. You cannot have economic development unless you have certain supportive political realities, one of which is some degree of self-determination.

The Dividends

What economic gratuities would flow from self-determination? Let us consider the massive budgets provided to pay for the goods and services of a single black community (which are then almost always poorly distributed in that community). Take the schools, for example. In a community like Harlem, close to a hundred million dollars is spent yearly for goods and services to supply the schools. We must assume, in fact we know, that in almost every instance those goods and services are purchased from sources outside the community. Now we in the black community pay taxes that are intended to be used to pay for these commodities, so that nominally, all tax monies are returned to us in this form. But what really happens is that our tax monies are returned to agents of the urban centers—the mayor and his commissioners and department heads—who will then use that money to enhance the economic interest of the white-dominated urban center by buying goods and services outside the black communities they are meant to serve.

That same hundred million dollars could have gone, let us say, to a corporation in Harlem put together by two or three black entrepreneurs and awarded a contract to supply books for the Harlem schools. It is immaterial that this hypothetical corporation does not own a publishing house or a printing plant. Neither do the white corporations that presently supply books to the public school system in Cleveland, or New York, or any place else across this country. They are merely middlemen. They buy from someone else and sell to the schools. They move paper from one side of their desk to the other and turn a handsome profit. That kind of profit could be turned just as easily within the black community, to increase its income by the millions. Multiply the massive budgets for the schools by the massive budgets in health and hospital services, sanitation, and all the other urban services, and you get a massive amount of money that represents a guaranteed market.

The name of this in economics is guaranteed market. That is what you have when you are selling to your own institutions: there will always be a demand for your goods and services. If you have control of these institutions you are able to determine who will get the contracts, and you can direct them back to your own people.

So here we see at least one route by which the black people can get a running start in economic development without huge investments in machinery, materials, technical expertise, and without most of the other impediments that are immediately cited when we talk about economic development. And it is a way in which we could secure a maximum return to our community from those precious tax dollars that we pay year after year.

Of course, this same division of interest and diversion of profit has social as well as economic consequences. We must control our schools if we are to upgrade education and pass on positive values to our children. We must control health facilities if we are to cut down our mortality rate. We must control the law enforcement in our areas if the police are to serve their proper function—which is protection, not oppression. In short, we must control every single institution that takes our tax moneys and is supposed to distribute goods and services equitably for us.

20 James Forman and the "Black Manifesto"

At New York City's Riverside Church in May 1969, James Forman interrupted Sunday morning services to read a 2,500-word "Black Manifesto," which claimed that the nation's "racist churches and synagogues" owed African Americans $500 million in hardship reparations. He later upped the ante to $3 billion. The document had been adopted in late April by a 187 to 63 vote of delegates attending the National Black Economic Development Conference, a three-day, blacks-only gathering sponsored by a coalition of major religious organizations interested in promoting job training, voter education, and community improvement programs. But it was the SNCC official's dramatic reading that made frontpage news. Soon thereafter, national debate began over the issue of whether wealthy mainstream institutions should be required to provide blacks with compensation for past suffering and exploitation. Never resolved—at least not in a manner likely to win the approval of staunch Black Power advocates—issues central to the reparations debate continue to stir passions whenever they are revisited. The following excerpts are taken from a pamphlet version of the manifesto distributed by TACT, San Marino, California, and reprinted by permission.

1969 *From* Manifesto to the White Christian Churches and the Jewish Synagogues in the United States of America and All Other Racist Institutions

Black Manifesto

James Forman

We, the black people assembled in Detroit, Michigan for the National Black Economic Development Conference, are fully aware that we have been forced to come together because racist white America has exploited our resources, our minds, our bodies, our labor. For centuries, we have been forced to live as colonized people inside the United States, victimized by the most vicious, racist system in the world. We have helped to build the most industrial country in the world.

We are, therefore, demanding of the white Christian churches and Jewish synagogues which are part and parcel of the system of capitalism, that they begin to pay reparations to black people in this country. We are demanding $500,000,000 from the Christian white churches and the Jewish synagogues. This total comes to $15 per nigger. This is a low estimate for we maintain there are probably more than 30,000,000 black people in this country. $15 a nigger is not a large sum of money, and we know that the churches and synagogues have a tremendous wealth, and its membership—white America—has profited and still exploits black people. We are also not unaware that the exploitation of colored people around the world is aided and abetted by the white Christian churches and synagogues. This demand for $500,000,000 is not an idle resolution or empty words. Fifteen dollars for every black brother and sister in the United States is only a beginning of the reparations due us as people who have been exploited and degraded, brutalized, killed, and persecuted. Underneath all this exploitation, the racism of this country has produced a psychological effect upon us that we are beginning to shake off. We are no longer afraid to demand our full rights as a people in this decadent society.

We are demanding $500,000,000 to be spent in the following way:

1. We call for the establishment of a Southern Land Bank to help our brothers and sisters who have to leave their land because of racist pressure, for people who want to establish cooperative farms, but who

have no funds. We have seen too many farmers evicted from their homes because they have dared to defy the white racism of this country. We need money for land. We must fight for massive sums of money for this Southern Land Bank. We call for $200,000,000 to implement this program.

2. We call for the establishment of four major publishing and printing industries in the United States to be funded with $10,000,000 each. These publishing houses are to be located in Detroit, Atlanta, Los Angeles, and New York. They will help generate capital for further cooperative investments in the black community, provide jobs and an alternative to the white dominated and controlled printing field.

3. We call for the establishment of four of the most advanced scientific and futuristic audio-visual networks to be located in Detroit, Chicago, Cleveland, and Washington, D.C. These TV networks will provide an alternative to the racist propaganda that fills the current television networks. Each of these TV networks will be funded by $10,000,000.

4. We call for a research skills center which will provide research on the problems of black people. This center must be funded with no less than $30,000,000.

5. We call for the establishment of a training center for the teaching of skills in community organization, photography, movie making, television making and repair, radio building and repair, and all other skills needed in communication. This training center shall be funded with no less than $10,000,000.

6. We recognize the role of the National Welfare Rights Organization, and we intend to work with them. We call for $10,000,000 to assist in the organization of welfare recipients. We want to organize the welfare workers in this country so that they may demand more money from the government and better administration of the welfare system of this country.

7. We call for $20,000,000 to establish a National Black Labor Strike and Defense Fund. This is necessary for the protection of black workers and their families who are fighting racist working conditions in this country.

8. We call for the establishment of the International Black Appeal (IBA). This International Black Appeal will be funded with no less than

$20,000,000. The IBA is charged with producing more capital for the establishment of cooperative businesses in the United States and in Africa—our Motherland. The International Black Appeal is one of the most important demands that we are making for we know that it can generate and raise funds throughout the United States and help our African brothers. The IBA is charged with three functions and shall be headed by James Forman:

    (a) Raising money for the program of the National Black Economic Development Conference.

    (b) The development of cooperatives in African countries and support of African liberation movements.

    (c) Establishment of a Black Anti-Defamation League which will protect our African image.

9. We call for the establishment of a Black University to be funded with $130,000,000 to be located in the South. Negotiations are presently under way with a Southern University.

10. We demand that IFCO allocate all unused funds in the planning budget to implement the demands of this conference. . . .

Brothers and sisters, we no longer are shuffling our feet and scratching our heads. We are tall, black, and proud.

And we say to the white Christian churches and Jewish synagogues, to the government of this country, and to all the white racist imperialists who compose it, there is only one thing left that you can do to further degrade black people and that is to kill us. But we have been dying too long for this country. We have died in every war. We are dying in Vietnam today, fighting the wrong enemy.

The new black man wants to live and to live means that we must not become static or merely believe in self defense. We must boldly go out and attack the white Western world at its power centers. The white Christian churches are another form of government in this country, and they are used by the government of this country to exploit the people of Latin America, Asia, and Africa. But the day is soon coming to an end. Therefore, brothers and sisters, the demands we make upon the white Christian churches and the Jewish synagogues are small demands. They represent $15 per black person in these United States. We can legitimately demand this from the church power structure. We must demand more from the United States Government.

But to win our demands from the church which is linked up with the

United States government, we must not forget that it will ultimately be by force and power.

We are not threatening the churches. We are saying that we know the churches came with the military might of the colonizers and have been sustained by the military might of the colonizers. Hence, if the churches in colonial territories were established by military might, we know deep within our hearts that we must be prepared to use force to get our demands. We are not saying that this is the road we want to take. It is not, but let us be very clear that we are not opposed to force, and we are not opposed to violence. We were captured in Africa by violence. We were kept in bondage and political servitude and forced to work as slaves by the military machinery and the Christian church working hand-in-hand.

We recognize that in issuing this manifesto, we must prepare for a long range educational campaign in all communities of this country, but we know that the Christian churches have contributed to our oppression in white America. We do not intend to abuse our black brothers and sisters in black churches who have uncritically accepted Christianity. We want them to understand how the racist white Christian church with its hypocritical declarations and doctrines of brotherhood has abused our trust and faith. An attack on the religious beliefs of black people is not our major objective, even though we know that we were not Christians when we were brought to this country, but that Christianity was used to help enslave us. Our objective in issuing this Manifesto is to force the racist white Christian church to begin the payment of reparations which are due to all black people, not only by the church but also by private business and the U.S. Government. We see this focus on the Christian church as an effort around which all black people can unite.

Our demands are negotiable, but they cannot be minimized. They can only be increased, and the church is asked to come up with larger sums of money than we are asking. Our slogans are:

ALL ROADS MUST LEAD TO REVOLUTION

UNITE WITH WHOMEVER YOU CAN UNITE

NEUTRALIZE WHEREVER POSSIBLE

FIGHT OUR ENEMIES RELENTLESSLY

VICTORY TO THE PEOPLE

LIFE AND GOOD HEALTH TO MANKIND

RESISTANCE TO DOMINATION BY THE WHITE CHRISTIAN
CHURCHES AND THE JEWISH SYNAGOGUES

REVOLUTIONARY BLACK POWER

WE SHALL WIN WITHOUT A DOUBT

21 Black Power and Black Labor: The League of Revolutionary Black Workers

During the Black Power years, the labor movement's traditional rallying song, "Solidarity," took on new meaning as African American workers expressed their grievances by forming independent black unions and joining black caucuses within established unions. Complaining of dehumanizing treatment as wage slaves on modern-day industrial plantations, they leafletted at factory gates, picketed convention halls, and disrupted production lines nationwide. Such job actions were particularly numerous—and volatile—within the auto industry. Here, young black workers challenged established patterns of authority by pledging allegiance to militant organizations such as DRUM (Dodge Revolutionary Union Movement), GRUM (at General Motors), and FRUM (at Ford). To sustain and give direction to these separate units, an umbrella support organization known as the League of Revolutionary Black Workers was established in 1969. It remained a force within the industry for the next two years—until organizational problems, internal disagreements, ideological disputes, and industry-wide layoffs occasioned by a slumping economy drained group energies. The first two selections are reprinted from the league's *General Policy Statement and Labor Program* (Highland Park, MI: League of Revolutionary Black Workers, 1970), by permission. They detail the shortcomings of the white-run labor movement and outline the league's broad, "anti-imperialist" agenda—in both narrative and poetic form. The third document, an interview with league officials Ken Cockrel and Mike Hamlin conducted by Jim Jacobs and David Wellman, originally appeared in *Leviathan* (June 1970). The present text is taken from *"Our Thing Is DRUM!"* (Detroit: Black Star Printing, 1970), by permission. It provides a graphic account of the oppressive working conditions that motivated disgruntled black autoworkers to join the liberation struggle.

1970   General Program (Here's Where We're Coming From)

League of Revolutionary Black Workers

The League of Revolutionary Black Workers is dedicated to waging a relentless struggle against racism, capitalism, and imperialism. We are struggling for the liberation of black people in the confines of the United States as well as to play a major revolutionary role in the liberation of all oppressed people in the world.

In U.S. society, a small class owns the basic means of production. There aren't any black people in this class, nor are the masses of whites; however, they are not in the same position as blacks.

Our black community is virtually a black working class, because of our relationship to the basic means of production. Black workers comprise the backbone of the productive process in this country. Since slavery, we have been the major producers of goods and services. In addition, we've produced goods under the most inhumane conditions. Our black community is comprised of industrial workers, social service workers, our gallant youth, and many ad hoc community groups.

The racist subordination of black people and black workers creates a privileged status for white people and white workers. While the imperialist oppression and exploitation of the world creates a privileged status for the people and workers of the U.S., the white labor movement has failed to deal with the worsening conditions of black workers and the key role of black workers in the economy and the working class. The white labor movement has turned its back on black worker problems such as less job security, speed-up, less pay, bad health (silicosis, in particular), the worst kind of jobs, and in most cases, exclusion from skilled trades.

These two systems of privilege become the basis for the aristocracy of white labor which gives white labor a huge stake in the imperialist system and renders white labor unable and unfit to lead the working class in the U.S.

United States society is racist, capitalist, and imperialist by nature. It is aggressively expansive, exploitative, and oppressive. The expansion of U.S. imperialism is primarily by means of worldwide financial penetration, backed up by a worldwide military regime. This gives a monopoly control of the resources, wealth and labor of the capitalist world to U.S.

finance capital. They use the most barbarous methods of warfare and subversion to maintain its billions of dollars in profit.

U.S. imperialism supports every reactionary and fascist regime in the world by means of subversion, CIA assassinations, invasions, terror bombings, and criminal means of warfare. U.S. imperialism also resorts to nuclear blackmail, to intimidate the revolutionary peoples of the world. Imperialism faces its inevitable destruction as the national liberation struggles, currently focused in Southeast Asia, become worldwide. This involves the rest of Asia, including populous India, along with the emerging struggles in Latin America and the developing struggles in Africa. The workers and peoples of Europe are also drawn into the anti-imperialist struggle as the grip of U.S. imperialism loosens on Europe as the result of the struggles waged in the rest of the world.

The oppressive, imperialist nature of U.S. society is evidenced at home in the suppression of the black liberation struggle, workers' struggles, and anti-war struggles, in an increasingly militaristic fashion. One of the essential domestic props of U.S. imperialism is the white labor aristocracy which shares in the spoils of the plunder of the world and is based in the domestic subordination of black workers.

The white labor aristocracy collaborates with the U.S. imperialist government in its aggressive wars, its CIA subversion and supports its political line. It also colludes with monopoly corporations at home to allow speed-up and unsafe working conditions, inflation that outstrips any wage gains, leaves most workers unorganized, and supports the brutal subordination of black workers.

The League of Revolutionary Black Workers emerged specifically, out of the failure of the white labor movement to address itself to the racist work conditions and to the general inhumane conditions of black people.

Our strength comes from the historical and heroic struggles of our people, our inspiration comes from the revolutionary upsurges of the international struggles, and our convictions are guided by the principles of Marxism-Leninism.

The League of Revolutionary Black Workers is a political organization. We relate to the total black community. Our actual practice involves us with industrial and service workers, youth, and several ad hoc groups; these categories make up the League of Revolutionary Black Workers. Our duty is to plan the most feasible means to insure freedom and justice for the liberation of black people based on the concrete conditions we relate to. In addition, we have the task of training our people for leadership and other special capacities that make a viable organization. Most importantly, the direction of our organization is clear. We're not talking about dealing with a single issue as the only factor, nor are we talking about reforms in the system; but we are talking about the seizure of state power.

It is clear to us that the development of our struggle based on concrete realities, dictates the need for black peoples' liberation political party. We state, unequivocally, that this must be a black Marxist-Leninist party, designed to liberate black people, dedicated to leading the workers' struggles in this country, and resolved to wage a relentless struggle against imperialism.

The League's program for building a black Marxist-Leninist party is as follows:

1. Organizing of black workers on the broadest possible scale into the League and its component parts.
2. Politicizing and educating the masses of black people to the nature of racism, capitalism, and imperialism, to further outline the solution to these problems in League programs and documents.
3. Supporting the efforts of our people to develop a broad economic base within the community to aid the revolutionary struggle.
4. Developing a broad based self-defense organization in the community.
5. Carrying on unceasing struggles on behalf of black workers and the total community.
6. Forming principled alliances and coalitions, on the broadest possible base, with other oppressed minorities, organizations, movements, and forces, black or white, which struggle against the evils of racism, capitalism and imperialism.

Our short range objective is to secure state power with the control of the means of production in the hands of the workers under the leadership of the most advanced section of the working class, the black working class vanguard.

Our long range objective is to create a society free of race, sex, class, and national oppression, founded on the humanitarian principle of from each according to his ability, to each according to his needs.

1970 Our Thing Is DRUM

League of Revolutionary Black Workers

Deep in the gloom
of the firefilled pit
Where the Dodge rolls down the line,
We challenge the doom
of dying in shit
While strangled by a swine. . . .
. . . For hours and years
we've sweated tears
Trying to break our chain—
But we broke our backs
and died in packs
To find our manhood slain. . . .
But now we stand—
For DRUM's at hand
To lead our Freedom fight,
and from now til then
we'll unite like men—
For now we know our might—
and damn the plantation
and the whole Dodge nation
For DRUM has dried our tears. . . .
and now as we die
we've a different cry—
For now we hold our spears!
U.A.W. is scum—
OUR THING IS DRUM!!!!!

1970 *From* **Fight on to Victory**

Interview with Ken Cockrel and Mike Hamlin

LEVIATHAN: How was the League of Revolutionary Black Workers formed? What are the origins of the League?

MIKE: The League began with the formation of the Dodge Revolutionary Union Movement in May of 1968. What it represented was the coming together of various elements of the black community: those elements being the black workers, the black students and intellectuals, and the lumpen proletariat—the black street force. It happened at a time when many of us who have had histories of radical involvement in this city for some time had just begun to develop a newspaper as a means of getting ourselves together. The newspaper was called the *Inner City Voice.* But we always had an understanding that what was necessary was that we organize black workers. And though we had never had a successful entrée into the plants with the workers and we really didn't understand how to go about it, we attracted to us a group of nine workers from the plant just by virtue of us producing a newspaper and projecting certain ideas. We had certain radical ideas and a certain revolutionary line: that black workers would be the vanguard of the liberation struggle in this country. And we had a series of meetings with these workers to get to know them, for them to get to know us, and to begin to develop a common understanding of how to proceed. They came to us because of the objective conditions in the plant, conditions that they had tried to deal with in a number of ways, primarily through the formation of caucuses. And obviously these efforts had been unsuccessful. So, kind-of in desperation, they came to us as the last hope and the only alternative to the approaches that they understood that they could take. And we developed a relationship which led to the formation of DRUM. We decided to use the newsletter as a means of organizing the workers in that we could establish a means of communication among the workers throughout the plant. We wrote about incidents, events and conditions of racism, brutality, and other kinds of bad working conditions, which began to build a sense of resentment among the workers and began to develop a sense of unity among them. It was a unity based on this resentment against these kinds of conditions, especially the racist practices in the plants.

LEVIATHAN: Mike, you said that they came to you as a last resort. I take it that they were in UAW locals. How did the UAW deal or not deal with the problems that these black workers had which left them no alternative but to turn to a more revolutionary direction?

MIKE: Well, let's look at it this way. When I was younger I worked at Ford's in the stamping plant. I worked for six weeks and then the lay-off came. So I began to look for a job. You have to understand that there's a grapevine in the black community that tells you where people are being hired on a given day. And if I was circulating in the same set that I was at the time, I could probably tell you today where they're hiring people. It gets around all over the city. When you show up there, you see the long lines of the same people that you saw the day before at Ford, or the day before at Cadillac's or whatever. So there's these long lines and you go out there and stand and they hire a few people and then they send the rest of them away. Now, what happens is there may be two or three whites in that line. And once you get into the employment office, they may hire a large number of blacks and a few whites.

But then you go in and see what kind of jobs they're giving. The whites generally get the easy jobs: inspection or jobs on small stock. The blacks go in and get the heavy jobs, the hard jobs, and the dangerous jobs. The reason for that is kind of interesting. First of all, whites won't work on those kinds of jobs. That's a fact. In plants where blacks are in the majority, for example, the Ford engine plant in Dearborn, the line runs at a back-breaking pace. The same operation in another Ford engine plant, where there is a majority of white workers, the line runs, you know, at the agreed upon rate. In the Mahwah, New Jersey Assembly Plant, the line runs at 52 units an hour. And it doesn't vary because the work force is 80 per cent white. If they speed it up, the white workers are going to walk out. But they know that we are so up-tight for jobs, and there's such a large supply of reserve labor, black labor, cheap labor available for them, that they can speed it up on us as much as they want to. And if we quit, they can always bring somebody in at the new rate. So in the Mahwah plant, they run 52 units an hour. In the Ford plant here, the agreed upon rate is something like 64. But in actuality, the line goes up to 76 in certain instances, depending on whether or not the foreman is meeting his quota, or whether or not he thinks he can slip one over on the workers.

LEVIATHAN: What's the union agreement about productivity?

MIKE: At the Ford Dearborn I think it's 64. But it doesn't mean anything because, first of all, when you're working there, you're working so hard, the line's going so fast that you're not counting. And secondly the union is not counting. The union has no power and no real concern about controlling that line. If the foreman can get away with it without the workers knowing that, then that's cool. What happens is, the workers can tell when they get really ridiculous because you're working so fast. And, like, some lines, you know, go on several floors. And sometimes a guy will be trying to run downstairs. He gets so far behind he'll be trying to run downstairs trying to catch up with the cars that he's supposed to be working on. So, that's why those departments are overwhelmingly black in almost every instance. The same applies for the foundry where work is dirty and dangerous, and a lot of workers get lung diseases. Little's done about it.

We also found out in certain instances, like last summer during the time of economic boom, that the guys were being rotated from plant to plant. They would hire a lot of people, keep them for 89 days since you're on probation 90 days, and the 89th day, you're discharged and you had to go to another plant. So this inflated the employment figures. In actuality, what they're doing was rotating guys from plant to plant. They fire them on various charges, trumped-up charges. At Ford Rouge they would fire six hundred workers per week. You know, six hundred workers per week. I mean that's every week. And at the Dodge Main plant they were firing 300 per week. And at Eldon they were firing 300 a week. And none of these people ever got back. They didn't even bother to fight. First of all, those who have 89 days don't have any recourse: they're not in the union even though they paid the initiation fees and paid dues for those three months. But they don't have full union rights. And then the other people are people who are "undesirable" people. At that time they were firing them for Afro hairdos, you know, or for any kind of sign of militancy or any kind of resistance to the harassment that was going on.

Before we came along they were constantly intimidating the workers, constantly threatening them with being fired, giving them time off and that kind of thing. They always had them in a state of intimidation, in a state of fear. And in certain instances, we have reversed that. It's now the foremen and the labor relations people who are intimidated, who are afraid to do the kind of things that they did before. And I think that's going to be the pattern throughout these plants as we continue to organize.

But, you know, the actual individual foremen were bold on the line: calling them names and walking up and kicking them. Up until that time there were not too many instances, excepting at the Ford Foundry, of people actually hurting or jumping on the foremen and killing 'em or anything like that. Ford has always been so bad that the foundry has a history of supervisors and union stewards getting killed and a few white workers too. They'd come up and tell some guy: "you're not catching them fast enough, speed up the line," you know and trying to get at them that way. I mean if they're going to speed it up, at least they don't have to add insult to injury. Come up and start talking about kicking you in the behind or something if you don't keep up. So that has been changed in Dodge. It still exists at Ford. . . .

These kinds of things resulted in actions like a number of wildcat strikes, which resulted in a number of people being fired. One of the wildcat strikes which involved black and white workers ended up with all of the workers going back except one of the founders of DRUM. But he continued working on the executive committee of the League.

Besides the strikes, an organization was formed called the "Concerned Unionists" which was a caucus but which was doomed to failure because the union apparatus was unresponsive. There was nothing being done about any of these abuses being heaped on the workers. So after they had gone all these routes, they didn't have any other option but to come seek an alliance with us and an involvement with us. One of the mistakes that we did not make was to set ourselves apart from the workers. What we did in fact was to involve ourselves and integrate ourselves with the workers.

KEN: See people don't understand that workers have been resisting for years man. Dig the whole characterization that black people give jobs man: It's a "yoke," it's a "hang," it's a "slave," you got to meet that motherfucking "mule" on Monday morning. That's what bloods talk about on the weekend, man. The whole week too! And the minute you get off that motherfucker on Friday, you living in dread and anticipation of that motherfucking Monday, man.

22   Liberating the "Subjugated Territory"

Believing that black Americans constituted a nation—a "community of suffering" whose differences were overshadowed by a wealth of shared experiences and a common relationship to the politically powerful white race—territorial nationalists of the Black Power era sought to realize the long-standing dream of establishing a national homeland. Among the most ambitious plans to acquire sovereign territory within the existing boundaries of the United States was that formulated by brothers Milton and Richard Henry (Gaidi and Imari Obadele), leaders of the Detroit-based Republic of New Africa (RNA). Their position on separatism was clear and unambiguous. The states of South Carolina, Georgia, Alabama, Mississippi, and Louisiana constituted "the subjugated territory" of the black republic. A primary objective of Afro-Americans should be to liberate this land upon which black people long had lived and, with their blood and sweat, had helped develop. Once sovereignty was achieved, the RNA's "government-in-exile" would work to "consolidate the Revolution" by constructing new institutions guaranteed to improve the lives of residents. *Ujamaa,* the Tanzanian model of cooperative economics and community self-sufficiency, would serve as a guide for the structuring of the republic's economy. U.S. government reparations payments of land and $400 billion in start-up funds would sustain the new nation during its infancy. If federal officials rebuffed their demands, the RNA was prepared to utilize the power of the black ballot or, alternatively, to fight a "people's war" in support of the black homeland ideal.

The following selection is part of the "Anti-Depression Program" that RNA officials presented to members of Congress in 1972. It is reprinted from Imari Abubakari Obadele I, *Foundations of the Black Nation* (Detroit: House of Songhay, 1975), by permission. Here, the RNA makes a case for black freedom and sovereignty as the solution to both racial unrest and "black dependence," outlines the "New African" lifestyle and worldview, and places the organization's separatist goals in the context of white America's legendary (and often romanticized) frontier experience of "building a new world on virgin land."

1972 *From* The Anti-Depression Program of the Republic of New Africa

The Solution to the Problem

. . . If black life—now a burden on the American nation—is to change qualitatively for the better, then the black man, the African in America, must have power. His problem is powerlessness. Its solution is power. The time for palliatives is past. The time has come for fundamental and far-reaching change. It has come because black men, represented in this by the Republic of New Africa, will no longer abide things as they are and, to change things for the better, will price our ambition so high and sell our very lives so dearly and with so much craft that America, should America fail to abet the change, will cease to exist for want of ability to pay the price. But this is no threat. It seems to us that the truth is We all have been waiting for the word, that clear and abrupt breaking of the vicious cycle, that desertion of the half-truths and patchwork programs, that bold new turning toward the light that will bring the people of this land up out of that abyss into which—because of racism and black dependence—black and white, now bound together, are fitfully sinking. This program is that word. It is that turning toward the light. It is this land's chance for racial peace and new progress for all. But the Congress must seize the courage to make three essential commitments. They are the following:

Removal of the Hands

If, as Historian Bennett suggests, the American tragedy began after 1660 when American planters decided to separate white servant from black and fasten slavery irrevocably to race and, to accomplish this, decided upon "the laying of hands on the mind of a whole people," then it must end now, in 1972, with a taking off of the hands. And this may be, for whites, the most difficult part. Whites, so used to us as "our Negroes," must remove their hands from our culture, our economics, our schools, government, persons. We say that the idea, the idea itself, that the black nation is a colony and that American cooperation must be extended only in some such way as to bring an economic return to Americans must end. The essence of reparations is that reparations are given as a debt due, *without* strings. Would America today truly prefer an obsequious and economically colonized Japan or an obsequious and economically colonized Europe? What General George Marshall said for Europe—and what became U.S. policy—must now be said for the African nation in America: "It would be neither fitting nor efficacious for this government to undertake to draw up unilaterally a program to place Europe on its feet economically. This is the business of the Europeans. The initiative, I think, must come from Europe. The role of this country should consist of friendly aid. . . ."

Acknowledgement of Land and Sovereignty for the New African Nation

Created here out of necessity, the New African nation *will* be free and sovereign; our challenge—together—is to determine how that freedom and that sovereignty may be secured amicably and rationally. (Amicability is a matter of will and men; We *can* achieve it.) Today We estimate that ten million black people in America wish to be a part of an independent New Africa, more than half of whom do not now live in the five states. No one must be coerced or made to come to New Africa, nor will the ten million who choose New Africa constitute all of the black poor, all of the oppressed or hope-lost—though many will be; many others will be the gifted, the well stationed, the ordinary man and woman with a desire for a life better. But by creating a marked environmental change for all ten million, and a physical *relocation for at least five million of these ten,* We shall bring about a new dimension in breathing and growing space for those who remain where they are; We shall immensely relieve pressure on the crowded northern and western ghettoes and spacially and materially restructure and abolish the growing black slums of the South. What is important is that America not choose the path of meanness, that America recognize the right (and beauty) of those of us who want independence and sovereignty and do whatever is necessary, with grace, not to interfere—indeed to help—with the realization of that sovereignty. And sovereignty is inseparable from independent land.

Toleration of New Africa's New Forms

The white American must reject the notion that everything that is different is hostile or inimical. It is not. The New African life-style will certainly be different from the American, but the emphasis of the design is to benefit the New African, not to harm anyone else. Our economics will be different. Certainly We cannot look toward laissez-faire capitalism in the Twentieth Century doing for New African development what it did for American development in the Nineteenth Century. The Nineteenth Century and most of its conditions are (fortunately) gone. In 1968 workshops of the National Black Economic Development Conference in Detroit agreed that black economic activity—even without benefit of a sovereign nation—should be for need, not profit. The means of production in New Africa will be in the trust of the state to best accomplish this end, and the further ends of rapidly ending want and creating surpluses. The system is New African and is called Ujamaa. Inevitably there are important social as well as economic relations that Ujamaa implies. Kenneth Clark (op. cit.) suggests the rationale: "The Roots of the multiple pathology in the dark ghetto are not easy to isolate. They do not lie primarily in unemployment. In fact, if all of its residents were employed it would not materially alter the pathology of the community. More relevant is the status of the jobs held. Nor do the primary roots lie in the frustrations of bad housing. There is correlation between social pathology and housing, apparently confirming the earlier hypothesis that while better housing heightens morale, it does not affect the more fundamental variable of economic status, broken homes, and lowered aspirations, that more important than having *a* job, is the *kind* of job it is. And more important than housing—once human beings are removed from substandard housing—is fundamental social change." The Ujamaa social relationships, to bring that necessary "fundamental social change," arise largely from these key excerpts from the New African Declaration of Independence and Creed:

From the Declaration. "Ours is a revolution against oppression—our own oppression and that of all people in the world. And it is a revolution for a better life, a better station for mankind, a surer harmony with the forces of life in the universe. We therefore see these as the aims of our revolution:

—*to assure all people in the New Society maximum opportunity and equal access to that maximum;*

—*to promote industriousness, responsibility, scholarship, and service;*

—*to protect and promote the personal dignity and integrity of the individual and his natural rights;*

—*to encourage and reward the individual for hard work and initiative and insight and devotion to the Revolution;*

From the New African Creed. The growth of new social relationships, rooted in the Declaration, is nourished by a set of personal objectives set for the New African in *The Creed.* Key among these objectives are these:

12. *I will love my brothers and sisters as myself.*

13. *I will steal nothing from a brother or sister, cheat no brother or sister, misuse no brother or sister, inform on no brother or sister, and spread no gossip.*

14. *I will keep myself clean in body, dress, and speech, knowing that I am a light on a hill, a true representative of what we are building.*

15. *I will be patient and uplifting with the deaf, dumb, and blind, and I will seek by word and deed to heal the black family, to bring into the Movement and into the Community mothers and fathers, brothers and sisters left by the wayside.*

Racial Peace

None of this implies limitless or unreasoning animosity toward America. In turn, it need not—and should not—be met by such. Actually there are too many bonds of language, culture, history, and (yes!) race between white and black in America that argue for friendship and unity for reasonable men to accept permanent hostility and dislocation. But separation is necessary first. An end to the "laying on of the hands" must come first. It may seem difficult, but something like it happened before: when Americans a quarter-century ago by mutual agreement ended the fifty-year-old colonization of the Philippines.

The Rise of Self-Esteem, the Release of Creativity

For the greater part of American history white Americans had a frontier, which, for them, continually offered the possibility of almost limitless opportunity. Black people in America have never had this. In slavery-days to flee to the Indians afforded only temporary sanctuary, for the white man never left the Indian at peace, and whenever it was learned a slave had refuged there, the result was almost always the raid-of-return. To flee North in time of slavery was much as it is today: a journey to a land of disappointment. We have never had a frontier. The independent sovereign nation will be that frontier, a place where a man can go and be respected and rise as high as hard work, ambition, and ability can carry him; a place, moreover, where a family can have a really fine life. We can expect that just as the frontier notion, the *idea* of building a new world on virgin land, released a long-lived gusher of creativity for the white American, so, too, the sovereign black nation will release lush and long-lived creativity for black people—both for those in the nation, building, and for those who remain where they are—like the Americans who never left the East—but identify.

23 "First of All and Finally Africans"

Black Power–era exponents of Pan–Africanism posited the existence of a transoceanic continuum of thought and experience that bound black Americans to their forebears even as it distanced them from stereotypical images of Africans as primitives. Africa, they said, not the United States, was their true home. To end white deception and promote racial unity, African Americans had to "return" to the land of their ancestors. For those who understood this concept to have connotations beyond the philosophical or cultural, Pan–Africanism might mean an actual physical journey. Hoping to establish direct lines of communication with contemporary African leaders and to assist in their struggles against neocolonialism, supporters of repatriation talked often of establishing a land base on the continent. Here, with a territorial foothold far more secure than they would have in any black nation-state located in North America, black expatriates would be able to develop their maximum human potential. In return, they would employ their technical expertise in the cause of national development. It was hoped that when African states began to increase in strength, dark-skinned peoples worldwide would gain new status and pride. Such a triumph might even cause skeptical "stay-at-home" types to conclude that Pan-Africanism was the highest political expression of the separatist ethic.

In the following essay, onetime SNCC and Black Panther Party leader Stokely Carmichael describes the various artificial "divisions" imposed on African peoples by whites. Concluding that "the only position for black men is Pan-Africanism," he advocates an activist program that proposes to alleviate this problem by (1) working to acquire a land base on the continent, and (2) teaching black people everywhere that they are "first of all and finally Africans." Acting on these beliefs, Carmichael (now Kwame Ture) emigrated to Guinea early in 1969, where he was made the special guest of that nation's socialist leader, Sekou Toure. Encouraged by his discussions with both Toure and exiled Ghanaian president Kwame Nkrumah, he organized the All-African People's Revolutionary Party (AAPRP) in support of Pan-African unity and black revolutionary struggle. The essay is reprinted from *Black Scholar* (November 1969), by permission.

1969 Pan-Africanism—Land and Power

Stokely Carmichael

Whether we want it or not, there are divisions among black Africans living in the United States, the Caribbean and on the African continent, divisions which have been imposed on us by Europeans. There are geographical divisions, countries such as Senegal and Mauritania, Mozambique and Guinea, created by Europeans as they struggled for the wealth of Africa. Then there are political divisions and economic divisions, again imposed on us by Europeans.

Now they are planning to impose on us grave cultural divisions and, most of all, to divide us by naming us different things. If you are in San Francisco, for example, and you see a Japanese or a Chinese walking down the street, you do not say that there goes an American Japanese or a Japanese-American. You say simply that there goes a Japanese—period. Yet, probably, that Japanese cannot speak Japanese at all: he may be third or fourth generation in America. But no one calls him a Japanese American. The first thing you call him is a Japanese; because a person is defined, really, at first by his physical presence, or in terms of his ancestral stock. Whether they are Chinese, Japanese or African. The same is true of the Indians. Even in America, when you see a red Indian, you do not say he is an American; you say he is an Indian. The same is true for East Indians; the same for Philippines. Wherever you see them, in any part of the world, you call them Chinese or what not.

The same is not true for Africans.

Let's ask ourselves why.

If you see an African in Europe, you do not say that he is an African. If you see him in America you do not call him an African. He may be Negro; he may be West Indian; he may be everything else but African. That is because Europe took its time to divide us carefully, quite carefully. And they gave us different names so that we would never, always never, refer to ourselves by the same name; which helped to insure that there would always be differences. If you say you are West Indian, it is fairly obvious that you are something different to be set apart from an African. An American Negro and an African also obviously are not the same thing.

One of the most important things we must now begin to do, is to call ourselves "African." No matter where we may be from, we are first of all and finally Africans. Africans, Africans, Africans. The same also happens to be true of North Africa. When they say "Algerians" or "Egyptians," they are talking about Africans because Africa happens to be one solid continent. Among Africans there will and must be no divisions. They are just Africans — period.

You must also understand that there are two types of oppression, basically. One is exploitation. Another is colonization. With exploitation one is economically raped; for example, in the 1930's the labor movement was a response to economic exploitation. Rich white people, in that instance, were exploiting poor white people. But there is another type of oppression — colonization. Colonization is not just the economic raping of someone, not merely taking a lot of money away. Colonization deals with destroying the person's culture, his language, his history, his identification, his total humanity. When one is colonized one is totally dehumanized. So that when the victims of colonization fight they are fighting for a process of humanization.

This is entirely different from the fight of people who are only exploited. The people who are exploited fight just for economic security. The colonized fights beyond economic security, far beyond. And so, it seems to me that as we begin the search for allies and coalitions we can only form alliances and coalitions based on whether those people are fighting for the same thing, fighting the same fight that we who have been colonized are fighting. In other words, people who are fighting for their humanity. This means, for example, that all non-white peoples who have been colonized can join hands, understanding of course that our fights remain entirely different.

The people who have been colonized by white folk, let us say, in Asia, are fighting the same fight but a different fight because of culture, humanity. Their way of life is and will be entirely different from ours. But they are fighting nonetheless and fighting for a humanity of their own, albeit the same thing in a sense that we are fighting for, to affirm our humanity. We are fighting to affirm our humanity. With those non-white people we can begin to move so long as they understand precisely what the fight is all about and that we may differ in some respects.

In America, folk seem to think that the revolution there — if there is such a thing, or even if there will be such a thing — will all be over in five years, when actually we are talking about a generation of struggle. That is why they always have deep questions in their minds to trouble them.

They fail to understand that the struggle we are talking about inside America is only symptomatic of a world-wide struggle against Europe and its satellites. America, in fact, is nothing but Europe. The white people in America are not Americans but in fact Europeans. When we call them Americans we allow them to escape; we define them incorrectly. We should call them Europeans and understand that they never belonged in America, that they took that continent from somebody else. When you call them Americans you forget that they were Europeans because you give them in fact the theory of native origin, that they came out of America. Where did Americans come from? They come from America—that is, somebody you call American. But if you say that they are Europeans (which is what they are), then the question arises as to where they came from—Europe. What are Europeans doing in what is now called America?

We must understand that because it shows how deep our struggle really, really, really is. These are things we do not even think about, because, if you see what I have been saying up to now, you also will see that, in the final analysis, the struggle is going to be waged with Europeans against non-Europeans. And that means that America is European. That means that our struggle is not five or ten years but is, in fact, a generation. Once we understand that our struggle is at least a generation, then we do not even have to worry about so many little things. We will know, then, that we are not going to see any really concrete or substantive victories in our fight for at least five or ten years. I mean to say anything really concrete enough for us to look at and say that that is what we have been able to do.

At this point, it becomes important that you have people of African descent—scattered over the Western hemisphere by Europeans, scattered across the West Indies and used so long as slaves—bound together in a unified struggle for their liberation. This is not impossible inasmuch as we have people today all over the world moving forward in the quest for liberation against their oppressors.

Because I understand so clearly the foregoing factors, the ancestral roots of the problem, I have concluded that the solution has to be Pan-Africanism. Everybody—Du Bois, Padmore or whoever—always comes back at last to Pan-Africanism. Pan-Africanism is not just some nonsensical black nationalism. Even white philosophers understand this fact. For example, Plato in *The Republic* talks about the theory of Antaeus. The parable of Antaeus, says Plato, shows that the philosopher king has come up out of the earth, that the people grew out of the earth. They were asking "Where are we from?" Plato says that you must always answer that question: "Where are we from?" In his book he says that the people come out of the earth, have grown up there, so that they always fight for that earth; and for the ideas that come out of that earth. And they always will. So black people (us) come out of that earth, and we always will; and so black people (us) must stop running around in circles. We have to have our theory of Antaeus—where we are from. If black people in the States say "where are we from?" they must wind up at Africa. One must know one's beginning, who one is, before one knows where one is going.

People who regard Pan-Africanism negatively, who think that it is a racist theory, ought to read George Padmore's book, *Communism or Pan Africanism*. Padmore is clear on this. Writing around the 1930's, and one of the advisers to Dr. Nkrumah, Padmore was crystal clear on the point that we must talk about Pan-Africanism. I believe that people who talk about "Marxist-Leninism" so hard, in such a hard line, are people who are groping for an answer. They seize on "Marxist-Leninism" as if it were some sort of a religion. Marx becomes, in essence, Jesus Christ. Now anything you cannot answer you take over and bow to Marx. That, in my view, is absolutely absurd. At least for me.

I cannot claim to understand all of Marxist-Leninism. I have read very little of them and understand little of what I have read. So, for me to jump up and say that I am a Marxist-Leninist is for me to be intellectually dishonest and, in fact as well, a damn liar. And yet, though I do not fully understand all that you folk are talking about, I do have certain universal concepts which happen to agree with the things that Marx was talking about. But, just because I have these concepts does not mean that Marx was the man who taught them to me. I knew them before I read Marx. So, even if I agree with them, why now should I call myself a Marxist? Tunisian Ibn-Khaldun spoke of Marx's concept of surplus value, for example, as early as the fifteenth century. Why should I give Marx the credit for plagiarizing Khaldun? Marx only wrote down universal truths about oppression. He did not invent all of them.

Everybody can arrive at these truths themselves. I don't need necessarily to read Marx, though Marx wrote it down more fully. I give Marx the credit for writing it down, of course, for being a good writer. But Marx wrote down the universal truths of those who came way back before Marx. Right here in Algeria there was Ibn Khaldun. For me, to always look to Marx is once again to give the credit for everything good to Europe. Once again I continue to stress my own inferiority as an African. Ready to unify my country, I continue to look to a European, Marx, to unify me. I say "Marx, Marx, Marx," and once again I am looking to Europe. People with this approach do not believe that they themselves can originate something worthy, which becomes very damaging.

People in that frame of mind are going in circles and they of course are going to be aided by our oppressors. They are going to be aided whenever they travel in circles. When a man is lost and you know that he is going in circles trying to get to you, you do not tell him "Look, Man, you are going in circles." Even if you did you would be unable to show him the proper path. If you said "Look, man, you are going in circles," he would get mad at you and keep on moving. He would lay back and then he would say, "O.K. man, let's go." Don't get in a man's way when he's going in circles.

And yet, I view the struggle in the States as part and parcel of the entire world struggle, particularly the black world struggle. That is to say, I cannot see the struggle in the States as any different from the struggle anywhere else where men are fighting against a common oppressor. Our fight is clearly a fight against both capitalism and racism. One does not get rid of capitalism without fighting against racism.

I cannot agree with the ideology that says that capitalism and racism are two different entities unto themselves. I would have you struggle against both. To get rid of capitalism—I repeat—is not necessarily to get rid of racism. As a matter of fact, I think that black people ought to know this better than anyone else. I think that, in terms of reality and history and my own ideology, all of the movement that we have been building up in terms of black nationalism, from the sit-ins for coffee to "black power," runs straight to Pan-Africanism. We always come back to that.

It is clear now that the only position for black men is Pan-Africanism. We need a land base. We need a base. A land base. In the final analysis, all revolutions are based on land. The best place, it seems to me, and the quickest place that we can obtain land is Africa. I am not denying that we might seek land in the United States. That is a possibility, but I do not see it clearly in my mind at this time. We need land and we need land immediately, and we must go to the quickest place for it.

We need a base that can be used for black liberation, a land that we can say belongs to us. We do not need to talk too much about it. That will harm the struggle. When one needs a base one needs also to prepare for armed struggle. To seize any of the countries in Africa today that are dominated by white people who have physically oppressed us is to confront an armed struggle, a prolonged struggle.

But once we have seized a base we will be on our way. We will then have to demonstrate our willingness to fight for our people wherever they are oppressed. I believe that people basically defend their own kind, as America did during the Spanish Civil War. In the Middle East they did it even in 1967 with Israel. People who didn't have any rights in that country were flying in from all over the world to fight. There's nothing wrong with our doing the selfsame thing. It can be done and, most important, we are trying to secure a political ideology as we seek a state. We are beginning to understand our movements and to see how we can move politically, so that we begin to talk clearly and critically now about Pan-Africanism. It is a discussion that must begin.

There are many people who live in Europe and America who support lands which do not belong to them. Concretely. They wage so large a propaganda campaign that one cannot say anything about their country without being automatically labeled "anti . . ." to the point where one is even afraid to move for fear of falling into that label. If we obtain a bigger base than they have we can do a better job than they do because we have more rights to be in Africa than they have to be where they are.

Malcolm X said that one fights for revolution but that in the final analysis revolution is based on land. He was absolutely correct. You have to have land in order to produce, in order to feed, shelter and clothe your people. People fight the revolution not solely for ideas; they fight also for a better way of life, and they incorporate new ideas introduced to them that promise a better way of life. People do not just fight for ideas, unless they are sure that they can see a better way of life coming out of those ideas.

Thus, unless one can feed and clothe and shelter people who want to fight for these better ideas, there is nothing for them to fight for. In order to have a revolution one must have a clear and viable alternative for the masses, one they can understand and follow, one that can move them to struggle. I do not think that in the States there can be a clear and viable alternative for black people. I am almost convinced that there cannot be. That is not to say that the struggle cannot and will not continue.

But we cannot begin to understand clear and viable alternatives until we first obtain a land base. We have to have a land base. I think that the best place for that is Africa and in Africa the best place is Ghana. Black people in the United States meanwhile must begin to understand that there needs now to be a clear sharpening of our ideologies. Our ideology must be Pan-Africanism, nothing else. I am almost convinced of that. Once we get a land base we can begin to experiment with it and develop it and go about the concrete tasks of nation building.

One of the problems of black people is that we are afraid, always, to put up leaders. I don't know why. We have some fear of putting up leaders and following a leader. What we always look for instead is merely someone who has an idea. We all will agree with the idea but fail nonetheless to give concrete support to that man. We keep saying that the man is not important, that the idea alone is important, but that is not necessarily true. You have to have someone who is capable of implementing the idea. Our enemies have recognized that and, whenever they find someone able to implement a viable idea, they move to destroy him. All the time. They kill him physically; or isolate him politically or ruin his name among us.

We allow that to happen and only after he has been destroyed does he become a hero for us. By that time it is too late. Now everybody is wearing Malcolm X T-shirts and Malcolm X, blah, blah, blah. But Malcolm today would be more important to us alive than dead, although in death he has become more famous. We need him now and we need to know what he would do in the present case, because at least he had some ideas about where he was going, before the rest of us did. He was ahead of us. We have caught up with him today in a sense but he would still be ahead of us, hopefully growing at the same rate that we are growing. But we never protect our leadership while our leaders are alive. We are afraid to do that.

We never understand history because history is always moved forward by a single person. China would not be China were it not for Mao Tse-tung. That is not to say that somebody else would not have led China, but it would not be what China is today without Mao. Vietnam would not be Vietnam without Ho Chi-minh. France would not be France without De Gaulle. England would not be England without Winston Churchill. We have to understand that. Now I have traveled all around the world. I have looked and I have seen. I have been waiting for and seeking for a black man outside of our generation who knows what is going on. I have found one—Dr. Nkrumah. He knows precisely what the struggle is. We should bring Dr. Kwame Nkrumah back to Ghana. I would not deny that he made some mistakes. But he was the first person to talk about Pan-Africanism as a concrete term. And he demonstrated his willingness to fight. He sent his troops to the Congo and mobilized his troops to move to Zambia when problems developed there. He trained many guerillas. He was the first to give Lumumba assistance. He gave his country as an open base for every African freedom fighter or liberation movement. He trained his youth in the concept of Pan-Africanism. It was he who started the whole drive for African nationalism. Dr. Nkrumah was one of the first people to wake me up. It was he who began to wake up everyone. He is the person who can bring our fight together and give us some direction to fight. We need such a person and Dr. Nkrumah happens to be that person as far as I am concerned.

But the fact that we start in Ghana does not mean that we stop in Ghana. We must fight for the unification of Africa. That's what Pan-Africanism is all about. The unification of the mother continent at this time must take priority. The unification of the African continent is entirely different from African unity. They are two different things. They are two different terms and they are two different things. African unity means you have different states who come together and talk, talk, talk, talk. Unification of Africa means you have one state—Africa. Everybody speaks the same language, one government, one army.

So that you start in Ghana for the unification of Africa and you recognize, if you are intelligent, that South Africa is not going to be removed by talk. It is not going to be removed by talk. It is not going to be removed by Britain, by the UN, or by anybody. Nor is it going to be removed by a handful of guerillas. It is only going to be removed by the entire black world standing up against it, because when in fact the final confrontation over South Africa for example, takes place, the black man will see that he is not just fighting whites in South Africa. He is fighting all of Europe, because all of Europe is going to actively defend South Africa.

We must begin to move. The whole black world must begin to move, though we will not even be able to see anything concrete for at least five to ten years. Then you begin to understand precisely our direction. We are coming closer; we are more sharply defined now. We have always been moving. Let's go back to the 1960's; we start a move for integration—a cup of coffee. Even before we got the cup of coffee, we recognized where else we were going. We were moving for the vote. By the time they were getting ready to give us the vote, we recognized that that was not it either. So now we recognize that it is Pan-Africanism.

It becomes more and more sharply defined now. It has taken since the 1960's, almost ten years, to understand precisely where we are going. Ten years to take us to Pan-Africanism, and it will probably take us another ten to sharply define what that is all about. We mistakenly believe that we can solve the problems of the United States in five years. Then, when the five years have come and gone and the problem remains unsolved, our people grow tired and say: "Well, you've been jiving me. You said five years." We should prepare ourselves for twenty-five years. We should always say twenty-five, at least twenty-five. One generation will have to fight, because there are people who are always attuned to fighting if you have indoctrinated one generation thoroughly, prepared them to fight. Then all subsequent generations are prepared to fight. Vietnam is clearly a case of that readiness.

I believe that as you study you struggle and struggle. It's like a math problem. If you are given a math problem, you may sit up all night working with it before, finally, things click and the problem is solved within five minutes. But that does not mean that you could come here and solve it in five minutes whenever you please. Before you solve it in five minutes, you have to sat down and go through that whole process of trying everything you know. If you have tried and you have eliminated all the possibilities, you now come to the one correct one. The same is true for us; that's what we have been doing in our struggle.

Pan-Africanism wants to save as many black people as possible. We will lose some. Some will even die in the struggle. We know that, but there's no need for us to emphasize those deaths. We want to emphasize what is alive. Revolution is not about dying; it is about living. People do not understand that. You kill to live; you die to live. It is not just about dying. We no longer have to prove that we are bad by dying. We want to live. Fratricide, for instance, is something that we must not in any way encourage. It is okay to back down from a fight with one's people. The impression of Pan-Africanism especially is that one must be aggressive and intolerant against the enemy; but, with one's people one must always be humble. If one says one is really serving the people, one must be humble. You are always humble to him whom you serve.

We must always be political. I think that culture, for example, is always very political. It always has been and always will be. We must understand that this conference is really a political conference, especially for our people. It means that at this point Africa is ready to launch its real liberation. In order to launch its liberation, it must have a culture because a culture represents the values, the values for which one fights. If one is fighting for a revolution, one is talking about more than just changing governments and power, and that is changing the value system. What carries that value system is one's culture. What we have here is the beginning of people who are trying to grope for a real fight with the culture.

Culture is a cohesive force. It is what keeps people together. Culture is very important in the fight because a lot of people have fought against their oppressors yet maintained the culture of their oppressors and culturally they are the same as their oppressors. They haven't fought for anything actually. All they have done is change powers, but that is not a revolution. You have to understand that changing powers is not a revolution.

Black people in America, Africans who live in America, especially must understand that and begin to alienate our people completely from the culture and values of Western society. That is going to be particularly difficult because all of us live within those values and it is going to be hard for us to root them out. I mean that it is like people who say that they want to be black. But being black is an awfully hard job in the United States.

It is very, very difficult, and we have to constantly try to understand the rejection of Western values and the picking up of new values. It is very, very difficult. But our first task is all the more to alienate our people at every chance we get from the Western culture and values, because once they are alienated there will be no influence over them. That is what we are seeking. We are seeking to stop all influence of Western culture on our people—completely. We must stop it; so we move to alienate. That is number one. Then number two: we move to give a concrete ideology that the people in the United States will adopt. They have a lot of technical skills and a lot of information which they could begin to put to the aid of the unification of Africa—spiritually, morally and politically.

At the same time, there will be struggles inside the United States, always moving on different levels as black people keep trying to get a better way of life. These struggles will continue. I cannot say that I know exactly which way to go, but I think that some trends are very important. For example, the trends in black studies are very, very important and they must continue because what is at stake is not the subjects but the attitude, the attitude of black people having the right to have the education that will benefit black people.

Those are the skirmishes. They are the beginnings because the rulers are not going to let us have a truly black studies or a truly black university. In the final analysis one can not have a black university in any other society than a black society because the job of the university is to propagate the values and institutions of that society. In the United States, a black university, a truly black university, is going to be totally anti-American, not just possibly anti-American, but anti-American to the point where it urges people to destroy, dismantle, disrupt, tear down, level completely in America. So you cannot have that, but that is precisely the job of the black educator, to train his people how to dismantle America, how to destroy it.

What those black study groups should now do is not just talk about Africans living in Africa, but Africans living all over the world, so that the subjects will become concrete subjects related to Africans, in Africa, Africans in the Caribbean, Africans in the United States, Africans in Canada. We have to understand also that Egypt is in Africa; Algeria is in Africa. They are African and even the Arabs are going to find that the African world must come first because that is where they are continentally. They are African. That's the roots, and that's where we all have to come from.

24 Black Art and Black Nationalism

Cultural nationalists held that their unique literary, artistic, and musical creations reflected a "special consciousness." Neither European nor African, the black aesthetic was said to be Afro-Americans' most important natural resource—the essence of their collective psyche. In this conceptualization, black culture *was* Black Power. Organically connected to the lives and traditions of black people, its vitality and grandeur challenged white cultural particularism and invalidated claims of Euro-American superiority. Its depth and scope provided a blueprint for the development of an authentically black value system. Diverse in format and manner of presentation, black cultural expression promoted racial unity, encouraged self-actualization, and facilitated the transmission of revolutionary messages to all manner of Afro-Americans. To the confirmed cultural nationalist, picking up a gun in support of black liberation without reaffirming the beauty of black culture seemed the height of irrationality. It was believed that the subordination of culture to economics or politics would eviscerate the revolution by denying its supporters access to the movement's lifeblood, its creative soul.

In the following article, Jeff Donaldson, a founding member of Chicago's AFRI-COBRA (African Commune of Bad Relevant Artists) arts collective has harsh words for the creators and disseminators of mainstream cultural expression—including those responsible for the content of late 1960s television programs and college textbooks. Constrained by a narrow, outmoded white aesthetic sensibility, most, he said, had yet to explore the "beauty and dignity of black life." Evidencing his agreement with the basic AFRI-COBRA/cultural nationalist tenet that held that the function of art is to liberate its audience and define and reveal a national black consciousness, Donaldson claims that any black-created work of art that fails to serve the cause of Black Power is "a waste of valuable time and creative energy."

This belief is reflected in Murry N. DePillars's dramatic 1968 pen and ink work entitled "Aunt Jemima." Here, a longtime household icon breaks the bonds of racial and gender-based stereotypes to join the revolution. Baring her breasts and wielding a lethal-looking spatula as a weapon, Jemima makes it clear that she no longer will submit to domestication or be constrained by convention.

"The Role We Want for Black Art" is reprinted from *College Board Review* (Spring 1969), by permission. "Aunt Jemima" is reproduced by permission of the artist.

1969 *From* The Role We Want for Black Art

Jeff Donaldson

Two psychiatrists who have spent the better part of their professional lives treating black men mentally crushed by the weight of America have written a book based on their work called *Black Rage*. I'm sure you've read it, but if you haven't, if there's one person here who hasn't, I suggest you do. In *Black Rage,* brothers William H. Grier and Price M. Cobbs suggest that black men defensively equipped with paranoic personalities survive the experience of America much better than those who are not so fortunately afflicted. And if this is true, if black paranoia is a requisite for black sanity, I have no anxiety regarding my own mental health. For I feel that there are forces all around me that constantly deny my humanity and even question the very fact of my existence.

These dehumanizing forces are present in every visible manifestation of the "American culture," from popular media to scholarly textbooks. If you examine a typical newspaper, you will find that black people are only newsworthy when they are restricted, convicted, or evicted. One rarely sees a black human-interest story, and I dare say that there are today more occurrences of genuine human interest in any black community on any given day than in most white communities in a whole week. For the black community is today enjoying a rejuvenation of the spirit and a sense of belonging and becoming which is overwhelming in its goal, its tempo, and its momentum.

But maybe I shouldn't complain about newspapers, because we raised a lot of hell recently about television and about how we were completely omitted and excluded from it. So this year the TV industry decided to do something about it. You know, there was a time when if we saw a black face on television, we ran to the telephone and called all our friends and said, "Hey, there's one on!" But if we did that nowadays, the result would be the greatest communications snarl in the history of A.T.&T. "Negroes" are everywhere. And I meant to use that word "Negroes" because they are "Negroes" to be sure, from the background of the deodorant commercial to full-fledged starring roles in serials. But they are "Negroes." They are all doing what we call a white thing. Not a single one of the new programs celebrates the beauty and dignity of black life style.

The White Television Thing

For instance, we have *Julia,* the simple, heart-warming story of a Negro nurse living in a white community, working for a white doctor in a white clinic. We have *Ironside,* the courageous story of an invalid white police detective whose wheelchair is cheerfully manned by an erstwhile black militant. We have *NYPD,* the story of a black detective who has completely turned his back on the Harlem of his youth. And finally, one more of the many, we have *The Outcasts,* saddle partners, one a white ex-slaveholder, one a black ex-slave. Now, if that combination is not implausible enough for you, they are bounty hunters—the most despicable profession in the whole West.

Now, I mention all this because all these shows have one thing in common, and that is an insidious, subliminal message. And the message is this: "Let bygones be bygones—all is forgiven—let's all work together in the spirit of law and order for the protection of private property, and three cheers for the old red, white, and blue." Well, bygones are not bygones, all is not forgiven, for justice still takes a back seat to law and order in this country. White people are still the haves and we the have nots; and until there are some fundamental changes in the structure of this society, the black cheers for the old red, white, and blue will be Bronx cheers.

Black Imagery Is Excluded

But more to the point of your immediate interests, we enter the sacred or semi-sacred halls of academe, and we experience a mere change in setting because even here dispassionate scholarship works hand in hand with the "hot" media in the promotion of the white thing. We observe the almost total exclusion of African and Afro-American artistic materials from school and college curriculums. And here I refer specifically to the Greco-Roman Renaissance art work adorning classrooms and campuses. I refer to that black imagery which is excluded from textbooks and also that which is negatively distorted by the approach to the subject when it *is* presented.

In my own special field, art history, I am constantly confronted with assaults on the dignity of my past and the creative worth of my present, and my future. I find that the art of my forebears was not art after all, but rather the intuitive expression of a people whose system of government was "tribal," whose artistic output is in the "curio" class and categorized as "primitive art," and this despite the heavy debt that modern Euro-American art owes to the work of my ancestors. Indeed, we may even lay strong claim to a sort of step-parentage to classical Western art as well, since archaic Greek art sprang from the loins of Egyptian art. All this, despite the significant expression of black craftsmen during the slave period, the extensive creative output of the Negro Renaissance artists of the 1920s and '30s, the Atlanta school of painting of the later '30s and '40s, the outstanding black murals of the depression years, and the artistically and socially important work done by black artists in the period since World War II.

"Art for the People's Sake"

Despite all these facts, the most extensive college-level reference work on American art, published as late as 1966, makes a one-paragraph reference to one contemporary black painter and one mulatto (that's the author's word) carpenter of the colonial period. No other black mark stains the pages of this scholarly ode to white supremacy, and the book is 706 pages long. Now while my remarks have reflected the situation in art history, similar cases could be made for black music, the black spoken and written word, black dance, the entire spectrum of what we call the arts.

But I don't tell you this in a "woe-is-me" attitude. I tell you how a substantial number of us feel about what we see, and I tell you we don't like it, and here are some of the things we're doing about it. Black image makers are creating forms that define, glorify, and direct black people— an art for the people's sake. Those of us who call ourselves artists realize that we can no longer afford the luxury of "art for art's sake." Black scholars are reassessing the relevance of their studies in the light of black peoples' present and future realities. We will no longer permit so-called higher learning to separate us from our people. We will no longer permit academic degrees to function as wedges between us and our peoples' needs and desires. We will no longer permit scholarly language, useless theoretical doubletalk, and esoteric dilettantism to make our academic and artistic exercises unintelligible to our people. In other words, art or knowledge that does not serve the cause of the black struggle is a waste of valuable time and creative energy. Black artists and black scholars who do not respond positively to the cause of black mental and physical liberation will be considered irrelevant by their grandchildren, if I may paraphrase brother LeRoi Jones. And as we work to define and direct ourselves, as we respond to the challenge of black needs, you must realize, if you are men and women of good will, that you have an equally important challenge facing you. You must realize that race relations in this country will never be the same as they were "in the good old days." Actions must be taken by whites as well as blacks, if we are to remain in the same country (and there is some question as to that). And you must realize that our roles as blacks and whites are clearly defined.

Gradualism Is Suicidal

Universities and colleges must not respond to our need with gradualism, for gradualism would be foolish and perhaps nationalistically suicidal at this moment in our history. You must not respond with tokenism because there you only delude yourselves. You must not respond with moderation because this will only make a bad situation worse, and at best will only forestall the inevitable cataclysmic confrontation that arises from hopeless frustration. And so for the sake of us all, if we are to remain one nation, divided even though we may be, we must propose programs that will immediately put right past wrongs and give directions for the future. . . .

On the question of visual imagery I wish to propose a program—and this is just the beginning, or an interim aspect, of what some of us consider to be the black agenda for higher learning in visual art. This program should be implemented immediately in the colleges and universities of this country.

We Need a New Esthetics

In art, we are calling for the revamping of the present system of esthetics and a purifying of the language employed in describing art forms of cultures which fall outside the purview of the Greco-Roman-Renaissance tradition. Black and white are undesirable synonyms for evil and purity. The term primitive is inadequate for describing a nonliterate culture, and physical beauty is not best defined by blond hair and blue eyes. We are seeking universal standards of beauty and excellence that are truly universal and not limited to Europe and its cultural colonies. We insist on the inclusion of histories of African and Afro-American art in all the colleges and universities that serve black people. And these histories must be written by black scholars and not by well-intentioned white ones. For there is a qualitative difference between being sympathetic and being empathetic.

And the emphasis I place on visual art is necessary, because visual art expression is the most profound reflection of a culture, and our people must become more aware of their rich cultural heritage. Finally, the inclusion in the total college curriculum of visual materials which reflect our long-standing and invaluable presence in the development of this country is an urgent request, and black visual artists, designers, painters, sculptors, and photographers must be employed in meeting this requirement.

25 The Black Church and Black Power

Throughout the Black Power years, leaders of the black church made development of an effective political voice a top priority. Collectively, they challenged all members of the African American religious community to be "reborn into involvement in the liberation of black people." If this could be accomplished, the faith would remain relevant to all those seeking rapid socioeconomic change. Thus, to spur both societal and church renewal, black caucuses were established in predominantly white denominations. "Plantation" theology was roundly condemned and a variety of activist-oriented, race-specific alternatives formulated. God, it was said, sided with the oppressed on issues of social justice. Therefore, it was legitimate to treat religious belief as a present-minded doctrine of empowerment.

Founded in 1966 as a nationwide ecumenical organization of clergy and laity committed to assisting the African American community in its freedom struggles, the National Committee of Black Churchmen (NCBC) coordinated the activities of black caucuses, supported both African liberation movements and James Forman's "Black Manifesto," and spoke out boldly against the racism and economic selfishness of white churches. On Independence Day eve, 1970, the committee issued the following position paper enumerating the many injustices to which black Americans had been subjected and invoking the collective spirit of past racial heroes in support of black liberation. Modeled in language and style after the original Declaration of 1776, the NCBC document—with the names and affiliations of its forty-one signatories attached—was published in the *New York Times* of 3 July 1970 and is reprinted here with permission. It was "ratified" later that year at a Black Solidarity Day rally held in New York City.

In the second document, as well as in works such as *The Black Messiah* (1968) and *Black Christian Nationalism* (1972), the Reverend Albert B. Cleage, Jr., pastor of Detroit's Shrine of the Black Madonna, speaks of the need to make the black church "relevant to the black revolution." Here, the outspoken minister's stinging rebuke of "slave Christianity" is joined to a decidedly nationalist interpretation of Scripture. He holds that rediscovery and acceptance of a black Messiah is intimately related to African Americans' rediscovery of themselves. Once rid of the self-hatred fostered by the worship of a white God, they could reclaim their religious heritage by uniting to build a strong black nation. Throughout the Black Power era, Cleage's unorthodox teachings spurred the growth of racial pride and served as an encouragement to both secular and church-based activism. The selection is reprinted from *Quest for a Black Theology,* ed. James J. Gardiner and J. Deotis Roberts, Sr. (Philadelphia: Pilgrim Press, 1971), by permission.

1970　The Black Declaration of Independence

National Committee of Black Churchmen

In the Black Community, July 4, 1970 a Declaration by concerned Black Citizens of the United States of America in Black Churches, Schools, Homes, Community Organizations and Institutions assembled:

When in the course of Human Events, it becomes necessary for a People who were stolen from the lands of their Fathers, transported under the most ruthless and brutal circumstances 5,000 miles to a strange land, sold into dehumanizing slavery, emasculated, subjugated, exploited and discriminated against for 351 years, to call, with finality, a halt to such indignities and genocidal practices—by virtue of the Laws of Nature and of Nature's God, a decent respect to the Opinions of Mankind requires that they should declare their just grievances and the urgent and necessary redress thereof.

We hold these truths to be self-evident, that all Men are not *only* created equal and endowed by their Creator with certain unalienable rights among which are Life, Liberty and the Pursuit of Happiness, but that when this equality and these rights are deliberately and consistently refused, withheld or abnegated, men are bound by self-respect and honor to rise up in righteous indignation to secure them. Whenever any Form of Government, or any variety of established traditions and systems of the Majority becomes destructive of Freedom and of legitimate Human Rights, it is the Right of the Minorities to use every necessary and accessible means to protest and to disrupt the machinery of Oppression, and so to bring such general distress and discomfort upon the oppressor as to the offended Minorities shall seem most appropriate and most likely to effect a proper adjustment of the society.

Prudence, indeed, will dictate that such bold tactics should not be initiated for light and transient Causes; and, accordingly, the Experience of White America has been that the descendants of the African citizens brought forcibly to these shores, and to the shores of the Caribbean Islands, as slaves, have been patient long past what can be expected of any human beings so affronted. But when a long train of Abuses and Violence, pursuing invariably the same Object, manifests a Design to reduce them under Absolute Racist Domination and Injustice, it is their Duty radically to confront such Government or system of traditions, and to provide, under the aegis of Legitimate Minority Power and Self

225

Determination, for their present Relief and future Security. Such has been the patient Sufferance of Black People in the United States of America; and such is now the Necessity which constrains them to address this Declaration to Despotic White Power, and to give due notice of their determined refusal to be any longer silenced by fear or flattery, or to be denied justice. The history of the treatment of Black People in the United States is a history having in direct Object the Establishment and Maintenance of Racist Tyranny over this People. To prove this, let Facts be submitted to a candid World.

The United States has evaded Compliance to laws the most wholesome and necessary for our Children's education.

The United States has caused us to be isolated in the most dilapidated and unhealthful sections of all cities.

The United States has allowed election districts to be so gerrymandered that Black People find the right to Representation in the Legislatures almost impossible of attainment.

The United States has allowed the dissolution of school districts controlled by Blacks when Blacks opposed with manly Firmness the white man's Invasions on the Rights of our People.

The United States has erected a Multitude of Public Agencies and Offices, and sent into our ghettos Swarms of Social Workers, Officers and Investigators to harass our People, and eat out their Substance to feed the Bureaucracies.

The United States has kept in our ghettos, in Times of Peace, Standing Armies of Police, State Troopers and National Guardsmen, without the consent of our People.

The United States has imposed Taxes upon us without protecting our Constitutional Rights.

The United States has constrained our Black sons taken Captive in its Armies, to bear arms against their black, brown and yellow Brothers, to be the Executioners of these Friends and Brethren, or to fall themselves by their Hands.

The Exploitation and Injustice of the United States have incited domestic Insurrections among us, and the United States has endeavored to bring on the Inhabitants of our ghettos, the merciless Military Establishment, whose known Rule of control is an undistinguished shooting of all Ages, Sexes and Conditions of Black People:

For being lynched, burned, tortured, harried, harassed and imprisoned without Just Cause.

For being gunned down in the streets, in our churches, in our homes, in our apartments and on our campuses, by Policemen and Troops who are protected by a mock Trial, from Punishment for any Murders which they commit on the Inhabitants of our Communities.

For creating, through Racism and bigotry, an unrelenting Economic Depression in the Black Community which wreaks havoc upon our men and disheartens our youth.

For denying to most of us equal access to the better Housing and Education of the land.

For having desecrated and torn down our humblest dwelling places, under the Pretense of Urban Renewal, without replacing them at costs which we can afford.

The United States has denied our personhood by refusing to teach our heritage, and the magnificent contributions to the life, wealth and growth of this Nation which have been made by Black People.

In every stage of these Oppressions we have Petitioned for Redress in the most humble terms: Our repeated Petitions have been answered mainly by repeated Injury. A Nation, whose Character is thus marked by every act which may define a Racially Oppressive Regime, is unfit to receive the respect of a Free People.

Nor have we been wanting in attentions to our White Brethren. We have warned them from time to time of Attempts by their Structures of Power to extend an unwarranted, Repressive Control over us. We have reminded them of the Circumstances of our Captivity and Settlement here. We have appealed to their vaunted Justice and Magnanimity, and we have conjured them by the Ties of our Common Humanity to disavow these Injustices, which, would inevitably interrupt our Connections and Correspondence. They have been deaf to the voice of Justice and of Humanity. We must, therefore, acquiesce in the Necessity, which hereby announces our Most Firm Commitment to the Liberation of Black People, and hold the Institutions, Traditions and Systems of the United States as we hold the rest of the societies of Mankind, Enemies when Unjust and Tyrannical; when Just and Free, Friends.

We, therefore, the Black People of the United States of America in all parts of this Nation, appealing to the Supreme Judge of the World for the Rectitude of our Intentions, do, in the Name of our good People and our own Black Heroes—Richard Allen, James Varick, Absalom Jones, Nat Turner, Frederick Douglass, Marcus Garvey, Malcolm X, Martin Luther King, Jr., and all Black People past and present, great and small—Solemnly Publish and Declare, that we shall be, and of Right ought to be, FREE AND INDEPENDENT FROM THE INJUSTICE, EXPLOITATIVE

CONTROL, INSTITUTIONALIZED VIOLENCE AND RACISM OF WHITE AMERICA, that unless we receive full Redress and Relief from these Inhumanities we will move to renounce all Allegiance to this Nation, and will refuse, in every way, to cooperate with the Evil which is Perpetrated upon ourselves and our Communities. And for the support of this Declaration, with a firm Reliance on the Protection of divine Providence, we mutually pledge to each other our Lives, our Fortunes, and our sacred Honor.

1969 *From* **The Black Messiah and the
Black Revolution**

Albert B. Cleage, Jr.

In the midst of a black revolution in which black people are struggling
for power, slave Christianity no longer meets their needs. Slave Christianity is the Christianity that old master gave black people back on the
plantation. He defined Jesus, and showed pictures of Jesus with his
flowing golden locks and his blue eyes. The obvious absurdity of the
portrait never even occurred to black people. There was no way in the
world Jesus could have looked like the pictures in the Bible, having been
born in the part of the world reserved for black people by God. The
whiteness of Jesus and Israel was basic to slave Christianity. Old master
taught black people that God was primarily concerned with petty little
sins (you don't fornicate, you don't smoke, you don't play cards, you
don't drink). A petty morality too trivial for God's concern were the
basic elements of slave Christianity. The whole idea of Christianity had
to do with an individual kind of salvation. Two thousand years ago on
Calvary a mystic event took place. Jesus was crucified, and somehow he
rose from the dead. In this redemptive act, God made salvation possible
for individuals who believed in all generations. This meant then that
each individual must fight for his own little individual salvation. Black
people took this slave Christianity and made of it an instrument for
survival. They put into it a vitality which the white man did not have in
his own church. They believed fervently because they needed to believe;
they needed a dream of escape in a world in which there was no real
possibility of escape. They could conceive of no way to end their oppression so they used this slave theology as one way of maintaining sanity.
Slave Christianity made it possible for black people to survive. The
slaves took the idea of going to heaven seriously. They took their pain
and suffering to Jesus. The slave could stand anything that the white
man did, saying, "The white man can beat me, he can rob me, he can
cheat me, he can rape my wife and my daughters, he can do anything,
but I can take it all to Jesus and I know that ultimately Jesus will
triumph because through his sacrifice God has already redeemed me. So
whatever the white man does I can accept." He went to church on
Sunday and shouted with joy, running up and down the aisles in sheer
ecstasy. The most effective Christian preaching in America was in black

pulpits with ignorant black preachers preaching slave Christianity as no one in the world ever preached it before, to people who had to believe because they had no alternative for this mystical religious escape.

The black slave church was also destroying black people. Black people suffered discrimination because they were black. They were persecuted, they were brutalized, they were discriminated against, they were exploited, solely because they were black. And then in church on Sunday morning the black slave preacher, would say, "God is concerned about each one of you. You think that all week he hasn't been looking at you, but he's been watching everything that the white man has been doing to you. God knows what white people have done to you and someday he is going to shake them over hellfire. One of these days God is going to do for you what you can't do yourself. So get along with these white people as best as you can, because soon you are going to be taken up yonder to God and then you can sit at his right hand, and look down into hell where white people are roasting over hellfire." That was a beautiful message with simple basic eloquence and power about it. I only wish that it were true! But then you remember that black people had been working all week for nothing, being beaten up by policemen and exploited in every possible way. The preacher helped them to forget by telling them how beautiful it was going to be up there, and pretty soon they would be running up and down the aisles, shouting and screaming, and for the moment each individual escaped from his everyday problems, and for the moment was completely out of this world. The church and slave Christianity has perpetuated our individualism. We don't have any sense of being a people fighting our problems together. We're waiting for God to save us individually. We're running up and down the aisle shouting and singing and hoping that Jesus will speak to our individual needs, not the needs of black people. We do not really ask God to help us change the basic conditions under which black people live. This is the weakness of the black church. It was a survival instrument. It helped maintain sanity, but it destroyed the possibility of a united black liberation struggle. The black preacher preached escapism and individualism. He destroyed the possibility of black people fighting together to change oppressive conditions. There were exceptions. There was Nat Turner who was a black preacher who understood that the lynching of Jesus on Calvary two thousand years ago did not stop him from trying to kill white people who were oppressing his people. He was a black preacher who somehow saw the inadequacies and the contradictions of slave Christianity. But his revolt failed because some good Christian brother betrayed him along the way to guarantee his salvation in glory. As long as black people could see no possibility of changing the world, escapism was good old religion. It was all that a black preacher could preach to a black congregation. As long as there was no way for black people to change their condition it was natural to concentrate on the possibility of a good life after death.

As soon as black people began to see the world in which they lived realistically, they began to see white people as they really are—corrupt, brutal, and oppressive. When black people began to look at white people and see them as they were they said we can change this world ourselves, we don't have to wait for Jesus. And that marked the beginning of a whole new way of life for black people. Then black people began to try to change the world day by day, not waiting either for Jesus or for the redemption of white people. This new attitude could not fit into the slave church. The new black militant talked about people working together to change the black man's condition. The slave preacher still talked about sending individuals to heaven one by one. The two can't mix. In Harlem half a million black people crowd into thousands of little churches every Sunday, and nothing is done to change the black man's condition in New York City. The ineffectiveness of the black church is reflected in the condition of Harlem. The black church could change Harlem any day it offered black people leadership here on earth by bringing black people together. The white power structure has a vested interest in keeping slave Christianity alive. No one will ever organize a black community for united action as long as black preachers stand up on Sunday morning and take people to heaven one by one. As soon as black people began to conceive of the possibility of changing the world, the absolute necessity for a new interpretation of the Bible and a new black theology became obvious. Now there were other possible solutions. Black people could just leave the church, and I think many white people would rather that we did just that. But Christianity belongs to us. We are not going to give it up just because white people have messed it up.

So when we began to see that we could change the world we began to see that the church offered a broad institutional power base that could be useful in the black revolution. The only institution black people have is the church. We don't have anything else. All of our money is tied up in religious structures and a good part of our trained personnel is tied up in religious institutions. We cannot just turn and leave it. We need it in the liberation struggle. Which means that we must change the church radically. We must make the church relevant to the black revolution.

The black revolution consists from day to day of those people who have severed their identification with white people, who realize that white people are the enemy, and are engaged in a struggle for power to control black communities. The black revolution must somehow take over the black church because the black revolution needs the black church. The black revolution will continue no matter what happens to the black church. But the black church can be helpful to the black revolution. Many young black militants think that the black church is too much trouble. They say that it is more trouble than it is worth. They would rather just leave it. But I am in it, I have a vested interest in it, and I am determined to take it along with the revolution. I am convinced that it can serve a valuable purpose if we will take the time to restructure it.

Everything must be restructured—its historical analysis, its biblical interpretation, its theology, its ritual, its preaching, everything. We can't just say we're going to change it a little bit, we're going to patch it up a little here and a little there. The whole basic Pauline interpretation of Christianity is historically false. The theology built on it has no relationship with the teachings of Jesus at all. You can ask, "How do you know?" I can reply, "That's a good question because none of us knows very much about what Jesus taught." All that we know about Jesus was filtered through the eyes of the early church after it had already been corrupted by the apostle Paul who was an Uncle Tom who wanted to identify with his white gentile Roman oppressors. Paul was very proud of his Roman citizenship although he was an oppressed Jew. Just like a black man today talking about his American citizenship. And I dare say that Paul's Roman citizenship did him just about as much good as a black man's American citizenship does him today. But that doesn't have anything to do with the way a man feels. Paul wanted to feel like a Roman. He wanted to be part of the pagan Roman world, so he took something that happened, the history and the person of Jesus and distorted them to make them acceptable to a pagan heathen world. There was some controversy about it. The disciples who remained in Jerusalem knew that he was preaching a false doctrine that had nothing at all to do with the Jesus with whom they had walked and talked. They tried to hold him accountable for his white corruptions. He tricked them just like people do today. He raised money from the churches he had organized and went back to Jerusalem with enough money to persuade the original disciples to overlook the fact that he was teaching a false doctrine. This is true. Paul does not follow in the footsteps of Jesus.

The black church must go back to the beginning and seek to rediscover the original teaching of Jesus and the nation Israel. There is very little historicity in the gospels and in the New Testament. In the Old Testament we have a little history intermingled with much fantasy and myth. Let's just admit that we don't have much, except insofar as we can understand the conditions out of which Jesus came and the role which he played in his day. We can find a few historical fragments in the Synoptic Gospels. We depend upon the Old Testament to validate the New Testament. Preachers don't quite know what to do with the Old Testament except to go back at Christmas-time and find passages which prove that Jesus was the Messiah. All of which have nothing to do with Jesus. Essentially the Old Testament contradicts the New. The easy way to get around that of course is to say that the New Testament is an expansion and development and takes the Old Testament to new heights, which we also know is a lie. It says something entirely different. The New Testament does not take the Old Testament to new heights. It is a complete contradiction of the Old Testament, and Jesus came to fulfill the Old Testament.

We go back to the beginning of the Old Testament and we find mythology of course. Moses did not write the first five books of the Old Testament. At some point Israel became a nation. At some point the process began. We like to begin with Abraham. We have the basic outline of his wanderings. In the beginning he was a Chaldean. Most of you who have seen Chaldeans know that they are not nearly so white even to begin with as the pictures of Jesus in our Sunday school literature, and this Chaldean and his family wandered into Africa at the beginning of putting together the nation Israel. He went down into Egypt where his wife had an affair with pharaoh to save Abraham's neck. Pharaoh finally discovered the deception and ordered Abraham and Sarah out of Egypt. To avoid God's displeasure, he gave him gifts including animals, slaves, and concubines. Abraham continued his wandering. Sarah was unable to have a child, and so she suggested that he have a child by Hagar, an Egyptian servant girl. And so Ishmael, Abraham's heir, was born of an Egyptian slave, Hagar. Obviously the relationships were close and friendly. Later they tried to get rid of Hagar and Ishmael. But certainly the Jews did not have any racial prejudice in the sense that they held themselves apart from other peoples. Wherever they went they tended to mingle, to intermarry, and to become part of the people. So as Israel wandered in Africa Israel became blacker and blacker. Some of you may want to argue that the Egyptians were not black. That is a ridiculous argument which could only arise in America.

Studies have been made which prove beyond a shadow of a doubt that most of the pharaohs were negroid. I use the word so you won't think that I am saying only "nonwhite." I'm talking about black. Most of the pharaohs had negroid blood that even now can be discovered by doing X rays of the mummies of the pharaohs. The percentage of pharaohs who obviously had negroid blood was markedly high in a study done recently by the University of Michigan Dental School. Studies of poor Egyptians indicate an even higher percentage as would be expected. The Egyptians were black. The intermingling of the Egyptians with Israel in the building of the nation Israel indicates that Israel was in the process of becoming black and everywhere that Israel went Israel grew blacker and blacker. Finally Joseph was sold into slavery and ended up back in Egypt. Israel went back into Egypt to escape from famine and settled there and became part of the people until "there arose a pharaoh who knew not Joseph." The mingling and intermixture is obvious. Then there were four hundred years of slavery. The Egyptians were the great slave traders of the ancient world and they made regular forays into the Sudan, into the land of the black people, and brought back slaves. And so in slavery in Egypt there were black people and there were the Israelites who were in the process of becoming black. For four hundred years they lived together and intermingled as slaves. At the time of their escape across the Red Sea, the black nation Israel was blacker than the Egyptians from whom they were fleeing.

Moses went off into Midian and married a black woman, the daughter of Jethro, and from Jethro, the high priest of Midian he borrowed the Yahweh religion which became the religion of the Israelites. Israel not only intermarried with the black peoples of Egypt and the Sudan but adopted the ideas and culture of black people. Moses brought back a concept of God from the Midianites. The God who spoke to Moses from the burning bush defined himself as the Midianite God. Jethro later visited Moses and gave him basic ideas of political organization. The Old Testament is the history of the development of a black nation. Perhaps you know many Jewish people today who do not look black. That's because the Jewish people in the Western world are the descendants of Jews who were converted to Judaism about one thousand years after the death of Jesus, in Europe, in Russia, and in other places in the white world. But even these "white Jews" retain physical signs of their black beginnings. A few communities have maintained an unbroken continuity since the fall of Jerusalem in A.D. 70. A Jewish community in India has descendants of the original black Jews who came to India directly from Israel, after the fall, and who are still black. The community also has some white Jews who migrated from Europe as merchants. There is constant conflict in this little Jewish community. The white Jews feel themselves superior to the black Jews. Particularly the white Jews don't want their daughters to marry the young black Jewish men. There are black Jews scattered throughout the world especially in Africa and in areas near to Israel. General Dayan's daughter recently complained in the world press that she was very upset because her house in Israel had depreciated in value because black Jews had purchased property on either side of her. The existence of black Jews is still a reality. White Jews are Zionists who needed Israel as a homeland, but are not of the bloodline of Abraham, Isaac, and Jacob.

Black Jews, as they became a people in their wandering, developed basic ideas which were important to them. The history and religion of Israel is dominated by the concept of nation. God was concerned not with individuals but with the black nation Israel. God supported the efforts of the black nation Israel. The black nation Israel made up the chosen people of God. God had a relationship with the nation Israel, and the nation Israel was to be saved or the nation Israel was to be punished. God spoke to a prophet that he might bring a message to the nation Israel. It is this concept of nation which Christianity loses entirely because of the apostle Paul's identification with the pagan white world. Black people of the nation Israel depended upon God to support them in every struggle. The Old Testament is a Black Power document that no modern book can equal. God would even hold the sun still while the black nation Israel killed its enemies. God would do anything necessary to help the black nation Israel find the promised land and keep it.

Jesus the black Messiah, lived in the midst of this kind of black liberation struggle. The Maccabean revolt freed Israel from white gentile oppression for a period, but by the time of Jesus, the Jews had again become an enslaved people who had lost much of their sense of nationhood. Jesus was born into a situation comparable to that in which black people in America live today. A situation in which black people were oppressed by a white gentile oppressor and were exploited in every way possible. Jesus found an underground revolutionary movement led by the Zealot extremists. The baptism of Jesus obviously marked his introduction into this revolutionary Zealot movement. When John the Baptist was arrested and about to be killed he sent disciples to talk to Jesus to find out whether or not he was the new leader who was to take over the movement. The terse reply of Jesus indicated quite clearly that he considered himself to be the new leader and that he was willing to be judged in terms of the things he was doing. Tell John and let him decide whether or not I am the Messiah. Following the death of John the Baptist, Jesus became the visible head of the revolutionary Zealot movement. Certain radical phases of the movement remained underground and certainly Jesus was forced to walk a tightrope in his relationships with an oppressed people who were fighting for liberation by any means necessary, and those who were in collaboration with the white oppressors and who expected certain benefits from this relationship. It is this kind of situation which is revealed in the little incident in which Jesus is asked about paying taxes to Caesar. The revolutionaries advocated paying no taxes to Caesar. They argued that this was one way of ending oppression. Jesus could have replied, "No, don't pay taxes to Caesar"; that would have been a popular answer and would have satisfied the movement, but would have led to his immediate arrest by the government. Upon the other hand he could have said, "Pay taxes to Caesar." Then he would have alienated the movement and endangered his life, but Rome would have been satisfied. He said neither. He pointed to Caesar's picture on the coin and said, "Give unto Caesar the things that are Caesar's and unto God the things that are God's." This is the kind of double-talk that preachers still use whenever they do not consider a question really important.

One of the most confusing teachings of Jesus has to do with the love ethic which the apostle Paul attempted to universalize. Jesus was defining a tribal ethic for the black nation Israel. He was trying to bring together a people who were oppressed, and who had been fragmented by their oppression. Any oppressed people are filled with self-hate and tend to identify with their oppressors. Psychological studies of modern Jews in concentration camps under Hitler, indicate that the greater the oppression, the greater the identification. In concentration camps the Jews identified totally with their guards who exercized the power of life and death. They were not even permitted to take care of their bodily needs without the guard's permission. So the guard became for them a kind of God with whom they identified completely. This is true with any oppressed people. Jesus understood the many forces which separate an oppressed people from each other and make them betray brothers to serve the interests of their oppressors. So in dealing with his own people he had to talk much about love. And in this sense, many of the things that Jesus said sound remarkably like the things that I've heard Stokely Carmichael say in talking to a black group. Stokely Carmichael could come into a meeting jammed with thousands of people and his first reaction would be in terms of the people's relationships with one another. If there were brothers sitting down and sisters standing along the wall Stokely would ask the brothers to please get up and let the sisters have their seats, saying that a people must learn to respect their women. That might have sounded like hate to white people, but to black people it pointed out a whole new approach to the possibilities of black people living together. Most of his talk would be in terms of how black people must love each other and build whatever they were going to build in terms of new human relationships, which could protect black people from the white man's materialism and selfishness. Listening to Stokely, I understood the kind of thing that Jesus had to do to unite the black people of Israel. He had to talk to them about the transforming and redemptive power of love within the black nation. If a black brother strikes you upon one cheek turn to him the other cheek, because we must save every black brother for the nation if we are to survive. We can't say that this group of black people is not important or that group of black people is not important. Every black brother or sister has to be saved and brought into the black nation. This is what Jesus was talking about. Turn the other cheek, go the second mile, go a hundred miles if necessary, if in this way you can save a black brother. In the parable of the good Samaritan, Jesus is trying to make the same emphasis. The Samaritans were Jews. They were a lost tribe, despised because they rejected the temple in Jerusalem. Jesus said, this, too, is part of the Jewish nation and it must be saved.

Jews could no longer look down on any part of the black nation. The parable of the good Samaritan was merely an effort to show Israel that these people could no longer be despised. Jesus said it straight out when the brother came and asked what he ought to do if a brother refused to treat him properly. Jesus said, "Take another brother and go and talk to him. If he still refuses to do right take another brother and talk to him again. If he still refuses, put him out of the nation and treat him like a gentile." We try to forget that Jesus talked about white gentiles in this way. Put him outside the nation. Treat him like a gentile. If Jesus had been preaching universal love when he said, "Go the second mile" and "Turn the other cheek" he would not possibly have understood that the black nation Israel was separate and apart from its white gentile enemies. Jesus made the same point with the gentile woman who came to have her daughter healed. Jesus explained that he had come to the house of Israel. She replied that a rich man throws crumbs from the table to feed the dogs. Jesus healed the child, but not out of love or concern for the white gentile. Jesus had come to the nation Israel. He tried to build the nation Israel. He labored to bring together a people who could stand against their oppressors.

We could say that this doesn't sound very revolutionary. He engaged in little physical combat except in the almost symbolic act of driving the money changers out of the temple. He didn't shoot a gun, he didn't use a sword. Even in Gethsemane when the soldiers came to arrest him and Peter drew his sword, Jesus stopped him in a very practical way. A battle would have been futile. The disciples were neither equipped nor trained for battle. If he had planned to fight, Jesus would have been putting together an army all the way to Jerusalem. But to turn what he had been trying to do for the nation into a military struggle at the last moment would have been ridiculous. Jesus was primarily concerned with building a people, bringing them together, and forming a nation. And this task to which Jesus gave his full commitment is profoundly revolutionary. Everything that Jesus taught, everything that he said is relevant to the liberation struggle in which black people are engaged. Instead of telling black people about escaping from the world and going home to God on high, the black church must begin to involve black people in the black liberation struggle, using the teachings of Jesus in the Synoptic Gospels, and the Old Testament concept of nation to show black people how coming together with black pride and Black Power is basic to survival. The black church must become central in the black revolution. Jesus was a black Messiah not in terms of his death on Calvary, but in terms of his dedication to the struggle of black people here on earth. In the black church the sacraments can take on a new meaning. At the Shrine of the Black Madonna we baptize into the nation. We die to the old Uncle Tom life. We die to the old identification with white people. To be baptized into a black church must symbolize a complete rejection of the values of a hostile white world and a complete commitment to the struggle of black people. When we take the sacrament of Holy Communion it symbolizes our total rededication to personal participation in the strug-gle of black people and total rededication to the black nation. The sacraments and ritual of the church then become for black people an intrinsic part of the revolutionary struggle.

Since all the great religions of the world derive from the black experi-ence, we could turn to another religion if we wished. They all belong to us. Or we could put together a new religion suitable to our present needs and true to our historic revelations of God. But for black people in America, Christianity is part of our past. Its reinterpretation in terms of its historic black roots is a joyful task which we have undertaken. To finally realize that Jesus is a black Messiah, that the things he taught are still relevant to us, and that the distortions which we have learned are deliberate distortions perpetrated by the white man for his own benefit and convenience, is to realize that the restoration of the original Christianity taught by Jesus, is a task which we cannot put aside. We can restructure theology, making it something that black people can understand and appreciate. In many places young black people are honestly ashamed to be seen going in or coming out of a church. Understandably so because the black church has been an Uncle Tom institution, committed to the preservation of the white status quo and the pacification of black people. A revolutionary black church must be a place to which black people come with pride, knowing that Jesus was black, that the nation Israel was black, and that we are following in the footsteps of a black Messiah. Even now we are restructuring the black church that it may become the foundation upon which we build the black Christian nationalist liberation struggle and the emerging black nation.

26 Revolutionary Nationalism: The Black Panther Party and the Revolutionary Action Movement

Many nationalists felt that black empowerment had to be accompanied by a thoroughgoing socialist transformation of society. The basic tenets of Black Power–era revolutionary nationalism held that the right to self-determination was inherent in all nations, including the black "internal colony" of the United States. In order to end their exploitation, African Americans had to gain control of land and political power through national liberation, establishing revolutionary socialism as their operative creed. But since a nationalist revolution would be considered reactionary if concerned only with the problems of a single group, control of the black nation-state had to be viewed as part of a worldwide, anticapitalist liberation movement, not as an end in itself. There could be no separate peace with the oppressor. Instead, alliances were to be made with Third World peoples, and, after careful scrutiny, with white radicals. Within these working relationships, the black "peasantry" (variously defined as the laboring class or the underclass) would compose a leadership vanguard. Eventually, through revolutionary struggle, the downtrodden would banish neocolonial imperialists from the globe and usher in an era of unprecedented gains for humanity. International in scope, but Afrocentric in its promotion of black Americans as the liberating vanguard, this basic ideology was flexible enough to be adapted to meet the needs of all those who conceptualized the black nationalist struggle as one of both race and class.

The following documents show how two of the best known Black Power–era revolutionary nationalist organizations interpreted and applied these theoretical concepts. The first three reveal both the anticapitalist and the community-centered service orientation of the Black Panther Party for Self-Defense (BPP). To Panther leaders such as minister of information Eldridge Cleaver, the police were the armed guardians of an exploitative, imperialistic social order. Serving the same function within urban black America as foreign troops occupying conquered territory, they were duty-bound to keep the peace and protect the powerful by maintaining black oppression. The Panthers sought to effect a change in the behavior of "racist pig cops" by organizing armed citizens' patrols of black living areas—by policing the police. Other BPP "survival" initiatives involved the creation of educational, medical care, legal assistance, and free food programs. Since "the people and only the people make revolutions," it was believed that revolutionary nationalist goals could be achieved only if the residents of black communities could be kept from perishing from lack of care and sustenance. The first selection, "Armed Black Brothers in Richmond Community," is reprinted from the inaugural issue of the *Black Panther*, 25 April 1967, by permission. Cleaver's "On Meeting the Needs of the People" was written from exile in Algiers—where he had fled rather than be imprisoned on charges stemming from a 1968 shoot-out with Oakland police. It appeared in *Ramparts* (September 1969). "What We Want, What We Believe" is reprinted from the pamphlet *On the Ideology of the Black Panther Party*, pt. 1 (San Francisco: Black Panther Party, ca. 1970), by permission. The text differs from minister of defense Huey P. Newton's and chairman Bobby Seale's original version of the BPP ten-point platform and program in that "CAPITALIST" has been substituted for "white man" in paragraph 3.

The final document, "The African American War of National-Liberation," details the rationale behind the Revolutionary Action Movement's (RAM) call for unceasing "war with the white world." Organized in 1963, three years prior to the founding of the BPP, RAM also engaged in protests against police brutality and developed various programs to educate the grassroots in the basic tenets of political revolution. Guided by the neo-Garveyite motto, "One Purpose, One Aim, One Destiny," RAM activists were committed to building racial solidarity and were not averse to promoting the use of guerrilla warfare tactics against their racial and class foes. Considered dangerous anarchists by law enforcement authorities, they saw themselves as "the pivotal point for the destruction of world imperialism." History, they were convinced, "will absolve us and dissolve the enemy." The document is reprinted from the summer–fall 1965 issue of *Black America*, by permission.

15 Black Brothers, most of them armed; with Magnum 12 gauge shot guns, M-1 rifles, and side arms, held a street rally at the corner of Third and Chesley in North Richmond last Saturday afternoon about 5 P.M. The nice thing about these Bloods is that they had their arms to defend themselves and their Black Brothers and Sisters while they exercised their Constitutional Rights: Freedom of Speech, and the right to Peacefully Assemble. And while they exercised another Constitutional right: the right to bear arms to defend themselves.

The racist cops could only look on. The Dog Cops made no attempt to break up the meeting like they generally do when Black people get together to sound out their grievances against the white power structure. The point to get firmly into your mind is that both the Black Brothers and the racist cops had "POWER". They had righteous "GUN POWER", but the significant thing is that the Black Brothers had some of this POWER. In the past, Black People have been at the mercy of cops who feel that their badges are a license to shoot, maim, and out-right murder any Black man, woman, or child who crosses their gun-sights. But there are now strong Black men and women on the scene who are willing to step out front and do what is necessary to bring peace, security, and justice to a people who have been denied all of these for four hundred years.

At this rally, the Brothers were uptight and knew exactly what they were doing at all times. They knew that they were acting strictly within their rights. These Brothers have become aware of something that the white racists have been trying to keep secret from Black people all the time: that a citizen has the right to protect himself. They were ready to insure that the rally went ahead as planned, without any interference from outlaw cops who wanted to suppress the meeting so that other Black People would not get the message.

Black People must realize that the time is short and growing shorter by the day. Check it out. People talk about "Power". There is White Power, Black Power, Yellow Power, Green Power, etc. but all Black People want out of all these different forms of Power is BLACK POWER, Black People want and need the power to stop the white racist power structure from grinding the life out of the Black Race through the daily operation of this system which is designed to exploit and oppress Black People.

The beautiful thing about the Brothers who held the rally is that they are organized, disciplined and politically aware of all the ins and outs of the problems facing Black People throughout the Bay Area in particular. When the cops came rolling up looking, the brothers spread out all across the street waiting for some fool cop to try and start something. The brothers were *organized*.

So, Brothers and Sisters everywhere: righteous BLACK POWER *organized* is where it's at. The BLACK PANTHER PARTY FOR SELF-DEFENSE really has something going. These brothers are the cream of Black Manhood. They are there for the protection and defense of our Black Community. The Black Community owes it to itself, to the future of our people, to get behind these brothers and to let the world know that black people are not stupid fools who are unable to recognize when someone is acting in the best interest of Black People. These Brothers have a political perspective. Most important, they are down here on the GRASS ROOTS LEVEL where the great majority of our people are. The BLACK PANTHER PARTY FOR SELF DEFENSE *moves*. The PARTY takes action. Everybody else just sits back and talk. All Black People know what needs to be done, but not all of them are willing to do it. The White man has instilled fear into the very hearts of our people. We must act to remove this fear. The only way to remove this fear is to stand up and look the white man in his blue eyes. Many Black People are able nowadays to look the white man in the eyes—but the line thins out when it comes to looking the white cops in the eye. But the white cop is the instrument sent into our community by the Power Structure to keep Black People quiet and under control. So it is not surprising that the action these days centers around the conduct of these white cops who come from way across town to patrol our communities for 8 hours a day. But Black People have to live in these communities 24 hours a day. So it is time that Black People start moving in a direction that will free our communities from this form of outright brutal oppression. The BLACK PANTHER PARTY FOR SELF DEFENSE has worked out a program that is carefully designed to cope with this situation.

BLACK MEN!!! It is your duty to your women and children, to your mothers and sisters, to investigate the program of the PARTY. There is no other way. We have tried everything else. This is the moment in history when Black People have no choice but to move and move rapidly to gain their freedom, justice, and all the other ingredients of civilized living that have been denied to us. This is where it is at. Check it out, Black Brothers and Sister! This is our Day!!!!!

1969   On Meeting the Needs of the People

Eldridge Cleaver

Back during the days when I was still running around in Babylon talking crazy about the pigs, if anyone had told me that someday I'd find myself in this exile situation trying to send a message back about the Black Panther Party's Breakfast for Children program and the white radicals of Berkeley with their People's Park, I probably would have taken it as a put-down. But it's all for real, and what is more I find myself very enthusiastic about these developments.

Both of these actions expose the contradiction between the pretenses of the system and the needs of the people. They stand as an assertion that the pigs of the power structure are not fulfilling their duties and that the people are moving, directly, to fill their own needs and redress their grievances. And the pigs in turn, with their hostile response to both of these programs, clearly expose themselves as enemies of the people.

Breakfast for Children and the People's Park are qualitatively different types of actions from anything we have been into in the past. They represent a move from theory to practice and implementation. The pigs cannot argue against the substance of these programs, even though they hate the forces that have brought them about. In fact, they will move to co-opt the programs and to drive a wedge between the programs and the vanguard forces that launched them. This has been the strategy of ruling classes all through history, because they really have no other choice—given their determination to hang on to power until it is wrenched from their grasp—and even this never really works, except to buy them time. It can only be tragic when the vanguard forces allow themselves to get co-opted. On the one hand, the pigs will pressure the vanguard—they will make liberal use of the Big Stick—but at the same time they will use the carrot. For instance, they will try to get Jerry Rubin to become the director of a City Park, and Bobby Seale to become the headwaiter in a statewide Nutrition Supplement program.

I have a question: Will my child ever be able to sit down to a Black Panther breakfast, and will Kathleen and I, with our child—and I'm counting this Panther before he claws his way out of the womb—ever be able to visit the People's Park? What we need is some liberated territory in Babylon that we are willing and prepared to defend, so that all the exiles, fugitives, draft-dodgers, and runaway slaves can return to help finish the job.

The black and white communities are controlled by the same ruling class. Towards black people this ruling class uses racism as a tool of oppression, turning this oppression into a National Question. In the white community, oppression is a Class Question, provoking the response of Class Struggle. And when we see clearly that we're only dealing with Dr. Jekyll and Mr. Hyde, we recognize the beauty of the response of the people. We recognize that the Breakfast for Children program and the People's Park are authentic and accurate responses to the situations of black people and white people in Babylon.

Breakfast for Children pulls people out of the system and organizes them into an alternative. Black children who go to school hungry each morning have been organized into their poverty, and the Panther program liberates them, frees them from that aspect of their poverty. This is liberation in practice. In the white mother country where class struggle is the appropriate tactic and expropriation of the expropriators the proper means to revolution, the act of seizing that land and establishing a People's Park could not have been more to the point. So it is clear that the people are always able to discover a way of moving. Out of their practice they develop new theory that sheds light on future ways of moving.

If we can understand Breakfast for Children, can we not also understand Lunch for Children, and Dinner for Children, and Clothing for Children, and Education for Children, and Medical Care for Children? And if we can understand that, why can't we understand not only a People's Park, but People's Housing, and People's Transportation, and People's Industry, and People's Banks? And why can't we understand a People's Government?

It is very curious that the Breakfast for Children program was born in West Oakland, which can be categorized as one of the most oppressed areas in Babylon, and that the People's Park, on the other hand, was born in Berkeley, which can be categorized as one of the least oppressed areas. I think this is how we have traditionally looked upon these two contrasting areas. Of white people, those in Berkeley thought that they were amongst the freest in the land, and of black people, those in West Oakland knew that they were amongst the most oppressed. So we have these two very significant developments one, in the most oppressed area and the other in the least oppressed area. And it's very instructive to notice that on the one hand there is an attempt to fill the emptiness of want, of need, and of deprivation that the system of oppression and colonization leaves in the lives of a people. Here people are fighting for the essentials of survival, fighting for food for children, fighting for what it takes just to survive. On the other hand, in the least oppressed area, we see a fight which at a superficial glance can be mistaken for a fight for leisure. But we must look upon the fight for the People's Park as an in-road into the system, because it poses the question of basic re-arrangements in the system itself. And this is really the crucial question in our overall struggle, for in Babylon there is not really a scarcity of goods, and there is, objectively, no real reason why there can't be people's parks, because the land is available and the wherewithal to build such parks is there in abundance. But the capitalists, who must first see the prospects of a profit before they make any distribution of the resources, do not see a profit in a park for the people. And they see no percentage, beyond underwriting some marginal goodwill in the community or good public relations, in the Breakfast for Children program. They see this program as a threat, as cutting into the goods that are under their control. They see it as cutting into the expendable portion of their possessions. These two questions pose the basic problem that radicals have to deal with in Babylon; ultimately, they both pose precisely the same question. It is only because they start from such divergent sources that they give the appearance of being worlds apart. One springs from needs that are obvious and basic, and people can relate to them on that basis, while the other springs from an area that we are not accustomed to looking upon as basic to survival. People can readily relate to the need to eat breakfast, but it is possible that they cannot see the need for a park. They can see life continuing without a park but they would be more concerned about attempting to perpetuate life without food.

Revolution, in its essence, means precisely the rearrangement of a system. Many people think of revolution only as overt violence—as guns shooting and conflagrations, as flames leaping into the air, bodies in the streets and the uprising masses storming city hall. This is only one phase of the revolutionary process, and the violence is not an end in itself but only the means through which the necessary power is seized so that the rearrangements in the system can be carried out. It is the means for expropriating the land, the natural resources, the machines, all the means of production, the institutions of society—for taking them out of the control, out of the hands of those who now have them and who have abused them, who have perverted these things and have converted them into instruments with which to pursue their own private gain at the expense of the wider public good.

Ironically, many of the oppressed people themselves do not feel that they have a right to the things that a revolutionary program demands in their name. They have guilt feelings about it. They recognize and relate to people having food to eat and a park for their children to play in. But when the pigs of the power structure oink their lying tears, bemoaning the outlaw nature of the movement, these politically unaware people who are not firm in their ideology will get up-tight and feel guilty. They can even be made to feel that they are doing something wrong or something that is immoral, and they can be manipulated because of this feeling. It is necessary to dispel this feeling, because what it flows from is indoctrination with the myth of private property, the myth and the cluster of beliefs that have been spawned by the soothsayers of greed in order to sanctify their possession of the earth under the guise of private property.

We are trapped between our visions of what life could be like and what it really is: a People's Government in which a rational arrangement is made, and the present reality—helicopters dispatched over college campuses to spread clouds of noxious gasses in order to intimidate the people and to stifle their protests; troops marching in battle formation down our streets; sharpshooters in the uniforms of the guardians of the law, taking aim, taking deadly aim, at citizens, actually aiming at vital spots of the body, actually pulling triggers, and actually killing people. And we stare dumbly, and we wonder, and we feel impotent and intimidated because we know that they have the guns, and they have the courts, and they have the prisons.

In a recent issue of the Black Panther Party newspaper which reported on the first casualty of the battle for the People's Park, an essential question was raised: "The white mother country radicals have demonstrated that they are willing to lay down their lives in the struggle, but the question still begs an answer—are they willing to pick up the gun?" This gives rise to another question. After picking up the gun, whom do we shoot?

We must get it clear in our minds that we will shoot anyone who uses a gun, or causes others to use guns, to defend the system of oppression, racism, and exploitation. And the issues of the People's Park and the Breakfast for Children program clearly convey that we are moving beyond the racist pig cops to confront the avaricious businessmen and the demagogic politicians, because we have to ask ourselves who sends the cops and the National Guard, and who they are there to protect.

We have nothing to gain by deluding ourselves or by seeking ways to evade the reality, the terrible reality, that confronts us. We must face the fact that we are at war in America. Not everyone realizes that there is a war going on. Some of us understand theoretically that in a capitalistic economy the relationship between the ruling class and the ruled has been defined as a relationship of struggle, of war, but even so it is as though we have been reading some mysterious sociological poetry that stimulates the fat inside our skulls and gives us some sort of secret thrill. Others of us are so nitpickingly fanatical that we cannot assess the reality before our very eyes—the reality in which we ourselves are participants and which our own work has helped bring about—unless we can read it in a book written a hundred years ago in another country, under vastly different circumstances which do not begin to approximate the gigantic proportions of the task which rests so smotheringly upon our shoulders.

The principles that have been learned from our experience with the People's Park and the Breakfast for Children program, I think, will take root in the minds of radicals all over the United States. Myself, I'm tired of using the terms "radicals" and "militants," and I prefer to use the term "revolutionaries," because if we are not involved in a Revolution, and if we don't understand ourselves to be revolutionaries, then there is very little that we can really hope to do. But if we understand ourselves to be revolutionaries, and if we accept our historic task, then we can move beyond the halting steps that we've been taking, beyond the Stupid Revolution, and gain the revolutionary audacity to take the actions needed to unlock and focus the great revolutionary spirit of the people. All they need is to get their teeth into a pig's ass, or to see the ace up the avaricious businessman's sleeve or the lies in the teeth of the demagogic politicians. Then there will be a new day in Babylon, there will be a housecleaning in Babylon, and we can halt the machinery of oppression, purge our institutions of racism, and put the oppressors up against the wall—or maybe more appropriately, up against the fence that they have built around the People's Park.

POWER TO THE PEOPLE!

1966 What We Want, What We Believe

Black Panther Party Platform and Program

1. We want freedom. We want power to determine the destiny of our Black Community.
We believe that black people will not be free until we are able to determine our destiny.

2. We want full employment for our people.
We believe that the federal government is responsible and obligated to give every man employment or a guaranteed income. We believe that if the white American businessmen will not give full employment, then the means of production should be taken from the businessmen and placed in the community so that the people of the community can organize and employ all of its people and give a high standard of living.

3. We want an end to the robbery by the CAPITALIST of our Black Community.
We believe that this racist government has robbed us and now we are demanding the overdue debt of forty acres and two mules. Forty acres and two mules was promised 100 years ago as restitution for slave labor and mass murder of black people. We will accept the payment in currency which will be distributed to our many communities. The Germans are now aiding the Jews in Israel for the genocide of the Jewish people. The Germans murdered six million Jews. The American racist has taken part in the slaughter of over fifty million black people; therefore, we feel that this is a modest demand that we make.

4. We want decent housing, fit for shelter of human beings.
We believe that if the white landlords will not give decent housing to our black community, then the housing and the land should be made into cooperatives so that our community, with government aid, can build and make decent housing for its people.

5. We want education for our people that exposes the true nature of this decadent American society. We want education that teaches us our true history and our role in the present-day society.
We believe in an educational system that will give to our people a knowledge of self. If a man does not have knowledge of himself and his position in society and the world, then he has little chance to relate to anything else.

6. We want all black men to be exempt from military service.

We believe that Black people should not be forced to fight in the military service to defend a racist government that does not protect us. We will not fight and kill other people of color in the world who, like black people, are being victimized by the white racist government of America. We will protect ourselves from the force and violence of the racist police and the racist military, by whatever means necessary.

7. We want an immediate end to POLICE BRUTALITY and MURDER of black people.

We believe we can end police brutality in our black community by organizing black self-defense groups that are dedicated to defending our black community from racist police oppression and brutality. The Second Amendment to the Constitution of the United States gives a right to bear arms. We therefore believe that all black people should arm themselves for self-defense.

8. We want freedom for all black men held in federal, state, county and city prisons and jails.

We believe that all black people should be released from the many jails and prisons because they have not received a fair and impartial trial.

9. We want all black people when brought to trial to be tried in court by a jury of their peer group or people from their black communities, as defined by the Constitution of the United States.

We believe that the courts should follow the United States Constitution so that black people will receive fair trials. The 14th Amendment of the U.S. Constitution gives a man a right to be tried by his peer group. A peer is a person from a similar economic, social, religious, geographical, environmental, historical and racial background. To do this the court will be forced to select a jury from the black community from which the black defendant came. We have been, and are being tried by all-white juries that have no understanding of the "average reasoning man" of the black community.

10. We want land, bread, housing, education, clothing, justice and peace. And as our major political objective, a United Nations-supervised plebiscite to be held throughout the black colony in which only black colonial subjects will be allowed to participate, for the purpose of determining the will of black people as to their national destiny.

When, in the course of human events, it becomes necessary for one people to dissolve the political bands which have connected them with another, and to assume, among the powers of the earth, the separate and equal station to which the laws of nature and nature's God entitle them, a decent respect to the opinions of mankind requires that they should declare the causes which impel them to the separation.

We hold these truths to be self-evident, that all men are created equal; that they are endowed by their Creator with certain unalienable rights; that among these are life, liberty, and the pursuit of happiness. That, to secure these rights, governments are instituted among men, deriving their just powers from the consent of the governed; that, whenever any form of government becomes destructive of these ends, it is the right of the people to alter or to abolish it, and to institute a new government, laying its foundation on such principles, and organizing its powers in such form, as to them shall seem most likely to effect their safety and happiness. Prudence, indeed, will dictate that governments long established should not be changed for light and transient causes; and, accordingly, all experience hath shown, that mankind are more disposed to suffer, while evils are sufferable, than to right themselves by abolishing the forms to which they are accustomed. But, when a long train of abuses and usurpations, pursuing invariably the same object, evinces a design to reduce them under absolute despotism, it is their right, it is their duty, to throw off such government, and to provide new guards for their future security.

1965 *From* **The African American War of National-Liberation**

Revolutionary Action Movement

Revolutionary Nationalism—Philosophy for the Afroamerican

Black people must realize that they are at war with the white world. The white man has distorted history and everything else to fit his needs to stay in power. The white man is an international white nationalist thinking of the white race, first, foremost and only. As Mrs. Amy J. Garvey stated in Garvey and Garveyism, "The only ground on which white people are really united is race, neither language, religion, nor political system . . . divide them." In order for black people to survive in a white, hostile, evil, reactionary world they must unite to destroy the universal slavemaster. Our philosophy must be that no black person is free until all black people are free. We must unite in a universal black liberation movement to strike the universal slavemaster at *one time, one blow, one war*— the war of armageddon. We must have *one purpose, one aim, one destiny.* One purpose meaning—to be free black people from the universal slavemaster (slang for capitalist oppression), one aim—to develop black people through struggle to the highest attainment possible, one destiny—to follow in the spirit of black revolutionaries such as Gabriel Prosser, Toussaint L'Ouverture, Denmark Vesey, Nat Turner, Sojourner Truth, Harriet Tubman, Frederick Douglass, Marcus Garvey, Dr. Du Bois, Patrice Lumumba, Robert Williams, and Brother Malcolm, to create a new world free of colonialism, racism, imperialism, exploitation, and national oppression. . . .

Why White Americans Fear Black Nationalism

Most white Americans either don't understand or fear nationalism among black Americans because they usually have paranoid tendencies concerning the racial situation in the U.S. and around the world. This comes from their guilt complex and is usually covered by paternalism. White America knows what their ancestors have done to the Afroamerican and they usually feel that one day they will have to pay for their deeds. When blacks start talking about killing whites and destroying the U.S. so-called white radicals say that we are not talking about "real" revolution.

What Is "Real" Revolution?

"Political power comes from the barrel of a gun." "Real" revolution is a political economic war that is a war with political objectives waged by the oppressed to destroy the oppressor's power over them. When white radicals talk about revolution without destroying the existing American society they are not talking about "real" revolution. What they fail to understand is that you have to destroy the old society in order to create a new one. They fail to understand that the racist ruling class oligarchy stays in power because of its machine. This machine controls all of the institutions of American society. If one is serious about "real" revolution he will realize that American society as it exists must be destroyed. Blood flows in "real" revolution. Millions of Americans' blood will flow — both white and black — in the coming revolution. This description is built on realism not utopianism. It is built on the concept of two different ways of life clashing, essentially two different nations — white America vs. Black America. Our concept of revolution is not designed to frighten off punks, spineless and gutless people. It is important for us to know what "real" revolution means. Once knowing what "real" revolution is we can estimate who will be on our side and who will be against us. To do this we must know what has been the relation between Black America and white America.

The Historical Relationship between White America and Black America

The American white working class has benefited for over one hundred years from the super exploitation of the Afroamerican. The white working class has been those who have led lynch parties and castrations against us. The only time the white working class has ever united with the Black man, (something the ofay left always brags about) is when it could use the black man to attain a higher status in American society. Ever since the African-American was stolen from Africa this has been happening. Whether the movements were successful or not, the African-American never gained from his alliance and still remained an outcast.

During the revolutionary war, the Black man was promised freedom from chattel slavery if he fought on the side of the American patriots. This promise was left unfulfilled. In fact so blatant was the racism of the American patriots that they classified the African-American as 3/8 human to justify their continued enslavement of him in their newly found constitution of the United States of America. The U.S.A. government of the people, for the people and by the people; that is . . . white people. During the civil war the African-American was promised if he fought on the side of the union he would get, "forty acres and a mule." Again the promise was broken. Historians say that there were clashes between the Blacks who seized the land and federal (union) troops after the war. So it goes on and on. The Populist movement "united" with the African-American as small farmer movement but when its bid for power was defeated it turned racist again. The labor movement developed along similar lines and the American communist movement which even promised the African-American a "Negro nation" ended up selling out to the Roosevelt machine.

The present day left promises the Afroamerican everything from racial, economic and political equality (integration) in a socialist America to the right of self-determination ("Negro" nationhood in southern states) and the right to separate (one or more states as a nation). The relationship of unity even in radical ranks has been of an exploitative nature; to use the African in America as a propaganda tool to get its (ofay left) program across. . . .

The Nature of Our Struggle

As the Afroamerican war baby generation attempts to fight for integration (an impossible goal under the racist capitalist system) and becomes frustrated from such, it will begin to repudiate white America's value and lean towards nationalism. By the nature of oppression and struggle they will realize that they must seize, control and maintain state power before achieving *any goal* (integration, separation, migration back to Africa, black nationhood, assimilation, etc). The faster the African-American struggles for assimilation in racist America, the faster he will become discouraged about integration as a goal as counter-revolution (so called white backlash) grows in white America. As the southern Afroamerican pushes for the right to vote, raising the question of self-determination; he will receive more resistance from the southern state apparatus and it will be easier to show him it is to his advantage to seize state power. . . .

The Responsibility and Theoretical Position of the Afroamerican Revolution

The Afroamerican revolutionary being inside the citadel of world imperialism and being the Vanguard against the most highly developed capitalist complex has problems no other revolutionary has had. His position is so strategic that victory means the downfall of the arch enemy of the oppressed (U.S. imperialism) and the beginning of the birth of a new world.

The African-American revolutionary awaits the day when Black humanism will prevail over white decadent materialism; for on that day the oppressed will see the sunrise again, the redeemers will walk the earth, Hiram shall awaken and the meek shall inherit the earth! Up you mighty revolutionaries, you can accomplish what you *will!*

27 Black Women and Liberation

With the formation of groups such as the National Black Feminist Organization in 1972 and the Combahee River Collective in 1976, more and more African American women began to revise their perceptions of both the white-dominated women's liberation movement and the predominantly male Black Power leadership elite. Before long, it became clear that many no longer would tolerate gender-based discrimination, submit to "revolutionary servitude," or remain silent when male activists referred to them as "bitches," "bimbos," or "babymakers for the revolution." Forwarding a gender-specific variation of the movement's gospel of self-definition and empowerment, black feminist activists accused the men of being sexists—of taking instruction in male-female relations from white, bourgeois models. Such behavior, they said, was narcissistic, chauvinistic, and counterrevolutionary. Black women's liberation had to be considered an integral part of the movement for the liberation of all black people.

The first selection, a group interview originally circulated as a four-page press leaflet, is reprinted from the *Movement* (September 1969), by permission. Here, women of the Black Panther Party offer a gender-specific reading of black liberation. In the process, they cite examples of male "backwardness" and chauvinism that, if unaddressed, threatened to compromise the ideal of a "United Front" working for revolutionary change. Firm in the belief that a "black man's manhood is not dependent upon the subordination of black women," they also assert that no organization working to relieve the black woman's "special oppression" should do so outside the context of the national liberation struggle.

The second document is a transcription of an address made by former Black Panther Assata Shakur on 4 July 1973. Known at the time as JoAnne Chesimard, she was awaiting trial on charges that she and other members of a small, closely knit revolutionary band known as the Black Liberation Army had engaged in a series of terrorist acts against police. In 1979, after serving two years of a life sentence, Shakur escaped from the maximum-security unit of New Jersey's Clinton Correctional Institution for Women. After going "underground," she was granted political asylum in Cuba in 1984. Shakur's personal statement reveals that her adopted African name was well chosen. Here, "She Who Struggles" turns the table on her accusers, charging members of the white establishment with numerous crimes against black humanity. The speech is reprinted from Assata Shakur, *Assata: An Autobiography* (Westport, CT: Lawrence Hill, 1987), by permission.

1969　Panther Sisters on Women's Liberation

MOVEMENT: HOW HAS THE POSITION OF WOMEN WITHIN THE BLACK
PANTHER PARTY CHANGED? HOW HAVE THE WOMEN IN THE PARTY DEALT
WITH MALE CHAUVINISM WITHIN THE PARTY?

PANTHER WOMEN: I've only been in the Party about ten months and when
I got in the Party the thing about Pantherettes was squashed, we sort of
grew out of it. Then there's Ericka Huggins. The brothers had to look on
Ericka with a new light because she had been thru a lot of things that some
Brothers hadn't even been thru. The sisters looked up to her and we all
saw what we had to do. The sisters have to pick up guns just like brothers.
There are a lot of things the sisters can do to change society.

We realize that we have a role to play and we're tired of sitting home
and being misused and unless we stand up, male chauvinism will still
show itself and be something that's just passed over. Unless we speak
against it and teach the brothers what's correct and point out what's
wrong, then it'll still be here.

There used to be a difference in the roles (of men and women) in the
party because sisters were relegated to certain duties. This was due to
the backwardness and lack of political perspective on the part of both
sisters and brothers. Like sisters would just naturally do the office-type
jobs, the clerical-type jobs. They were the ones that handled the mailing
list. You know all those things that go into details. They were naturally
given to the sisters and because of this, because the sisters accepted it so
willingly because they had been doing this before, this is the type of
responsibilities they've had before, it was very easy for male chauvinism
to continue on. The only examples we had of sisters taking responsibility
were probably in Kathleen or one or two people who exercised responsibility in other areas of Party work.

We've recognized in the past 4 or 5 months that sisters have to take a
more responsible role. They have to extend their responsibility and it
shouldn't be just to detail work, to things women normally do. This, I
think, has been manifested in the fact that a lot of sisters have been
writing more articles, they're attending more to the political aspects of
the Party, they're speaking out in public more and we've even done
outreach work in the community, extensive outreach work in that we've
taken the initiative to start our own schools—both brothers and sisters

now work in the liberation schools. It's been proven that positions aren't relegated to sex, it depends on your political awareness.

I can remember that when I came into the Party over a year ago at that time David Hilliard was National Headquarters Captain, and there was another sister in the Party who was the National Captain for women and even though most of the people related to David Hilliard as being National HQ Captain, most of the women related to this other sister for directives because she was the National Captain for women. Under her were sergeants and lieutenants who were all sisters and in their ranks were other sisters. There was almost a separation between the brothers and the sisters.

Reorganization

When that was abolished, when there were no longer any separate positions for sisters and brothers, when we all had to relate to the brothers or sisters who were in the specific positions, there wasn't just a reaction on the part of certain brothers cause they didn't like having to relate to certain sisters, who were in leadership positions. There was also a reaction on the part of some sisters, who because they had to relate to some brothers, because they did not have ranks above certain brothers, they wanted to quit the Party. So it wasn't just a matter of brothers being male chauvinistic in not wanting to relate to sisters as leaders over them—but it was also the sisters because of conditioning wanted to continue to submit to other sisters, rather than to leaders of the Party per se, regardless of sex.

And I can see since the time I joined the Party that the Party has undergone radical change in the direction of women leadership and emancipation of women. Even though Ericka Huggins provides us with a very good example, it's not so much Ericka and the realization that Ericka poses a strike example. It's the fact that the political conscious-ness and the political level of members of the Party have risen very much since I joined the Party and because of the fact that we're moving toward a proletarian revolution and because we have come to realize that male chauvinism and all its manifestations are bourgeois and that's one of the things we're fighting against. We realize that in a proletarian revolution, the emancipation of women is primary. We realize that the success of the revolution depends upon the women. For this reason, we know that it's necessary that the women must be emancipated.

Importance of Women's Liberation

MOVEMENT: Could you explain what you mean when you say that the success of the revolution depends on the emancipation of women.

PANTHER WOMEN: It's because of the fact that women are the other half. A revolution cannot be successful simply with the efforts of the men, because a woman plays such an integral role in society even though she is relegated to smaller, seemingly insignificant positions.

I think conditions outside the Party have forced us to realize that we have to get rid of male chauvinism. As Panthers, we cannot separate ourselves and divide ourselves and work as Pantherettes, and on the other hand have brothers work as Panthers and expect to present a United Front against Facism or against the enemy or against outside forces. There has to be unity within the Party. We can't be divided on the basis of sex and we can't be divided on the basis of principles or anything.

Ericka became a good example because the pigs realized she was a revolutionary. Maybe we didn't realize that, in the sense that we thought about it all the time or brought her up as an example of a strong woman. But, I think the pigs realize that and this outside condition has forced us to realize that we can't operate as two halves, separate, apart from each other—we have to be unified.

Vietnamese Women Lead

MOVEMENT: You once said that the Vietnamese women were your example. Could you explain more concretely what that means in terms of the struggle of women in the United States?

PANTHER WOMEN: We feel that the example given us by the Vietnamese women is a prime example of the role women can play in the revolution. The Vietnamese women are out there fighting with their brothers, fighting against American imperialism with its advanced technology. They can shoot. They're out there with their babies on their backs, as the case may be, and they're participating in the revolution wholeheartedly just as the Vietnamese men are participating in the revolution, in the national liberation struggle. The success of their national liberation struggle is just as much dependent upon the women continuing struggle as it is dependent on the Vietnamese men. So there we see in Vietnam where the struggle today is the sharpest in terms of struggling against US imperialism, the women in fact, play the role of the other half—not the weaker half, not the stronger half, but the other half of the Vietnamese men. We hold them up as our example and we hope that the revolutionary women in the U.S. can follow that example and live up to the goal that they have set.

Right now the issue of male chauvinism is rather sharp and kind of out of place. We're starting to talk about it and everybody is sensitive about it—but once women find their place in terms of their roles as revolutionaries and use the example of the Vietnamese women, then I don't think it will be such a sharp issue. I think we'll begin to function and make it very natural for a woman to behave as a revolutionary and not as a subordinate or as a submissive half.

Special Role of Black Women

MOVEMENT: Black women are considered to be the most oppressed group in the US, as blacks and as women. That special oppression gives them a special, even vanguard, role. Do you want to talk about that a little?

PANTHER WOMEN: I think, historically, even at this time, even for women in the Party, to say we want full share and full responsibility is kind of difficult and kind of touchy because of our society. Our men have been sort of castrated, you know. The responsibilities that they rightfully should have had before, were taken away from them—to take away their manhood. We've had to fight all this before. Our men are constantly thinking or saying that maybe if we assume a heavier role, a more responsible role, that this, in turn, will sort of take away their responsibility and it's such a touchy thing, that we have to be very sure that the roles are evenly divided.

It shouldn't have to be one certain role for a man and one certain role for a woman—we're all gonna participate in the struggle and whatever we can do best, we do it, whether it's at a higher level or not. This is very touchy and presents some problems in combatting a specific thing like male chauvinism, because some brothers still have this fear of women dominating the whole political scene. It may not be voiced that often, but I think it's a very real fear, and we're going to have to be sensitive enough to recognize it. We're going to have to be sensitive enough to say that we're going to take more of a share of the poltical arena but, at the same time, we're going to have to keep these things in mind.

I think it's important that within the context of that struggle that black men understand that their manhood is not dependent on keeping their black women subordinate to them because this is what bourgeois ideology has been trying to put into the black man and that's part of the special oppression of black women. Black women as generally a part of the poor people of the US, the working class, are more oppressed, as being black, they're super oppressed, and as being women they are sexually oppressed by men in general and by black men also.

So, in this context we see that black women are especially oppressed in this country and it's very important that black women understand and black men understand that black man's manhood is not dependent upon the subordination of black women, but rather his manhood is, in fact, dependent on his own strength and the strength he also gets from a revolutionary relationship. A relationship is more fruitful when, in fact, the woman is the other half and not the weaker half. They (the men) get more out of the relationship, just as the women.

Unity in Struggle

MOVEMENT: What are your ideas on the strategy for women's liberation in terms of separate women's organizations, the priority of women's liberation in relation to other issues like imperialism and racism?

PANTHER WOMEN: I think it's important that the separate women's liberation groups not all be lumped into one category. Their effectiveness and their value is dependent upon to what extent their work is furthering revolutionary goals in this country. I think that there are all different kinds of organizations in existence now. There are some people who talk about the contradiction among men and women as one of the major contradictions in capitalist society and therefore they take that contradiction (and even if they don't talk about it, some of them put it into practice) and develop it into an antagonistic contradiction, when actually it is a contradiction among the people. It's not a contradiction between enemies.

An example of this is at the UFAF Conference where occasions arose from time to time where women would want to have a caucus and a man would come around and they would get very uptight that a man was there and were practically ready to jump on him, just because he happened to be listening around. I think that's an example of how the women's struggle is taken out of perspective—it is separated from class struggle in this country, it's separated from national liberation struggles and it's given its own category of women against men. Sometimes people say, "It's within a revolutionary context," but in practice, if all their rhetoric and all their practice is anti-men, it is not a revolutionary program and, as a matter of fact, it hinders the revolutionary forces.

The contradiction between men and women is a contradiction that has to be worked out within the revolutionary forces. It is not at all comparable to the class contradictions. It's the class struggle that takes priority. To the extent that women's organizations don't address themselves to the class struggle or to national liberation struggles they are not really furthering the women's liberation movement, because in order for women to be truly emancipated in this country there's going to have to be a socialist revolution. And there's going to have to be ideological struggle for decades and probably for centuries before male chauvinism is overcome. If women don't understand this, they're not going to truly be able to overcome their special oppression.

Roberta is correct and even those women's organizations who do address themselves to the struggles that are at hand, the strategy of having autonomous women's liberation organizations is incorrect because, as Roberta says, it seems as if those organizations look upon women's liberation as a priority when in actuality the struggle towards socialist revolution is a priority. Women can only become emancipated, not through their own efforts as a particular group, but through their participation on an equal plane in the existing organizations which are comprised of men and women who are struggling for the same cause. It's not a separate struggle and women's liberation does not take priority, but in fact is part and parcel of the overall struggle.

Female Chauvinism

Any organization that's being formed for women's liberation, like Rosemary said, has got to take into consideration that they can't operate separately and by themselves. They must also understand the definition of chauvinism. Chauvinism isn't just relegated to the male. Chauvinism is an undying or unreasoning or irrational love for one's sex and if a women's liberation organization gets uptight because a man comes around, that's unreasoning and irrational. It's not being realistic and looking at things as a whole in terms of a man too functioning as a revolutionary and a woman functioning as a revolutionary. If they're not careful, they will go to an extreme and they will become female chauvinists. They will have an undying love for their sex and totally negate revolutionary struggle.

Unfortunately, if we don't be careful, I think that the women's liberation struggle can be coopted by opportunists. It can become just like a style or a fad and the whole revolutionary struggle will be set back because of this. This is one reason why the revolutionary practitioners, because of the repression we're suffering, can't take time out to go off by ourselves to solve some of our backwardness. This would be just another dividing tactic as far as I can see.

Women's Liberation in Practice

I think it's important to recognize the dangers that separate women's groups face immediately, just because they're women's groups and there's a good chance that they're going to get off base in terms of what the primary struggle is. However, I think we have to be very careful in terms of condemning forms that are used in the movement. I think that there is room for special organizing of women. There are positive things that these kinds of groups can do: for example, canneries, special plants where there's primarily women, electronics and this sort of thing in terms of working class organizing, in terms of organizing cooperative nurseries to liberate the energies of women.

But, they are always facing certain dangers in terms of turning in on themselves, in terms of becoming a very petit bourgeois little clique where they just talk about how they have to take care of the kids all the time or become a gripe session. So, I think, while we as Panthers, while we integrate the struggle of the brothers and sisters within the Party, we still will see how these separate women's liberation groups do thru their practice. And that's where our judgment of them will come in.

We have a phrase that says that the only culture worth keeping is a revolutionary culture. Now, our culture dictates that we become revolutionaries. Irregardless of what the brothers say, like Rosemary says, we should function in a position that furthers revolution and revolutionary culture. The women's liberation groups that are separating away from the men (I think Roberta said there is some room for them and we can't vacillate on whether there is or not, we have to judge them on their practice) should take into consideration that we're here to liberate the people and like we said, it's a socialist liberation struggle and we can't operate as halves.

If women's liberation is going to exist, it should exist with the goal in mind to channel the energies they liberate into a united liberation of the men and women together—not as a bourgeois cult, because this has happened many times. They've become extremist organizations of female superiority and have totally forgotten about the people's struggles and oppressed people and have, themselves become oppressors.

Panther Programs

MOVEMENT: Do the Panthers have any specific programs directed at women in the community to get them involved in the struggle?

PANTHER WOMEN: The Black Panther Party does not have any program that is specifically addressed to women per se. There is, on the National Committee to Combat Fascism, a committee on the national steering committee of women. But the primary function of this committee is to channel those women who are proponents of women's liberation into areas of work integrated into the liberation movement.

Even though the Panther Party doesn't have a women's program per se, (I don't know whether we will in the future or not) I think we realize that the best effort is thru practice and that our liberation is gonna come thru the realization on the part of the brothers that they can't practice male chauvinism, but even more important, it comes from a conscious effort on the part of the sisters to educate themselves and not to accept menial positions or relegate themselves to submissive positions. The brothers can be non-chauvinistic as much as they want, but unless the sisters realize that they have to accept an equal position or act as a revolutionary, then this isn't going to do any good. So I think the best criterion for that is practice.

In addition to that—simply because of the fact that we are members of the Black Panther Party and are therefore in the vanguard, does not necessarily mean that we can deem ourselves champions of women's liberation. We believe that male chauvinism must be stomped out, because we have come to realize that it is bourgeois. Bourgeois ideas are those which are perpetuated upon us by the bourgeois class and is something we're fighting against. But because we've come to realize all these things just recently, we're very new at it. So that whether or not we will become champions of women's liberation, whether or not we'll be able to provide the example to lead other organizations towards women's liberation will come thru our practice.

Women's Caucuses

MOVEMENT: What do you think about all women's caucuses inside the organization? Some people say that within movement organizations there's male chauvinism and women must deal with it from a position of power, so they should organize their own caucuses. They also say there's a parallel between women's liberation and black liberation and just like black people had to get themselves together without whites first, so women have to get themselves together without men. Movement organizations have always been dominated by men, the way civil rights organizations used to be dominated by white people.

PANTHER WOMEN: I don't know, that sounds illogical to me because you can't solve the problem apart from the problem. You can't be liberated from male chauvinism if you don't even deal with it—if you run away from it. And I think forming any separate organization with that in mind is negating, or contradicting what you're setting out to do. I think any type of inside organization that deals with women's liberation should take into consideration that women's liberation is important, but what is primary is the People's liberation. If they want a women's club, those have existed for centuries—they should form that, instead of calling themselves revolutionaries.

MOVEMENT: One of the arguments that's been made is that the movement has failed to attract a lot of women because of the chauvinism within the movement and because of the intimidation that's found in a lot of political organizations. We fail to attract the other half because men dominate. Women have to get together to talk about their special problems in order to involve more women in the struggle.

PANTHER WOMEN: I think our judgment of caucuses, just like independent groups, is going to have to depend on whether or not they forward the revolutionary movement in the end. I mean if their purpose for caucusing among themselves is to make a more efficient organization and if they, in fact, are able to do that thru their practice, then Right On. But if they fall into a trap of just getting by themselves and just complaining about the situation and are unable to put forth a positive program, then that form is not viable. Again, their practice is going to have to tell—whether or not they further the revolutionary organization PERIOD.

Role for Advanced Women

Also for a person to use the argument that the struggle does not ATTRACT women to the organization, I think, is coming from a subjective point of view. Because if they understand that it's not a women's or a man's struggle, it's not an attraction for a man or a woman, but we're here for the liberation of oppressed people, irregardless of whether male chauvinism exists, the women would still come into the Party or movement because they agree or are willing to support the revolutionary principles that exist. If they find male chauvinism, they should be willing to fight it on the basis of principle and unity. And to say, "they're not attracted to it"—there's no advertisement for getting rid of oppression. It's an attraction based on principles, not based on some subjective wishes or wants. So I say that women who say that they don't want to come into the struggle because they're not ATTRACTED to the struggle aren't really interested in the first place.

MOVEMENT: No, they say the movement doesn't deal with their special oppression.

PANTHER WOMEN: Well, that may be true, but still, if you're interested in the struggle of oppressed people, you can come into an organization and bring that question in yourself, instead of staying away from it. You can fight on the basis of unity within an organization, not on the basis of, "well, they're not dealing with the women's question and they're not dealing with the special oppression of women, so therefore I'm not going to participate". They're still being subjective.

Well, I think that's one place where women who are already advanced are going to have to take a strong stand. The fact is because of objective conditions in this society women are more backwards, because of their positions in their home, or in school, even working women who are more exposed to what's happening in the world, are still relegated at home and to the family jobs to the children, etc, etc, and their perspective in terms of the world is more limited. So it's very important that women who are more advanced, who already understand revolutionary principles, go to them and explain it to them and struggle with them. We have to recognize that women are backwards politically and we have to struggle with them. And that can be a special role that revolutionary women can play.

From **To My People**

Assata Shakur

Black brothers, Black sisters, i want you to know that i love you and i hope that somewhere in your hearts you have love for me. My name is Assata Shakur (slave name joanne chesimard), and i am a revolutionary. A Black revolutionary. By that i mean that i have declared war on all forces that have raped our women, castrated our men, and kept our babies empty-bellied.

I have declared war on the rich who prosper on our poverty, the politicians who lie to us with smiling faces, and all the mindless, heartless robots who protect them and their property.

I am a Black revolutionary, and, as such, i am a victim of all the wrath, hatred, and slander that amerika is capable of. Like all other Black revolutionaries, amerika is trying to lynch me.

I am a Black revolutionary woman, and because of this i have been charged with and accused of every alleged crime in which a woman was believed to have participated. The alleged crimes in which only men were supposedly involved, i have been accused of planning. They have plastered pictures alleged to be me in post offices, airports, hotels, police cars, subways, banks, television, and newspapers. They have offered over fifty thousand dollars in rewards for my capture and they have issued orders to shoot on sight and shoot to kill.

I am a Black revolutionary, and, by definition, that makes me a part of the Black Liberation Army. The pigs have used their newspapers and TVs to paint the Black Liberation Army as vicious, brutal, mad-dog criminals. They have called us gangsters and gun molls and have compared us to such characters as john dillinger and ma barker. It should be clear, it must be clear to anyone who can think, see, or hear, that we are the victims. The victims and not the criminals.

It should also be clear to us by now who the real criminals are. Nixon and his crime partners have murdered hundreds of Third World brothers and sisters in Vietnam, Cambodia, Mozambique, Angola, and South Africa. As was proved by Watergate, the top law enforcement officials in this country are a lying bunch of criminals. The president, two attorney generals, the head of the fbi, the head of the cia, and half the white house staff have been implicated in the Watergate crimes.

They call us murderers, but we did not murder over two hundred fifty unarmed Black men, women, and children, or wound thousands of others in the riots they provoked during the sixties. The rulers of this country have always considered their property more important than our lives. They call us murderers, but we were not responsible for the twenty-eight brother inmates and nine hostages murdered at attica. They call us murderers, but we did not murder and wound over thirty unarmed Black students at Jackson State—or Southern State, either.

They call us murderers, but we did not murder Martin Luther King, Jr., Emmett Till, Medgar Evers, Malcolm X, George Jackson, Nat Turner, James Chaney, and countless others. We did not murder, by shooting in the back, sixteen-year-old Rita Lloyd, eleven-year-old Rickie Bodden, or ten-year-old Clifford Glover. They call us murderers, but we do not control or enforce a system of racism and oppression that systematically murders Black and Third World people. Although Black people supposedly comprise about fifteen percent of the total amerikkkan population, at least sixty percent of murder victims are Black. For every pig that is killed in the so-called line of duty, there are at least fifty Black people murdered by the police.

Black life expectancy is much lower than white and they do their best to kill us before we are even born. We are burned alive in fire-trap tenements. Our brothers and sisters OD daily from heroin and methadone. Our babies die from lead poisoning. Millions of Black people have died as a result of indecent medical care. This is murder. But they have got the gall to call us murderers.

They call us kidnappers, yet Brother Clark Squires (who is accused, along with me, of murdering a new jersey state trooper) was kidnapped on April 2, 1969, from our Black community and held on one million dollars' ransom in the New York Panther 21 conspiracy case. He was acquitted on May 13, 1971, along with all the others, of 156 counts of conspiracy by a jury that took less than two hours to deliberate. Brother Squires was innocent. Yet he was kidnapped from his community and family. Over two years of his life was stolen, but they call us kidnappers. We did not kidnap the thousands of Brothers and Sisters held captive in amerika's concentration camps. Ninety percent of the prison population in this country are Black and Third World people who can afford neither bail nor lawyers.

They call us thieves and bandits. They say we steal. But it was not we who stole millions of Black people from the continent of Africa. We were robbed of our language, of our Gods, of our culture, of our human dignity, of our labor, and of our lives. They call us thieves, yet it is not we who rip off billions of dollars every year through tax evasions, illegal price fixing, embezzlement, consumer fraud, bribes, kickbacks, and swindles. They call us bandits, yet every time most Black people pick up our paychecks we are being robbed. Every time we walk into a store in our neighborhood we are being held up. And every time we pay our rent the landlord sticks a gun into our ribs.

They call us thieves, but we did not rob and murder millions of Indians by ripping off their homeland, then call ourselves pioneers. They call us bandits, but it is not we who are robbing Africa, Asia, and Latin America of their natural resources and freedom while the people who live there are sick and starving. The rulers of this country and their flunkies have committed some of the most brutal, vicious crimes in history. They are the bandits. They are the murderers. And they should be treated as such. These maniacs are not fit to judge me, Clark, or any other Black person on trial in amerika. Black people should and, inevitably, must determine our destinies.

Every revolution in history has been accomplished by actions, although words are necessary. We must create shields that protect us and spears that penetrate our enemies. Black people must learn how to struggle by struggling. We must learn by our mistakes.

I want to apologize to you, my Black brothers and sisters, for being on the new jersey turnpike. I should have known better. The turnpike is a checkpoint where Black people are stopped, searched, harassed, and assaulted. Revolutionaries must never be in too much of a hurry or make careless decisions. He who runs when the sun is sleeping will stumble many times.

Every time a Black Freedom Fighter is murdered or captured, the pigs try to create the impression that they have quashed the movement, destroyed our forces, and put down the Black Revolution. The pigs also try to give the impression that five or ten guerrillas are responsible for every revolutionary action carried out in amerika. That is nonsense. That is absurd. Black revolutionaries do not drop from the moon. We are created by our conditions. Shaped by our oppression. We are being manufactured in droves in the ghetto streets, places like attica, san quentin, bedford hills, leavenworth, and sing sing. They are turning out thousands of us. Many jobless Black veterans and welfare mothers are joining our ranks. Brothers and sisters from all walks of life, who are tired of suffering passively, make up the BLA.

There is, and always will be, until every Black man, woman, and child is free, a Black Liberation Army. The main function of the Black

Liberation Army at this time is to create good examples, to struggle for Black freedom, and to prepare for the future. We must defend ourselves and let no one disrespect us. We must gain our liberation by any means necessary.

> It is our duty to fight for our freedom.
> It is our duty to win.
> We must love each other and support each other.
> We have nothing to lose but our chains.

PART THREE

*Black Nationalism
and Contemporary Society*

28 Maulana Karenga: "Keeper of the Tradition"

Founder of the West Coast cultural nationalist organization Us in 1965, Maulana Karenga survived the sometimes bloody infighting within the Black Power movement to become one of America's most influential black studies educators. Taking his adopted Swahili name literally, he sought to be a "keeper of the tradition"—working to wean his black brothers and sisters from white cultural forms and the values they reflected. In their place, he would substitute a cultural system that continually generated uplifting, ennobling images. In Karenga's formulation, to return to tradition was the first functional step toward a greater African American future.

A leader in the late 1960s "back to black" movement in clothing and hairstyles, Karenga promoted the teaching of Swahili as a "nontribal" language of self-determination. He developed the *Nguzo Saba,* a set of seven key values by which blacks seeking liberation were to order their lives. He also instituted the celebration of *Kwanzaa* as an alternative to the gross materialism that characterized white America's approach to the Christmas season. Initially observed in Los Angeles from 26 December 1966 to 1 January 1967, this African American holiday of the "first fruits" was derived from the harvesttime festivals of African agriculturalists. Both the *Nguzo Saba* and *Kwanzaa* are constituent components of the ideology and practice of *Kawaida,* the theory of cultural and social change adopted by members of Us.

Today, Karenga chairs the Department of Black Studies at California State University, Long Beach, is executive director of the Kawaida Institute of Pan-African Studies and the African American Cultural Center, Los Angeles, and continues to head Us. In the following selection, he explains the purpose and meaning of the *Nguzo Saba*. The document is excerpted from Maulana Karenga, *The African American Holiday of Kwanzaa: A Celebration of Family, Community and Culture* (Los Angeles: University of Sankore Press, 1988), by permission.

From **The Nguzo Saba (The Seven Principles)**

Their Meaning and Message

Maulana Karenga

In terms of the interest and aspirations of African American people, the Nguzo Saba were developed and offered as an Afrocentric value system which would serve the following basic functions: 1) organize and enrich our relations with each other on the personal and community level; 2) establish standards, commitments and priorities that would tend to enhance our human possibilities as persons and a people; 3) aid in the recovery and reconstruction of lost historical memory and cultural legacy in the development of an Afrocentric paradigm of life and achievement; 4) serve as a contribution to a core system of communitarian ethical values for the moral guidance and instruction of the community, especially for children; and 5) contribute to an ongoing and expanding set of Afrocentric communitarian values which would aid in bringing into being a new man, woman and child who self-consciously participate in the ethical project of starting a new history of African people and humankind. With these observations in mind, we can now turn to the rich meaning and message of the Nguzo Saba themselves, both in the context of Kwanzaa and daily life.

Umoja (Unity)

To strive for and maintain unity in the family, community, nation and race.

This is the First and foundational Principle of the Nguzo Saba, for without it, all the other Principles suffer. Unity is both a principle and practice of togetherness in all things good and of mutual benefit. It is a principled and harmonious togetherness not simply a being together. This is why value-rootedness is so important, even indispensable. Unity as principled and harmonious togetherness is a cardinal virtue of both classical and general African societies. In ancient Egypt, harmony was a cardinal virtue of Maat, i.e., righteousness, rightness. In fact, one of the ways to translate Maat is to define it as harmony—harmony on the natural, cosmic and social level. Likewise, cieng among the Dinka, means both morality and harmonious living together. Thus in both ancient Egyptian and Dinka society, one cannot live a moral life without living in harmony with other members of the community.

If unity is in essence a Principle, it is no less a practice as are all the other Principles. For practice is central to African ethics and all claims to ethical living and commitment to moral principles are tested and proved or disproved in relations with others. Relations, then, are the hinge on which morality turns, the ground on which it rises or falls . . . Character development is not simply to create a good person abstracted from community, but rather a person in positive interaction, a person whose quality of relations with others is defined first of all by a *principled* and *harmonious* togetherness i.e., a real and practiced unity.

Another way of discussing unity is to see it as active solidarity. This essentially means a firm dependable togetherness that is born, based and sustained in action. It is usually applied to groups, organizations, classes, peoples and expresses itself as building and acting together in mutual benefit. The key here is again practice. In the end practice proves everything. No matter how many books one reads on swimming, sooner or later s/he must get into the water and swim. This may be called, on this level, the priority of practice. Finally, unity means a oneness, a similarity and sameness that gives us an identity as a people, an African people. And inherent in this identity as a people is the ethical and political imperative to self-consciously unite in order to define, defend and develop our interests.

Unity as principle and practice begins in the family but presupposes value-orientation of each member. Adults and children must respect and approach unity as a moral principle of family and community not simply a political slogan. As principle and practice, this means principled and harmonious living with brothers and sisters, mothers and fathers—sharing and acting in unison. It means avoidance of conflict and quick, willing and principled resolution when it occurs . . . The family must reject harshness and practice gentleness, stress cooperation and avoid conflict, and be very attentive to things that would divide or create differences negative to togetherness.

Especially important is the unity of the father and mother, for they are the models for the children and the foundation for the family in every sense of the word. Here the African concept of complementarity of male and female as distinct from and opposed to the concept of conflict of the genders is instructive and of value. As Anna J. Cooper, educator and social theorist, taught "there is a feminine as well as masculine side to truth (and) these are related not as inferior and superior, not as better or worse, not as weaker or stronger, but as comple-ments—complements in one necessary and symmetric whole." The rec-ognition of this truth and responding creatively to it is necessary, she says, to give balance to the individual, and to save the nation from its extremes. It also is a shield against sexism, i.e., the social practice of using gender to establish and/or justify exploitation, oppression or un-equal relations. . . .

Finally the family must be, as in African culture, the focal point of unity not simply of siblings and of genders, but also of generations. One of the most important expressions of family unity is the respect and collective concern and care for the elders. Respect for elders . . . is a cardinal article of the code of behavior of African society. One who does not respect his/her elders is seen as immoral and uncultured. Elders are respected, like the ancestors they will become, for their long life of service to the community, for their achievement, for providing an ethical model and for the richness of their experience and the wisdom this has produced. Thus, elders are seen as judges and reconcilers. It is they who hear cases of conflict and problems and offer solutions. One of the most important aspects of African respect for elders is that it makes them useful and active in the community, unlike the worst of European society which deprives them of meaningful roles and places them to the side, leaving them with only failing memories.

Also, the active participation and involvement of elders in the daily life of the family not only benefits them but the younger people. For it teaches them to understand and appreciate the process of growing old, gives them access to seasoned knowledge and experience and helps prevent the so-called generation gap so evident and advertised in Euro-pean society. Key to this linking of young and old is the concept of lineage which links all the living, the departed and the yet unborn. This is translated in practice into the extended family and the protocol, ritual, reciprocity and remembrance this involves and requires. Early in life continental African children are taught to memorize and recite their family tree as far back as any ancestor is known. This keeps historical memory alive and reaffirms respect for those living and departed who contributed to their coming into being and cultural molding.

Now, if one starts with the family when discussing unity, the commu-nity becomes of necessity the next level of the concern and practice of unity. The family, as it is written, is the smallest example of how the nation (or national community) works. For the relations, values and practice one has in the family are a reflection and evidence of what one will find in the community. Likewise, the strengths and/or weaknesses of the family are those of the community. Unity in the community, then, begins in the family but it extends to organizational affiliation and then the unity of organizations, i.e., African American united fronts. Malcolm X taught that community unity first depended on everyone's belonging to an organization, then all organizations uniting on the basis of common interests and aspirations. He posed community unity—in its two-level form—as morally compelling. It was for him irresponsible and self-destructive not to unite around common interests and instead glory in differences. What African Americans needed to do, he taught, is to forget their superficial organizational differences and even differences of religion and unite around their common identity as Africans, and their common interests, especially the interests of liberation.

Unity of the nation is unity of the national community as distinct from the local community. The above applies in equal measure to the national community. In terms of "racial" unity, when one says race, one means the world African community. Thus, when Garvey says "Up you mighty race; you can accomplish what you will," he is talking to the world African community. The form of unity this takes is Pan-Africanism, i.e., the struggle to unite all Africans everywhere around the common interests and make African cultural and political presence on the world stage both powerful and permanent. Pan-Africanism requires and urges that we see ourselves and act in history as an African people, belonging to a world community of African peoples. In this way, we self-consciously share in both the glory and burden of our history. And in that knowledge and context act to honor, preserve and expand that history in the struggle for liberation and ever higher levels of human life.

Kujichagulia (Self-Determination)

To define ourselves, name ourselves, create for ourselves and speak for ourselves instead of being defined, named, created for and spoken for by others.

The Second Principle of the Nguzo Saba is self-determination. This too expresses itself as both commitment and practice. It demands that we as an African people define, defend and develop ourselves instead of allowing or encouraging others to do this. It requires that we recover lost memory and once again shape our world in our own image and interest. And it is a call to recover and speak our own special truth to the world and raise images above the earth that reflect our capacity for human greatness and progress. . . .

To answer the question of "Who am I?" correctly, then, is to know and live one's history and practice one's culture. To answer the question of "Am I really who I am?" is to have and employ cultural criteria of authenticity, i.e., criteria of what is real and unreal, what is appearance and essence, what is culturally-rooted and foreign. And to answer the question of "Am I all I ought to be?" is to self-consciously possess and use ethical and cultural standards which measure men, women and children in terms of the quality of their thought and practice in the context of who they are and must become—in both an African and human sense.

The principle and practice of self-determination carries within them the assumption that we have both the right and responsibility to exist as a people and make our own unique contribution to the forward flow of human history. This principle shelters the assumption that as fathers and mothers of humanity and human civilization in the Nile Valley, we have no business playing the cultural children of the world. So it reminds us of the fact that African people created and introduced the basic disciplines of human knowledge—science, technology, geometry, math, medicine, ethics, advanced architecture, etc. And it urges us as a people not to surrender our historical and cultural identity to fit into the culture of another. Openness to exchange is a given, but it presupposes that one has kept enough of one's culture to engage in exchange, rather than slavishly follow another's lead . . . .

Ujima (Collective Work and Responsibility)

To build and maintain our community together and make our sister's and brother's problems our problems and to solve them together.

The Third Principle is Ujima (Collective Work and Responsibility) which is a commitment to active and informed togetherness on matters of common interest. It is also recognition and respect of the fact that without collective work and struggle, progress is impossible and liberation unthinkable. Moreover, the principle of Ujima supports the fundamental assumption that African is not just an identity, but also a destiny and duty, i.e., a responsibility. In other words, our collective identity in the long run is a collective future. Thus, there is a need and obligation for us as self-conscious and committed people to shape our future with our own minds and hands and share its hardships and benefits together.

Ujima, as principle and practice, also means that we accept the fact that we are collectively responsible for our failures and setbacks as well as our victories and achievements. And this holds true not only on the national level, but also on the level of family and organization or smaller units. Such a commitment implies and encourages a vigorous capacity for self-criticism and self-correction which is indispensable to our strength, defense and development as a people.

The principle of collective work and responsibility also points to the fact that African freedom is indivisible. It shelters the assumption that as long as any African anywhere is oppressed, exploited, enslaved or wounded in any way in her or his humanity, all African people are. It thus, rejects the possibility or desirability of individual freedom in any unfree context; instead it poses the need for struggle to create a context in which all can be free. Moreover, Ujima rejects escapist and abstract humanism and supports the humanism that begins with commitment to and concern for the humans among whom we live and to whom we owe our existence, i.e., our own people. In a word, real humanism begins with accepting one's own humanity in the particular form in which it expresses itself and then initiating and sustaining exchanges with others in the context of our common humanity. It also posits that the liberation struggle to rescue and reconstruct African history and humanity is a significant contribution to overall struggle for human liberation.

In the context of a communitarian social order, cooperation is another key aspect of Ujima. It is based on the assumption that what one does to benefit others is at the same time a benefit to him/her. Likewise, "one who injures others in the end injures him/herself" as the Yoruba proverb states. In the Lovedu community in South Africa, children are taught not to be aggressive or competitive but to be cooperative and share responsibility. Even their language reflects the cooperative thrust. For even when no one has just been given something, the child says when asking for something, "give me also." Likewise, their prayer is never just for themselves but for all's health, blessing, prosperity. In fact, to ask for the personal without at the same time asking for the collective is both improper and immoral.

The lesson of the Lovedu is that harmonious living, as with the Dinka, is of paramount importance. Thus, being quarrelsome or contentious is one of the worst offenses. And striving for uncoerced or free and willing agreement is the model of behavior. Reconciliation of conflict is patient and never coercive, and always done keeping the person in mind. And the fundamental objective in conflict is not to mechanically apply the rule but to reconcile the people. For they believe that "if people do not agree, there can be no relationship." And if they have to be coerced, there cannot be genuine agreement. In such a context collective work and responsibility is facilitated and sustained.

Finally, collective work and responsibility can be seen in terms of the challenge of culture and history. Work—both personal and collective—is truly at the center of history and culture. It is the fundamental activity by which we create ourselves, define and develop ourselves and confirm ourselves in the process as both persons and a people. And it is the way we create culture and make history. It is for this reason, among others, that the Holocaust of Enslavement was so devastating. For not only did it destroy tens of millions of lives, which is morally monstrous in itself, but it also destroyed great cultural achievements, created technological and cultural arrest and thus eroded and limited the human possibility Africa offered the world. In fact, the effects of this Holocaust are present even today both in terms of the problems of the Continent and those of the Diaspora.

The challenge of history and culture then is through collective work and responsibility, to restore that which was damaged or destroyed and to raise up and reconstruct that which was in ruins as the ancient Egyptians taught. It is also to remember we are each cultural representatives of our people and have no right to misrepresent them or willfully do less than is demanded of us by our history and current situation as a community-in-struggle. We must accept and live the principle of shared or collective work and responsibility in all things good, right and beneficial to the community.

Ujamaa (Cooperative Economics)

To build and maintain our own stores, shops and other businesses and to profit from them together.

The Fourth Principle is Ujamaa (Cooperative Economics) and is essentially a commitment to the practice of shared social wealth and the work necessary to achieve it. It grows out of the fundamental communal concept that social wealth belongs to the masses of people who created it and that no one should have such an unequal amount of wealth that it gives him/her the capacity to impose unequal, exploitative or oppressive relations on others. Sharing wealth is another form of communitarian exchange, i.e., sharing and cooperating in general. But it is essential because without the principle and practice of shared wealth, the social conditions for exploitation, oppression and inequality as well as deprivation and suffering are increased. . . .

Ujamaa also stresses self-reliance in the building, strengthening and controlling of the economics of our own community. President [Julius] Nyerere [of Tanzania] has said self-reliance in Ujamaa means "first and foremost . . . that for our development we have to depend upon ourselves and our own resources." The assumption here is that we must seize and maintain the initiative in all that is ours, and that we must harness our resources and put them to the best possible use in the service of the community. This, he says, does not mean denying all assistance from or work with others but of controlling policy and shouldering the essential responsibility for our own future.

Closely related to this concept of self-reliance and the responsibility it requires is the respect for the dignity and obligation of work. To respect work is to appreciate its value, reject its exploitation and engage in it cooperatively for the common good of the community. Also, inherent in Ujamaa is the stress and obligation of generosity especially to the poor and vulnerable. . . .

. . . In fact, throughout the sacred teachings of ancient Egypt in particular and Africa in general, the ethic of care and responsibility is expressed in the concept of shared social wealth and service to the most disadvantaged. This, of course, finds its modern philosophical expression in our social thought and struggles, as a people, around and for social justice. And this struggle is not simply to be generous to the poor and vulnerable but ultimately to end their poverty and vulnerability, so that they too can live a decent, undeprived and meaningful life. For only in such a context will they be able to pursue the truly human without the limitation imposed by poverty, deprivation or the debilitating struggle for just life's basic necessities. To share wealth and work, then, is to share concern, care and responsibility for a new, more human and fulfilling future.

Nia (Purpose)

To make our collective vocation the building and developing of our community in order to restore our people to their traditional greatness.

The Fifth Principle of the Nguzo Saba is Nia (Purpose) which is essentially a commitment to the collective vocation of building, developing and defending our national community, its culture and history in order to regain our historical initiative and greatness as a people. The assumption here is that our role in human history has been and remains a key one, that we as an African people share in the great human legacy Africa has given the world. That legacy is one of having not only been the fathers and mothers of humanity, but also the fathers and mothers of human civilization, i.e., having introduced in the Nile Valley civilizations the basic disciplines of human knowledge. It is this identity which gives us an overriding cultural purpose and suggests a direction. This is what we mean when we say we who are the fathers and mothers of human civilization have no business playing the cultural children of the world. The principle of Nia then makes us conscious of our purpose in light of our historical and cultural identity. . . .

. . . We are both *heirs* and *custodians* of a great legacy. This means first that we must not simply receive the legacy as a formal historical and cultural transmission, but recognize and respect its importance. Secondly, it means that far from being simple heirs we are also custodians. And this implies an even greater obligation.

To inherit is to receive as legacy, place adequate value on and make a part of one's life. But to be a custodian of a great legacy is to guard, preserve, expand and promote it. It is to honor it by building on and expanding it and in turn, leaving it as an enriched legacy for future generations. . . . It is a call for us to see ourselves not as simple ghetto dwellers or newly arrived captives of the suburbs, but more definitively as a world historical people who have made and must continue to make a significant contribution to the forward flow of human history. . . .

Finally, Nia suggests that personal and social purpose are not only non-antagonistic but complementary in the true communitarian sense of the word. In fact, it suggests that the highest form of personal purpose is in the final analysis, social purpose, i.e., personal purpose that translates itself into a vocation and commitment which involves and benefits the community. As we have noted elsewhere, such level and quality of purpose not only benefits the collective whole, but also gives fullness and meaning to a person's life in a way individualistic and isolated pursuits cannot. . . .

. . . For again our purpose is not to simply create money makers, but to cultivate men and women capable of social and human exchange on a larger more meaningful scale, men and women of culture and social conscience, of vision and values which expand the human project of freedom and development rather than diminish and deform it.

Kuumba (Creativity)

To do always as much as we can, in the way we can, in order to leave our community more beautiful and beneficial than we inherited it.

The Sixth Principle is Kuumba (Creativity) and logically follows from and is required by the Principle of Nia. It is a commitment to being creative within the context of the national community vocation of restoring our people to their traditional greatness and thus leaving our community more beneficial and beautiful then we, i.e., each generation, inherited it. The Principle has both a social and spiritual dimension and is deeply rooted both in social and sacred teachings of African societies.

Nowhere is this principle more clearly expressed than in the literature and culture of ancient Egypt. Creativity here is both an original act or imitation of the Creator and a restorative act also reflective of the Creator constantly pushing back the currents of chaos and decay and revitalizing and restoring the natural, spiritual and cosmic energy of the world. In ancient Egypt, there was a spiritual and ethical commitment and obligation to constantly renew and restore the great works, the legacy of the ancestors, and the creative energy of the leader and nation. This was considered doing Maat, i.e., reaffirming and restoring truth, justice and righteousness, harmony, balance, order, rightness, etc. Each pharaoh saw his or her reign, then, as one of restoration of Maat, i.e., the reaffirmation, reestablishment and renewal of the Good, the Beautiful and the Right. . . .

It is interesting to note here that my creation of Kwanzaa falls within the restorative conception of creativity. For when I say I created Kwanzaa, the term "created" does not imply or mean "made out of nothing", for it is clearly not the case as the above discussion on the Continental African origins of Kwanzaa shows. What one has, then, is rather a *creative restoration* in the African spirit of cultural restoration and renewal in both the ancient Egyptian and African American sense of the practice as used in the 1960's.

It is, in fact, a restoring that which was in ruins or disuse in many parts of Africa, and especially among Africans in America and attempting to make it more beautiful and beneficial than it was before as the Principle of Kuumba (Creativity) requires. This . . . contains the interrelated principles of *restoration* and *progressive perfection*. To restore is what we called in the 60's "to rescue and reconstruct". Progressive perfection is a Kawaida concept that assumes an *ability* and *obliga-*

tion to strive always to leave what one inherits (legacy, community, etc.) more beautiful and beneficial than it was before. It is again, in this context and spirit of the cultural project of recovering and reconstructing African first fruit celebrations that Kwanzaa was conceived and constructed.

The stress, then, is on leaving a legacy which builds on and enriches the legacy before you. It is again stress on generational responsibility. Kwanzaa reminds us of the ancient Egyptian teaching that if we wish to live for eternity we must build for eternity, i.e., do great works or serve the community in a real, sustained and meaningful way. . . .

. . . The lesson here is that creativity is central to the human spirit and human society, that it causes us to grow, restores and revitalizes us and the community and insures our life for eternity. . . .

Imani (Faith)

To believe with all our heart in our people, our parents, our teachers, our leaders and the righteousness and victory of our struggle.

The Seventh Principle is Faith which is essentially a profound belief in and commitment to all that is of value to us as a family, community, people and culture. In the context of African spirituality, it begins with a belief in the Creator and in the positiveness of the creation and logically leads to a belief in the essential goodness and possibility of the human personality. For in all African spiritual traditions, from Egypt on, it is taught that we are in the image of the Creator and thus capable of ultimate righteousness and creativity through self-mastery and development in the context of positive support. Therefore, faith in ourselves is key here, faith in our capacity as humans to live righteously, self-correct, support, care for and be responsible for each other and eventually create the just and good society. . . .

. . . Also, . . . faith in the masses of our people is central to our progress as a people. . . . As a community-in-struggle there is no substitute for belief in our people, in their capacity to take control of their destiny and daily lives and shape them in their own image and interests. This is fundamental to any future we dare design and pursue.

Especially we must believe in the value and validity, the righteousness and significance of our struggle for liberation and a higher level of human life. This must be tied to our belief in our capacity to assume and carry out with dignity and decisiveness the role [Frantz] Fanon and history has assigned us. And that role is to set in motion a new history of humankind and in the company of other oppressed and Third World peoples pose a new paradigm of human society and human relations. Fanon says we can do anything as long as we don't do two basic things: 1) try to catch up with Europe (after all where is it going—swinging between spiritual and nuclear annihilation); and 2) imitate them so that we become "obscene caricatures" of them. We must, he says, invent, innovate, reach inside ourselves and dare "set afoot a new man and woman." The world and our people are waiting for something new, more beautiful and beneficial from us than what a past of oppression has offered us. Let us not imitate or be taught by our oppressors. Let us dare struggle, free ourselves politically and culturally and raise images above the earth that reflect our capacity for human progress and greatness. This is the challenge and burden of our history which assumes and requires a solid faith.

We must, then, have faith in ourselves, in our leaders, teachers, parents and in the righteousness and victory of our struggle, faith that through hard work, long struggle and a whole lot of love and understanding, we can again step back on the stage of human history as a free, proud and productive people. It is in this context that we can surely speak our own special truth to the world and make our own unique contribution to the forward flow of human history.

29   Afrocentricity

As black studies educators struggled to legitimize and institutionalize their programs, the marketplace of ideas became a highly competitive arena for the testing and development of model curricula. One of the most widely adopted approaches to black studies education at all levels was the Afrocentric model. Developed, promoted, and theoretically refined by Temple University professor Molefi Kete Asante, Afrocentricity posits the necessity of shifting the pedagogical spotlight away from its traditional focus on Euro-American achievements, allowing it to shine full force on the lives and accomplishments of black people. It is held that such a newly "centered" curriculum reorients alienated African American students by validating feelings of individual and group self-worth, promoting cultural awareness, and inculcating homegrown, humanistic values. Critics contend that Afrocentricity takes a "cheerleader" approach to the study of the black experience, that it "tribalizes" the educational process, and that its focus on ancient African peoples and civilizations does little to improve the life chances of today's students. The following selection makes the case for the Afrocentric idea as an essential "stepping-stone" to the development of modern, nonhierarchical, multicultural curricula. It is reprinted from the *Journal of Negro Education* (spring 1991), by permission.

1991 *From* The Afrocentric Idea in Education

Molefi Kete Asante

Introduction

Many of the principles that govern the development of the Afrocentric idea in education were first established by Carter G. Woodson in *The Mis-education of the Negro* (1933). Indeed, Woodson's classic reveals the fundamental problems pertaining to the education of the African person in America. As Woodson contends, African Americans have been educated away from their own culture and traditions and attached to the fringes of European culture; thus dislocated from themselves, Woodson asserts that African Americans often valorize European culture to the detriment of their own heritage. Although Woodson does not advocate rejection of American citizenship or nationality, he believed that assuming African Americans hold the same position as European Americans vis-à-vis the realities of America would lead to the psychological and cultural death of the African American population. Furthermore, if education is ever to be substantive and meaningful within the context of American society, Woodson argues, it must first address the African's historical experiences, both in Africa and America. That is why he places on education, and particularly on the traditionally African American colleges, the burden of teaching the African American to be responsive to the long traditions and history of Africa as well as America. Woodson's alert recognition, more than 50 years ago, that something is severely wrong with the way African Americans are educated provides the principal impetus for the Afrocentric approach to American education . . .

Definitions

. . . In education, *centricity* refers to a perspective that involves locating students within the context of their own cultural references so that they can relate socially and psychologically to other cultural perspectives. Centricity is a concept that can be applied to any culture. The centrist paradigm is supported by research showing that the most productive method of teaching any student is to place his or her group within the center of the context of knowledge. For White students in America this is easy because almost all the experiences discussed in American classrooms are approached from the standpoint of White perspectives and history. American education, however, is not centric; it is Eurocentric. Consequently, non-White students are also made to see themselves and their groups as the "acted upon." Only rarely do they read or hear of non-White people as active participants in history. This is as true for a discussion of the American Revolution as it is for a discussion of Dante's *Inferno;* for instance, most classroom discussions of the European slave trade concentrate on the activities of Whites rather than on the resistance efforts of Africans. A person educated in a truly centric fashion comes to view all groups' contributions as significant and useful. Even a White person educated in such a system does not assume superiority based upon racist notions. Thus, a truly centric education is different from a Eurocentric, racist (that is, White supremacist) education.

Afrocentricity is a frame of reference wherein phenomena are viewed from the perspective of the African person. The Afrocentric approach seeks in every situation the appropriate centrality of the African person. In education this means that teachers provide students the opportunity to study the world and its people, concepts, and history from an African world view. In most classrooms, whatever the subject, Whites are located in the center perspective position. How alien the African American child must feel, how like an outsider! The little African American child who sits in a classroom and is taught to accept as heroes and heroines individuals who defamed African people is being actively de-centered, dislocated, and made into a nonperson, one whose aim in life might be to one day shed that "badge of inferiority": his or her Blackness. In Afrocentric educational settings, however, teachers do not marginalize African American children by causing them to question their own self-worth because their people's story is seldom told. By seeing themselves as the subjects rather than the objects of education—be the discipline biology, medicine, literature, or social studies—African American students come to see themselves not merely as seekers of knowledge but as integral participants in it. Because all content areas are adaptable to an Afrocentric approach, African American students can be made to see themselves as centered in the reality of any discipline.

It must be emphasized that Afrocentricity is *not* a Black version of Eurocentricity. Eurocentricity is based on White supremacist notions whose purposes are to protect White privilege and advantage in education, economics, politics, and so forth. Unlike Eurocentricity, Afrocentricity does not condone ethnocentric valorization at the expense of degrading other groups' perspectives. Moreover, Eurocentricity presents the particular historical reality of Europeans as the sum total of the human experience. It imposes Eurocentric realities as "universal"; i.e., that which is White is presented as applying to the human condition in general, while that which is non-White is viewed as group-specific and therefore not "human." This explains why some scholars and artists of African descent rush to deny their Blackness; they believe that to exist as a Black person is not to exist as a universal human being. They are the individuals Woodson identified as preferring European art, language, and culture over African art, language, and culture; they believe that anything of European origin is inherently better than anything produced by or issuing from their own people. Naturally, the person of African descent should be centered in his or her historical experiences as an African, but Eurocentric curricula produce such aberrations of perspective among persons of color.

Multiculturalism in education is a nonhierarchical approach that respects and celebrates a variety of cultural perspectives on world phenomena. The multicultural approach holds that although European culture is the majority culture in the United States, that is not sufficient reason for it to be imposed on diverse student populations as "universal." Multiculturalists assert that education, to have integrity, must begin with the proposition that all humans have contributed to world development and the flow of knowledge and information, and that most human achievements are the result of mutually interactive, international effort. Without a multicultural education, students remain essentially ignorant of the contributions of a major portion of the world's people. A multicultural education is thus a fundamental necessity for anyone who wishes to achieve competency in almost any subject.

The Afrocentric idea must be the stepping-stone from which the multicultural idea is launched. A truly authentic multicultural education, therefore, must be based upon the Afrocentric initiative. If this step is skipped, multicultural curricula, as they are increasingly being defined by White "resisters" . . . will evolve without any substantive infusion of African American content, and the African American child will continue to be lost in the Eurocentric framework of education. In other words, the African American child will neither be confirmed nor affirmed in his or her own cultural information. For the mutual benefit of all Americans, this tragedy, which leads to the psychological and cultural dislocation of African American children, can and should be avoided. . . .

The Condition of Eurocentric Education

Institutions such as schools are conditioned by the character of the nation in which they are developed. Just as crime and politics are different in different nations, so, too, is education. In the United States a "Whites-only" orientation has predominated in education. This has had a profound impact on the quality of education for children of all races and ethnic groups. The African American child has suffered disproportionately, but White children are also the victims of monoculturally diseased curricula.

The Tragedy of Ignorance

During the past five years many White students and parents have approached me after presentations with tears in their eyes or expressing their anger about the absence of information about African Americans in the schools. A recent comment from a young White man at a major university in the Northeast was especially striking. As he said to me: "My teacher told us that Martin Luther King was a commie and went on with the class." Because this student's teacher made no effort to discuss King's ideas, the student maliciously had been kept ignorant. The vast majority of White Americans are likewise ignorant about the bountiful reservoirs of African and African American history, culture, and contributions. For example, few Americans of any color have heard the names of Cheikh Anta Diop, Anna Julia Cooper, C. L. R. James, or J. A. Rogers. All were historians who contributed greatly to our understanding of the African world. Indeed, very few teachers have ever taken a course in African American Studies; therefore, most are unable to provide systematic information about African Americans. . . .

Correcting Distorted Information

Hegemonic education can exist only so long as true and accurate information is withheld. Hegemonic Eurocentric education can exist only so long as Whites maintain that Africans and other non-Whites have never contributed to world civilization. It is largely upon such false ideas that invidious distinctions are made. The truth, however, gives one insight into the real reasons behind human actions, whether one chooses to follow the paths of others or not. For example, one cannot remain comfortable teaching that art and philosophy originated in Greece if one learns that the Greeks themselves taught that the study of these subjects originated in Africa, specifically ancient Kemet. The first philosophers were the Egyptians Kagemni, Khun-anup, Ptahhotep, Kete, and Seti; but Eurocentric education is so disjointed that students have no way of discovering this and other knowledge of the organic relationship of Africa to the rest of human history. Not only did Africa contribute to human history, African civilizations predate all other civilizations. Indeed, the human species originated on the continent of Africa—this is true whether one looks at either archaeological or biological evidence.

Two other notions must be refuted. There are those who say that African American history should begin with the arrival of Africans as slaves in 1619, but it has been shown that Africans visited and inhabited North and South America long before European settlers "discovered" the "New World." Secondly, although America became something of a home for those Africans who survived the horrors of the Middle Passage, their experiences on the slave ships and during slavery resulted in their having an entirely different (and often tainted) perspective about America from that of the Europeans and others who came, for the most part, of their own free will seeking opportunities not available to them in their native lands. Afrocentricity therefore seeks to recognize this divergence in perspective and create centeredness for African American students.

Conclusion

The reigning initiative for total curricular change is the movement that is being proposed and led by Africans, namely, the Afrocentric idea. When I wrote the first book on Afrocentricity, now in its fifth printing, I had no idea that in 10 years the idea would both shake up and shape discussions in education, art, fashion, and politics. Since the publication of my subsequent works, *The Afrocentric Idea* and *Kemet, Afrocentricity, and Knowledge,* the debate has been joined in earnest. Still, for many White Americans (and some African Americans) the most unsettling aspect of the discussion about Afrocentricity is that its intellectual source lies in the research and writings of African American scholars. Whites are accustomed to being in charge of the major ideas circulating in the American academy. . . .

Afrocentricity provides all Americans an opportunity to examine the perspective of the African person in this society and the world. The resisters claim that Afrocentricity is anti-White; yet, if Afrocentricity as a theory is against anything it is against racism, ignorance, and monoethnic hegemony in the curriculum. Afrocentricity is not anti-White; it is, however, pro-human. Further, the aim of the Afrocentric curriculum is not to divide America, it is to make America flourish as it ought to flourish. This nation has long been divided with regard to the educational opportunities afforded to children. By virtue of the protection provided by society and reinforced by the Eurocentric curriculum, the White child is already ahead of the African American child by first grade. Our efforts thus must concentrate on giving the African American child greater opportunities for learning at the kindergarten level. However, the kind of assistance the African American child needs is as much cultural as it is academic. If the proper cultural information is provided, the academic performance will surely follow suit.

When it comes to educating African American children, the American educational system does not need a tune-up, it needs an overhaul. Black children have been maligned by this system. Black teachers have been maligned. Black history has been maligned. Africa has been maligned. Nonetheless, two truisms can be stated about education in America. First, some teachers *can and do* effectively teach African American children; secondly, if some teachers can do it, others can, too. We must learn all we can about what makes these teachers' attitudes and approaches successful, and then work diligently to see that their successes are replicated on a broad scale. By raising the same questions that Woodson posed more than 50 years ago, Afrocentric education, along with a significant reorientation of the American educational enterprise, seeks to respond to the African person's psychological and cultural dislocation. By providing philosophical and theoretical guidelines and criteria that are centered in an African perception of reality and by placing the African American child in his or her proper historical context and setting, Afrocentricity may be just the "escape hatch" African Americans so desperately need to facilitate academic success and "steal away" from the cycle of miseducation and dislocation.

30 Melanin and the Dynamics of Genetic Survival

For the past quarter century, psychiatrist Frances Cress Welsing has stirred debate over her theories about the link between whites' "genetic color inferiority" and their attempts to dominate and oppress peoples more richly endowed with the ability to produce skin-darkening melanin. In Welsing's conceptualization, the underlying purpose of white supremacy is to prevent white genetic annihilation in a world where (in terms of skin coloration) nonwhites are genetically dominant. This, she holds, helps explain both the historical course of international politics and the current urban drug epidemic. Inevitably, the "white genetic survival imperative" leads to a program of genocide directed, most visibly, at African American males. In "The Neurochemical Basis for Evil," written in 1988, Welsing discusses the "observable differences in behavior" that can be attributed to the relative presence or absence of melanin. The article is reprinted from *The Isis (Yssis) Papers: The Keys to the Colors* (Chicago: Third World Press, 1991), by permission.

1988   The Neurochemical Basis for Evil

Frances Cress Welsing

The American philosopher William James has stated, "There is no doubt that healthy mindedness is inadequate as a philosophical doctrine, because the evil facts which it positively refuses to account for are a genuine portion of reality, and they may after all be the best key to life's significance, and possibly the only openers of our eyes to the deepest level of truth."

The Kabbalah, which literally means "tradition," is the sum of Jewish mysticism, the tradition of things divine. The Book Bahir, an 1180 A.D. document on the Kabbalah concerning Satan, states,

> It teaches that there is in God a principle that is called 'Evil', and it lies in the north of God, of it is written [Jer. I:14]: 'Out of the north the evil shall break forth upon all the inhabitants of the land,' that is to say, all evil that comes upon all the inhabitants of the land breaks forth out of the north. And what principle is this? It is the form of the hand [one of the seven holy forms which represent God as the original man], and it has many messengers, and all are named 'Evil', . . . And it is they that fling the world into guilt for the *tobu* is in the north, and the *tobu* means precisely the evil that confuses men until they sin, and it is the source of all man's evil impulses.

In early Egyptian (African) tradition, evil was associated with Set, the brother of Osiris ("Lord of the perfect black"). Set eventually killed his brother Osiris and dismembered his body, which his sister/wife (Isis) helped restore to life. Osiris was the great Egyptian God figure. Set is considered the white brother.

In contrast, the early Christian religion and the Bible related evil to the *fallen* angel Lucifer, a word that means light and that can be construed to mean white. However, in the Middle Ages, for some Europeans, the devil took on an appearance of a Black man with a long phallus, which has been modified as the present red colored figure with a long *tail* and a long *fork*.

In keeping with each of the above perspectives of evil, *Webster's Dictionary* defines "evil" as: "1. morally bad or wrong; wicked, depraved, 2. causing pain or trouble; harmful; injurious, 3. threatening or bringing misfortune; unlucky; disastrous; unfortunate; as an evil hour, 4. resulting from or based on conduct regarded as immoral; as an evil reputation."

The Cress Theory of Color Confrontation and Racism (White Supremacy), links whites' unjust behavior towards people of color (black, brown, red and yellow) to whites' inability to produce melanin skin pigment in the skin melanocyte. The whites' numerical minority status in the world and, ultimately, their fear of global white genetic annihilation by the genetically dominant, skin melanin producing, non-white world majority are pointed out as additional reasons for white aggression towards people of color. This thesis helps to explain the evil "kill or be killed" behaviors of the global white collective in relation to non-white people.

In 1972, I presented a paper entitled, *Melanin: The Neurochemical Basis for Soul,* at the annual meeting of the National Medical Association Section on Neurology and Psychiatry. I theorized that the presence of melanin in high concentrations in Blacks accounted for some of the observable differences in behavior between Black and white people (i.e., religious responsiveness, rhythm, emotional responsiveness, sensitivity levels), noting the familiar saying amongst older Black people, "The blacker the berry, the sweeter the juice; if it ain't got no soul, it ain't got no use." Also, I emphasized the song by James Brown, "We Got More Soul." Further, I pointed out that the most sensitive body areas are the areas most highly pigmented.

Fifteen years ago in a paper entitled, "Blacks, Hypertension and the Active Skin Melanocyte" (*Journal of Urban Health,* 1975), I posited melanin, among other things, as a possible neurotransmitter and the skin melanocytes as the foundation of the sixth sense—the basis for knowledge of the unseen, including a deeper knowledge of "bad." I explained that if the melanocytes were sense receptors and melanin was a neurotransmitter, then the darker the skin, the higher the levels of hypertensions found. Primarily, this is true because people with darker skins are more sensitive to the energy currents around them. If those energy currents are stressful, they will be more stressed, increasing *levels* of hypertension.In 1987, at the first Melanin Conference, I discussed The Cress Theory on the George Washington Carver Phenomenon, suggesting that the skin melanocytes of this very Black-skinned scientist (high level concentration of melanin skin pigment) enabled him to communicate with the energy frequencies emanating from plants. Thus, he was able to learn their secrets and purposes.

Since my 1972 presentation on the neurochemical basis for soul, the neurochemical basis of evil has periodically come to my mind, begging that I outline my thoughts on evil as the anti-thesis of soul. I relate soul to order, spirituality and the affirmation of life. I equate evil with chaos and destruction, especially the destruction of life. (The word *evil* when spelled backward is, *live*.) The discussion of evil takes on even more significant proportions in light of the increasing number of persons in this society who openly are proclaiming themselves to be worshippers of the Devil—Devil being the arch doer of evil—in contrast to worshipping God. Reportedly, these persons participate in the ritual murder of human beings.

The concept of evil is not at all unusual in religious and philosophical discourse. Also, evil has been a frequent subject for literary exploration. (The novel *Moby Dick* by Herman Melville is an example of the symbolic discussion of evil in classical American literature.) Evil is approached less often in the natural sciences, including modern medicine. However, psychiatry is the one branch of modern medicine that has major antecedents in both religion and philosophy and thus, the topic of evil has found discussants who consider themselves scientists and scientific.

The role of the psychiatric-physician or physician-scientist is to attempt to comprehend, bringing greater clarity and insight, the total spectrum of human behavior, which would include the special category of behavioral phenomena recognized as evil. Further, I believe that the challenge of modern psychiatry, like the challenge of modern physics, is to approach, if possible, a view of the "unified field."

Modern physics, since Albert Einstein, has sought to unite the spectrum of forces—gravity, electromagnetism, weak and strong forces—in a unified field, viewing these separate forces as outgrowths from or manifestations of a whole (a unified force field). Likewise, modern psychiatry should seek to discover if there is a united behavioral force field that can explain evil as well as other dominant behavioral phenomena.

For the ant, the greatest evil consists of killing ants. For the human being, the greatest evil consists of the obsessional degrading and killing of other human beings. All lesser evils are simply added to this (i.e., destruction of other life forms, destruction of the planet and destruction that extends beyond planet Earth). With evil so defined, clearly there is an overwhelming atmosphere of evil in the world. In fact, the entire planet exists in an atmosphere of degradation and murder. To ignore this evidence of evil, this obsession with mass killing and death, is only to participate in the establishment and the maintenance of its reality— in effect, to participate in evil. On the other hand, to address this obsession with mass death and the degradation of human life in hopes of countering it is to affirm the dignity of human beings and the universe.

Ernest Becker, in his book *Escape From Evil*, had the following to say about evil: "All organisms want to perpetuate themselves, continue to experience and to live. . . . For all organisms, then, opposing and obliterating power is evil—it threatens to stop experience." He continues, "So we see that as an organism man is fated to perpetuate himself and as a conscious organism he is fated to identify evil as the threat to that perpetuation. And what then would be the highest development and use of those [man's] talents? To contribute to the struggle against evil."

However, before there can be effective struggle against evil, the following questions must be answered: 1) What are the dynamic conditions in a society or culture that would stimulate such activity as announced as devil worship? 2) What are the dynamics in a society and culture wherein increasing numbers of Black males are being killed daily/yearly at epidemic levels? 3) What are the exact causation dynamics in a society and culture wherein the greatest percentage of its resources are used in the development and production of instruments of death and destruction? 4) What are the exact dynamic conditions in a power system or culture wherein 50 million people can be destroyed in the course of slave trade, as on the continent of Africa? 5) What are the exact dynamic conditions in a power system or culture wherein six million Semites of the Jewish religion can be destroyed deliberately or 20 million people killed in the course of a war, such as in the Soviet Union during World War II? 6) What are the dynamics in a society and culture in which hundreds of thousands, possibly millions, are doomed to die of infection with a virus that increasing numbers are concluding was deliberately man-made?

These are questions that the psychiatrist should be motivated to answer in the context of understanding the issue of evil, especially when it is recalled, as stated by Thomas Merton in his *Raids on the Unspeakable* that,

One of the most disturbing facts that came out in the [Adolph] Eichman trial was that a psychiatrist examined him and pronounced him *perfectly sane*. We equate sanity with a sense of justice, with humaneness, with prudence, with the capacity to love and understand other people. We rely on the sane people of the world to preserve it from barbarism, madness, destruction. And now it begins to dawn on us that it is precisely that sane ones who are the most dangerous. It is the sane one, the well adapted one, who can without qualms and without nausea aim the missiles and press the buttons that will initiate the great festival of destruction that they, the sane ones, have prepared.

Psychiatrist M. Scott Peck, in his nationwide best selling book, *People of the Lie, The Hope for Healing Human Evil,* contends, "Science has also steered clear of the problem of evil because of the immensity of the mystery involved. . . . we do not yet have a body of scientific knowledge of human evil deserving of being called a psychology." He also states,

> Those of us who are Caucasians seem to have fewer compunctions about killing blacks or Indians or Orientals than we do in killing our fellow white men. It is easier for a white man to lynch a 'nigger' than a 'redneck'. . . . The matter of the racial aspects of intraspecies killing is yet another one deserving significant scientific investigation.

He concludes, "War today is at least as much a matter of national pride as of racial pride."

Even though Peck suggests that science has steered clear of the subject of evil because of the "immense mystery involved," Herman Melville, the 19th century novelist, perhaps subconsciously, went directly to the subject of evil. He approached "evil" through the symbolism of the white whale, Moby Dick, and the crippled white ship captain who pursued him, Ahab (who is often compared to Satan). Melville uses an entire chapter of his book to discourse on "The Whiteness of the Whale." He begins,

> What the White whale was to Ahab, has been hinted; what, at times, he was to me, as yet remains unsaid. Aside from those more obvious considerations touching Moby Dick, which could not but occasionally awaken in any man's soul some alarm, there was another thought, or rather vague, nameless horror concerning him, which at times by its intensity completely overpowered all the rest; and yet so mystical and well nigh ineffable was it, that I almost despair of putting it in a comprehensible form. It was the whiteness of the whale that above all things appalled me. But how can I hope to explain myself here; and yet, in some dim, random way, explain myself I must, else all these chapters might be naught.

Melville proceeds to detail many positive associations with whiteness: "and though this pre-eminence in it [whiteness] applies to the human race itself, giving the white man ideal mastership over every dusky tribe." He continues,

> . . . yet for all these accumulated associations, with whatever is sweet, and honorable, and sublime, there yet lurks an elusive something in the innermost idea of this hue, which strikes more of panic to the soul than that redness which affrights in blood. . . . That ghastly whiteness it is which imparts such an abhorrent mildness even more loathsome than terrific, to the dumb gloat-

ing of their aspect. So that not the fierce-fanged tiger in his heraldic coat can so stagger courage as the white-shrouded bear or shark.

Further on, Melville contemplates,

What is it that in the Albino man so peculiarly repels and often shocks the eye, as that sometimes he is loathed by his own kith and kin! It is that whiteness which invests him, a thing expressed by the name he bears. The Albino is as well made as other men—has no substantive deformity—and yet this mere aspect of all-pervading whiteness makes him more strangely hideous than the ugliest abortion. Why should this be so?

Again referring to whiteness, Melville writes, ". . . it is at once the most meaning symbol of spiritual things, nay, the very veil of the Christian's deity; and yet should be as it is, the intensifying agent in things the most appalling to mankind."

Melville's Captain Ahab sees the white whale as all evil of which he is in pursuit. In a letter to Nathaniel Hawthorne, Melville referred to *Moby Dick* as a "wicked book." My own interpretation of the symbolism in this novel, which has been regarded as the greatest of all American novels, is that the crippled white Captain Ahab represents the mutant (global) white population, afflicted with albinism (whiteness). The white whale is symbolic of racism (white supremacy), the major pursuit of the global white collective—the evil destructive goal of the global white collective. This furious, evil pursuit in *Moby Dick* ends in a disaster for all: a deadly end in which the white ship captain and all of his crew, whites and non-whites alike, are destroyed. Yet, one survived to tell the tale, foretelling the end of white supremacy as a specified power dynamic.

It is not surprising that this novel containing the symbolism of albinism and white supremacy was written prior to the great bloody conflict (The American Civil War) that had so much to do with the relationships between white (albino) and Black people. This conflict ended the power of the slaveholders as well as the formal enslavement of Black people by whites.

Melville's linkage of evil and dread with the condition of albinism parallels my own thesis that the absence of the neuropeptide melanin— the absence of this black pigment in the skin and other aspects of the nervous system—critically impairs the depth sensitivity of the nervous system and the ability to tune in to the total spectrum of energy frequencies in the universe. This deficiency of sensory awareness sets the stage for the absence of harmony (the chaos and destruction), which is evil.

Thus, the injustice and evil of white supremacy not only has its foundation in the numerical minority status of the global white population and its genetically recessive status in terms of melanin pigment production, but the very absence of melanin in the nervous system in significant degrees (decreasing sensory input and thus sensitivity) is an additional contributing factor in the problem of white supremacist injustice. White supremacy is the greatest known evil on Earth. Likewise, racism (white supremacy) is the unified force field that encompasses all of the lesser evils we now recognize. Indeed, if the absence of melanin obstructs the nervous system's ability to tune in to the total spectrum of frequencies in the universe, rendering those lacking melanin incapable of acting in harmony with those frequencies, then it becomes incumbent upon those possessing melanin to counteract the evil.

31 Black Theology and "The Dream of Freedom"

A major contributor to the late 1960s debate over the validity and relevance of conceptualizing Black Power as an expression of the Christian gospel, Union Theological Seminary professor James H. Cone published *Black Theology and Black Power* at the height of the furor over James Forman's "Black Manifesto." Forwarding an essentially classical interpretation of the faith, but one that took the African American experience seriously, Cone's conclusion that Black Power and black religion were inseparable—that both sought to free the oppressed from white racism—was widely influential. His concept of a nationalistic black theology, developed more fully in later works, provided many activist clergy with scholarly ammunition for use against those who could find nothing in the Afro-American historical experience that would justify a "blackenization" of traditional Christian beliefs. Refusing to lose the "particular" in the "universal," Cone taught that a black theology was equally a Christian theology precisely *because* it has "the black predicament" as its point of departure.

"Black Theology and the Black Church" originally was prepared for presentation to the Black Theology Project of the Theology in the Americas Conference (1977). It is reprinted from *Black Theology: A Documentary History, 1966–1979,* ed. Gayraud S. Wilmore and James H. Cone (Maryknoll, NY: Orbis, 1979), by permission. Here, after revisiting the debates of the 1960s, Cone describes subsequent efforts to develop a black religious "frame of reference"—a "radical and creative" black theology that is "not afraid of truth from any quarter." In addition to actively supporting Afro-America's historical quest to actualize the "dream of freedom," such a belief system also should, he says, speak to the needs of other oppressed peoples and nations. By endowing black religious expression with a global vision, he refutes claims that a race-specific theology necessarily promotes selfishness and sectarianism.

1977 Black Theology and the Black Church

Where Do We Go from Here?

James H. Cone

Since the appearance of black theology in the late 1960's, much has been
written and said about the political involvement of the black church in
black people's historical struggle for justice in North America. Black
theologians and preachers have rejected the white church's attempt to
separate love from justice and religion from politics because we are
proud descendants of a black religious tradition that has always interpreted its confession of faith according to the people's commitment to the
struggle for earthly freedom. Instead of turning to Reinhold Niebuhr
and John Bennett for ethical guidance in those troubled times, we
searched our past for insight, strength and the courage to speak and do
the truth in an extreme situation of oppression. Richard Allen, James
Varick, Harriet Tubman, Sojourner Truth, Henry McNeal Turner and
Martin Luther King, Jr. became household names as we attempted to
create new theological categories that would express our historical fight
for justice. . . .

. . . The cry of Black Power by Willie Ricks and its political and
intellectual development by Stokely Carmichael and others challenged
the black church to move beyond the models of love defined in the
context of white religion and theology. The black church was thus faced
with a theological dilemma: either reject Black Power as a contradiction
of Christian love (and thereby join the white church in its condemnation
of Black Power advocates as un-American and unchristian), or accept
Black Power as a socio-political expression of the truth of the gospel.
These two possibilities were the only genuine alternatives before us, and
we had to decide on whose side we would take our stand.

We knew that to define Black Power as the opposite of the Christian
faith was to reject the central role that the black church has played in
black people's historical struggle for freedom. Rejecting Black Power
also meant that the black church would ignore its political responsibility
to empower black people in their present struggle to make our children's
future more humane than intended by the rulers in this society. Faced
with these unavoidable consequences, it was not possible for any self-
respecting church-person to desecrate the memories of our mothers and
fathers in the faith by siding with white people who murdered and

imprisoned black people simply because of our persistent audacity to assert our freedom. To side with white theologians and preachers who questioned the theological legitimacy of Black Power would have been similar to siding with St. George Methodist Church against Richard Allen and the Bethelites in their struggle for independence during the late 18th and early 19th centuries. We knew that we could not do that, and no amount of white theological reasoning would be allowed to blur our vision of the truth.

But to accept the second alternative and thereby locate Black Power in the Christian context was not easy. First, the acceptance of Black Power would appear to separate us from Martin Luther King, Jr., and we did not want to do that. King was our model, having creatively combined religion and politics, and black preachers and theologians respected his courage to concretize the political consequences of his confession of faith. Thus we hesitated to endorse the "Black Power" movement, since it was created in the context of the James Meredith March by Carmichael and others in order to express their dissatisfaction with King's continued emphasis on non-violence and Christian love. As a result of this sharp confrontation between Carmichael and King, black theologians and preachers felt themselves caught in a terrible predicament of wanting to express their continued respect for and solidarity with King, but disagreeing with his rejection of Black Power.

Secondly, the concept of Black Power presented a problem for black theologians and preachers not only because of our loyalty to Martin Luther King, but also because many of us had been trained in white seminaries and had internalized much of white people's definition of Christianity. While the rise and growth of independent black churches suggested that black people had a different perception of the gospel than whites, yet there was no formal theological tradition to which we could turn in order to justify our definition of Black Power as an expression of the Christian gospel. Our intellectual ideas of God, Jesus, and the Church were derived from white European theologians and their textbooks. When we speak of Christianity in theological categories, using such terms as revelation, incarnation and reconciliation, we naturally turn to people like Barth, Tillich and Bultmann for guidance and direction. But these Europeans did not shape their ideas in the social context of white racism and thus could not help us out of our dilemma. But if we intended to fight on a theological and intellectual level as a way of empowering our historical and political struggle for justice, we had to create a new theological movement, one that was derived from and thus accountable to our people's fight for justice. To accept Black Power as Christian required that we thrust ourselves into our history in order to search for new ways to think and be black in this world. We felt the need to explain ourselves and to be understood from our own vantage point and not from the perspective and experiences of whites. When white liberals questioned this approach to theology, our response was very similar to the bluesman in Mississippi when told he was not singing his song correctly: "Look-a-heah, man, dis yere *mah song*, en I'll sing it howsoevah I pleases."

Thus we sang our Black Power songs, knowing that the white church establishment would not smile upon our endeavors to define Christianity independently of their own definitions of the gospel. For the power of definition is a prerogative that oppressors never want to give up. Furthermore, to *say* that love is compatible with Black Power is one thing, but to demonstrate this compatibility in theology and the praxis of life is another. If the reality of a thing was no more than its verbalization in a written document, the black church since 1966 would be a model of the creative integration of theology and life, faith and the struggle for justice. But we know that the meaning of reality is found *only* in its historical embodiment in people as structured in societal arrangements. Love's meaning is not found in sermons or theological textbooks but rather in the creation of social structures that are not dehumanizing and oppressive. This insight impressed itself on our religious consciousness, and we were deeply troubled by the inadequacy of our historical obedience when measured by our faith claims. From 1966 to the present, black theologians and preachers, both in the church and on the streets, have been searching for new ways to confess and to live our faith in God so that the black church would not make religion the opiate of our people.

The term "Black Theology" was created in this social and religious context. It was initially understood as the theological arm of Black Power, and it enabled us to express our theological imagination in the struggle of freedom independently of white theologians. It was the one term that white ministers and theologians did not like, because, like Black Power in politics, black theology located the theological starting point in the black experience and not the particularity of the western theological tradition. We did not feel ourselves accountable to Aquinas, Luther or Calvin but to David Walker. Daniel Payne and W. E. B. Du Bois. The depth and passion in which we express our solidarity with the black experience over against the western tradition led some black scholars in religion to reject theology itself as alien to the black culture. Others, while not rejecting theology entirely, contended that black theologians should turn primarily to African religions and philosophy in order to develop a black theology consistent with and accountable to our historical roots. But all of us agreed that we were living at the beginning of a new historical moment, and this required the development of a *black* frame of reference that many called "black theology."

The consequence of our affirmation of a black theology led to the creation of black caucuses in white churches, a permanent ecumenical church body under the title of the National Conference of Black Churchmen, and the endorsement of James Forman's "Black Manifesto." In June 1969 at the Interdenominational Theological Center in Atlanta and under the aegis of NCBC's Theological Commission, a group of black theologians met to write a policy statement on black theology. This statement, influenced by my book, *Black Theology and Black Power,* which had appeared two months earlier, defined black theology as a "theology of black liberation."

Black theology, then, was not created in a vacuum and neither was it simply the intellectual enterprise of black professional theologians. Like our sermons and songs, black theology was born in the context of the black community as black people were attempting to make sense out of their struggle for freedom. In one sense, black theology is as old as when the first African refused to accept slavery as consistent with religion and as recent as when a black person intuitively recognizes that the confession of the Christian faith receives its meaning only in relation to political justice. Although black theology may be considered to have formally appeared only when the first book was published on it in 1969, informally, the reality that made the book possible was already present in the black experience and was found in our songs, prayers, and sermons. In these outpourings are expressed the black visions of truth, pre-eminently the certainty that we were created not for slavery but for freedom. Without this dream of freedom, so vividly expressed in the life, teachings, and death of Jesus, Malcolm, and Martin, there would be no black theology, and we would have no reason to be assembled in this place. We have come here today to plan our future and to map out our strategy because we have a dream that has not been realized.

To be sure, we have talked and written about this dream. Indeed, every Sunday morning black people gather in our churches, to find out where we are in relation to the actualization of our dream. The black church community really believes that where there is no vision the people perish. If people have no dreams they will accept the world as it is and will not seek to change it. To dream is to know what "is ain't suppose to be." No one in our time expressed this eschatological note more clearly than Martin Luther King, Jr. In his "March on Washington" address in 1963 he said: "I have a dream that one day my four children will live in a nation where they will not be judged by the color of their skin but by the content of their character." And the night before his death in 1968, he reiterated his eschatological vision: "I may not get there with you, but I want you to know tonight that we as a people will get to the promised land."

What visions do we have for the people in 1977? Do we still believe with Martin King that "we as a people will get to the promised land"? If so, how will we get there? Will we get there simply by preaching sermons and singing songs about it? What is the black church doing in order to actualize the dreams that it talks about? These are hard questions, and they are not intended as a put-down of the black church. I was born in the black church in Bearden, Arkansas, and began my ministry in that church at the early age of sixteen. Everything I am as well as what I know that I ought to be was shaped in the context of the black church. Indeed, it is because I love the church that I am required, as one of its theologians and preachers, to ask: "When do the black church's actions deny its faith? What are the activities in our churches that should not only be rejected as unchristian but also exposed as demonic? What are the evils in our church and community that we should commit ourselves to destroy?" Bishops, pastors, and church executives do not like to disclose the wrong-doings of their respective denominations. They are like doctors, lawyers, and other professionals who seem bound to keep silent, because to speak the truth is to guarantee one's exclusion from the inner dynamics of power in the profession. But I contend that the *faith* of the black church lays a claim upon all church people that transcends the social mores of a given profession. Therefore, to cover-up and to minimize the sins of the church is to guarantee its destruction as a community of faith, committed to the liberation of the oppressed. If we want the black church to live beyond our brief histories and thus to serve as the "Old Ship of Zion" that will carry the people home to freedom, then we had better examine the direction in which the ship is going. Who is the Captain of the Ship, and what are his economic and political interests? This question should not only be applied to bishops, but to pastors and theologians, deacons and stewards. Unless we are willing to apply the most severe scientific analysis to our church communities in terms of economics and politics and are willing to confess and repent of our sins in the struggle for liberation, then the black church, as we talk about it, will remain a relic of history and nothing more. God will have to raise up new instruments of freedom so that his faithfulness to liberate the poor and weak can be realized in history. We must not forget that God's Spirit will use us as her instrument only insofar as we remain agents of liberation by using our resources for the empowerment of the poor and weak. But if we, like Israel in the Old Testament, forget about our Exodus experience and the political responsibility it lays upon us to be the historical embodiment of freedom, then, again like Israel, we will become objects of God's judgment. It is very easy for us to expose the demonic and oppressive character of the white church, and I have done my share of that. But such exposure of the sins of the white church, without applying the same criticism to ourselves, is hypocritical and serves as a camouflage of our own shortcomings and sins. Either we mean what we say about liberation or we do not. If we mean it, the time has come for an inventory in terms of the authenticity of our faith as defined by the historical commitment of the black denominational churches toward liberation.

I have lectured and preached about the black church's involvement in our liberation struggle all over North America. I have told the stories of Richard Allen and James Varick, Adam Clayton Powell and Martin Luther King. I have talked about the double-meaning in the Spirituals, the passion of the sermon and prayer, the ecstasy of the shout and conversion experience in terms of an eschatological happening in the lives of people, empowering them to fight for earthly freedom. Black theology, I have contended, is a theology of liberation, because it has emerged out of and is accountable to a black church that has always been involved in our historical fight for justice. When black preachers and laypeople hear this message, they respond enthusiastically and with a sense of pride that they belong to a radical and creative tradition. But when I speak to young blacks in colleges and universities, most are surprised that such a radical black church tradition really exists. After hearing about David Walker's "Appeal" in 1829, Henry H. Garnet's "Address to the Slaves" in 1843, and Henry M. Turner's affirmation that "God is a Negro" in 1898, these young blacks are shocked. Invariably they ask, "Whatever happened to the black churches of today?" "Why don't we have the same radical spirit in our preachers and churches?" Young blacks contend that the black churches of today, with very few exceptions, are not involved in liberation but primarily concerned about how much money they raise for a new church building or the preacher's anniversary.

This critique of the black church is not limited to the young college students. Many black people view the church as a hindrance to black liberation, because black preachers and church members appear to be more concerned about their own institutional survival than the freedom of poor people in their communities. "Historically," many radical blacks say, "the black church *was* involved in the struggle but today it is not." They often turn the question back upon me, saying: "All right, granted what you say about the historical black church, but *where* is an institutional black church denomination that still embodies the vision that brought it into existence? Are you saying that the present day AME Church or AME Zion Church has the same historical commitment for justice that it had under the leadership of Allen and Payne or Rush and Varick?" Sensing that they have a point difficult to refute, these radicals then say that it is not only impossible to find a black church denomination committed to black liberation but also difficult to find a local congregation that defines its ministry in terms of the needs of the oppressed and their liberation.

Whatever we might think about the unfairness of this severe indictment, we would be foolish to ignore it. For connected with this black critique is our international image. In the African context, not to mention Asia and Latin America, the black church experiences a similar credibility problem. There is little in our theological expressions and church practice that rejects American capitalism or recognizes its oppressive character in Third World countries. The time has come for us to move beyond institutional survival in a capitalistic and racist society and begin to take more seriously our dreams about a new heaven and a new earth. Does this dream include capitalism or is it a radically new way of life more consistent with African socialism as expressed in the *Arusha Declaration* in Tanzania?

Black theologians and church people must now move beyond a mere reaction to white racism in America and begin to extend our vision of a new socially constructed humanity for the whole inhabited world. We must be concerned with the quality of human life not only in the ghettos of American cities but also in Africa, Asia and Latin America. Since humanity is one, and cannot be isolated into racial and national groups, there will be no freedom for anyone until there is freedom for all. This means that we must enlarge our vision by connecting it with that of other oppressed peoples so that together all the victims of the world might take charge of their history for the creation of a new humanity. As Frantz Fanon taught us: if we wish to live up to our people's expectations, we must look beyond European and American capitalism. Indeed, "we must invent and we must make discoveries.... For Europe, for ourselves and for humanity, we must turn over a new leaf, we must work out new concepts, and try to set afoot a new [humanity]."

New times require new concepts and methods. To dream is not enough. We must come down from the mountain top and experience the hurts and pain of the people in the valley. Our dreams need to be socially analyzed, for without scientific analysis they will vanish into the night. Furthermore, social analysis will test the nature of our commitment to the dreams we preach and sing about. This is one of the important principles we learned from Martin King and many black preachers who worked with him. Real substantial change in societal structures requires scientific analysis. King's commitment to social analysis not only characterized his involvement in the civil rights movement but also led him to take a radical stand against the war in Vietnam. Through scientific analysis, King saw the connection between the oppression of blacks in North America and the United States involvement in Vietnam. It is to his credit that he never allowed a pietistic faith in the other world to become a substitute for good judgment in this world. He not only preached sermons about the promised land but concretized his vision with a political attempt to actualize his hope.

I realize, with Merleau-Ponty, that "one does not become a revolutionary through science but through indignation." Every revolution needs its Rosa Parks. This point has often been overlooked by Marxists and other sociologists who seem to think that all answers are found in scientific analysis. Mao Tse-tung responded to such an attitude with this comment: "There are people who think that Marxism is a kind of magic truth with which one can cure any disease. We should tell them that dogmas are more useless than cow dung. Dung can be used as fertilizer."

But these comments do not disprove the truth of the Marxists' social analysis which focuses on economics and class and is intended as empowerment for the oppressed to radically change human social arrangements. Such an analysis will help us to understand the relation between economics and oppression not only in North America but throughout the world. Liberation is not a process limited to black-white relations in the United States; it is also something to be applied to the relations between rich and poor nations. If we are an African people, as some of the names of our churches suggest, in what way are we to understand the political meaning of that identity? In what way does the economic investment of our church resources reflect our commitment to Africa and other oppressed people in the world? For if an economic analysis of our material resources does not reveal our commitment to the process of liberation, how can we claim that the black church and its theology are concerned about the freedom of oppressed peoples? As an Argentine peasant poet said:

> They say that God cares for the poor
> Well this may be true or not,
> But I know for a fact
> That he dines with the mine-owner.

Because the Christian church has supported the capitalists, many Marxists contend that "all revolutions have clashed with Christianity because *historically* Christianity has been structurally counter-revolutionary." We may rightly question this assertion and appeal to the revolutionary expressions of Christianity in the black religious tradition, from Nat Turner to Martin Luther King. My concern, however, is not to debate the fine points of what constitutes revolution, but to open up the reality of the black church experience and its revolutionary potential to a world context. This means that we can learn from people in Africa, Asia and Latin America, and they can learn from us. Learning from others involves listening to creative criticism; to exclude such criticism is to isolate ourselves from world politics, and this exclusion makes our faith nothing but a reflection of our economic interests. If Jesus Christ is more than a religious expression of our economic and sexist interests, then there is no reason to resist the truth of the Marxist and feminist analyses.

I contend that black theology is not afraid of truth from any quarter. We simply reject the attempt of others to tell us what truth is without our participation in its definition. That is why dogmatic Marxists seldom succeed in the black community, especially when the dogma is filtered through a brand of white racism not unlike that of the capitalists. If our long history of struggle has taught us anything, it is that if we are to be free, we black people will have to do it. Freedom is not a gift but is a risk that must be taken. No one can tell us what liberation is and how we ought to struggle for it, as if liberation can be found in words. Liberation is a process to be located and understood only in an oppressed community struggling for freedom. If there are people in and outside our community who want to talk to us about this liberation process in global terms and from Marxist and other perspectives, we should be ready to talk. But *only* if they are prepared to listen to us and we to them will genuine dialog take place. For I will not listen to anybody who refuses to take racism seriously, especially when they themselves have not been victims of it. And they should listen to us *only* if we are prepared to listen to them in terms of the particularity of oppression in their historical context.

Therefore, I reject dogmatic Marxism that reduces every contradiction to class analysis and thus ignores racism as a legitimate point of departure in the process of liberation. There are racist Marxists as there are racist capitalists, and we must struggle against both. But we must be careful not to reject the Marxist's social analysis simply because we do not like the vessels that the message comes in. If we do that, then it is hard to explain how we can remain Christians in view of the white vessels in which the gospel was first introduced to black people.

The world is small. Both politically and economically, our freedom is connected with the struggles of oppressed peoples throughout the world. This is the truth of Pan-Africanism as represented in the life and thought of W. E. B. Du Bois, George Padmore, and C. L. R. James. Liberation knows no color bar; the very nature of the gospel is universalism, i.e., a liberation that embraces the whole of humanity.

The need for a global perspective, which takes seriously the struggles of oppressed peoples in other parts of the world, has already been recognized in black theology, and small beginnings have been made with conferences on African and black theologies in Tanzania, New York, and Ghana. Another example of the recognition of this need is reflected in the dialogue between black theology in South Africa and North America. From the very beginning black theology has been influenced by a world perspective as defined by Henry M. Turner, Marcus Garvey, and the Pan-Africanism inaugurated in the life and work of W. E. B. Du Bois. The importance of this Pan-African perspective in black religion and theology has been cogently defended in Gayraud Wilmore's *Black Religion and Black Radicalism*. Our active involvement in the "Theology in the Americas," under whose aegis this conference is held, is an attempt to enlarge our perspective in relation to Africa, Asia, and Latin America as well as to express our solidarity with other oppressed minorities in the United States.

This global perspective in black theology enlarges our vision regarding the process of liberation. What does black theology have to say about the fact that two-thirds of humanity is poor and that this poverty arises from the exploitation of the poor nations by rich nations? The people of the United States compose 6 percent of the world's population, but we consume 40 percent of the world resources. What, then, is the implication of the black demand for justice in the United States when related to justice for all the world's victims? The dependent status we experience in relation to white people, Third World countries experience in relation to the United States? Thus, in our attempt to liberate ourselves from white people in North America, it is important to be sensitive to the complexity of the world situation and the oppressive role of the United States in it. African, Latin American, and Asian theologians, as well as sociologists and political scientists can aid us in the analysis of this complexity. In this analysis, our starting point in terms of racism is not negated but enhanced when connected with imperialism and sexism.

We must create a global vision of human liberation and include in it the distinctive contribution of the black experience. We have been struggling for nearly four hundred years! What has that experience taught us that would be useful in the creation of a new historical future for all oppressed peoples? And what can others teach us from their historical experience in the struggle for justice? This is the issue that black theology needs to address. "Theology in the Americas" provides a framework in which to address it. I hope that we will not back off from this important task but face it with courage, knowing that the future of humanity is in the hands of oppressed peoples, because God has said: "Those that hope in me shall not be put to shame" (Isa. 49:23).

32 Louis Farrakhan and the Nation of Islam

After Elijah Muhammad succumbed to congestive heart failure at the age of seventy-seven in 1975, his son and successor, Wallace D. (Warith Deen) Muhammad, began to implement major changes in the Nation of Islam. Before long, members could salute the American flag, serve in the U.S. armed forces, and engage in electoral politics. Pronouncing the Koran—not his father's doctrines—the group's supreme authority, the new leader closed the theological gap between the Nation and orthodox Islam. Even bolder directives changed the organization's name (to World Community of Al-Islam in the West/American Muslim Mission), scrapped the goal of a separate black state, and opened places of worship to the faithful of all races.

Late in 1977, minister Louis Farrakhan announced his disagreement with these changes and left to form a competing organization grounded in the teachings of Elijah Muhammad. Resurrecting the Nation of Islam designation, the former national spokesman and head of Temple No. 7 in Harlem made clear his belief in the continuing need for a race-specific theology and a self-defining, separatist approach to economic and social relations. A powerful articulator of African American dissatisfaction with the status quo, the sixty-two-year-old Farrakhan became the nation's best-known contemporary proponent of black nationalism after successfully organizing the "Million Man March" on Washington, DC in 1995.

Here, in a speech delivered at Washington's John F. Kennedy Center in 1985, the Muslim leader discusses the Nation of Islam's People Organized and Working for Economic Rebirth (P.O.W.E.R.) program in the context of America's troubled racial history. Noting the inability of African Americans to effect the establishment of a separate nation-state, he urges his listeners to "come out of Egypt" and create a "new world order" by (1) developing "an autonomy of mind and spirit"; (2) increasing their economic productivity; and (3) redirecting group purchasing power. The selection is reprinted from *Back Where We Belong: Selected Speeches by Minister Louis Farrakhan,* ed. Joseph D. Eure and Richard M. Jerome (Philadelphia: PC International Press, 1989), by permission.

1985 *From* P.O.W.E.R. at Last and Forever

Louis Farrakhan

Historical Solutions Offered for Racial Problems

There have been many solutions that have been offered to the problems that exist between black and white people. *George Washington the first president of the United States, "feared that blacks would become a most troublesome species of property before too many years had passed over our heads." Thomas Jefferson believed, "that there were indelible lines in nature that forbade us from getting along in terms of social equality." And Abraham Lincoln believed, "that as long as we were present in America we could never hope for social equality, and that blacks suffer from being in America, and that whites suffer from our very presence." And therefore Abraham Lincoln felt that the two people should be separated.* His first white house conference with black leaders was based on the question of separation. Mr. Lincoln desired that blacks be resettled either in Africa or somewhere in Central America. Mr. Lincoln felt that if we returned to Africa with the knowledge that the intellectuals had gained from our sojourn in America we could be a blessing to the continent of Africa. Our black intellectuals rejected that solution.

Although Liberia was formed, and is there struggling for existence today, the Honorable Elijah Muhammad said that the black man could never go free here or anywhere without a profound knowledge of self, and even though white America will not expose to the world the crime that has been committed against black people, to rob us of the characteristics of human beings. That they could so destroy us and then put it in their Constitution that we are three-fifths of a human being, then they amended the Constitution, but they never amended the damage that their fathers had done to destroy a whole people.

As there were many white statesmen who wanted to resettle black people, there were many black leaders who have emerged to offer solutions. If you remember Frederick Douglass told us, "that power concedes nothing without a demand, it never has and it never will." That great black orator wanted black people to demand justice and equity within America. Of course Booker T. Washington believed, "that blacks should be trained to develop skills and trades that we might drop our buckets down where we are." And W. E. B. Du Bois believed in the concept of the talented tenth, "that among black people there is a talented tenth that should be trained in language, in philosophy, in government, in law, in science, that the talented tenth might lead the way to freedom for the others." W. E. B. Du Bois and Booker T. Washington were engaged in great and bitter conflict, and the residue of that conflict is with us today.

So, among these arose a great debate, and out of that debate came the great and honorable Marcus Garvey. Marcus Garvey developed the strongest mass movement of black people in our history in America. And his cry was, "Africa for the Africans at home and abroad." He desired to see blacks return to Africa. Again a black man now is echoing the sentiment of Abraham Lincoln, of Tom Jefferson, and other white statesmen. The masses of black people rallied to Marcus Garvey and it frightened the government, and they moved to destroy that man's reputation, and destroy his movement. Then came the Honorable Elijah Muhammad, my leader, teacher, and guide who advocated that the time for separation had arrived, and that blacks could no longer stay in America under the same conditions that we had lived under. And that this hypocritical friendship called integration was nothing more than a trick to make us believe that our 400 year old enemies had all of a sudden become our friends. So Elijah Muhammad advocated separation in a state or territory of our own either here or elsewhere, and he advocated that America should take care of us in that state or territory for the next 20 to 25 years until we were able to go for ourselves.

Since we have reached that time in history that we must make an exodus we must ask ourselves in light of the realities of today, what kind of exodus must we make? If you say we must return to Africa, what nation in Africa is willing to receive 40 million of us in the condition that we are in? Let's be reasonable. And if 40 million of us said tonight we want to leave right now, it would take all of the navies of the whole world, plus their air force, plus whatever barges or ships they could manage, and then it would take generations to get 40 million of us to return to Africa. And there is no government on the African continent at present that will accept such a challenge. We must be realistic.

And of course that represents an extreme posture, but it's just. *You don't have anything for us to do? Why play with us? Let us go. If you don't want us, let us go. Don't use us in your army to fight wars for your good and not for ours. Don't leave us walking the streets of America with no jobs or no hope for a job, that our young men have to involve themselves in crime to make a living, so that the jails are filled with* blacks, and the army is filled with blacks, and the streets are filled with black men who have no where to go and no hope. We can't continue to live like this! The Black man is just about a destroyed man, because America cannot countenance a Black man that is strong and independent. And therefore America, like pharaoh, has said "They're multiplying too fast, come let us deal wisely with them, lest they multiply and join on to an enemy of ours and remember the evil that we have poured upon them and come against them." So they have decided to kill all the boy babies and spare the female. And so the black man is being killed wholesale, not necessarily with a gun, but he's being killed in his mind. The little children are being killed in the classrooms. The little boy babies that have talent and promise are being crushed mentally, and if they escape high school they get crushed when they get told, "that all you have to do is get an education and the world will accept you." And then they go and spend their parents' money, or get a grant or a loan and when they come out of the colleges and universities there are no jobs for them. Either they are too well educated or they are too undereducated for the job so they are frustrated, walking the streets. Walking time bombs. Angry and disillusioned.

America has disillusioned black people in the same way as a master quarterback must hide the football, make you think the halfback's got it, make you think the fullback's got it, make you think that somebody else got it, then he craftily waits for his opening and then moves on to make a touchdown.

Economics Is the Answer

White folks have told us, "get education, you'll make it." Then after we got education and didn't make it they said, "seek political power and you will make it." We went and we have black mayors, we have black this, black that, still powerless. *Now we found out what the real deal is, where the real ball is, and the real deal and the real ball is* ECONOMICS, ECONOMICS, ECONOMICS, ECONOMICS, ECONOMICS. *All praise is due to Allah.*

White folks don't mind you hollerin' and shoutin' in the church. You can jump and run up and down the aisle saying you got the ghost, as long as you leave the ghost in the church, don't come out of the church with power in the street. You can go to the Mosque or the Masjid and say your jumah prayers, they don't mind if you say ten rakahs, twenty rakahs, pray all night seven times a day, don't get up from the prayer rug with power and come out with economic development for your people. *This government can tolerate religion as long as religion is a do good religion. A religion that makes you sanctimonious, holy looking, but powerless in your actions. I respectfully say to my Muslim brothers and sisters, Islam has never been a sanctimonious religion. Islam has never been a religion where men and women pray and go to Mosque, and have no bearing on the society. Islam has always been a force that dispels tyrants and tyranny, oppression and exploitation. Islam has always been a force that militates for justice. And whenever a religion becomes so religious that it cannot be militant for the oppressed against the oppressor; or the exploited against the exploiter; or the slave against the master, then that religion has become good for nothing. And most of you have a good for nothing religion. And as long as Farrakhan prays the way the Muslim world prays, goes to the Mosque or the Masjid, and puts on a sanctimonious front, you say he's a good Muslim. But I am a better Muslim than 99 percent of all the Muslims that are on the Earth, because I, I like Prophet Muhammad, I like Jesus, I like Moses will stand for truth and justice against the oppressor even if it costs my life.*

And so I challenge the Muslim world to rise up to that covenant that Prophet Muhammad took for you and fight against oppression wherever it is, and start right in your own country.

Black people it's time to make an exodus. We got to come out, come out. "Come out of what? And if we come out where do we go?" We must come out of Egypt. Egypt only means a land of bondage. America has been and is a land of bondage to black people. We must come out of the mind, the spirit, the way, the values, the norms, the folkways, the mores, the culture of our former slavemasters and their children. You must come out of this mind of dependency. You must come out of this mind of inferiority. You must come out of this bondage of sin and ignorance, and we must develop an autonomy of mind and spirit. Almighty God is gradually bringing us out from under the authority of our former slavemasters and their children, and this is manifested in our children's unwillingness to go along with their teachers of education. You can't handle the children today in the school. They are rebelling against your authority. They are rebelling against the authority of the church. There is a breakdown of order and discipline in the society. This is because it is time. It is time that the black people of America come out from under the authority of their former slavemasters.

The Need to Develop New Relationships

And we must make a new relationship with America. For the old relationship is dead. *"You say Farrakhan are you trying to break up the old relationship between Jews and blacks?"* I most certainly am. I ask you in truth, what kind of relationship do you have? A relationship of a master to a slave. You are the tenant and they are the landlord. They own the house and you clean it. They are the merchant you are the consumer. You are the talent they are the agent. You are the actor they are the producer and the owner. Break up that relationship and let's begin a new one. Break up that relationship. Break up the present relationship with the government of America. Break it up and begin a new one. I don't like the relationship we have with America, it's a slave/ master relationship. They use us and we get nothing in return. Break up that relationship. OUR TIME HAS COME!

God wants us to build a new world order. A new world order based on peace, justice and equality. Where do we start? Since there is great fear on the part of some powerful white Americans that if we separate there is the possibility that we might join on to an enemy and come against them, and there's a great fear of our increasing birth rate and what this portends for the future. So physical separation is greatly feared, and it is not now desired by the masses of black people, but America is not willing to give us eight or ten states, or even one state. Let's be reasonable.

Discusses Palestine

Look at what happened in Palestine. When you take land from somebody, give it to somebody because of a claim that they say they have. Look at the anguish of the Palestinians. Look at the anger in the Palestinians. Look at the hurt of the Palestinians. Look at the desire in the Palestinians to return to their native land again. If America were to move white people out of Alabama, and Mississippi and say "Because you have suffered black people, here's Alabama, here's Mississippi", what will the whites say who have lived there all their lives. Yes, you may move them out, but their anger will be kindled; their hatred would be kindled, and America would have violent revolution within her borders. So asking America for a separate state, even though it is a just request, it is a request that America can not give. But it is just.

Discusses Conservatism in the U.S.

So what can be done since the time has arrived, and all efforts to integrate has met and is meeting with a dismal failure. Look, you prayed for Mondale, and God gave you Reagan. What is the matter? Is it that your prayers have fallen on deaf ears? God answers prayer, but he gave you Reagan because he knows what you want, but he knows what you need. Can't you see this conservative mood growing in the country? Why is there a rise in the Ku Klux Klan, the Nazi Party, and white's rights groups. Why has the Supreme Court struck down affirmative action, and reversing all of the gains that the Civil Rights movement made in '64, '65, and '66. It is because it is time, and all of the conditions are right to justify our exodus. And you know when it's time for a baby to come to birth, it's not only that the baby's head turns down and the rightful head takes its rightful place. The head was where the feet used to be, but when the right time comes a turn takes place, and the right head comes down and begins to forge the way to freedom, but the mother has to start pushing down. There must be contractions. Can't you feel the contractions? Can't you feel America contracting, and re-stricting, and pushing? It's time. There's no need to cry, it's time. There's no need to weep, it is time. There is no need to lament it is time. There is no need for despair, hopelessness, and bitterness, it is time. It is time for you to come out with great substance.

Reasons for Black Economic Underdevelopment

So now you are coming out of dependency, ignorance and fear. You are being forced to stand up and do for ourselves. What we propose tonight is a solution that is in between two extremes. If we cannot go back to Africa, and America will not give us a separate territory, then what can we do here and now to redress our own grievances? You must understand that blacks are the mammies of this society. You know what a mammy is don't you? The mammy is that black woman that nursed little white babies to strength from the milk from her breasts. And that white baby would ultimately grow up to disrespect that mammy that nursed it to strength. So with the purchasing power that we have in America we have nursed many people to strength.

The Jews came at the turn of the century and they saw that you had a purchasing power, but you were not producing goods and services for yourself. So they came into the black community providing us with goods and services. And they took our purchasing power, took it back into their community, built up their community. They became strong nursing from the breast of the black community, growing up to disrespect the very breast that they sucked milk from. Then with the riots and rebellions in '64, '65, and '66, Jews made an exodus out. And with the torment in the Middle East the Arabs came in, and took up the stores in the black community. And there they nursed from the black breast. Now the Arabs are becoming economically strong, but ofttimes disrespectful of the very people whose breast they are sucking to gain economic strength. Now the Asians and boat people are coming in. The Koreans are there, the Southeast Asians are there.

You should not blame the Jews. You should not blame the Arabs. You should not blame the Koreans and the Southeast Asians. You have a breast, but you won't put yourself on your own breast. So no wonder you are weak and powerless, but since you've nursed everybody else to strength, don't you think that we could nurse our own self to strength? Yes we can!

So we propose that we use the blessings that we have received from our sojourn in America to do for ourselves what we have been asking the whites in this nation to do for us.

The P.O.W.E.R. Program

P.O.W.E.R., people organized and working for economic rebirth. P.O.W.E.R. works very simply. It puts the consumer together with the black producer in a way that gives us both equal benefits, through a system of distribution that we set up. That we become the producer, we are the distributor, we are the consumer, and the money stays within our circle. Then we can build our own community up and become a strong and powerful people right within the land where we were sold as slaves. P.O.W.E.R., people organized and working for economic rebirth. *According to* Black Enterprise *magazine, we will get out of the American economy this year 204 billion dollars. That's a great purchasing power. And if we compare our purchasing power with the gross national product of the nations of the Earth, we would be the 12th richest nation on the Earth. Here we are crying, and pleading, saying to C.B.S. and N.B.C. and A.B.C., "you don't tell our story, you don't do anything right for us, you portray us in a bad light. You ugly television stations." Last year you poor people, you poor people spent 9 billion dollars on alcohol,*

poor people, 4 billion dollars on tobacco, and nearly 15 billion dollars
estimated in illicit drugs, reefer, cocaine, heroin, pills. You poor people
threw away nearly 30 billion dollars last year on death dealing drugs,
and spent only 10 billion dollars to maintain your health. No wonder
you are getting sick.

But look, you complain about the television, but A.B.C. was taken
over with 3.5 billion. Ted Turner is trying to take over C.B.S. and can
do it with less than 5 billion. N.B.C. can be taken over with another 5
billion. You threw away enough money last year, where this year you
could have owned A.B.C., N.B.C., and C.B.S., and told your own story.
You got power but it is misdirected. We've got power but our leaders
need to address our power, organize our power, redirect that power, but
the leaders must not be vain, self seeking, egotistical maniacs that only
want self aggrandizement. The leaders must work for the masses of the
people. The leaders must live to see the masses empowered.

Need for Redirecting Black Purchasing Power

The redirecting of our 204 billion dollar purchasing power will allow us
to strengthen the institutions we already have, and build new institutions. No black college would have to close, and you could add more
and more black colleges and hospitals. You got the money but you're
throwing it away, as the prodigal son in riotous living. The redirecting
of this vast purchasing power would allow us to rebuild the wasted
cities. You live in the cities and the cities are decaying beneath our feet,
but we have the resources in our hands to rebuild them, to own them, to
take them over, but you sitting around here looking for sympathy.
Crying and wailing and begging at the feet of white people like a lazy
begger when you can get up and do these things for yourself.

The redirecting of this vast purchasing power would allow us to
compete not only for the market of our people, but we will become
productive enough to compete for the American market and the world
market. This productivity of black people will cause us to address our
own unemployment concerns. It will enable us to rebuild a stable black
family life. It will drastically reduce the involvement of black people in
crime and drugs. *You don't need to be a criminal when you're making*
money. You don't need to be high off of drugs when you can be high off
of accomplishment. Everybody else is doing it in America, the law
doesn't forbid you to do it. We must be able to take advantage of the
law and build for black people right inside America, we can do it.

And if we do it, it would make the streets of the cities of America safer for all. And at the core it would strengthen America, for the condition of black people in America makes us the Achilles heel of this nation.

Here's how it works, simply this. Every black man or woman that is in business, that is an entrepreneur, we are going to sign up in the next year and a half, a million members of P.O.W.E.R. When you belong to P.O.W.E.R., people organized and working for economic rebirth, you get what is called a P.O.W.E.R. membership card. Only ten dollars and you're a member of P.O.W.E.R. The businesses, the entrepreneurs become members of P.O.W.E.R., then the P.O.W.E.R. member trades with another P.O.W.E.R. member at a reduced price. This actually encourages the masses of black people to spend their money with their own, but the black business people must live up to certain standards. You must not expect black people to spend their money with you and you are disrespectful of them. You must know and you must learn how to serve your own people. How to be kind and bend over backwards. Travel in the South and see how white people say sir. "Yes suh, no suh, yes ma'm, no ma'm." They "suh" you to death to get that money. You should love each other enough that you should want to serve your own people. And when they come into your place of business have your business well lit, your shelves well stocked, and you be there on time, smiling at the door to greet your people.

Blacks as Manufacturers

Doctors can live, lawyers can live, teachers can live, just don't suck the blood of your people. Let it be a fair exchange, the consumer with the entrepreneur. Yes, but not only that, we must begin to produce some of the things that we consume. And so we have hooked up black manufacturers whose plants are now ready to begin to produce some of the things that we consume. *Last year we spent nearly 3 billion dollars on toothpaste, mouthwash, liquid soap, liquid detergent, body oils, deodorant, etc. What's wrong with us? Don't we have chemists that can produce this? Of course we do. And so we propose, and we are working now feverishly that by the first quarter of 1986 we will have a line of products that black folk consume, but this time we'll be the producer, we'll be the distributor, and we'll be the consumer.* Look, all of you use toothpaste. Don't you think we can make a toothpaste that is sweet and nice, conquering halitosis and fixing up cavities? Can you see black folk on television saying, "I brushed this morning with POWER." Huh? Look here, can you see a football player that just got finished a hard days work in the stadium. He goes in the back and he looks up and he says, "I understand how you feel but it'll be taken care of in a minute, I use POWER deodorant." Huh?

I ask you will you buy your own product? And all we have to do is buy from ourselves, support our own and within five years we will have a one billion dollar corporate entity. And where do you go from there? You go to the Earth, you go to the Earth, you go to the Earth. You buy up the farmers' land. The farmers in America are tired of farming, they're not getting a good break. We'll go to them and say, "Mr. Farmer, I know you're having it hard. I'll buy this, I'll buy that." Look down in Florida, a bug started biting on the crop, then God sent frost down there. Then in a few days we can go down and say, "I'll buy the orange orchard, I'll buy the grapefruit orchard. We'll buy it all." Why you gonna buy it Black man? Because the book says, *"If you will repent, and if you will return to me, and if you will obey the law, the statutes that I give you in this day, blessed shall you be in the city, blessed shall you be in the country. Blessed shall be your basket and blessed shall be your store. Blessed shall be the fruit of your womb, blessed shall be the fruit of the ground."* We are the people of God, and if we turn back to God, the rain will come down in abundance. The elements of time are on our side if we will only get up and do for ourselves. Black people are you ready to do for yourself? You are ready?

The International Scope of the P.O.W.E.R. Program

Brothers and sisters hold on a minute. If you are ready, I want to tell you your worldwide commitment. Because P.O.W.E.R. cannot be national, P.O.W.E.R. must be an international movement. Do you know why? The same way you are suffering, Africa is suffering, the Caribbean is suffering, from economic dependency. But here in America we have some of the most brilliant minds anywhere to be found on the Earth. But what are you doing with your mind? You are giving it to the multinational corporations who are the bloodsuckers of the poor people of the Earth. You must give your time, you must give your mind to Africa, to the Caribbean. We must strike a relationship with the Caribbean. We must ask the Caribbean, "what do you need?" And we will set up a P.O.W.E.R. skills bank, and all of you that have skills, and you are not using your skills properly, we will ask you to put in a year's service to three years service working in the Caribbean, working in Africa, to develop the economies of Africa and the Caribbean, and the Middle East. Let us not forget the American Indians. For the American Indian is our own flesh and our blood. He is sitting on the last energy resources in America. We must strike up a strategic relationship with the American Indians and use our vast technological skill in harmony with the Indians to develop their resources. *So as the Indians rise, and the Mexicans rise, and the Blacks rise, and the Caribbean rises, and Africa rises, a whole new world is on its way in, a whole new world is on its way in.*

What Should America's Response Be?

Now as I conclude. Some of you may ask, "Why would America permit you to do this?" I say to you, it is in America's best interest to permit us to do this. For right now blacks are becoming increasingly disenchanted, and we are a social tinderbox. And if black people rise up in an evil manner, we could foment revolution inside this country, and so weaken America that she could not entertain war with her enemies on the outside. It is not in America's best interest to leave Black people in this condition, but America does not know how to solve the problem. Here we are, we have the solution. America open up your ears it is the *Final Call*. Listen, I want to say to all of you who are here tonight, *we contribute to white supremacy by not being involved in black productivity. You make white people think that they are better than you, and you are genetically inferior, and you look at them and say, "Why do they think this way?" They think this way because you keep on permitting it. And the reason you permit it is because you refuse to become a productive people. But when we become productive two things happen; we begin to destroy the mind and the myth of white supremacy, which is crippling America. We give America her chance to make her exodus. Since the book says, "a mixed multitude went out", America has a chance to make an exodus out of the crippling arrogance of white supremacy that has made her hated all over the world. She has a chance today to look human again. If she will permit the slaves, that have been brought to these shores to come up under the blessing of Almighty God, and to come out with great substance.* Then we, the children of slaves, using what we have learned, sharing it with the Caribbean, and sharing it with Africa, and sharing it with the Middle East, and sharing it with the oppressed peoples of the world. Then America, through us, takes on a new image. An image that will be the rebuilding of America. This productive activity on the part of black people will make us that which Joseph became, it will make us great in the land in which we were sold as slaves. This is the only way. If you won't let us go, you won't give us states, then you must let us now do something for ourselves.

33   The Black Belt Question Revisited

In *The Making of Black Revolutionaries*, "Black Manifesto" champion James Forman's 1972 memoir of an activist in midcareer, Black Power was described as "a concept pointing the way to a revolutionary ideology." For Forman, the belief system in question owed a great deal to Frantz Fanon; Forman called for "colonized" blacks and "all the other wretched of the American earth" to form a vanguard force in support of worldwide socialist revolution. In the following selection, the onetime SNCC, Black Panther Party, and League of Revolutionary Black Workers official outlines an updated version of the Marxist-Leninist rationale and program for winning autonomy for African Americans in the Southern Black Belt and in those parts of the United States where they compose a "national minority" population. He concludes that such struggles for self-determination will help bring about a world order in which both national boundaries and all forms of inequality and discrimination are abolished. Forman's conceptualization originally appeared as a component of his 1980 Cornell University master's thesis and is reprinted from James Forman, *Self-Determination: An Examination of the Question and Its Application to the African-American People* (Washington, DC: Open Hand Publishing, 1984), by permission.

1984   *From* **Which Way for the Black Belt Thesis?**

James Forman

This thesis contends that the African-American people in the United States of America are an oppressed nation of people in the Black Belt area of the southern part of the United States. This area has definable boundaries and limits as set forth in this thesis. Outside of this area in the United States, the African-American people constitute national minorities. This thesis advocates, moreover, that the African-American oppressed nation and its national minorities are entitled to self-determination. This self-determination is not something for the future. The African-American oppressed nation and its national minorities are entitled to self-determination now without any further struggle for its realization.

Consequently, as step one in this direction, negotiations with the United States government by various representatives of the oppressed African-American nation and its national minority areas should begin immediately with the expectation that autonomy, already described in chapter one, under the existing socio-economic arrangement of the United States will be successfully arranged for the oppressed African-American nation and its national minority areas. Autonomy under existing arrangements would provide for a form of self-government consistent with forms of self-government for many other oppressed nations that currently have seats in the United Nations, a world body of more than 150 nations with headquarters in New York. This body should also be notified of the efforts of the oppressed African-American nation and its national minority areas to negotiate autonomy now as the first step in the full realization of its self-determination. . . .

In order to implement autonomy now this thesis urges the formation of a call committee that would prepare an agenda for a conference of African-American organizations. This small group would also prepare a list of organizations that would be invited to such a conference. Hopefully, one of the items on the agenda of the conference would be ways and means to carry out political education about the meaning of autonomy now and the necessary steps to negotiate its fulfillment. The possibility of holding a plebiscite to further determine the wishes of the African-American people concerning their self-determination might also be an agenda item. A necessary third agenda item would entail a discussion of the advantages and methods for involving more and more organizations and institutions in the negotiating process, including representatives of other nationalities.

What are the positive factors and advantages involved in negotiating autonomy now as the first step in the full realization of self-determination for the African-American oppressed nation and its national minority areas? Historians usually record the first presence of the African-American people on the soil of the United States in 1619. Captured in Africa, many African-American people were forced to work the land of the United States as slaves. Many other captured African people were also forced to work as slaves in other parts of the new world. Through the suppression of the history of the African-American people, their contributions to world culture, their origins in Africa, their scientific discoveries and through various methods of torture, control, brainwashing, psychological warfare, and attempted genocide, the United States government has consistently tried to forcibly subjugate the African-American oppressed nation. African-American family life has been systematically made difficult by forces of reaction. In many cities the African-American family cannot go out to dinner or to other public places without enduring racial insults. In some places the names of various institutions are a constant affront to the African-American people and other people of good-will. Statistics on the length of life in the United States tend to show that the African-American male lives the shortest number of years of all people in the United States; the pressures of life in the United States on the African-American male are very great, a contributing factor to a short life: This thesis suggests that these conditions and many others faced by the African-American people can be resolved through the exercise of self-determination by the oppressed African-American nation and its national minority areas, for the African-American oppressed nation has continuously resisted any efforts to force it into subjugation, amalgamation, or annihilation. This resistance is also true for all the other oppressed nations and minorities in the United States.

Petitions for redress of grievances to the United States government, nevertheless, to resolve these problems, are constantly made and should continue. The options of life for an oppressed nation, however, and its national minority areas are not just limited to petitions to the oppressing government for changes. An oppressed nation can negotiate its self-determination as outlined in this thesis. Within the context of autonomy now under the existing socio-economic arrangement of the United

States, the African-American people will have a better chance to gain experience in resolving the racial, national, class, sexual, psychological, and religious problems with which they are confronted. These problems exist in various forms for all nations, oppressed or not oppressed.

What is most likely the main opposition to the proposed efforts to negotiate autonomy now for the oppressed African-American nation and its national minority areas as the first step in exercising self-determination? This thesis maintains that the most vigorous opposition will come from those who say the African-American people are not a nation and never were a nation. They are simply a minority in the United States and they do not have any right to self-determination. They must learn to live and to adjust to their status as it currently exists. Various officials of the United States government will often speak as the representatives of this group. The next most vigorous opposition may come from those who assert that the will of the African-American people has not been expressed. Agents of this opposition group may work in various ways to block the expression of a national will toward autonomy now. Opposition to autonomy now may also come from sectors of the leadership of various parties.

As is true for all opposition groupings, this resistance can be overcome through the political education of the membership, most of whom have been denied the correct history and theory of self-determination. Every effort will also be made to prove conclusively to any opposition that autonomy now will be very beneficial to all the people of the United States and the people of other countries. Conversely, efforts will be made to show where the failure to sit-down and negotiate an end to the misery of the people of the United States and to the African-American people, in particular, will only prolong and worsen the agony and pain that the people of the United States are currently experiencing: high rates of inflation, massive unemployment, overseas runaway plants, urban blight, consistent rise in drug addiction among all races and all classes of people, the systematic destruction of the youth of the United States through successive war efforts that are counter-productive for everyone, and many other problems that are directly related to the forcible retention and suppression of oppressed nations and national minorities in the United States of America.

In order to win over the main opposition it will be necessary to unite more and more African-American people around the concept of autonomy now as the first step toward self-determination and to extend the struggle for autonomy now for the oppressed African-American nation and its national minority areas to all other oppressed nations, colonies, and national minorities of the United States government. Such an effort is just, correct, and strengthens the negotiations for all the representatives of oppressed nations, colonies and national minorities. Conversely, to limit negotiations simply for the oppressed African-American nation and its national minority areas weakens the negotiating power of oppressed nations, colonies, and national minorities of the United States government. This thesis holds, moreover, that all of what are usually called immigrant groups in the United States are in fact national minorities. The term national minorities is therefore not limited to people of color in the United States such as the Chinese, Japanese, Mexican, Filipino, Vietnamese, or Haitians. Rather, the Greek-Americans, Italian-Americans, Ukrainian-Americans, Polish-Americans, and other immigrant people and descendants of immigrants from the white race are also national minorities. As national minorities they have the right wherever possible to re-unite with their nation or to live in peace as national minorities in the United States and other countries. They also have the right to live and develop the positive aspects of their national culture and languages as essential guarantees in developing trust and overcoming differences between people of various cultures, races, and religions. As the representatives of the oppressed African-American nation and its national minority areas who seek to negotiate autonomy now involve more and more members of other oppressed nations, colonies and national minorities in the negotiating process, the opposition to autonomy now for the African-American oppressed nation and its national minority areas will lessen and forms of autonomy now for all oppressed nations, colonies, and national minorities will become more certain.

34 The "New Afrikan" Case
for Reparations

In recent years, African American interest in winning federal reparations
payments for the descendants of ex-slaves has been heightened by the
successful campaign of Japanese Americans to win financial redress for
their internment during World War II. Petitions have been circulated,
lawsuits filed, and quantitative studies of the "costs" of slavery and of
the nation's accrued "debt" published. Several cities, including Detroit,
Cleveland, and the District of Columbia, have passed resolutions endorsing basic reparationist tenets. As seen by the members of N'COBRA
(National Coalition of Blacks for Reparations in America), an activist
support group founded in 1989, such payments are more than justified
because slavery's cruel legacy still can be seen in the poverty, family
disintegration, crime, and other problems plaguing modern-day black
communities. A major federally sponsored redistribution of wealth along
racial lines would materially improve black America's chances of achieving economic parity with whites.

The following document, authored by the Republic of New Africa's
Imari Obadele and presented to members of Congress in 1987, makes
the case for reparations as (1) partial compensation for past suffering;
(2) a stimulus to economic growth; and (3) a mechanism for improving
the financial and political situation of the RNA. It is reprinted from
Chokwe Lumumba, Imari Abubakari Obadele, and Nkechi Taifa, *Reparations Yes!* (Baton Rouge: House of Songhay, 1993), by permission.

1987   **An Act to Stimulate Economic Growth in the United States and Compensate, in Part, for the Grievous Wrongs of Slavery and the Unjust Enrichment which Accrued to the United States Therefrom**

Imari Obadele

Preamble

WHEREAS the Congress of the United States has never accorded ultimate political justice to New Afrikans in this country—New Afrikans being all the descendents of Afrikans held as slaves in this country—by authorizing a plebiscite and a process of registration whereby collectively and individually New Afrikans could exercise their right to self-determination by freely and with full information voting collectively on their future, and registering individual political options, and

WHEREAS the Congress of the United States recognizes the Thirteenth Amendment as protecting this right of New Afrikan people to self-determination, and

WHEREAS the illegal transportation to, and the enslavement of Afrikan people in the United States was carried out under authority of the U.S. Constitution for seventy-seven years, and for a total of 200 years under the antecedent authority of the Articles of Confederation, and the Colonial law, and

WHEREAS the authority in the United States Constitution for enslavement of the New Afrikan people was contained in clause three, Section Two of the Fourth Article, commonly known as the fugitive slave provision, which placed the full force of the United States military, executives, and courts against even the most inoffensive person held as a slave who quietly slipped away to freedom, and against the entire New Afrikan people, and

WHEREAS the United States further dehumanized the New Afrikan by holding her/him to have the status of three-fifths of a white person in clause three, Section Two of Article One of the U.S. Constitution, and

WHEREAS that most heinous war against Afrika, commonly known as the slave trade, was authorized for United States principals for 20 years more after the ratification of the United States' Constitution by clause one in Section Nine of the First Article of the United States Constitution, and

WHEREAS principles of international law and a reconciliation of the peoples require that the United States attempt a good faith, if partial, reparation for the unjust war waged against the New Afrikan people for 200 years, and for cultural destruction, and for labor stolen, and

WHEREAS the concept of reparations is recognized in United States law, and the United States has sponsored and paid reparations for other victims, and

WHEREAS the Congress finds that New Afrikan people, descendants of persons kidnapped from Afrika and held here against their will, currently residing in the United States, are entitled to exercise collective and individual rights to self-determination, and

WHEREAS the Congress is aware that the options regarding political future which are open to the New Afrikans include (a) return to Afrika, (b) departure for some country other than one in Afrika, (c) acceptance of U.S. citizenship, and (d) creation of an independent New Afrikan state in North America, and

WHEREAS the Congress is convinced that some New Afrikan people will choose each of these four options, and

WHEREAS, moreover, the Congress is further convinced that some New Afrikan people will never forsake the three-centuries-old desire to create an independent New Afrikan state in North America and have, in fact, duly elected a Provisional Government to protect the interests of the New Afrikan nation, as a nation, and to establish an independent New Afrikan state by means sanctioned by international law, and

WHEREAS the Congress finds that various international covenants and resolutions affirming that all peoples have the right to self-determination apply to Afrikan people born in North America, and

WHEREAS the Congress recognizes that the necessary foundation for effectuating the results of an act of self-determination by the New Afrikan people is the means and resources to achieve those results, and

WHEREAS the authority for providing such means and resources lies in Section Two of the Thirteenth Amendment, and

WHEREAS this legislation affects only those parties under domestic United States jurisdiction and is not to be construed as discharging the obligation owed to Afrikan people by other countries and governments.

THEREFORE the following provisions are enacted into law under the authority of the Thirteenth Amendment to the United States Constitution.

Title I. Reparations

1. The United States accepts the obligation of the United States to pay reparations to the descendants of Afrikans held as slaves in the United States and undertakes to make such payments to the New Afrikan nation as political unit, to compensate in part for the destruction and/or damage to Afrikan political units in Afrika and for the abortion and the destruction of New Afrikan political units in the United States during the era of slavery, and payments to New Afrikan organizations to compensate in part for the deliberate subversion of the New Afrikan social structure, and the obligation to pay directly to each New Afrikan, descendant of Afrikans held as slaves in the United States and born on or before the date of ratification of this Act, and still living on the date of each appropriation, the total sum of _____ dollars.

2. Congress is authorized to appropriate and pay annually sums of money and credit to discharge this obligation over a period of years, not less than three-billion dollars annually.

    a. One-third of the annual sum shall go directly to each individual, except that the sum due a person not yet 17 years of age who is not the head of an independent household shall be paid to the head-of-household who stands as such person's parent or guardian or jointly to such persons in the case of husband and wife. Social Security records, Internal Revenue Service records, and Aid to Dependent-Children records, or records of successor agencies, shall be available to facilitate determination of heads-of-household, as consistently as possible with the provisions of the Privacy Act, its conflicting provisions hereby being waived. This program shall be administered by the Internal Revenue Service.

    b. One-third of the annual sum shall go directly to the duly elected government of the Republic of New Afrika, and to any other state-building entity of New Afrikan people, provided that elections for the RNA Provisional Government or for the officers of such other

New Afrikan state-holding entity are observed by the United Nations or other distinguished international body and deemed by said international body to be open, honest, and democratic, for purposes of the economic, social, cultural, and educational development of the New Afrikan nation-state or states. This payment shall be made by the United States Treasury.

c. One-third of the annual sum shall be paid directly to a National Congress of Organizations, consisting of all the New Afrikan churches and other New Afrikan organizations which for a period of two years prior to the enactment of this legislation have engaged in community programs designed to end the scourge of drugs and crime in New Afrikan communities and advance the social, economic, educational, or cultural progress and enrichment of New Afrikan people. Programs serving New Afrikan communities shall be eligible to participate in local conventions of the National Congress of Organizations, provided that these programs are led by New Afrikans and have been so led for at least three years prior to enactment of this legislation. The United States Treasury shall administer this payment.

Title II. Plebiscites and Self-Determination

1. Pursuant to the Thirteenth Amendment, the United States President is authorized and directed to arrange with the President or appropriate body of the Provisional Government of the Republic of New Afrika and/or other state-building entity the holding, within five years after the enactment of this legislation, of independence plebiscites in all such counties or major portions of such counties in the states of South Carolina, Georgia, Florida, Alabama, Mississippi, Louisiana, Arkansas, and Tennessee, where ten percent of Afrikans, aged 16 or over, within such counties or major portions thereof signify their desire for the holding of such plebiscites.

2. Such ten-percent petitions may be certified by special *Status Courts,* hereby created in the same districts as the now-established districts for United States courts, within the states enumerated in Paragraph One of this Title, and Regional Status Courts are hereby created in New York, Chicago, Atlanta, and Los Angeles. The judges of these Article One-Thirteenth Amendment *Status Courts* shall be three in number: one appointed by the President of the United States, one appointed by the

Republic of New Afrika, and one which the General Assembly of the United Nations shall be invited to appoint.

3. The jurisdiction of said Status Courts shall be limited to (1) determination of the validity of petitions for plebiscites and their certification, (2) the certification of Election results, and (3) such other matters as are set out in this Act. Such Status Courts, established under Article One and the Thirteenth and Fourteenth Amendments of the United States Constitution, and the agreement of the Provisional Government of the Republic of New Afrika, insofar as the authority of the United States is concerned, shall have power to compel the appearance and testimony of witnesses, issue process for production of evidence, make findings of fact and conclusions of law, conduct trials, and issue judgements.

4. Such Status Courts shall have power through a conference, presided over by a Chief Judge elected by the Conference of all Status Court judges, to issue rules, consistent with the rules of the federal courts of the United States, the Judicial Statute of the Republic of New Afrika, and the Statute of the International Court of Justice. Such rules shall become effective if not returned for further consideration by the United States or the Republic of New Afrika sixty days after the date of promulgation by the Chief Judge of the Status Courts. In the event of such return, the Chief Judge may amend the Rules and promulgate them de novo, under the same conditions of veto. Judges of the Status Courts shall have power to conduct contempt proceedings and assess penalties upon findings of contempt, which penalties should not exceed five years in prison and a $10,000 fine.

5. Compensation for Status Court judges shall be the same as that of District Judges of the United States. The United States shall promptly and regularly pay these salaries and provide for adequate staffing and support services for the Status Courts. Such compensation and expenses shall be included in the regular budgeting and appropriations for the U.S. Courts and shall not be treated as a charge against the appropriation for reparations.

6. *Change of Sovereignty.* Whenever a simple majority of voters in a county or a portion of a county pre-designated for plebiscite, shall during a plebiscite on status vote in favor of a majority of Republic of New Afrikan candidates for the legislative or governing body of such county, or a portion thereof, that area shall be deemed to be under the

sovereignty of the Republic of New Afrika. The provisions of this Section, paragraphs 6,7, and 8 apply not only to the RNA Provisional Government but to any New Afrikan state-building entity filing ten-percent petitions in accordance with paragraphs 1 through 5 of Title II of this act.

7. The United States shall undertake to secure agreement from the Republic of New Afrika that all persons residing in an area where the Republic of New Afrika wins sovereignty shall be guaranteed all the rights set forth in the United Nations Covenant on Civil and Political Rights, to the same extent that the United States guarantees these rights to all persons residing in the United States.

8. Immediately after the first plebiscite which results in a confirmation of Republic of New Afrika sovereignty, the President of the United States shall invite the President of the Republic of New Afrika and the Secretary General of the United Nations to join in a request to the Status Courts that they open official *Status Registers*. These *Registers* shall permit individual New Afrikans who, living in the United States, do not wish to accept United States citizenship, and New Afrikans who, living in New Afrika, do not wish to retain New Afrikan citizenship, to register these personal options. A New Afrikan who does not register a personal option shall be deemed to have the citizenship of the sovereignty—New Afrikan or United States—under which he or she lives, but this fact for New Afrikans who remain in the United States does not obliterate New Afrikan citizenship in the context of *dual* citizenship. Such registration of personal choice must take place within three years of a status plebiscite in the area in which a person resides, where a change of sovereignty occurs. In all cases New Afrikans wishing to exercise a personal option for citizenship in the Republic of New Afrika but living in an area where no plebiscite has been held or where no status court is established, must do so within ten years after the date of the enactment of this legislation. For this purpose the United States Postal Service shall provide secure *Status Letters* which, after execution, shall be delivered to the appropriate Regional Status Courts in New York, Chicago, Atlanta, or Los Angeles. Persons may file personally at these Regional Status Courts. The citizenship of a child, 15-years-old or younger, shall be the same as that of his or her parents, parent, or guardian who stands as head-of-household, unless such person maintains an independent household.

Title III. Freedom for Black Liberation Army Soldiers

1. The Congress of the United States finds that the continued imprisonment of the following Black Liberation Army soldiers and certain other persons is contrary to the national interests of the United States and a substantial impediment to the successful fulfillment of the intent of this legislation under the Thirteenth Amendment, that intent being to stimulate economic growth in the United States, compensate in part victims and heirs for past wrongs, facilitate racial healing and reconciliation in the United States, and provide for the long-delayed exercise of the right to self-determination by the New Afrikan people. The Congress finds that the Continued imprisonment of these persons is contrary to fulfillment of United States obligations under the Thirteenth Amendment. The Congress therefore directs the immediate release of these persons from prison without condition:

Sundiata Acoli
Assata Shakur
Herman Bell
Albert Nuh Washington
Jalil Muntuaqin
Geronimo ji Jaga (Pratt)
Mutulu Shakur
Dhoruba Ben Wahad
Kubwa Obadele
Kwablah Mthawabu
Sekou Odinga
Veronza Bowers
Atiba Shanna
Bashir Hameed
Abdul Jamid
Haroun Abdul Rauf

2. The United States Congress, for its part, further provides to the Status Courts, hereinabove established, jurisdiction to accept applications from persons similarly situated and the power to make prompt and just decisions on their application for release.

Title IV. Administrative Funds

Funds for the administration of the provisions of the Act shall be appropriated from the general treasury of the United States and included in the budgets of the Status Courts and the executive agencies responsible for carrying out the provisions of this legislation, without any charges against the sums appropriated for the payment of reparations under Title I of this Act.

35 Toward African Liberation

Founded in 1983 following a split within Stokely Carmichael's All-African People's Revolutionary Party, the Pan-African Revolutionary Socialist Party (PRSP) adopted a program calling for "all people of African descent, no matter where they were born, or where they live" to help build a revolutionary political movement in support of the liberation and unification of their ancestral homeland. As the following selection reveals, while concerned with issues of both racial and class oppression, the PRSP chose to highlight "the primacy of Africa" in their "scientific socialist" version of black liberationist thought. Like numerous revolutionary and territorial nationalists before them, PRSP activists sought to speed the end of "neo-" and "settler-" colonialism. Under Pan-Africanism, control of the continent would return in full to indigenous leaders. "Wage slavery" and unequal trade relationships would end. Neither divided allegiances nor "ideological confusion" would prevent the people of Africa from returning to the "glory days" of the early black kingdoms. Influenced greatly by the writings of African political leaders such as Ghanaian president Kwame Nkrumah, groups like the PRSP had a major role to play in keeping the question of South African independence in the forefront of international debate throughout the 1980s. The following editorial appeared in the *Nkrumaist* (November–December 1984), and is reprinted by permission.

1984   A Plan of Action

Pan-African Revolutionary Socialist Party

The PRSP, at its founding Congress in November 1983, adopted a three-pronged strategic thrust. This line of struggle flows from an analysis of the major contradictions confronting our people—national oppression and class exploitation. It was determined that we would focus our energies on highlighting the primacy of Africa (Pan-Africanism) neo-colonialism and settler-colonialism. Furthermore, it was decided that during the positive action offensive, that will last until our first Congress in 1985, we would place major emphasis on the issue of settler-colonialism while showing the interconnection with neo-colonialism and the necessity for Pan-Africanism.

The issue of the primacy of Africa is critical because it centers around the issue of land and the attending questions of identity and land base. Control of the land is vital to the destiny of a people. From the land evolves all of the essential elements—the natural resources—that a people need to develop and sustain themselves. As victims of slavery and the colonial experience, our people have had the land stolen from our domain by the European colonial powers. In fact, it has been 100 years since the capitalist/imperialist divided up Africa for the purposes of exploitation.

Using our labor and resources, the European ruling class has amassed great wealth in Europe, the U.S. and wherever they have settled. As a result, our people suffer. Materially we lack food and shelter, economically, we who can find work are wage slaves; politically we are divided as a nation, many owing allegiance to some artificial identity such as Ghanian, Afro-American, Jamaican, etc. Socially, the institutions are capitalist in character and consequently our education and our health suffer as we are still viewed in an inferior manner. The dilemma that all of these maladies create psychologically is what Nkrumah called the crisis of the African personality.

For us the answer to these problems is very simple. Africa is our land, we are Africans and the crisis plaguing our people can only be solved when the masses of our people reclaim control of our land and achieve Pan-Africanism—the total liberation and unification of Africa under a scientific socialist government is achieved.

For that to occur we must struggle against the phenomena of neo-

343

colonialism. In the early 1950's African people had waged struggle against the colonial powers for independence. Europe and the U.S. became concerned with the possible loss of Africa's resources. As a result a system of sham independence was devised in which political control of the territories was granted to Africans, while the control of the economy remained in the hands of foreign corporate interests in collaboration with their local African puppets. This system was a 'new' or neo-colonialism. Today we find Barclay's Bank, British Petroleum, Lonrho Corp., Standard Oil and other corporate giants dominating the African economy. We find our land, Africa, still divided by European drawn boundaries that finds, for example, the Wolof tribe divided by a Gambia-Senegal border.

Neo-colonialism prevents the African people from solving the economic, social and political chaos that plagues us. Rather than pulling together and utilizing the vast resources for the betterment of the people, the African puppet rulers mortgage our land and resources to the capitalist powers for a few pennies, to maintain their extravagant lifestyles. Consequently, to use our land for the development of the people's class means we must wage class struggle to gain dominance and control from the oppressor's class.

Meanwhile there still remain vestiges of colonialism called settler-colonialism. Namibia and South Africa, (Azania) are the last two vestiges where a settler class has managed to maintain control of the people's land. In each of these areas the European minority has imposed vicious racial (apartheid) and economic policies to seek to prevent our people from controlling our own destiny. (Many of the repressive policies used in South Africa were modelled after policies used by the U.S. against the Indians and the Africans.) The Afrikaners with the support of the capitalist/zionist connection in recent months have intensified their efforts to halt our people's quest for freedom sparked by our valiant warriors of SWAPO, ANC & PAC. Simultaneously the capitalist/imperialist support sparked by the U.S. policy of constructive engagement has served as a source of encouragement for the Afrikaner to seek to destabilise the socialist oriented liberated zones of Zimbabwe, Angola and Mozambique.

Again we see where our division plagues our struggle for liberation. Over 22 micro-states in Africa trade with the Afrikaner regime. Clearly a united concerted effort to support the freedom fighters of Namibia and Azania would quickly bring the Afrikaner regime to its knees.

The question for us in the PRSP is how do we move to extricate ourselves from our plight. We concluded that the only way to solve our people's problems is to build an organization dedicated to establishing Pan-Africanism. This objective solves the question of having a land that we can develop for the betterment of our people—a land base that allows us to feed, clothe and shelter our people and simultaneously provides us the material base with which we can restore the African personality to a place of glory and pride and to once again be able to make major contributions freely to the development of society as had our ancestors in Egypt, Monopotopa, Ghana, Mali, Songhay and other early kingdoms.

Obviously to do this we must wage struggle in a scientific manner against the forces of oppression. An analysis of our plight indicated that the control by the oppressor of the minds of our people could be more readily broken by placing emphasis on the brutality of the settler colonial regime while moving continuously towards the major battle of removing the African neo-colonial puppets and finally uniting our land under one socialist government.

Make no mistake that we believe this to be an easy task. But have no doubts that we believe this to be a challenge that must be and will be fulfilled. The historically determined resistance of our people is evidence of the success that is to come from our struggle. We urge you to assume your responsibility to our people. Whatever your status today, it is the direct result of the oppression of our land and our people. You owe it to our people to organize for our children's tomorrow.

FORWARD EVER

36 "Political Prisoners and Prisoners-of-War"

In the following interview conducted by German journalist Heike Kleffner in October 1992 and published in *Race & Class* (July–September 1993) (reprinted by permission), former Black Panthers Geronimo ji-jaga Pratt and Mumia Abu-Jamal respond to a series of questions concerning the party, FBI counterintelligence (COINTELPRO) activities, and their personal experiences as "political prisoners and prisoners-of-war." At the time of the interview, Pratt—who once served as deputy minister of defense for the Panthers' Los Angeles chapter and whose political writings on guerrilla warfare circulated widely throughout revolutionary nationalist circles during the 1970s—had been incarcerated for twenty-two years. The much-decorated Vietnam War hero had been convicted of first-degree murder in 1972. Abu-Jamal was a freelance reporter who began his career in journalism by writing for the Black Panther newspaper during the late 1960s. He later supported MOVE, the Philadelphia-based separatist group whose fortified communal headquarters were beseiged by authorities and firebombed (via state police helicopter) in May 1985; eleven people were killed in the bombing. Abu-Jamal was found guilty of the 1981 murder of a Philadelphia police officer; his death sentence was interpreted by many as punishment for his radical political views. Over the years, both men have garnered considerable support for the reduction or overturning of their sentences. Their cases continue to spur debate over both the role played by race and class in the criminal justice system and the wisdom and morality of capital punishment.

Interviews with Geronimo ji-jaga Pratt and
Mumia Abu-Jamal

HEIKE KLEFFNER: How did you get involved with the Black Panther
Party (BPP) and what did you do before that?

GERONIMO JI-JAGA PRATT: I am from a small town in Louisiana, part
of the national territory we feel should be liberated, and I grew up in a
segregated situation. It was very much like you probably imagine a Black
nation to be. The situation was pretty racist, on the one hand; on the
other, it was full of integrity and dignity and the pride of being a part of
this community. So, I grew up witnessing lynchings and other activities
that you have probably heard about, that the Ku-Klux-Klan performed.
There was an atmosphere of fear like that, but, too, of a close-knit
family—the values, the work ethic, very respectful to everyone. Eventually, I joined the US army and ended up in Vietnam. This was during the
'60s when a lot of change was taking place in the country. That change
was interpreted to us down South in a different kind of way—because
there, you grew up fighting; there was a constant state of warfare,
because of the racial polarisation. Martin Luther King, the civil rights
movement, etc., was not that popular there, because we were raised on
the self-defence principle of fighting and defending our people from
those kinds of racist attacks. That stayed with me all my life through the
service and back out and eventually in the BPP.

HK: When did you first get introduced to the BPP?

GP: When I got out of the US army, I enrolled at UCLA and I was
befriended by a brother who was the Deputy Defense Minister of the
Southern California chapter, named Bunchy Carter. In fact, we ended
up being room-mates. We were both taking the same classes at UCLA
and, as a result, I became very familiar with the BPP and the movement
as a whole. Being fresh from Vietnam, plus being from the South, opened
my eyes to a lot of things. At that time, I was not a member, I was just a
friend of Bunchy's; everybody thought that I was a member, because I
was always with Bunchy. I had attended some meetings of the BPP with
Bunchy—the national meetings in Oakland—and helped implement a
lot of student programmes in conjunction with the BPP. But I had not

joined. When Bunchy was killed in January 1968, he left a recording that resulted subsequently in my helping to rebuild their Ministry of Defense.

So, when you say 'joining the BPP', there was never really a formal joining. It was a coming together of different forces under the auspices, the banner of the BPP—it was not as cut-and-dried as people may think now.

HK: What did Bunchy's recording say?

GP: That if anything happened to him, he recommended that I take his place. It was a shock to me. I was blown away. I had already heard that he was dead and then, when I heard this . . . He had never asked me to join; he knew my position on things. It was like a coming together of two different worlds, two different sectors of a field of struggle and I wasn't so eager to join anything. I had grown up in an organisation that was based on the principles of liberation that the BPP were struggling to comprise. So, when he was killed and he left that recording, and Bobby and Kathleen and all heard it, and then asked me, would I do this—it kind of threw me off. After a while, I decided to help build the Ministry of Defense—the Party was made up of different ministries, the Ministry of Education, the Ministry of Culture led by Emory Douglass—and it became incumbent on me to take this task on.

HK: What did your job entail?

GP: I assumed the role of the Minister of Defense because Huey [Newton], who was the nominal Minister of Defense, was incarcerated. And I became a member of the first cadre of the Central Committee, the highest decision-making body of the BPP. I had to go to various locations and organise classes on defence—self-defence—and things of that nature. Also, we worked on technical defence and theoretical defence. Theoretical defence was comprised of more intellectual dialogue between individuals, so that you could understand the basics of warfare; the technical was the actual implementation of defence techniques, defending our offices, etc.

HK: Can you tell us a bit about the community programmes of the BPP?

GP: That commitment was ongoing. You had to contribute a certain amount of hours to the breakfast programme, to the clothing give-away programme, to the medical programmes. It was a constant thing, 24 hours, a full-time job. You had to maintain the political education classes, because those classes were primary, before anything we had to maintain political education. So, it was quite a busy time.

HK: When did you first learn about COINTELPRO and when did you first become one of its targets?

GP: We began to feel the effects of COINTELPRO-type operations from the start. Even before I had gotten out here to California, those kind of things were being felt throughout the country, throughout the movement. But it became more intense at the end of 1968 and the beginning of 1969, shortly after J. Edgar Hoover issued his infamous proclamation that we were the greatest threat to their national security.

HK: Can you describe when and how you felt the effects personally?

GP: When I was shot at in my bed, four days after the assassination of Fred Hampton in 1969. A very similar thing happened when a sister and I were in bed. They came and shot at the bed and they missed. Buckshots and an assassination attempt. A few months prior to that I had been shot at on the streets by unknown assailants—there were three whites in a car, in the ghetto on the East Side of LA. I was going through Memphis, doing some work there and was shot at. I had been shot at quite a bit in Vietnam, and when the bullets are close, they make a cracking sound. These were very close. I was just lucky that they didn't hit me.

HK: Did you foresee then the split that was going to happen in the BPP?

GP: We had signs of it—not a split that actually occurred, but there were always some infiltrators, some agents provocateurs, who were just omnipresent, who you had to try to weed out and identify, and who were constantly trying to provoke this kind of separation within the ranks. It would come from various directions. It might be played out through fratricidal warfare between other organisations and the Panthers, or the Peacetoll Nation and the Panthers in Chicago. Then you had the anti-Castro Cubans, who were known as the Guzanos and who were used pretty much against the Panthers; you had the Minutemen, and, of course, the Ku-Klux-Klan and the John Birch Society. There was always someone, some kind of force coming at you like this and it wasn't so clear during this period that it was coming directly from the FBI or the CIA. But it became a serious topic of our political education classes and studies. Quite a lot of the findings that came out of those studies were presented to the central committee. A few times they were laughed at, because a lot of the leaders didn't think that we were that important; that the US would waste time using the CIA and the FBI.

HK: Did you work with any white organisations and how did you feel about those alliances?

GP: We had good relations with some white organisations throughout that period. In effect, we were criticised quite a bit by a more narrow nationalist black organisation for even working with organisations such as SDS, the Weathermen, the communist New Left, the youth alliances, the labour parties—all the way to the Communist Party. There were problems. We had to find ways of working with various forces moving in the same direction. And we understood that our entire struggle was really based on a class struggle, and that our adversaries would try to use the race factor to manipulate and to divide and conquer—when all along those people of other nations, other ethnic backgrounds, are in fact our allies and our friends. We enjoyed good relations with white people, brown people, red people and encouraged a united front at all times. In fact, we had a couple of united front conferences that were pretty successful—back in 1969.

HK: At what point was the BPP split up nationally?

GP: We were growing like wildfire, so fast that the leadership really had to slow down and try to see who was coming up. It was growing so fast, it went national, then international when Eldridge Cleaver went overseas. We had chapters in Havana and Algiers and Copenhagen. It just spread all over. It wasn't that easy to try to provide the kind of leadership needed to try to function properly.

HK: Do you think that such an organisation needed a hierarchical structure?

GP: That's a good question. I often brought that up for a topic of discussion during that period and I was accused of being too militaristic, of thinking too militaristically. But it was Amilcar Cabral who gave us a lot of insight into vertical structures as opposed to more horizontal structures. And that was discussed quite a bit—a lot of the formulas were actually put into practice in certain areas and worked pretty good. But there was still the matter of hooking it all together, because sometimes you would hook it together—say we hooked up the Boston chapter and the chapter in Jamaica, NY—the link that you would use would actually be an agent and you wouldn't know. That was the worst thing, being linked up through an agent, who was directly working for J. Edgar Hoover (FBI director at the time). So we had problems in security screening which became harder because we were naive; agents would actually come and advocate blowing up buildings, shooting police, doing things radically, going out and shooting somebody. And you would say, 'Oh, this guy, he is just crazy, but he is not an agent, just because he did some stuff like this.' Yet they were the ones provoking it all. A lot of the local leaders were suckered because of that.

HK: Did you think it was necessary to have hierarchical structures in order to control the organisation or to make sure that it stayed together?

GP: What we called vertical structures were more popular, and I was one of the ones who dissented from that. I thought that, since we were widespread, we needed a horizontal structure, based more on a cell system, that empowered the local leadership. But, because of the fear and the paranoia so prevalent among the national leadership, they would opt for the vertical. Their strong advocacy of this though was continually opposed by the actual practices of the police, who were constantly arresting and removing the national leadership. So, you had to reverse and revise and develop other forms of organisational control.

HK: What about the role of women in the BPP? It struck me in talking to different former Black Panthers and women, that sexism was right in there in the organisation. What is your perception of it in retrospect?

GP: When I became a member of the central committee, I was always in support of women's liberation issues, but we didn't have to be in support of anything, because the sisters would make sure that you respected them and that their points got across and were adhered to. One of the first sisters who comes to mind is sister Afeni Shakur and, of course, the sister they called my wife, known as Sandra Pratt. She was killed. Or Kathleen Cleaver—you are talking about some strong sisters, sisters you may not have heard about—like Amantelaba—but who were very beautiful, who you would listen to. We had to face our sexism and our machoism because of them. They would educate us—Joan Bird, Assata Shakur—and you would respect and love them, because they made you look into yourself; you became a better person because of them. So, the credit starts with them, because they took the initiative to educate us, to teach us. I wish I could sit here and name all of them.

HK: Can you describe how you ended up in prison, how you were framed and what the situation was over that?

GP: I was arrested on December 8th, 1970, in Dallas, Texas, on a warrant run out of what's known as the shoot-out in Los Angeles in 1969. I was extradited back to California a couple of months later to stand trial for those charges. At that time I was indicted for a murder— I was indicted for quite a few things and one of them was the murder that I am convicted of right now. At the time that I was indicted, it was just another charge that they threw in to maintain a no-bail situation. It wasn't taken too seriously, because they had done this before. Eventually, it became more and more obvious to us that the murder charge was something that they were really going to try and press.

HK: Looking at the rebellions in LA and speaking with young Black kids, it seems to me that they are mostly concerned with the everyday struggle for survival. How do you reach out to them, or do you see any force at this point that is organising these kids?

GP: There are quite a few forces out there that are organising them— conscious organisers like, in some situations, 'Educated Fools from Un-educated Schools', educating and organising them to lean right back on the system. Most of those children have stated very clearly that they are tired of being always in the position of 'we gotta ask him for a job; we gotta ask him for welfare; we gotta ask him for health care'. It is almost innate for them to speak of autonomy, and, although they don't even really understand what sovereignty and independence mean, their deep-est desire is to be on their own, to work for themselves. They are tired of asking the government. That is the strongest argument in favour of nationalism, national independence. Just listen to them, from the rappers to the ones that go to church every day. They want to have their own presidents or prime ministers, their own supreme courts, their own police forces, their own educational institutions. That is what I have been hearing every day. I get a lot of letters from them, and that is what they are looking for—someone who could help them build this vast nation of ours. There is kind of a rough, unrefined understanding that I sense from them, based on: they want theirs, not so much from the system, as from the hundreds and hundreds of years' wealth that was accumulated from slavery. I think there are a lot of ways that they can be organised and are being organised, whether we like it or not.

HK: How do you perceive the support for yourself and other political prisoners and prisoners-of-war from the Black liberation movement? A lot of young kids especially don't know about your case, or the cases of other Panthers.

GP: I think there is a conscious and systematic attempt on the part of the government to oppose any support that may be developing for us. The solution, I think, has to be based on our national efforts for liberation— that we are soldiers who fought for the liberation of our nation and our nation fights for the liberation of us. But if our nation does not realise it is a nation, then it's gonna constantly be victim of this kind of manipulation by our enemies. I don't now advocate so much 'Free Geronimo' as 'Free our Nation'; that our prisoners and our protectors and soldiers of that nation be provided for. The important thing is the freedom of our people. We were always sacrificial lambs for that, we understood that we were going to be killed, put in prison, or ostracised, because it is not a popular thing among those you fight against to fight for freedom and independence. And, in the process, support will come for Mumia Abu-Jamal and all other political prisoners and prisoners-of-war. One of the things that the white superstructure is afraid of is the coming together of various national forces such as the Native movement, the Chicano movement, what is called the white North American anti-imperialist movement, which are all based on the same principles, the principles of our independence. That is something I always try to make people aware of. We could talk about this a long time, but I know we don't have a lot of time.

HK: Do you feel that the support for yourself has got stronger in the last few years?

GP: Yes, it is constantly growing. But, if I could, I would take every ounce of support that I have for me and give it to Mumia and other prisoners-of-war. Mumia is a very beautiful brother. He was framed, his life is in imminent danger and we can ill afford to execute Mumia.

HK: Can you talk a bit about your prison conditions?

GP: My prison conditions are harsh. I am in maximum security imprisonment, and, after twenty-two years in prison, it is not common to be maintained in what is called a level-four prison. The conditions are very punitive and repressive, ranging from the food conditions to the violence of seeing a person arguing and the guards shooting him from a tower, killing him. There are constant lies and manipulations. Just think of a COINTELPRO on a microcosmic scale. In fact, we found in some of the files the existence of an operation called PRISAC programme; it is directed against prison activists and ranges over spreading rumours, falsely labelling you, taking your letters, poison-pen letters. It is a constant state of warfare.

HK: What about the Black elected officials—do they support the demand of freedom for Black political prisoners at all?

GP: They like to individualise prisoners, because, by and large, they buy into the system's propaganda, that there are no political prisoners. You have to understand that in the New Afrikan nation you have a class situation. Within this class structure, we have what we call the black bourgeoisie. Malcolm X would make the analogy that they were the house Negroes as opposed to the field Negroes. A field Negro lives in the field, hoping that something bad will happen to the master, whereas the house Negro is hoping that master lives for ever, because he lives in his house, eats of his table, etc. The house Negroes do all they can to try to preserve the very system that we try to get away from.

The Black bourgeoisie individualise a lot—they might take an Angela Davis because it is fashionable to get behind Angela Davis to help her get out of prison and then they feel as though they have contributed; but they turned away from Ruchell Magee, who was actually shot and almost killed. So, a few may get behind Geronimo ji-jaga, because he knows Danny Glover or he has been to Vietnam, but they might oppose Sundiata Acoli, who is a very beautiful brother who should be supported a thousand per cent and should be freed. They might get behind Dhoruba bin-Wahad and Mutulu Shakur and ignore Marilyn Buck and Laura Whitehorn. It is a matter of us trying to educate them to the reality, what is happening, so they could broaden their support and base their decisions on principles as opposed to personalities.

HK: How about your parole hearings? Do they ask you to disavow your political beliefs?

GP: Ordinarily, you wouldn't find a person being kept in prison as long as I have because of what they say they are keeping me in prison for. To me, the parole hearing is only a formality. They have, by law, to review your case a certain number of times every few years. Since I have been in prison, I have known prisoners who have come in for heinous murders who have gotten out three times—not just once, but for three different murders and have gotten out. It is all a political machine comprised of ex-law-enforcement individuals who are manipulated by their bosses. Every now and then you might run across one or two who seem to show a more humanistic understanding, but they are a minority.

It was a political situation that landed me in here, and it will be a political situation that releases me. And, after so many years, you cease to think so much about you yourself being released. Sure, I would love it, I love freedom, to be out of these places. But you don't dwell on that too much, you would go crazy. It is more broad; you think more about the liberation of society and your people, rather than this little, insignificant person who consciously joined a movement to struggle for liberation.

HK: What do you think about the explosion of the prison population in the last twenty to fifteen years?

GP: It was predicted. Huey Newton gave a lecture on that one time and we had foreseen that this was gonna happen. After the leadership of the BPP was attacked at the end of the '60s and the early '70s, throughout the Black and other oppressed communities, the role models for the upcoming generations became the pimps, the drug dealers, etc. This is what the government wanted to happen. The next result was that the gangs were being formed, coming together with a gangster mentality, as opposed to the revolutionary progressive mentality we would have given them. So, by eliminating or driving the progressive leadership—the correct role models—underground, killing them and putting them into prison—eliminating them—all of these younger generations were left prey to whatever the government wanted to put them into. It is another form of genocide, of killing off populations of Third World and progressive people who pose a threat to their system. And this is one of the reasons why people like me are kept in prison. They don't want me out there, because people like me will go out there and struggle to bring home the truth to those youngsters. They know those youngsters have a lot of respect for us, because we haven't betrayed anything, because we have stayed firm to our principles. Like I said, it is not just me, it is people like us who adhere to the basic principles of liberation and basic humanism for all people—for the Mexican people, for Indian people, for all the struggling peoples.

We have the biggest prison population anywhere in the world and the next one is in South Africa. Of course, there is racism involved. Here, in California, you have a lot of Mexicano and Brown people in prison. It's just so pathetic. They are being railroaded into prison, a lot of them don't speak English, and when they come to prison they are just branded—either you're in this or that gang—and, basically, they don't even know what they are talking about. Then they end up shooting themselves. We have been struggling for years to get the Crips and the Bloods together in prison. We were successful in that a few years ago; it spilled out on to the streets and we are happy about that. Now, since the state and the government can't get the Crips and the Bloods to fight each other, what you see is them trying to get Mexicans and Blacks against each other. It is all being manipulated from above, designed to keep that death factor high. The best way is to have them kill each other off. It is presenting again what existed when I first came in, which George Jackson and others struggled against, by trying to get the prisoners together across racial lines.

HEIKE KLEFFNER: Could you say how you got involved in politics and what got you started?

MUMIA ABU-JAMAL: Well, my political life formally began with the Black Panther Party. I've been in a sense thankful to the Philadelphia police department for kicking and beating me into the Black Panther Party (BPP). As a youth, prior to joining the BPP, I remember the 1968 presidential campaign when George Wallace [former governor of Alabama] was running for US president on the third party ticket; I think it was the American Independence Party. I and several other young Blacks felt that there was something improper about this. So, we went to demonstrate against him at the Spectrum, which is a large sporting venue in Philadelphia. After our very brief demonstration and our expulsion from the Spectrum, we were attacked, beaten and locked up and hospitalised by Philadelphia policemen, who protested our presence. It was from that point forward that my eyes were opened to the militant movements that existed. I wasn't a member of any organisation, but I felt the need hence to be a part of one, to try to change that reality. People speak about fundamental rights; but when you are beaten when you exercise them, then they are not rights, terror and fear will push you away from the need to demonstrate or the feeling that you can freely do so. As a member of the BPP, I was active in the Ministry of Information—the part of the Party that dealt with propaganda, putting out the Party newspaper, putting out leaflets and maintaining communications between chapters like New York, Philadelphia, Chicago, etc. Thereafter, when I left the Party, I continued, one could say, my propaganda efforts by going into journalism—broadcasting, writing and so forth.

HK: Why did you leave the BPP?

MAJ: Some reasons were personal, some political. Around the time of the fight between the East Coast and the West Coast Panthers, I felt that it was not my function, or my reason for joining the Party, to fight other

Black Panthers. I felt that it was proper to fight the system, but when the system can manipulate you into fighting your own, then the system wins and the people lose. I think that period really reflected the destruction of the Party as a national presence, because, once it was split between coasts—between the Central Committee and reigning Party members of the West Coast and some of the most active chapters of the East Coast—then, for all intents and purposes, it lost its effectiveness. Because, even though the Party began in the West, some of its most energetic and militant chapters existed in the East, because this is where some of the largest Black communities and some of the most dire conditions exist. Hence the call for, the need for, a Black Panther Party was very strong here—like the Philadelphia Chapter, like the Winston Salem, Baltimore and New Haven Chapters. Once that was split asunder, it could no longer function as the Black Panther Party, no matter what name it used. It was no longer a united Black political revolutionary organisation trying to achieve Black revolutionary political power.

HK: How would you describe your situation after you left the BPP? Did you feel that journalism was a way to go about your political aims?

MAJ: In some respects, but only to the extent that journalism is a tool to change people's consciousness, to give people insight, and, in another way, a kind of affirmation that their lives have value and purpose. When one reads the daily press or listens to what is broadcast on the regular 'white' radio stations and TV stations, you will perceive a picture, a slanted picture, of Black life that reflects it in the most improper terms. When media journalism and propaganda is used to reflect a positive side of people, the side that resists oppression, the side of people's inherent worth, no matter what their property or economic value, then that in itself is revolutionary, because this system tends to denigrate people who are poor. And most of the people on planet earth are poor. That is the kind of consciousness that drove me towards journalism. And, of course, through the Party I was trained in that field and was able to write from a radical revolutionary perspective.

HK: Your name is often linked to the radical MOVE organisation. MOVE was founded in 1970 in Philadelphia. During a time when the Panthers had already been destroyed by the state's counter-intelligence programme COINTELPRO and by internal infighting, MOVE attracted a lot of young Black as well as white and Latino people. MOVE describes itself as 'a radical, revolutionary organisation, fighting for life and against a system that destroys life and nature.' MOVE members live in communal houses, they do not send their children to public schools and they have a long history of confronting police brutality in the Black community and exposing the judicial system. As a result, MOVE was constantly involved in confrontations with the Philadelphia police, which resulted in several MOVE members being killed, as well as the imprisonment, over a decade ago, of thirteen MOVE members. When did you first meet MOVE?

MAJ: As a reporter. Of course, even prior to that I had read about them in the newspaper, like most people in Philadelphia, and had seen one or two MOVE people on the street. But when the confrontation started heating up in Philadelphia in 1977 and 1978—and it was a very naked level of repression that the Philadelphia police heaped on MOVE—I could not help but draw attention to it. The acting mayor of Philadelphia at the time, Frank Rizzo, and his police started a siege against a MOVE house in Powelton Village in 1977. The siege lasted over one year. By the end, police had cut off all water and electricity to the house, but people from the neighbourhood and supporters from the city supplied MOVE with the basic necessities. Finally, on August 8th, 1978, more than 700 policemen stormed the house. During their action, one policeman was hit in the crossfire of his colleagues. Nine MOVE members who were arrested in the house were later charged and convicted of having jointly killed this one cop. They were all sentenced to 30–100 years in prison, despite the fact that the judge admitted that he didn't know who had shot the cop.

Coming from the quasi-socialist, and in some respects paramilitary, background of the Party, my first impressions of MOVE were extraordinarily negative. I could not perceive them as revolutionary, because they didn't wear uniforms like the Panthers did. They weren't talking about Marxism, Leninism, Mao Tse-Tung thought, as the Panthers were doing. They weren't talking about building a socialist society as a solution to the economic, political and social problems in the US. So, therefore, in the same way that the Philadelphia Police Department beat me into the BPP, the Philadelphia Police Department's repression of MOVE attracted me to MOVE. Because, even though the repression was extraordinarily severe, brutal and devastating, MOVE continued to rebel and resist, and, as MOVE founder John Africa would say: 'Strength and commitment is attractive.'

HK: Can you say how it happened that you stood trial for allegedly having killed a cop? Do you feel that the Philadelphia police set you up on the night when you got shot and this cop got killed? I remember reading that the then mayor, Frank Rizzo, once said about you that your 'breed of journalism' needed to be stopped by any means.

MAJ: I think it is undeniable that elements of a set-up existed and that my background as a Panther and as what some people called a 'MOVE journalist' or a MOVE supporter were elements in that. There was never any time, before or after, when the police acted as if they didn't know who I was. For several months—the better part of a year—I worked at a public radio station, actually right next door to the Philadelphia Police Department's headquarters. So that every day, several times a day, I had to go that route to work. And I think that the work I did—because it was not done by other reporters in Philadelphia—put me down as a target to be neutralised. One must look back at the coverage of MOVE around the time of the police siege of their house in 1978 to see how demonised, how inhumane, how animalistic the portrayal of MOVE was. When interviews were done with them that showed that they were good, decent and committed people, it challenged the public perception of who they were. I did these interviews because I thought they needed to be done; I did them because I thought it was the right thing to do; and I did them because I thought that any journalist should have been doing them. If someone else had done it, I would have had no need.

I remember going to MOVE headquarters and making some phone calls, and going back to the job and being criticised by my boss for that. When I asked him why, he said that phone taps on the MOVE headquarters phone revealed that I had made several calls from there. I said: 'So what? I can call from wherever I want to call.' And he said: 'Well, it damages your objectivity. Other reporters are calling you Mumia Africa.' He meant that as a slur. So it is very clear that not only police intelligence but also intra-station intelligence had me marked as a MOVE operative, when it simply wasn't true. I was just a reporter who worked closely with my subjects.

HK: Do you believe that racism played a role in the fact that you were sentenced to death?

MAJ: What I believe is really immaterial. I think that the facts speak for themselves. The fact is that the state, by intent and design, selected a predominantly white jury, predominantly older, middle-aged jurors who, for the most part, hailed from north-east Philadelphia, which is a very white part of the town. Some jurors were related to cops, some jurors were actually friends of cops. When one takes that into account, as well as the intentional removal from the jury of African-Americans from the central city, I don't think any other result can come to mind.

HK: Do you see racism in general being reflected in the death penalty? How does it play out?

MAJ: Let's look at it this way: of around 2,800 people who are on death rows across the US, an estimated 40 per cent are African-Americans—for the most part men. Of the, say, 2,800 people on death row in the US, only 28 are women. So, that 40 per cent are Black men. The percentage of African-Americans in society is roughly 12 per cent, but when you slice it into half, by male and female, you are talking about 6 per cent. So, 6 per cent of the population become an estimated 40 per cent of people on death row. I don't think that those results can be obtained in any way without racism being a factor.

At all levels of the criminal justice system, whether in charging, the prosecution, the judging and the defence—not to mention the whole level of appeal—it is mostly white individuals in positions of power (magistrates, district attorneys, judges and appellate judges and defence lawyers, etc.) who make independent determinations about the worth of a person, the worth of their life and whether they should be exposed to the most extreme penalty. More often than not, when an African-American is placed in that position, all bets are off.

HK: Following on from that, and in regard to racism, I'd like to know what your impression is of the rebellion in LA. Is this just one 'spark,' which was quietened down, or do you feel that there is potential for the African-American community to start organising around police brutality again?

MAJ: In some respects, some level of organising has already begun as a response to LA. But the LA rebellions reflect, more than anything else, hopelessness. When people riot, they riot because they feel they have nothing to lose. Riot is an act of desperation, not of intent, not of planning. I just think that the forces that converge on African-American life from all levels of American society were symbolised in that case, where Rodney King was beaten and his tormentors and beaters were acquitted [first time round] by—people say a predominantly white jury—it was an all-white jury. People responded viscerally, in their guts, to what they knew was an injustice, a slap in the face of African-American people. Did it move people to organise? I think in some respects, yes. It showed that this system is not our system. It showed that when one is an employee or an agent of the system like a cop, that system will bend over backwards to protect those who are charged with assaulting, or even killing, someone, if that person is poor, African-American, without power, without influence or the like. It shows also how arrogant the system is. One might think they would bend over backwards the other way, given that there is an actual videotape of the crime, but the video meant absolutely nothing. It was as if it had happened in the dead of the night, as if there was no videotape capturing it all. Some people tended to take heart because the federal government stepped in after the rebellions to say, now we are going to start a federal prosecution. But when you look at it, this is the same federal government that, years before, promised to investigate that kind of behaviour across the nation. And, for years, there was silence. This is the same government that pulls its hair out and shrieks about how the federal judiciary, the federal courts, should not be allowed to hear people's appeals from death row. Well, it seems to me that if the federal courts can prosecute someone who was acquitted in a state court, then certainly they should have the authority, unabridged, to review people who were convicted in state courts. It seems only logical.

HK: For a number of years, African-Americans have often held power as heads of police departments, or the mayors of New York or LA. Do you think that the majority of the African-American community feels that here are members of their own community in positions of power, yet they obviously don't change the methods very much?

MAJ: I think that most folks in the African-American community know in their hearts and in their minds that there is a difference between the appearance of power and true power; that African-American political leaders can be mayors, police commissioners, governors, prison superintendents—it doesn't matter what the actual job is—they know they can have a position of power and lack real power. Power is the ability to enforce your will. When one looks at what happened in Philadelphia in 1985 under Mayor Goode and in New York in September of this year under Mayor Dinkins, one cannot come away from these situations without feeling that, in some respects, they were absolutely powerless. In the Goode situation, I refer to the May 13th, 1985, bombing of MOVE, when police bombed and burned eleven MOVE people to death and burned a whole neighbourhood. Mayor Goode accepted all the responsibility, but none of the blame. What he said lately in his recently published autobiography, *In Goode Faith,* was that the reason why he was not on the scene in Osage Avenue when police bombed and then incinerated and shot down MOVE people was that he had received intelligence that the Philadelphia Police Department had him marked for death. I believe him, especially when you look at what happened recently, when 10,000 policemen rioted in New York City and hurled racial slurs at their commander-in-chief, at the mayor of the city. Well, I don't care what your title is—if 10,000 people can come up to your office and call you everything but a child of god, or a bathroom attendant, then you have no power. It is unthinkable that any other white or European-American mayor or chief executive in a political system could be threatened with death by people who are his subordinates and that that white political figure would not have the skills or the contacts or the executive powers to isolate that threat and take care of it. None of these skills were demonstrated by Goode or Dinkins, who are, for all intents and purposes, fairly good politicians. But they happen to be African-American politicians, who have the appearance of power, but no real power.

HK: But, twenty years ago, African-Americans struggled to be represented in the political arena and demanded control over their communities and, on the surface, this demand seems to have been met.

MAJ: Well, twenty years ago, one of the goals of the Black Panther Party was the achievement of Black revolutionary political power. What the Party tried to do was make a distinction between Black revolutionary political power and Black political power; that putting a Black face in a high place was not a solution. In a very real sense, when an African-American person is placed in a position of power, he or she doesn't represent the interests of the poor, of the powerless; he or she represents the interests of the system and not the people. If you look back twenty years ago, the prospect of a Black mayor of New York or a Black mayor of Philadelphia, for that matter, or even of a Black police commissioner, was almost unthinkable. Now it is thinkable, but, in a very real sense, for people in the real world on the streets, life has not changed for the better. In fact, in some respects, it has probably changed for the worse.

HK: Can you describe what your legal situation is right now?

MAJ: We are preparing for a post-conviction relief petition. I am working with my attorneys on that. One of my attorneys, Leonard Weinglass from New York, has said—very accurately in my estimation—that, for all intents and purposes, I have never had any true representation. When you have a lawyer who is appointed, who doesn't want to be there or is denied the most fundamental tools of defence, then you have a lawyer in name, but in name only.

The *Philadelphia Inquirer*, Philadelphia's biggest mainstream newspaper, recently did a report, two pages, that dealt with the representation of people who are charged with capital offences in Philadelphia. What was revealed was that Philadelphia was at the bottom of the league; that in, let's say, Cleveland, Ohio, or San Francisco, as a matter of course, one would be supplied with two attorneys—one for the penalty phase and one for the guilt phase—jury selection specialists, a staff psychiatrist, a ballistics expert and an investigator. This is a matter of course, it goes with the programme. Lawyers from those cities who are defending capital cases get $10,000 at the very bottom to begin; lawyers from Philadelphia—at least in the early '80s—got $2,500 tops. Now, I hear, it has improved somewhat. The lawyer of someone who is charged with a capital offence in Philadelphia might get $4,500, but that is the highest. They are also appointed by the judge, so that, just as a matter of simple psychology or even politics, if I am the judge and I appoint you to the case, and I also determine how much you get paid, when you get paid or even if you get paid, then you had better not make me too angry. You'd better not challenge my rulings too strenuously and you'd better not do anything that will make me look questionable or bad.

HK: As I understand it, right now you are being held in disciplinary custody, because you refuse to cut your hair, which would be against your religious principles. Now the Commissioner of Corrections of Pennsylvania, Joseph Lehmann, has issued two new directives in regard to prison conditions for death row prisoners and prisoners in disciplinary custody. Could you describe how your already extremely harsh prison conditions are going to be restricted even further by those new directives?

MAJ: In a nutshell, the worst conditions on death row in America are just about to get worse. There are two new directives coming out of Harrisburg, Pennsylvania's capital, Directive 801 and 802, which further restrict visitation, correspondence, letters, magazines, newspapers. To those who write directives in Harrisburg, apparently if one is locked up twenty-two hours a day, that is one hour too many out of your cell, so they are cutting it down to twenty-three hours a day, and one hour outside of the cell in a steel cage. For those on disciplinary custody, like myself, it will be one non-contact visit a month, no phone calls at all, one newspaper—a legal newspaper only, and one must give an old newspaper to get the next one. The only commissary available is two packs of cigarettes a month.

One of the things that this brought to my mind was to look at African-American history, especially the case of El Hajj Malik El-Shabazz, known popularly as Malcolm X. When he was imprisoned, his behaviour was so negative that people called him 'Satan'. It was only through his ability to study the teachings of the Honourable Elijah Muhammad and his ability to study a dictionary that he was able to pull himself out of that dark well of negativity and began to build a positive core of self-being. That he did so is a tribute to his teachings as well as to his internal spirit, himself, his determination to come out of that well and to become something other than what society told him he was. Under these new directives, he would not be able to receive those teachings. He would not be able to have a dictionary. So that one who was called 'Satan' would never have been able to develop and metamorphose into a Malcolm X and later on El Hajj Malik El-Shabazz, because he would not be able to have the tools to develop, to grow, to read, to stretch, to learn. If one looks at how the state is developing its new Marionisation programme, it looks as if one of its intents is to stop that kind of growth and development and, indeed, to create, if not 'Satans,' then certainly beasts, bitter, angry, burnt-up people—as opposed to people who are growing, sensitive, insightful, better people. It seems to me that a system that dares call itself the Department of Corrections has a job to make people better as opposed to bitter.

HK: A lot of people seem to think that, under Clinton, everything will be better. From your perspective, is that true?

MAJ: Well, my perspective is a little biased. As an African-American on death row, I am not of that opinion. I would suspect that for most Blacks, and perhaps some white people on death row in Arkansas, they don't feel very heartened by that prospect. Clinton is a staunch supporter of the death penalty and has been responsible for at least four executions in Arkansas. Clinton also calls for more police and the building of new jails, despite the fact that there are already one million people in prisons throughout the US, which makes the US the country with the highest incarceration rate worldwide in regard to its overall population.

HK: Why did you think it was that, for many years, people even on the Left or in the African-American community never heard about political prisoners, and, in particular, about Black Panther and BLA political prisoners like you or Bashir Hameed or Nuh Washington from the BLA?

MAJ: I guess the reason is simple. In American consciousness, as well as in African-American consciousness, something is not real unless it's on TV. If it didn't happen on NBC, CBS or CNN, it didn't happen. Marshall McLuhan said that the medium is the message, and it is; that which the ruling class's communication network wishes to present and promote is what is carried over into popular consciousness. That which it does not wish to promote, it either ignores or slanders. People like myself, like Bashir Hameed, like Andul Majid, like Geronimo ji-jaga Pratt, like Chuckie Africa and Delbert Africa from MOVE, like all these political prisoners, are invisible to millions of Americans.

HK: At this point, do you see any force out there that has a revolutionary strategy, or that has the power to move people into action?

MAJ: There are several organisations in the US of varying ideological persuasions who have revolutionary theories that they believe will transform America's present social, political and economic reality. Do they have the power to enforce them and change the reality now? No. What it's going to take, more than anything, is the cohesion of many forces, the building of mass power to change those realities. In the sense that no *one* organisation has the power to transform it themselves. This is a huge, vast country with 260 million people and to suppose that an organisation of 200, 300 people is going to effect the deep degrees of transformation that need to take place is pretentious. Look at the fact that, at its height, the BPP had 15,000-16,000 members and was cooperating with other revolutionary organisations as well.

Unless and until a political gathering and grouping is able to galvanise the power of the masses of the people, then no immediate change is imminent—that is, positive change. There is a whole lot of negative change to come. One element of that is what we talked about earlier as 'Marionisation'. We are not just talking about the Marionisation of this prison here in Huntingdon or in Pennsylvania, but the Marionisation and the prisonisation of America. You have over one million people locked up in prisons and jails in the US right now. Indeed, if we break that down into percentages, over 38 per cent of that million are African-American men. So that, unless and until a popular force is built and welded that coheres something from here and something from there, a popular force that develops a counterforce to the 'mainstream' for real, then there will be no change. What you are looking at in the US when I say prisonisation is not just the million of people who are locked down. Increasingly, as industries flee this country, people find that their only option in terms of personal survival is to become a part of what has been called a 'fortress economy'. More and more, when people look for jobs, they find them in the security field, as prison guards, as cops, etc. So that, from the outside and the inside, America is becoming the prison house of nations.

37 "Forward Ever, Backward Never"

In recent years, the mainstream media and an assortment of disaffected radicals have taken great pleasure in highlighting the "changes" that time, travel, and graying temples have wrought in Black Power–era militants. But there is another equally compelling side to this story, one that suggests both the timelessness of the nationalist impulse and the determination and conviction of its adherents. In the volume's final selection, longtime UNIA president general Charles Lionel James reminisces about his early days with Garvey and posits the continuing need for an activist black nationalism. " 'Forward ever, backward never'— that is the UNIA today, we have not changed," he notes proudly in this 1987 interview. "We need to grasp certain principles, like those of Garveyism, in order to survive." The interview is reprinted from Jeannette Smith-Irvin, *Footsoldiers of the Universal Negro Improvement Association* (Trenton, NJ: Africa World Press, 1989), by permission.

1987 *From* Interview with Charles Lionel James

I was born in Antigua, April 26, 1905. In 1922 I left Antigua and went to New York to my brother George. He was an ardent Garveyite and he had bought about $250 worth of shares in the Black Star Line. I met Mr. Garvey April 19, 1922. After getting myself settled, I went to Harlem and found the office of the UNIA, which was located at 52–54 West 135th Street. About two weeks after that, I joined the New York Division.

When I was seventeen, I started taking a general education course after joining the UNIA. I had a part time job while attending school. I was elected first vice-president of the UNIA, the youngest ever to be elected to that position. In 1927, I was transferred to Newark, New Jersey and became president of the Newark Division from 1927 to 1928. I was also commissioner for the states of Kansas, Arkansas, and Ohio. There were two other branches in New Jersey, and I got them together and we purchased property at 35 Broome Street (Liberty Hall) for about $37,000. Our membership was from 150 to 1,000 members. In 1928, I was sent to Gary, Indiana . . . and became president of the Gary Division from 1928 until the war started. The Gary Division membership then was about 300, and while I was president the membership increased to about 2,000. We had a Liberty Hall located at 2128 Washington Street, Gary, Indiana.

While serving in the various capacities in the UNIA, I was compensated because it took all of my time. We were sent out on speaking engagements, and usually those who were sent out were able to bring money back to the international headquarters. World War II broke out in 1938, and I went into the service and was stationed at Fort Pickett, Virginia.

In 1922, when I met Mr. Garvey, I had explained to him that I had just come from the West Indies, and how the Black Star Line was so well known in Antigua. When I shook his hand, I was shook up because right then and there I felt the electricity. I saw a man with flashing eyes. There were many people in Antigua that he knew, and he told me that there was no height in the UNIA that I could not reach. My impression of him at that time was that I was in the presence of royalty. He wanted me to visit Liberty Hall and hear the program of the organization. I was able to see the organization in its bloom. His presence was irresistible and the first meeting was almost indescribable, and it drew me to him. I knew then my career had started with him.

While I was in the service, UNIA members were kept under surveillance for a long time. The United States government thought the UNIA was subversive. There were UNIA divisions all around Camp Pickett and I wanted to attend a meeting. At first the army said no, but later they gladly let me go to the Sunday meetings whenever I asked.

There were about 100,000 people in the New York Division. In the early years, the membership of divisions ran anywhere from 250 to 900. We had divisions in the South, a few in the far West. England and Canada had divisions, and all of the West Indian Islands were involved with the UNIA in some way.

As commissioner and first assistant president general, I traveled at the direction of Mr. Stewart, who was president general at the time. My duties were those of principal speaker on special occasions, and I also regulated the activities at the branches. Sometimes the divisions would request my presence, but other times the parent body would notify them I was coming. That was the understanding we had. Wherever I traveled as commissioner, I had a good relationship with the people. While in Gary, I was adopted by the John Amos family. They were the grandparents of John Amos, who is a famous movie star. They lived in Gary at the time. Mrs. Hattie Sears, who was a strong member of the UNIA and president of the Gary branch, also adopted me as her son. In each city I stayed, there was a family who provided for all my wants and needs and gave me the necessary support in order for me to carry out my duties while I was in the area.

My involvement in the UNIA engulfed my whole life. The idea of returning to Antigua has always been there, but my style and way of living in the United States was such that I could never return to stay on an island of 108 square miles, after becoming a world traveler. However, I made it a point—and it is my duty—to visit home as often as I can. The last time I went was in 1958 at the death of my brother. My social contacts were in the UNIA and I was scared to have contacts outside of the organization for fear someone might come in and move me out. My expectation of being in the organization was nothing more than the satisfaction of helping to keep the UNIA alive. All that I wanted I found in the UNIA.

The structure of the UNIA in the early years was as such: there was the top position of president general. The executive general consisted of the president general, the first assistant president general along with the second, third, and fourth assistant presidents general, the secretary general, the high chancellor, and the auditor general. The field officers (of which I was one) were the commissioners and special representatives.

The requirements for membership in the organization were that you had to be of African descent, be at least eighteen years old, and pay regular joining fees of thirty-five cents a month, which went into the charity fund. We raised funds by collecting individual pledges and donations. All of this was on a voluntary basis. We had a compulsory fee of one dollar per year, which was used to operate the parent organization. We also had a juvenile division for young people. When they became eighteen, they moved into the larger membership body.

The goals and objectives never changed. It is the same now as it was in the beginning in 1914. The ultimate objective was the freedom of Africa. The UNIA was to establish a confraternity among the race, promote the spirit of pride and love, and assist and administer to the needy, reclaim the fallen, and to do all in our power for the advancement of the race.

I had a close association with Marcus Garvey. . . . He picked me out because he recognized my ability to learn. He used me as a guinea pig many, many times and challenged my imagination. He would make me angry, knowing that I could not do anything about it. I was easy to cry and he let me know he made me angry in order to stir me. I soon recognized the fact, as I grew older, that he was testing me and preparing me for the battles after his death. Even when I took the course in African philosophy, he embarrassed me in front of my fellow students, and told me that I did not know anything. He shook his finger in my face, and I told him I did not need the course because I had read everything he wrote and that there was nothing that he could teach me. That was my ego coming out at that particular moment. But when I got in class the first day, I found out that I did not know. When all of us were supposed to defend our orations, and when I got up to make my speech, I was but five minutes into the speech when he stopped me and said, "That's alright James, you can stop now. I know that you know because I've taught you." That was the way he was.

I was in New York when Mr. Garvey was tried and convicted. At that time, I was an active officer in the Brooklyn Division, and my presence in the area gave me the opportunity to go to the court each day to listen to the case. I recall very vividly the trial. There were twelve jurors, only three of them Black. The trial was very dramatic. Mr. Garvey defended himself. The White attorney from the firm of Corman and Nagle was so bad that Mr. Garvey had to take the case over himself. I saw him pleading the case, questioning the witnesses and getting his defense and support. One of the things I saw was the time when the judge was charging the jury and indicating that Garvey was like a tiger, ferocious. In the midst of all that, I heard the attorney telling the jurors, "Gentlemen, are you going to let the tiger go?" Those words stuck deep in my mind. I never will forget how Marcus Garvey walked down in front of the jurors and said, "Gentlemen, one thing the judge and State attorney have done is against all of our judicial efforts." He pointed out several pieces of law and condemmed the judge and district attorney for uttering epithets and naming individuals, which was against the law.

His reply to the attorney general's question was, "I want you to know that you may cage the tiger but there are going to be thousands of cubs in the bushes that you've got to catch." Hearing him make that statement, I did not realize that I was going to be one of those cubs they were going to be hunting. I too have been hounded and put in jail. I was taken to the lynching ground and had to use the same powers of persuasion and confidence. I was in jail in New Jersey in 1928, and in the thirties, I was in jail in Missouri. It was after a meeting that five white men took me out and told me that they were going to lynch me. They took me from an audience of about four to five hundred, and they took me between two buildings. They began to call me all kinds of names, and I knew I could not fight because they had guns. They asked me why was I trying to upset the "niggers" and get them all excited. I had to use Marcus Garvey's philosophy and I asked them if they knew what the UNIA meant and when they said no, I explained it to them, I told them that the UNIA was trying to put backbone into Black folks so that they will be able to be in a position to do for themselves and depend upon others for nothing.

When Mr. Garvey went to jail, the organization rallied like they had never rallied before to Mrs. Garvey's aid. This is a fact, contrary to rumors that we did not. We raised hundreds and thousands of dollars for a bond which the court refused. We followed through with Mr. Garvey's appeal when he went to the penitentiary and left his wife in our charge. I personally can say that we, the UNIA, gave Mrs. Garvey support. I myself have raised money, and forwarded it to her. We did not let Mrs. Garvey suffer. There might have been individuals who did not do what they were supposed to do, but let the record show that we the members of the UNIA, those of us who believed in Marcus Garvey, did our part for the protection of the Garvey family.

After Mr. Garvey was convicted, there was a power struggle among the leaders; there was no question about the power struggle. Marcus Garvey had a personality that captivated people and when he was removed from the organization as an active leader, naturally some of our members felt that it was over, there was a falling off of the membership. There is no question about it, whether we like it or not—Garvey's personality was, and is, unmatched by any other leader. Whenever he asked something of you, you automatically found yourself saying, "Yes sir!" The officers he trusted felt it was their chance to seize power of the organization while he was in prison, and they did. That thwarted some of the efforts of those of us who were sincere and wanted him back. The enemies of Marcus Garvey, seeing this struggle, moved in and further contributed to the disintegration of the UNIA.

Our branches have fallen off in many states. We have had to adopt new methods to reach old goals. We had to change the long range program of the UNIA. There was nothing that we could do about that. That is the only thing that has kept the UNIA alive. The structure of the UNIA remains the same. Our membership diminished and that put a great strain upon those of us who are carrying on now. For instance, we had the Black Star Line, the Black Cross Nurses, the Black Star Navigation and Trading Company, and the Motor Corporation. We had the Liberian Land Development Association and the Negro Factories Corporation. But the biggest plus of all was that we had Marcus Garvey. We had "Liberty Halls" scattered all over the world. We had the Universal African Legions and the Royal Engineers. Now, most of those institutions have passed, and it puts the leadership in the position of having nothing to sell but the hardcore UNIA as Marcus Garvey advocated it.

The economic situation of our country today also plays a major part. During the Garvey days, he could easily talk about raising a million dollars and could easily say that at least a million people would give a dollar each, where now, to even think about raising $5,000 is a major, major effort. At that time, we attracted a certain politically conscious type of member, and we could demand certain things we cannot demand today. The enemies of Marcus Garvey who existed then were frustrated because of the power of the organization. We were the most powerful minority organization. The same enemies are here today, using every imaginable type of energy and propaganda to destroy the UNIA and the reputation and credibility of Marcus Garvey. "Forward ever, backward never"—that is the UNIA today, we have not changed. We are still in about twenty-five states and Canada, as well as the Caribbean and

Central America, and we have connections in Africa. We are not dead by any means. . . .

Overall, Mr. Garvey's greatest trouble was with the integrationists. It is not too much different today: only the scene has changed, and the actors have changed. Schuyler was one of Mr. Garvey's greatest enemies at the time; he was the foremost writer for the *Pittsburgh Courier*. Then there was Robert S. Abbott in Chicago. He used his column in the *Chicago Defender* to disrupt Garvey's program. Everything that was barbaric was written about Marcus Garvey. He used the lines of the paper to lie and write propaganda against Garvey. He was used by the White people who felt that Marcus Garvey's dream of nationalism and commercial enterprise was too much, and basically they were afraid that it was going to be accomplished. But Garvey and Garveyism have survived.

Du Bois was an effective individual in what he believed. I do not regard him as a traitor to the race, even though Mr. Garvey spoke of him in those terms. It was a philosophical difference between Garvey and Du Bois. But Garvey felt that Du Bois, with all of his pompousness, was sincere and wanted a better life for Black folks, but the route he was going always spelled disaster for other people and would do the same thing for us. Du Bois took more of an intellectual route, so much so that before he passed away he embraced the very ideas that he fought. He went to Ghana to live and admitted in writing that if he had to do it all over again he would do it differently. Mr. Garvey, in his last statement in Toronto, Canada, told us that Du Bois mistreated him, but that there was a move afoot to destroy Du Bois. Mr. Garvey, in the latter days of his administration, said not to deal harshly with Du Bois because, what he did, he did not know any better, but we should not let the white man destroy him as they were about to destroy Mr. Garvey.

The opportunity for nationalism is limitless. Nationalism is going to be the only hope for our young Blacks. The time has come when they must put down the hero worship of other races and begin now to emulate and create heroes of their own. They need to recapture their proud culture in order to survive. They need to read everything that they can read, digest it thoroughly and put it to action. The present leadership of the Black race is pointing to integration, and this is nothing but racial suicide. And if it is not checked, the race is not going to achieve politically.

The goal of Marcus Garvey was economic independence. It is the only way individuals can be totally independent. Our political and religious independence rests upon our economic independence. Garvey felt that if he needed a million dollars, he would have to have a million people and it worked. He dealt with the masses. I hope and pray that Marcus Garvey's vision of a free and redeemed Africa will become a reality. I am not unmindful of the past. The struggle is hard, but I am convinced that Marcus Garvey's ultimate objective is not as far to be reached now as it was then. Black folks in America or anywhere are not going to be able to achieve any substantial goal without quoting Marcus Garvey and the principles that he enunciated. We have to encourage unity here and abroad. We who are Garveyites have to live and preach his principles. Instead of driving the nationalist away by saying they do not do things the way we want, let us say to them, "You have now accepted Garveyism." Now let us together fashion this concept and make it work. Embrace the philosophy. You have the Black Muslims who are feeding off of Garveyism. The Honorable Elijah Muhammad of the Black Muslims was a former member of the UNIA. I remember when he first came; it was fashionable for you to refer to him as a follower of Marcus Garvey.

Reexamine the philosophies of all the Black leaders and put into action some of these positive ideas and goals, especially for the young Black man and woman. Endure, struggle, and read, and do whatever you can to achieve in the field of economics, for in the time we are living in, the system is an economic one. We need to understand it in order to survive. At the same time, we need to grasp certain principles, like those of Garveyism, in order to survive.

Index

Davis, Angela, 354
Deacons for Defense and Justice, 93, 135
Declaration of Rights of the Negro Peoples of the World, 23–31
De Gaulle, Charles, 210
Delany, Catherine, 9
Delany, Martin, 8, 9
DePillars, Murry N., 215–16, 222
Diop, Cheikh Anta, 292
Dodge Revolutionary Union Movement (DRUM), 188, 192–96
Donaldson, Jeff, 215–21
Douglas, Aaron, 56
Douglas, Emory, 348
Douglass, Frederick, 5–6, 70, 227, 252, 316
Du Bois, W. E. B.: in Africa, 47–50; birthday celebrated, 173; and double consciousness, 154; relations with Marcus Garvey, 373; promotes Pan-Africanism, 40–46, 206, 313; quoted, 140, 165; as revolutionary, 252; and the "talented tenth," 316–17; writings of, praised, 55, 306
Dumas, Alexandre, 9, 71
Dunbar, Paul Laurence, 54
Dunne, Bill, 60

Economics, black nationalism in: championed by Congress of Racial Equality, 178–81; Maulana Karenga on, 282–83; Nation of Islam and, 97, 104, 315–27; and National Black Economic Development Conference, 182–87; Organization of Afro-American Unity and, 112; and Republic of New Africa, 199–200; Universal Negro Improvement Association and, 11, 373–74. See also Buy Black campaign; Reparations
Education, black nationalism in: Black Panther Party and, 258–59; and Nation of Islam, 97, 104; and Universal Negro Improvement Association, 11.

See also Afrocentrism; Black Studies
Edwards, Harry, 14
Egypt: as black homeland, 6, 99, 233–34; greatness of, 39, 276–77, 280, 283–85, 293, 345
Eisenhower, Dwight D., 140
El-Shabazz, El-Hajj Malik. See Malcolm X
Emigrationism: distinguished from colonization, 17 n. 10; criticized by communists, 62; early organizations promoting, 8–10; Louis Farrakhan on, 317. See also Territorial nationalism; Universal Negro Improvement Association
Evans, Arthur, Sir, 68
Evers, Medgar, 270

Fanon, Frantz, 127–32, 286–87, 311, 328
Farrakhan, Louis, 315–27
Fauset, Jessie, 40
Federal Bureau of Investigation (FBI), 32–33, 133–35, 346, 350, 351
Fisher, Rudolph, 56
Forman, James, 182–87, 223, 303, 307, 328–32
Frobenius, Leo, 82

Garnet, Henry Highland, 6–7, 8, 309
Garvey, Amy Jacques, 51, 57, 252, 371
Garvey, Marcus Mosiah: influence on African Nationalist Pioneer Movement, 84, 88, 91–92; charisma of, 368, 372; criticized by communists, 59, 62; relations with W. E. B. Du Bois, 373; as educator, 370; targeted by FBI, 32–33; as hero, 227; as leader of masses, 317, 374; political enemies of, 372–73; quoted, 23, 279; as race savior, 57; as revolutionary, 252; in textbooks, 1; influence on theology, 313; trial and conviction of, 12–13, 370–71

Party, 358; Stokely Carmichael on, 207–8; and colonialism, 78, 131, 328; James Cone on, 311–13; and League of Revolutionary Black Workers, 190–91; and Pan-African Revolutionary Socialist Party, 342; and racial equality, 60. *See also* Communist Party of the United States; Revolutionary nationalism
Mays, Willie, 121
Meredith, James, 305
Merleau-Ponty, Maurice, 311
Million Man March, 315
Moore, Richard B., 78–83
MOVE, 346, 357–59, 361–62, 365
Muhammad, Elijah: death of, 315; and economics, 97, 103–4; targeted by FBI, 135; and Malcolm X, 106, 364; on self-knowledge, 99–100, 316; advocates territorial nationalism, 97–98, 104, 317; theological beliefs, 97, 99–102; and Universal Negro Improvement Association, 374; on whites as devils, 101–2
Muhammad, Wallace D., 315
Multiculturalism, 291

National Association for the Advancement of Colored People (NAACP), 12, 122–23, 153
National Black Economic Development Conference, 182–87, 200
National Black Feminist Organization, 256
National Black Political Convention, 136–44
National Coalition of Blacks for Reparations in America (N'COBRA), 333
National Committee of Black Churchmen (NCBC), 223, 225–28, 307
National Committee to Combat Fascism (NCCF), 265
National Conference of Black Churchmen. *See* National Committee of Black Churchmen

Nationalism: defined, 2–4. *See also* Black nationalism
National Urban League, 153
National Welfare Rights Organization, 184
Nation of Islam, 97–105, 135, 315–27, 374
Negro World, 12, 23, 33, 64
Neocolonialism. *See* Colonialism
Newton, Huey P., 241, 348, 355
Nguzo Saba, 275–87
Niagara Movement, 122–23
Nixon, Richard M., 141, 153, 269
Nkrumah, Kwame, 203, 207, 210–11, 342, 343
Nonviolence, 95. *See also* Civil rights movement; King, Martin Luther, Jr.
Nyerere, Julius, 283

Obadele, Gaidi, 197
Obadele, Imari, 197, 333–41
Organization of Afro-American Unity (OAAU), 106–15

Padmore, George, 206–7, 313
Pan-African Conference of 1900, 10
Pan-African Congress movement, 40
Pan-Africanism: and African Nationalist Pioneer Movement, 91; and black theology, 313; Stokely Carmichael on, 203–14; promoted by W. E. B. Du Bois, 40, 46, 206, 313; James Forman and, 185; Maulana Karenga on, 279; in nineteenth century, 8–9, 17 n. 10; and Organization of Afro-American Unity, 109–11. *See also* All-African People's Revolutionary Party; Pan-African Revolutionary Socialist Party; Universal Negro Improvement Association
Pan-African Revolutionary Socialist Party (PRSP), 342–45
Pan-Caribbean movement, 78–83
Parks, Rosa, 311
Payne, Daniel, 306, 310

Plato, 6, 206–7
Pluralism, 3
Politics, black nationalism in, 12, 136–57, 361–62
Powell, Adam Clayton, 309
Pratt, Elmer Gerard ("Geronimo"), 340, 346–56, 365
Prosser, Gabriel, 8, 252

Racial designations, preferred, 7, 27, 78, 84, 87, 115, 204–5
Randolph, A. Philip, 73–77
Reagan, Ronald, 321
Reiss, Winold, 55, 57
Religion, black nationalism in, 11. See also Black Manifesto; Black theology; Nation of Islam; National Committee of Black Churchmen
Remond, Charles Lenox, 9
Reparations: Black Panther Party on, 249; James Forman on, 182–87; and Republic of New Africa, 197–98, 333, 335–37
Republic of New Africa (RNA), 93, 197–202, 333–41
Revolutionary Action Movement (RAM), 93, 135, 241, 252–55
Revolutionary nationalism, 167–68. See also Black Panther Party for Self-Defense; Marxism-Leninism; Revolutionary Action Movement
Ricks, Willie, 304
Robeson, Paul, 55, 56
Robinson, Jackie, 121
Rogers, Joel Augustus, 64–72, 292
Roosevelt, Franklin D., 73, 75, 140
Rush, Christopher, 310
Russwurm, John Brown, 70

Seale, Bobby, 241, 244, 348
Self-definition. See Black Power movement, psychological aspects; Racial designations, preferred
Separatism: distinguished from nationalism, 168; distinguished from segrega-

tion, 14. See also Community control; Territorial nationalism
Shabazz, tribe of, 97, 99
Shakur, Assata, 256–57, 269–72, 340, 351
Shrine of the Black Madonna, 223
Singleton, Benjamin, 10
Smith, Bessie, 56
Smith, Clara, 54
Southern Christian Leadership Conference (SCLC), 122, 135
Squires, Clark, 270. See also Acoli, Sundiata
Stanford, Maxwell, 135
Student Nonviolent Coordinating Committee (SNCC), 119–26, 135

Talmadge, Herman, 74
Territorial nationalism: and Cyril Briggs, 34; Stokely Carmichael on, 208–10; Malcolm X on, 154–55, 209; of Elijah Muhammad, 97–98, 104, 317; in nineteenth century, 8–9; of Geronimo Pratt, 347. See also Black Belt Republic; Community control; Republic of New Africa
Third International Conference on Black Power, 159, 172–74
Till, Emmett, 270
Toomer, Jean, 54–55, 56
Toure, Sekou, 145, 203
Toynbee, Arnold J., 68
Truman, Harry, 140
Truth, Sojourner, 252, 304
Tubman, Harriet, 252, 304
Ture, Kwame. See Carmichael, Stokely
Turner, Henry McNeal, 10, 304, 309, 313
Turner, Nat, 8, 227, 230, 252, 270, 312

United Nations: and human rights, 113, 329; mentioned, 154; to supervise plebiscite, 250, 338–39; and South African liberation, 211
United Transatlantic Society, 10

Universal African Legion, 12, 84, 89–90, 372
Universal Ethiopian Anthem, 29–30
Universal Negro Catechism, 11, 23
Universal Negro Improvement and Conservation Association and African Communities (Imperial) League. *See* African Communities League; Universal Negro Improvement Association
Universal Negro Improvement Association (UNIA): and African Blood Brotherhood, 34, 36; aims and structure of, 10–13, 368–72; and communists, 59, 62; flag of, 18 n. 15; membership of, 17 n. 15, 368–69. *See also* Declaration of Rights of the Negro Peoples of the World; Garvey, Marcus Mosiah; James, Charles Lionel
Us, 275

Varick, James, 227, 304, 309, 310
Vesey, Denmark, 8, 252
Vietnam war: Martin Luther King, Jr., and, 311; Student Nonviolent Coordinating Committee on, 124; Robert F. Williams on, 94; role of women in, 260–61
Violence: in auto plants, 196; Amiri Baraka on, 146, 148, 151–53; and Buy Black campaign, 89–90; Eldridge Cleaver on, 246–47; and cultural nationalism, 215; gang-related, 355–56; against oppressors, 8, 27, 96, 113, 185–86, 250; psychological aspects of, 127–32; and Republic of New Africa, 197; Revolutionary Action Movement on, 252–53; societal, 298–99; of whites, 94–96, 103, 112–13, 226–27, 242, 269–71, 371. *See also* Guerrilla warfare

Walker, David, 8, 306, 309
Wanton, George, 70
Washington, Booker T., 85, 316–17
Washington, George, 65, 67, 151, 173, 316
Welsing, Frances Cress, 295–302
West Indies Federation, 78
White liberals: and Black Studies, 169–70; and black theology, 306; and civil rights movement, 14; political failures of, 140–41; and Student Nonviolent Coordinating Committee, 119–26. *See also* Alliances, feasibility of
Whitfield, James M., 7
Wilkins, Roy, 152, 157
Williams, Robert F., 93–96, 252
Wilmore, Gayraud, 313
Women's liberation movement, 256–68, 351
Woodson, Carter G., 289, 291, 294
World Community of Al-Islam in the West, 315

Yokinen, August, 59
Young, Whitney, Jr., 152